Organization Change

To Bobbi
And to the next generation . . .
Brian & Emily, Courtney & Darrin, and Donovan & Reni
And to the next generation after that . . .
William, Thomas, Julien, Adrian, Madeleine, and Maya

Organization Change

Theory and Practice

W. Warner Burke

Teachers College, Columbia University

Los Angeles | London | New Delhi
Singapore | Washington DC

Los Angeles | London | New Delhi
Singapore | Washington DC

FOR INFORMATION:

SAGE Publications, Inc.
2455 Teller Road
Thousand Oaks, California 91320
E-mail: order@sagepub.com

SAGE Publications Ltd.
1 Oliver's Yard
55 City Road
London EC1Y 1SP
United Kingdom

SAGE Publications India Pvt. Ltd.
B 1/I 1 Mohan Cooperative Industrial Area
Mathura Road, New Delhi 110 044
India

SAGE Publications Asia-Pacific Pte. Ltd.
3 Church Street
#10-04 Samsung Hub
Singapore 049483

Acquisitions Editor: Patricia Quinlin
Associate Editor: Maggie Stanley
Assistant Editor: Megan Koraly
Editorial Assistant: Dori Zweig
Production Editor: Stephanie Palermini
Copy Editor: Megan Markanich
Typesetter: C&M Digitals (P) Ltd.
Proofreader: Ellen Brink
Indexer: Kathy Paparchontis
Cover Designer: Candice Harman
Marketing Manager: Liz Thornton

Printed in the United States of America

Library of Congress Cataloging-in-Publication Data

Burke, W. Warner (Wyatt Warner), 1935-

Organization change : theory and practice / W. Warner Burke, Teachers College, Columbia University. — Fourth edition.

pages cm. — (Foundations for organizational science)
Includes bibliographical references and index.

ISBN 978-1-4522-5723-5 (pbk. : alk. paper) — ISBN 978-1-4522-5726-6 (web pdf) 1. Organizational change. 2. Leadership. I. Title.

HD58.8.B876 2014
658.4'06—dc23   2013023143

This book is printed on acid-free paper.

16 17 10 9 8 7 6 5 4 3

Contents

Preface

The bulk of what was written for the first three editions of this book remains the same in this fourth edition. Fundamentals of organization change are still fundamental. This fourth edition nevertheless has been revised with new chapters on loosely coupled systems and future priorities as well as other revisions here and there. These revisions are more about additions that I believed needed to be included—especially in the two new chapters: 12 and 16.

The purpose of this book, then, is to report on and interpret current knowledge of organization change. The knowledge comes from a variety of sources, as noted next. The interpretation comes from my understanding as an academic of what the literature seems to be telling us and from my experience of well over 40 years as an organization change consultant. Will Rogers is reported to have said, "All I know is what I read in the newspapers." All I know is what I have read in the organization literature and what I believe I have learned as a consultant to organizations. Both are limited. You, the reader, should therefore be forewarned. While I have made a concerted effort to present material from the literature as objectively as I could, in the end what I have written is biased, at least in two ways: (a) my selections from the literature are just that, selective, and are not comprehensive, and (b) my interpretations come from experience. It should be noted, however, that in the meantime I have coedited a book of readings that contains much of the literature that undergirds this text. With this book (Burke, Lake, & Paine, 2009) of some 52 entries, you, the reader, can go to the originals and make your own interpretations. In any case, the reader serves as a useful supplement to this fourth edition. Experiences as an organization consultant continue to influence my thinking and writing. For example, in the past few years I seem to have been drawn more and more to focus on leadership. There are two chapters on leadership: Chapters 13 and 14. Maybe I am coming full circle. My doctoral dissertation many years ago was on leadership. Allow me to describe briefly a few examples.

First, I continue to codirect our MA program in organizational psychology here at Teachers College, Columbia University, for a cohort of 24 U.S. Army officers at the U.S. Military Academy at West Point. On completion of this graduate degree in one year, most of these officers (captains and majors) will be assigned to cadet companies (about 130 students) as the regular army's officer-in-charge. They evaluate twice a year the cadets' military performance and also serve as mentors, coaches, and leaders for these cadets. They have considerable influence on future officers of the U.S. Army. Our faculty, therefore, have indirect influence through our classroom teaching. This experience has been significant and rewarding. No doubt I have been influenced as well.

Second, I have been involved for a few years now with a midwestern state university as a visiting professor but also as a consultant to the provost and dean of the one of the university schools. In this work, we have focused on the leader's (provost and dean) role in initiating and managing change. Being one of the state-supported universities in this particular state means that regulations and budgets are somewhat imposed, which in turn creates a "tightness" in how the institution operates. Yes, it is a university after all, which means that it is more of a loosely coupled system overall than a tight one. We therefore emphasize mission, change direction, shared values, and cooperative actions across units to ensure that even though looseness is recognized and informally rewarded, a system consisting of interdependent parts is the focus. In working with this organization, I was reminded of ideas from the 1930s expounded by Mary Parker Follett (as cited in Follett, 1996), an individual way ahead of her time. Her notion of the invisible leader is an excellent case in point. She stated that for organizational effectiveness, both the leader and the followers need to follow the invisible leader—the *purpose* of the organization. That way, leadership is organizationally focused and not so dependent on the persona of the leader. I am using this idea in discussing the leadership of this university.

Third, I have been involved in leadership transitions, trying to help organizations deal as effectively as possible with the change from an old to a new president and chief executive officer. This kind of transition provides a wonderful opportunity for organization change. We need to know more about matters of leadership transitions. Incidentally, quite a number of years ago, Michael Mitchell wrote a brief and useful article for the *Harvard Business Review* on how to facilitate a transition in leaders.

In sum, recent experiences with leader coaching and consulting have no doubt influenced choices and perspectives in this fourth edition. And, as before, my attempt has been to combine and to some degree integrate theory and research with application. After setting the stage in Chapters 1 and 2, then providing some background and history in Chapter 3, Chapters 4 to 8 are more about theory and research, and the remaining chapters deal more with application and practice.

Teaching Resources and Website to Accompany the Book

For the Instructor

The password-protected Instructor Site at **www.sagepub.com/burke4e** gives instructors access to a full complement of resources to support and enhance their courses. The following assets are available on the Instructor Site:

- A Microsoft® Word® test bank is available, containing multiple-choice, true–false, and essay questions for each chapter. The test bank provides you with a diverse range of prewritten options as well as the opportunity for editing any question and/or inserting your own personalized questions to effectively assess students' progress and understanding.
- A Respondus electronic test bank is available and can be used on PCs. The test bank contains multiple-choice, true–false, and essay questions for each chapter and provides you with a diverse range of prewritten options as well as the opportunity for editing any question and/or inserting your own personalized questions to effectively assess students' progress and understanding. Respondus is also compatible with many popular learning management systems so you can easily get your test questions into your online course.
- Editable, chapter-specific Microsoft® PowerPoint® slides offer you complete flexibility in easily creating a multimedia presentation for your course. Highlight essential content, features, and artwork from the book.

- **Sample course syllabi** for semester and quarter courses provide suggested models for use when creating the syllabi for your courses.
- EXCLUSIVE! Access is available to certain full-text **SAGE journal articles** that have been carefully selected for each chapter. Each article supports and expands on the concepts presented in the chapter. This feature also provides questions to focus and guide student interpretation. Combine cutting-edge academic journal scholarship with the topics in your course for a robust classroom experience.
- Carefully selected, web-based **video links** feature relevant interviews, lectures, personal stories, inquiries, and other content for use in independent or classroom-based explorations of key topics.

Acknowledgments

I have many people to thank, and I am very pleased to have this opportunity to do so. First and foremost is Ben Schneider, who insisted that I write this book. Throughout, he was incredibly supportive, patient, and persistent about my staying the course. Then there were my three official reviewers for Sage, beyond Ben, two of whom had reviewed my previous work (Burke, 1982). Len Goodstein was his true self and a true friend in holding my feet to the fire—that is, calling my attention to the need for (a) more examples, (b) better linkage between theory and practice, and (c) better logic as I went from A to C and assumed too much by skipping B. Craig Lundberg gave me feedback in two categories: (a) the "big stuff" and (b) the "little stuff," as he called it. I paid attention to all but particularly to the big stuff. All the "stuff" was on target and very helpful. The third Sage reviewer was David Whetten. As with the others, it was clear that he had given the manuscript a careful reading. First, he pointed out a major inconsistency in my coverage of theory, which I quickly corrected to alleviate my embarrassment. David and I share a strong interest in and reliance on models. His suggestions along these lines were most helpful. Also, his urging me, as Ben did, to talk about future research needs in the final chapter caused me to take action.

And then there were my friends and colleagues at Teachers College, all of whom amazed me by actually reading the entire first draft. I am immensely grateful. First, Roger Myers, now emeritus, the consummate psychologist who knows how to write and is a stickler about the bad habit of making nouns into verbs, helped to considerably improve my writing of this book. Caryn Block reminded me time and again to remind the reader about points made earlier and how they related to what I was stating. She also urged me to use examples. I did. Arthur Levine, former president of Teachers College and a change leader in the world of education, brought his experience and knowledge to my manuscript. His critique and questions were invaluable. Debra Noumair was my idea person. For example, she suggested that I declare myself in the second chapter. My "points of view" section was the result of that suggestion. She also helped me to think through the ordering of things. Her creativity was much appreciated. Victoria Marsick shares with me the excitement of ideas from chaos theory and the life sciences. I followed many of her suggestions for applying these ideas. Lee Knefelkamp, a scholar of the first order, is superb at helping one to see how seemingly disparate concepts actually intertwine. Her support in my attempt to "bring things together" was most beneficial.

Tony Petrella, a friend and colleague of many years who also read the manuscript, is a true organization change practitioner. What is unique about Tony is that as a consultant and practitioner, he understands and deeply appreciates theory. His comment about my ability to "push practice through the lens of theory" was very meaningful to me.

Finally, and most important for this fourth edition, was my right arm, Lynda Hallmark. She helped me to get this manuscript onto the computer and into readable form. I was fortunate to have her help and skills with the computer and her constantly positive attitude. Also helpful in all of these matters was our academic program secretary, Ambar Urena, and assistant administrator, Lebab Fallin.

It is appropriate for me to end these acknowledgments with the requisite caveat. Even with all the help that I received, I do in the end acknowledge that the final product is solely my responsibility.

ONE

Sources for Understanding Organization Change

Introduction and Overview

Organizations change all the time, each and every day. The change that occurs in organizations is, for the most part, unplanned and gradual. Planned organization change, especially on a large scale, affecting the entire system, is unusual—not exactly an everyday occurrence. Revolutionary change—a major overhaul of the organization resulting in a modified or entirely new mission, a change in strategy, leadership, and culture—is rare indeed. Most organization change is evolutionary. These two distinctions, planned versus unplanned and revolutionary versus evolutionary, represent core themes of this book. To be unequivocal here at the outset, the emphasis is more on planned and revolutionary change.

The reason for this emphasis is the clear and present need for a greater depth of understanding of organization change. Current and future trends in the external environment in which organizations function necessitate such an understanding. Unlike the situation a few decades ago, the external environment now changes much more rapidly than organizations do. Organizations today are playing catch-up, and certainly they will do so even more in the future. Capital markets, for example (see Chapter 2), are definitely changing more rapidly than the business organizations that depend on them. Moreover, business organizations in particular do not last as long as they have in the past. Thus, we need to know much more than ever before about how to understand, lead, manage, and, in particular, change organizations. And this gives rise to the purpose of this book.

In attempting to understand organizations in greater depth, another distinction is important. Organizations are created and developed on an assumption of continuity, to continue surviving, and to last. The external environment, while continuously "out there," is *not* continuous in the same sense that organizations are. Factors and forces in an organization's external environment are discontinuous, do not fit neatly together in a pattern, are not interdependent, homeostatic, linear, or highly predictable. Forces in the external environment can cause destruction but can cause creativity as well. This continuous–discontinuous theme also runs throughout the book and is analogous to the organizational theory literature; this body of books and articles addresses mainly continuity and stabilization, not discontinuity and change. Although not exclusively, many sources for help in writing this book had to come from the nontraditional literature.

First, as noted, the organizational theory literature is about continuity and stabilization. So one must search diligently for theory about organization change. Such literature exists, although not in abundance, and much of it is cited and relied on in this book. In addition to using theoretical references, I have also relied on models of organizations that come from the organization change literature. Models are important because they help to link theory with practice. In fact, models are covered in 4 of the 16 chapters in this book.

A *second* potential source for knowledge and assistance is the trade literature, professional books written by consultants, and experienced practitioners such as Peters and Waterman (1982) with their best seller, *In Search of Excellence,* and later, *Built to Last,* by Collins and Porras (1994). These writings typically focus on organization exemplars: This is what to learn from, to model, and to follow. The authors draw conclusions from these model organizations and sometimes even derive principles about how organizations should be led and managed. Peters and Waterman had eight such principles: for example, "stick to your knitting." Collins and Porras stressed the power of culture as facilitating continuity and stabilization over time. The problem here is that by using popular, actual organization cases as the base from which to derive principles, sooner or later—and today it is much sooner rather than later—the organizations studied and showcased no longer illustrate the principles because things have changed. The model organizations have perhaps fallen on bad times, have become acquired, or worse, have filed for Chapter 11. The principles become passé, are no longer (if they ever were) relevant, and are soon forgotten. Sticking to one's knitting in this day and age may be the opposite of what to do in business. In fact, in a recent article, Peters (2001) "confesses" that a number of the conclusions in the 1982 book were guesses and opinions rather than rigorously based on data.

Another form that trade books take is for the author(s) to distill "wisdom" from many years of experience as a consultant, a teacher, an executive, or some combination of these roles. The accumulated wisdom is based on lessons learned. Such books by executives include the following: Rudolph Giuliani's (2002) *Leadership*, Jack Welch's (2001) *Jack: Straight from the Gut*, and Larry Bossidy and Ram Charan's (2002) *Execution: The Discipline of Getting Things Done.*

A highly popular book on organization change by a consultant is the one by Peter Block (1981) on flawless consulting. The book is based on the author's many years of both internal and external consulting and provides a "guide for developing the necessary skills for 'flawless' consulting" (from the dust jacket). The author provides "suggestions for further reading" of other books; otherwise, there are no references to any research or theory about organization change.

An example of this form of book, distilling wisdom, is John Kotter's (1996) *Leading Change*. Kotter, an academic, a frequent speaker at conferences, and an occasional consultant, draws on his experience in executive programs discussing with participants' cases of organization change, and he wrote many of the cases himself. From these experiences, he declares that leading change consists of an eight-stage process:

1. Establishing a sense of urgency

2. Creating the guiding coalition

3. Developing a vision and strategy

4. Communicating the change vision

5. Empowering employees for broad-based action

6. Generating short-term wins

7. Consolidating gains and producing more change

8. Anchoring new approaches in the culture

Kotter (1996) provides many examples throughout his coverage of the eight stages. His book has been popular and can still be easily found at your local bookstore. The book's popularity is due in part to (a) Kotter's status and reputation in the field, (b) his ability to distill into eight stages a mass of case examples, and (c) the face validity of the eight stages—they sound plausible and relevant.

This form of trade book, based on author experience and wisdom, can be helpful to the reader but nevertheless is problematical. Following Welch's ideas for how to bring about organization change, Block's guide for how to facilitate change as a consultant and Kotter's eight stages can be helpful, but remember that the wisdom is based on one individual's experience and knowledge. In Kotter's book, for example, there are no references and bibliography. But it is in the trade book category, after all, and such things are not necessarily expected. Without independent veri-fication and validation that what these authors recommend actually works under a variety of circumstances, however, leaves me with some concerns and skepticism. Maybe it's just my nature. And can any of us achieve what Jack Welch did, even by following his advice? I seriously doubt it.

A *third* potential source is "story" books that have a clear and usu-ally simple maxim to teach. The book tells a story, perhaps based on a metaphor or in allegorical form. A best seller in this genre is *Who Moved My Cheese?* (Johnson, 1998). A more recent one is by our friend John Kotter (2005), written with his colleague Holger Rathgeber, titled *Our Iceberg Is Melting.* He now has published works in all three of my categories—organizational scholarly literature, trade books, and story-books. Kotter and Rathgeber's *Iceberg* book is about a colony of pen-guins whose home, a large iceberg, is slowly melting and they must find a new home; in other words, they must deal with change. The dust jacket notes the following:

> Their story is one of resistance to change and heroic action, confu-sion and insight, seemingly intractable obstacles, and the most clever tactics for dealing with those obstacles. It's a story that is occurring in different forms all around us today—but the penguins handle the very real challenges a great deal better than most of us.

The book includes attractive pictures and is indeed a charming story. Such books are easy and often fun to read. The author wants us to remember the maxim, and a story is a fine way to do it. These books often sell well. Unfortunately, they tend to *over*simplify the theme(s) they are addressing. Regardless of how charming it might be, organization change is far too complex for a simple story to teach us what we ultimately need to know.

There are some books that are not as easy to categorize. They represent a combination of categories. The book summarized in Chapter 2 and in the Appendix by Foster and Kaplan (2001), *Creative Destruction,* is both a trade book and a research-based one. The premise of their book is that the external environment for corporations, especially capital markets, changes today more rapidly and is more complex than ever before. Moreover, corporations today experience what Foster and Kaplan referred to as "cultural lock-in"; they cannot change themselves rapidly enough to remain a high-performing organization—assuming they were in the first place. The authors of this book amass an impressive amount of data to support their premise.

Another example is the book by Pascale, Milleman, and Gioja (2000), *Surfing the Edge of Chaos,* cited in this text and also summarized in the Appendix. This is a trade book that incorporates theory. The authors make their case for organization change and then assert that understanding the applicability of chaos theory and theory from life sciences will greatly facilitate successful change. Much of their book is devoted to cases from corporations around the world that support their arguments.

Yet another example of blending my categories and one that has been highly popular is *The Tipping Point,* by Malcolm Gladwell (2000). This book fits the trade category but is very effectively grounded in research, particularly from the social and behavioral sciences. In other words, Gladwell did his homework. *The Tipping Point* is applicable to organization change, as we will see in Chapter 15.

The sources for this book have therefore generally come from the type of organization literature that one would assume—organizational psychology, organization and management theory, and organizational behavior—but not exclusively. The life sciences have much to teach us about change and in fact have become a recent trend in the organization literature. Even the nontrendy *Harvard Business Review* published an article by Bonabeau and Meyer (2001) on "swarm intelligence." The behavior of ants, with their flexibility, robustness, and self-organization (as the authors summarize it), can be applied to certain aspects of running a business and result in significant increases in efficiency. The primary source for this book in this domain is *The Web of Life* by Capra (1996).

Other sources are literature from chaos theory, from nonlinear complex systems theory, and from as far afield (although highly relevant) as Gladwell's (2000) book, *The Tipping Point*. For an annotated bibliography of theses and other primary sources, see the Appendix.

To set the stage for the remainder of this fourth edition, let us consider a short story of launching an organization change effort.

A Short Story of Launching Organization Change

The president of Teachers College, Columbia University, holds regular meetings throughout the academic year of her President's Advisory Group, which is composed of the senior administrators of the college and the chairs of the 10 academic departments. As the current chair of the Department of Organization and Leadership, I am one of the attendees. At a recent meeting, the vice president for finance and administration presented an overview of a plan for refurbishing a significant portion of the physical plant of the college—that is, a reconstruction of classrooms, faculty, and staff offices. The reconstruction will require approximately two years. The need is obvious. Most of the Teachers College buildings are at least a century old. The faculty and staff occupying the affected space will have to move to temporary quarters for up to two years. About halfway through the VP's presentation, he was interrupted by one of my department chair colleagues. The chair stated rather emotionally that the change plan being presented was "very dangerous." This senior faculty member and department chair then elaborated on the "dangerous" comment by pointing out that people, especially faculty members, would not only be upset but their productivity and morale would plummet. Perhaps it goes without saying that this chair's department would be among those having to move to temporary offices.

In responding, the VP did not disagree about these possible consequences of the change; rather, he focused on the need to do something about our dated facilities—for example, taking advantage of new technology as well as creative and flexible use of space for our classrooms and offices. A few minutes later, another department chair, knowing something about my background and expertise, asked me to comment on the plan for change. Not daring to give a lecture on organization change to my colleagues, I limited my remarks to two points. *First,* I stated that for the person in a change leadership role—in this case, our VP—it was important to be as clear as possible about the future and what it would take to get there but in particular not to come across as defensive, to respond to questions as factually as possible, and to be patient. I added that in my opinion the VP had not been defensive. *Second,* it was also important for the change leaders to acknowledge that in the short run there would indeed be frustration, perhaps anger, and resentment. Maybe productivity would suffer for a period of time, but with a focus on the long term and what would be gained as a result, the whole effort would be worthwhile. The shorthand version of my point was "short-term pain for long-term gain."

After the meeting, a few attendees thanked me for my comments, but the aggravated department chair left without saying a word to anyone.

In the short hour of the VP's coverage of the plans for change at the college, quite a number of principles regarding the organization change process were either explicitly addressed, like vision for the future, or at least implied such as the changing external environment. Next are brief statements of these principles, noting where they are covered in more depth in the relevant chapters that follow.

- *External environment.* As noted in Chapter 2, we typically begin an organization change effort by considering what is happening in the organization's external environment. We need to be aware of the evidence that the external environment is changing more rapidly than ever before making it tougher and tougher for organizations to change themselves rapidly enough to keep up and stay competitive. Institutions of higher education are no exception. Being tuition dependent, Teachers College must be competitive by having state-of-the-art facilities and superb faculty. Thus, the reconstruction project is a response to this ever-changing, complex environment.
- *Expressing the need.* Organizational members must see the need for change for them to be willing to embrace it. Coupled with this expressed need is a way forward, what will address the need, what might be the goals. Thus, there are two actions that are required that can be expressed as (a) creating a sense of urgency and (b) providing a vision for the future. Chapter 5 provides more depth of coverage.

- *Consequences.* Spelled out in Chapter 2 is the paradox of planned change. We plan change in a linear fashion—Step 1, Step 2, Step 3, etc.—but quickly realize that the change itself is nonlinear. There are unintended consequences that we didn't anticipate. Moreover, the change will be experienced as messy if not chaotic. In the case of Teachers College, some of the interim facilities may not be satisfactory and lead to even more frustration and anger.
- *Resistance.* While not everyone is likely to be resistant to change, some if not many will be as in the case of our department chair's warning us of dangers ahead. There are individual differences regarding resistance and all resistances are not the same. So we take resistance seriously in this text in Chapter 6, and we revisit resistance in the final chapter—Chapter 16.
- *Change leader role.* Change, certainly planned change, is not likely to occur without leadership. The change leader needs to be transparent, nondefensive, persistent yet patient. Our change leader, the VP, is off to a good start by being clear, not defensive, and patient. But there are tough times ahead. Two chapters are devoted to leadership with one focusing specifically on leading change: Chapters 13 and 14, respectively.

By implication, our short case is based on the principle of an organization's being an open system influenced by its environment and context. This kind of thinking is based on open-system theory (Chapter 4). Also, the forthcoming change at Teachers College is more evolutionary than revolutionary and should be managed accordingly (Chapter 5), and the change is more at the larger system level than at the group or individual level although all levels are involved to some degree (Chapter 6). Other chapters not mentioned here—Chapters 1, 3, 7 through 11, and 14—cover history, theory, research, and practice all in support of the main principles of organization. We have much to cover, all of which is important and exciting, of course. So, let us proceed.

TWO

Rethinking
Organization Change

Most efforts by executives, managers, and administrators to significantly change the organizations they lead do not work. By "change significantly," I mean to turn the organization in another direction, to fundamentally modify the "way we do things," to overhaul the structure—the design of the organization for decision making and accountability—and to provide organizational members with a whole new vision for the future. And in the ever-increasing world of mergers and acquisitions, 75% fail at this (Burke & Biggart, 1997; "How Mergers Go Wrong," 2000). To survive, especially for the long term, organizations must change and adapt to their environments, but typical changes consist of fine-tuning: installing a new system for sales management; initiating a program to improve the quality of products or services; or changing the structure to improve decision making without first changing organizational strategy, which is, after all, the basis for decision making.

Examples of significant and successful organization change will be presented in this book. These examples, however, are exceptional. Most organization change is not significant or successful. Organizational improvements do occur, even frequently, and do work, but large-scale, fundamental organization change that works is rare. Why is this the case?

There are many reasons. First and foremost, deep organization change, especially attempting to change the culture of an organization, is very difficult. Second, it is often hard to make a case for change, particularly when the organization appears to be doing well. Nothing is broken, so what's to fix? A paradox of organization change is that the peak of success is the time to worry and to plan for and bring about significant change.

Third, our knowledge for how to plan and implement organization change is limited. The primary purpose of this book is an attempt to rectify this limitation, at least to some extent. Let's begin with a fundamental issue.

Accepted knowledge of organization change is that we plan the change according to steps or phases. Step 1 is, perhaps, to inform organizational members about the need for change. Step 2 might be to implement an initial project that gradually expands to a larger program of change, and so on. But the actual change itself does not occur according to steps. It's another paradox.

The Paradox of Planned Organization Change

In an Associated Press release on June 1, 2001, the Federal Communications Commission head at the time, Michael Powell, referring to the shift to digital technology, was quoted as saying that "it will be messy and it will be confusing, and we will get a lot of it wrong and we'll have to start over. But that's the creative process, that's the evolutionary process" (Srinivasan, 2001, p. 6A). *Revolutionary* process might have been more accurate; in any case, Mr. Powell described the change process very realistically. I thought at the time, this man knows what he is talking about.

As stated previously, when planning organization change, the process is usually linear, that is, Step 1 or Phase 1, then Step 2, 3, and so on. And although an attempt is made in the implementation of change to follow these steps or phases, what actually occurs is anything but linear. The implementation process is messy: Things don't proceed exactly as planned; people do things their own way, not always according to the plan; some people resist or even sabotage the process; and some people who would be predicted to support or resist the plan actually behave in just the opposite way. In short, unanticipated consequences occur. Leaders of change often say something like "for every step forward we take, we seem to fall back two steps; something always needs fixing to get us back on track."

Provided the change goals are clear and change leaders are willing to stay the course, over time, the process may end up being somewhat linear, or at least a pattern may emerge. But linearity is not what anyone experiences during the implementation process itself, in the thick of things, which may feel chaotic, with people in the organization constantly asking the question "Who's in charge here?" Figure 2.1 is a simple way of trying to depict this nonlinear process yet show at the same time the possibility of an emergent pattern. But no pattern will emerge unless there is a clear change goal or goals. The end in mind (although in organization change there are milestones that are reached but probably no *end* state) is what "pulls" or establishes a pattern.

Consider the figure further: We launch the change effort with some new initiative, for example, a different way of evaluating and rewarding performance from, say, results only as the index of performance to a "balanced scorecard" (Kaplan & Norton, 1996). In planning for the change, we were counting on a number of key executives to support it, and we

Figure 2.1   Depiction of the Nonlinear Nature of Organization Change

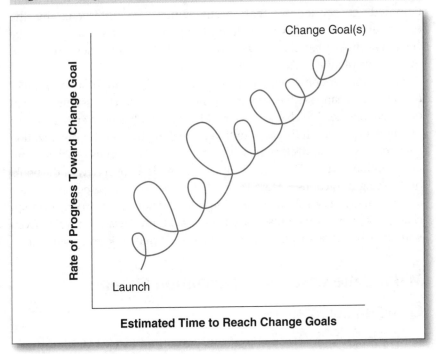

assumed that certain others would be resistant. Once the initiative was launched, to our surprise, we found that some of the executives that we were counting on for support actually resisted the change and some that we believed would be resistant turned out to be advocates. Thus, we faced a need to regroup, in a sense, and work hard on those now resisting who we had assumed would be supportive and at the same time rally around those now advocating the change who we thought were going to resist. In other words, we needed to "loop back." This occurrence, while unanticipated, does not necessarily represent a huge block or barrier to the change effort overall, and therefore the loop is not very large but requires a loop back to fix the problem nevertheless.

Note that the second loop is larger. It may have been necessary to install a new computer software program to facilitate the change to a different way of tracking and recording performance at the individual, work unit, business unit, and overall organizational levels. But what we found, let's say, was that the software package did not work satisfactorily. So, we have to loop back and fix the software problem. It represents a significant problem to fix and therefore the loop is larger. And so it goes. The managing change process as depicted in the figure is one of dealing with unanticipated consequences that occur when we intervene in the organization's normal way of doing things with a new way. Let us be clear: We must plan change yet understand that things never turn out quite as we planned. It's a paradox.

How organization change occurs, with particular emphasis on *planned* organization change, is the primary theme of this book. The assumption that organizations need to change is embedded in what has been stated so far. I will now expound on this assumption by making the case for organization change. Next, I will declare myself by explaining my points of view about organization change. These points of view provide an overview of the book, or "coming attractions." More than what is to come, these points of view also reveal my biases about what is important, if not critical, in organization change. So, here at the outset of our journey, I am declaring myself. Even with these biases on display, I hope you will continue the journey with me.

Making the Case for Organization Change

Changing Corporations

My primary source for this section is the volume by two McKinsey consultants, Foster and Kaplan, *Creative Destruction* (2001), referred to earlier in Chapter 1. In contrast to popular business books such as *In Search of Excellence* (Peters & Waterman, 1982) and *Built to Last* (Collins & Porras, 1994), Foster and Kaplan, with their data from more than 1,000 corporations in 15 industries over a 36-year period, argue that we now are clearly in the "age of discontinuity," as Drucker (1969) earlier predicted.

Consider the following points made by Foster and Kaplan (2001). The first *Forbes* top 100 companies list was formed in 1917. *Forbes* published its original list again in 1987. In 1987, 61 of the original 100 no longer existed. And of the remaining 39 companies, only 18 remained in the top 100: companies such as DuPont, General Electric (GE), Kodak, General Motors, Ford, and Procter & Gamble. These 18 companies survived but, according to Foster and Kaplan, did not perform. Long-term earnings returns by these companies for their investors from 1917 to 1987 were not exactly outstanding: 20% less than for the overall market. Today, only GE performs above the average.

Next, Foster and Kaplan (2001) refer to the Standard & Poor's (S&P) 500. Comparing the 500 in 1957 with those in 1998, only 74 remained on the list, with a mere 12 of those 74 outperforming the S&P index itself. Moreover, "if today's S&P 500 were made up of only those companies that were on the list when it was formed in 1957, the overall performance of the S&P 500 would have been about 20% less *per year* than it actually has been" (Foster & Kaplan, 2001, p. 8). As the authors then ask, how can it be that so many companies do not survive and that those that do survive, with few exceptions, perform below average?

Part of the answer rests with the pace-of-change phenomenon that Foster and Kaplan (2001) use as their opening lines. In 1917, the pace of change was indeed much slower than it is today. During that time and continuing on into the 1920s and 1930s, even with the climatic changes of the Great Depression, the turnover rate of companies in the S&P rankings averaged 1.5% a year. A new company making the list then could expect to remain for about 65 years. As Drucker (1969) pointed out, in those days, change was not a major concern. Continuity was the goal and the way of operating. Vertical integration was the name of the game—that is, owning as much of the production chain as possible, from raw materials to distribution to the customer. But in 1998, "the turnover rate in the S&P 500 was close to 10%, implying an average lifetime on the list of ten years, not sixty-five!" (Foster & Kaplan, 2001, p. 11). Times have changed, and we are living in the age of discontinuity for corporations, not continuity.

The larger answer to Foster and Kaplan's (2001) question about corporate survival and performance can be found in a corporation's external environment. Although any organization's external environment consists of many factors—customers, the general economy, changing demographics, and changing government regulations, to name a few—one of the most powerful factors or forces for business, especially those that are publicly owned, is the *capital market*. Capital markets are informal aggregations, not highly organized and structured as are corporations. Capital markets consist of buyers, sellers, and others who interact for the purpose of economic exchange. These businesspeople are loan officers in banks, investment bankers, stockbrokers, stock analysts, venture capitalists (those who often help to start companies), and anyone else who has money to invest. Although not acting in concert, these people decide whether your business, your company, and your vision for the future of your organization is worthy of investment. Is your company worth the risk of loaning you $1 million, of buying 1,000 shares of your stock, or investing money to help you with your desire to acquire another business? So, this informal aggregation of buyers and sellers forms a powerful force in the organization's environment, determining in part the long-term survival and success of a company. This world is largely a business-to-business arena, and a business can live or die from the vagaries of the marketplace. The point Foster and Kaplan make is that capital markets change far more rapidly than do corporations; are based on an assumption of discontinuity, not continuity; weed out poor performers; reward creativity and innovation; and encourage new business entries into the marketplace.

Before going too far with the concept of the power of capital markets to determine the fate of corporations, we should pause for a moment and make the most critical point of all, lest we overlook a fundamental one. In the end, it is the *consumer,* the customer out there in the organization's external environment, who determines the fate of any business. Will anyone, after all, actually buy our products and services?

By the time my son, Brian, was about 11 years old, he had amassed a huge collection of baseball cards. When I asked him why he had so many, he quickly told me that his collection was an investment. These cards, he informed me, would be worth far more money in a few years than what he'd paid for them. Ah, I thought, here is a teachable moment! So, I patiently explained that his investment would pay off if and only if someone in a few years were willing to buy these cards from him. Brian's reaction to my explanation was something like, "Dad, I don't think you really understand." Obviously, he had a huge psychological investment in those cards.

So, it is the consumer to whom the capital markets folks pay attention. Will anyone out there buy this stuff, pay for these services, and keep on doing so for the foreseeable future?

The primary point made by Foster and Kaplan (2001), then, is that capital markets outpace corporations, the rate of change is considerably different, and the basic assumptions of the two for long-term survival are opposites: discontinuity for the capital markets and continuity for corporations. For corporate survival and success, Foster and Kaplan argue that companies must abandon the assumption of continuity; corporations must understand and mitigate, as they call it,

> "Cultural lock-in," the inability to change the corporate culture even in the face of clear market threats—[this] explains why corporations find it difficult to respond to the messages of the marketplace. Cultural lock-in results from the gradual stiffening of the invisible architecture of the corporation and the ossification of its decision-making abilities, control systems, and mental models. It dampens a company's ability to innovate or to shed operations with a less-exciting future. Moreover, it signals the corporation's inexorable decline into inferior performance. (p. 16)

Changing Government Agencies

Government agencies are also having to deal with changes in their external environments. Take, for example, the National Aeronautics and Space Administration (NASA). The external environment for NASA is just as complex as a corporation's, if not more so. Every day, NASA deals with the public at large, the U.S. Congress, the president and the executive administration, contractors, vendors and consultants, the scientific community, and various watchdog organizations that constantly monitor how taxpayer dollars are spent. Daniel Goldin, the administrator of NASA for about a decade, significantly affected the organization as a change leader. His mantra of "faster, better, cheaper" permeated the agency. Goldin was quite clear about whom he and NASA served: the American public through its elected representatives, such as the president and Congress. His response to this critical part of NASA's external environment, under the banner of faster, better, cheaper, drove and continues to drive changes at this federal agency.

At the state level, a good example of significant change took place in Ohio, driven by the governor and a desire to be more efficient and customer focused for the people of the state; several separate agencies merged into a much larger one of about 4,000 state employees. The merged organization, the Ohio Department of Job and Family Services, has the responsibilities of providing for families in need, especially those on welfare and with children who require special care, and of contributing to the Ohio workforce through unemployment support, training, and development. With more federal tax dollars being delegated to the states for administration and services, these government organizations have had to deal with significant change.

Changing Higher Education Institutions and Nonprofit Organizations

Institutions of higher education no longer exist exclusively in the nonprofit sector. The University of Phoenix, for one, is a profit-making company and by all accounts is doing quite well. Even though it has a fairly sizable campus with classrooms in Phoenix, its forte is distance learning. It is more expensive than many of their competitors, but focuses on customer convenience and service. This relatively recent entrant into the world of higher education has caused a stir and has begun to call into question the long-term survival of many colleges, especially if they drag their feet on implementing technology. Moreover, with tuition increasing every year, many colleges and universities may be gradually pricing themselves out of the market. So, even in the domain of higher education, which includes some of the oldest, most traditional types of organizations in the world, the external environment is changing. Unless colleges and universities adapt, their traditions may not last, at least not for the centuries they have in the past.

With respect to the changing world for nonprofit organizations, consider the case of the A. K. Rice Institute (AKRI). This institute was founded in Washington, D.C., by a group of psychologists, psychiatrists, and related professionals who were keenly interested in the form of human relations and group dynamics training and education that had been developed by the Tavistock Institute in the United Kingdom. In the United States, the foundation took the name of A. Kenneth Rice because he was instrumental in bringing to this side of the Atlantic the methods and theory of this form of education. From 1965 until recently, AKRI has steadily grown and extended roots all across America through regional affiliates. AKRI has been both a membership organization (with dues) and an educational institute that holds national and regional conferences (learning laboratory groups) throughout the year. Qualified members of AKRI serve as staff for its educational conferences.

The primary point to be made with this example of an organization and its relation with its external environment is the distinct possibility that AKRI has not been sufficiently *in touch* with its external world. This insularity has been due in part to (a) the desire of members to work and, of course, earn money as staff for the conferences and (b) broader issues of membership per se; that is, what do we get in return for our dues, and who gets selected and why? These issues have been all-consuming. Members not selected, or not selected often enough, to staff conferences became angry and resentful. Blame was directed at the national organization, which was perceived to be overly restrictive and limited in its decision making. It is interesting that the exciting group process of the conferences—learning experientially about issues of authority, leadership, individual-group interactions, and the power of the group as a whole—became the mode members and committees used to attempt to deal with AKRI itself. In other words, the real work before the institute was often left undone because the sexier way of working was the conference learning process, as opposed to tackling tasks and accomplishing objectives on behalf of AKRI itself. Confronting AKRI, *the authority,* was more fun than dull and time-consuming committee work.

The problem, therefore, has been the dual and somewhat conflicting missions of the institute, that is, to be a membership organization and serve its members, while at the same time having an educational mission for the public at large. Membership issues often prevented effective accomplishment of the educational mission. And to be effective at the latter, AKRI's external environment needed to be monitored and responded to more directly, instead of indirectly via its members, who were often conflicted between an individual desire to earn money and a desire to give back to and serve AKRI. AKRI has recently launched a significant organization change effort to modify its bylaws and governance structure in support of one mission, the educational one, and to close down its membership structure. Among a number of other consequences, this change will force AKRI to be significantly more in touch with its external environment. And the likelihood is much greater that AKRI will indeed survive and perhaps be even more successful in the future, at least until the external environment changes again.

Summary

The sections in this chapter so far have been about changing corporations, changing government agencies, and changing higher educational institutions and nonprofit organizations, which have served as examples of the critical nature of organizations' external environment and their dependence on it for survival. These examples have also illustrated how organizations of all kinds today are having to deal with environments that are changing more rapidly than the organizations themselves. In fact, the remainder of this book could be filled with such examples alone. The ones covered are illustrative only, not comprehensive.

The primary purpose, therefore, of these sections has been to make the case for the need for a much greater depth of understanding about organization change across all major sectors of organizations. With the rate of change becoming faster and faster and the demands on organizations to adapt and change themselves becoming greater and greater, our learning curve is steep. This book, then, is an attempt to climb that curve and provide more depth of understanding. Our need is to understand organizations more thoroughly, but the greater need is to learn more about how to change them.

Another purpose in presenting these examples of changing organizations and their interactions with their external environments was to introduce, perhaps not so subtly, a particular point of view about organization change: that the process begins (and ends, for that matter) with the external environment.

The objective of the following sections is to be more explicit about points of view and to provide with these personal declarations a preview of coming attractions.

Personal Declarations and Points of View

The purposes of the final section of this chapter are (1) to provide personal points of view about organization change, especially planned organization change, and (2) to provide very briefly an overview of what is covered in each of the following chapters.

The Metaphor of Choice

As Gareth Morgan (1997) has so eloquently explained, we can understand an organization through a variety of metaphors, such as a machine, a brain, a psychic prison, or an organism. Morgan appropriately warns us about metaphors: that although they are a way of seeing, at the same time they are a way of not seeing. Metaphors can help but can also limit our perspective and ultimate understanding.

With this warning clearly in mind, the metaphor of choice for this writing effort is the organism. A major strength of this metaphor is the emphasis on the interactions between an organization and its external environment. An organization, therefore, is *not* a closed system, a fact that encourages viewing it as an open and flexible entity. A second strength, as Morgan (1997) has pointed out, is the emphasis on survival; that is, certain needs must be satisfied for the organization to survive:

> This view contrasts with the classical focus on specific organizational goals. Survival is a process, whereas goals are often targets or end points to be achieved. This reorientation gives management greater flexibility, for if survival is seen as the primary orientation, specific goals are framed by a more basic and enduring process that helps prevent them from becoming ends in themselves, a common fate in many organizations (p. 67).

One of the limitations of this metaphor is the fact that an organism is concrete; it is a fundamental of nature, with material properties that can be seen and touched. An organization, on the other hand, is socially constructed, a product of someone's ideas, vision, and beliefs. And although there may be buildings, land owned or leased, machines, and money, organizations depend on the actions of human beings for survival. It does not maintain itself through an autonomic process.

Also, this view suggests that organizations are totally dependent on their environments for survival, overlooking the fact that organizations *interact* with the external world: yes, being influenced, but influencing outwardly as well.

Another limitation of the metaphor is what Morgan (1997) calls functional unity. Organisms have highly interdependent parts, and each element supports other elements, as in the human being with a heart, lungs, glands, and so on, operating together to preserve the whole. Organizations rarely operate this way. We might argue that ideally they should, with an interdependence and harmony and all elements working for the good of the whole. Yet we know that creativity often stems from conflict and debate and that these kinds of actions by organization members may contribute more to its survival than harmony would.

The final limitation that Morgan (1997) notes is the danger that the metaphor might become an ideology: that organizations *should* be harmonious, that interdependence is always a *good* thing, or that individuals *should* get their needs met on the job.

Bearing in mind these limitations, the strengths of the organism metaphor support the points of view represented in this writing more than any other metaphor. Thus, the choice. Not becoming trapped by the metaphor is nevertheless a highly important pitfall to avoid as we proceed.

The Theories of Choice

It should come as no surprise that, with the metaphor of choice being an organism, the primary choice here is open system theory, which was, after all, derived from biology. Moreover, the point of view established in this book is that the life sciences, with their theoretical foundations, are more relevant to understanding organizations and change than are the physical sciences. Fritjof Capra's (1996) work is especially relevant, particularly his emphasis on the concepts of pattern, structure, and process. Chapter 4 is devoted to these theoretical foundations.

Types of Organization Change

Think first about evolution versus revolution, a gradual continuous process of change in contrast to a sudden event. That sudden event might precipitate massive turmoil, resistance, and planned change that could lead to eventual organization change. This contrast is actually a useful way to think about the different forms that organization change can take. The language that scholars and practitioners currently use is exemplified as follows:

Revolutionary versus Evolutionary

Discontinuous versus Continuous

Episodic versus Continuous flow

Transformational versus Transactional

Strategic versus Operational

Total system versus Local option

Stating this language in terms of one versus the other is for purposes of clarity and understanding, not to suggest that the conditions they describe are mutually exclusive. Pascale, Milleman, and Gioja (2000), for example, have stated:

> The point is: Over time (and even concurrently) organizations need evolution *and* revolution. When they have been limited exclusively to the restrictive precepts of social engineering [for example], they have been handicapped and largely unsuccessful in unleashing authentic revolutionary change. The principles of living systems offer a powerful new recourse. The trick is to clearly identify the nature of the challenge and then use the right tool for the right task. (p. 38)

Revolutionary change or transformation requires different tools and techniques for bringing about successful organization change than do methods for evolutionary or continuous change. The former requires total system events, such as (1) an initial activity that calls attention to the clear need for a dramatic modification of mission and strategy due to changes that have occurred in technology or (2) new, unforeseen forays by a significant competitor. The latter requires improvement measures in how a product is designed, how a service is delivered, or how quality is measured and upgraded. A transformation requires the immediate attention of all organizational members, whereas a continuous improvement action may require the attention of only a certain segment of the organizational population or a phased involvement of all organizational members over time. Chapter 5 provides further detail and examples of these two different forms of organization change. Chapter 7 also addresses this distinction from a theoretical and research perspective.

Levels of Organization Change

As in the case of the differences between transformational (revolutionary) and transactional (evolutionary) change, it is very important to understand the various effects of organization change across the primary levels of any social system. These primary levels are the *individual,* the *group* or work unit, and the *total system.* In many large corporations today there is an additional level—the business unit, which consists of multiple work units and teams and is a primary subsystem of the larger organization. In other words, a business unit is responsible for a significant piece of the overall corporation's business, such as a regional group—such as the southeastern United States—or a unit responsible for a primary segment of the larger market, such as a department of women's wear as part of a larger clothing and fashion business. The group level encompasses both local work units and may also include the larger business unit, which consists of local work units. In any case, the point here is that the way that organization change affects the individual differs from the way that groups are affected and from the way that the total system is affected. Furthermore, the major focus for change differs as a function of level. At the individual level, the focus of attention is on activities such as recruitment, replacement, and displacement; training and development; and coaching and counseling. At the group level, the focus is on, for example, team building and self-directed work units. At the total system level, the emphasis is on the more encompassing aspects of the organization such as mission, strategy, structure, or culture. In other words, components of the organization that will be affected sooner or later by the initial activity.

Chapter 6 is devoted to an examination of the levels of organization change, how resistance to change differs by level, and how change leaders need to deal with the resistances according to level. The process is not the same for all organizational levels.

How Organization Change Occurs

Let us assume that an organization needs to change itself significantly. With major shifts in its external environment, the organization must change its basic strategy and certain aspects of—if not most of—its mission statement, the organization's raison d'être. Change in mission and strategy means that the organization's culture must be modified if the success of the overall change effort is to be realized. Change in the culture is in *support* of the changes in mission and strategy; it is the "people" side, the emotional component of organization change, or what a seasoned organization change consultant calls "the change monster"—the human forces that either facilitate or prevent transformation (Duck, 2001). So, culture change is our focus. The point of view that I am presenting here is that you don't change culture by trying to change culture. Culture is "the way we do things around here" and concerns deeply held beliefs, attitudes, and values. Taking a direct, frontal approach to changing values is fraught with difficulty, resistance, and strong human emotion. We therefore start with behavior instead. We start with the behavior that will lead to the desired change in attitudes and values.

When talking about a desired organization change, leaders and managers often say something like, "We need to change people's mental sets." The implication is that attitude is the focus of change. As is the case with values, attempting to change an attitude, one's mental set, is difficult. So, we begin with behavior changes that, if enacted, will eventually lead to shifts in attitudes and beliefs and will subsequently affect values. Although it is absolutely necessary to be clear at the outset of a change effort about the desired values and about the modified culture that is the goal, we do not concentrate on the culture per se, but on the behaviors that will gradually influence the culture in the desired direction. Further thought about this point of view and the theory and research that support it is covered in Chapter 7.

The Content and Process of Organization Change

The *content* of organization change is one thing, and the *process* another. The distinction is important because the former, the *what*, provides the vision and overall direction for the change, and the process, the *how*, concerns implementation and adoption. Content has to do with purpose, mission, strategy, values, and what the organization is all about—or should be about. Process has to do with how the change is planned, launched, more fully implemented, and, once into implementation, sustained. The kinds of behaviors required for content differ from those required for process. Determining the *what* requires leadership in the form of taking a stand, declaring what the new world will look like, and composing the story of change that addresses issues of identity and purpose. Determining the *how* requires leadership that, for example, is participative, involves organizational members in the activities that will bring about the change, and recognizes accomplishments. So, for example, composing the story is the content, and telling the story is the process. This distinction between content and process, although useful for our understanding, is not pure. Composing the story of organization change is, after all, a process. In any case, the various ways of understanding the distinctions and overlaps is the subject matter of Chapter 8.

Organizational Models

In addition to theory about organization change, it is useful to have frameworks that help to simplify and focus: *simplify* in the sense of reducing the many parts and aspects of any organization into more manageable portions, and *focus* as a matter of determining which portions are the most important ones for our attention. A useful organizational model is one that simplifies and at the same time represents reality, a conceptual framework that makes sense to people who work in organizations and helps them to organize their realities in ways that promote understanding and action for change. Many organizational models or frameworks for understanding organizations exist in both the academic and applied worlds. The organizational models covered in Chapter 9 are highly selective. They are the ones most closely associated with organization change. For the most part, these models are steeped in open-system theory and convey an organismic perspective. They also help to integrate content and process of change.

The Organizational Model of Choice

In making a choice about a model to apply to an organization change effort, certain questions are important to consider. First, in what kind of theory is the model grounded? Organization theory in general or, say, open-system theory in particular? If the latter, then an input-through-output sequence, with a feedback loop from output to input and vice versa, is absolutely necessary. Second, does the model consist of the most relevant and key factors or components? For example, is the mission included? Third, is the model merely descriptive, or is it prescriptive? That is, for performance to be optimized or for change to be effective, are there certain components in the model that are more important or carry heavier weight than other factors? For example, is culture more important than strategy or structure, or vice versa? And finally, are there any unique features of the model?

Although the questions just posed are appropriate, they are also somewhat leading. The Burke 1–Litwin model of organizational performance and change, the model of choice for me, represents a positive response to these questions. Born from the world of practice, the model evolved and was defined from a major organization change effort in the 1980s at British Airways (BA). Theoretically, the model is grounded in the open system way of thinking. The components of the model come from original work on organizational climate by George Litwin, in the 1960s, and from experiences at BA. (On climate, see Litwin & Stringer, 1968; for BA, see Goodstein & Burke, 1991.) Also from these experiences, the model became both descriptive and prescriptive. The model is more normative than contingent on what actions should proceed what other actions in a large-scale transformation of an organization. Furthermore, the model is unique in that transformational or discontinuous change is addressed, as well as transactional or continuous change. A full description of the model is provided in Chapter 10.

Organization Change
Should Be Data-Based and Measured

With respect to planned organization change, it is imperative that the effort be based on data as much as possible to help ensure success. It is difficult to know what to do next if one does not know what the current situation is. Measures taken over time—Time 1 compared with Time 2, then with Time 3—help to (1) track progress, (2) establish priorities for next steps, and (3) determine what to celebrate when milestones are reached.

Planned Organization Change Requires Leadership

Change can emanate from any unit, function, or level within an organization. Regardless of its origin, leadership is required. There can be leaders anywhere in an organization. But if the organization change is large in scale and transformational in nature, requiring significant change in mission, strategy, and culture, then leadership must come from the top of the organization, from executives, particularly the chief executive. Chapter 13 addresses the importance of transformational leadership, and Chapter 14 concentrates on executive leadership and specifies the change leader's role for each of four sequenced activities: the prelaunch phase, the launch of the organization change, the implementation phase, and sustaining the effort. The perspective taken herein is that leadership should take the form of specified roles and behaviors rather than the form of a personality orientation. Is personality important? Yes, because leadership is far more personal than management. But charisma, for example, is not required for successful organization change. Neither should we attempt to emulate great leaders, such as Mohandas Gandhi, Margaret Thatcher, Martin Luther King Jr., Jack Welch, Ronald Reagan, Eleanor Roosevelt, or George Patton. Although lessons can be learned from the lives of these people, in the end, it is how each of us uses our *self* in its own unique formation that makes the difference. An article (Brooker, 2001) about Herb Kelleher, the fabled former CEO of Southwest Airlines, had the subtitle of "I Did It My Way." How else could he have done it? And how else could anyone else do it except his or her own way? That is what leadership is about, doing it one's own way, but for purposes of leading change according to key roles and sequenced activities.

Planned Organization Change Is Complex

Charles de Gaulle, the past president of France, once said, "I have come to the conclusion that politics are too serious to be left to the politicians." A similar statement could be made about the complexity of organization change. In other words, organization change is too complex to rely solely on the traditional literature in areas such as organization theory, organizational behavior, organization development, and strategic management. As stated in Chapter 1, sources for this book have not been exclusively the "usual suspects." The life sciences and theories related to chaos and nonlinear systems are more useful for our understanding and application. In Chapter 15, I will, for example, address Gladwell's principles and perspectives from his book, *The Tipping Point*, and apply them to organization change.

Summary

With these personal declarations and points of view, I have attempted to accomplish two objectives. First, I wanted to declare myself—to state my points of view about organization change with biases clearly presented. With these declarations, I have also shown what I consider to be the most important topics for understanding organization change in more depth. A second objective was to summarize in a few pages what the book addresses in the following 14 chapters. Now, as you will see in my closing request, I hope that I did not tip my hand too much.

A Closing Request

When you go to a movie theater, the film you came to see never begins at its designated time. What precedes it is a flood of previews and coming attractions attempting to entice you to return to the theater and see those movies as well. Some critics and pundits have been known to complain that these previews show the best parts of a forthcoming film, so that actually seeing the entire movie is not worth one's time. Whether this complaint is valid or not, the danger of having provided the previews of this book is that you, the reader, will now skip the details. But please read on. The richness of organization change is in the details.

THREE

A Brief History of Organization Change

Organization change is as old as organizations themselves. The pharaohs of ancient Egypt probably struggled with a need to change the organizations that built their pyramids. And imagine the degree of organization needed, with continual modifications, to successfully construct the Great Wall of China. What we call reengineering today was probably practiced in some form back then.

The first organization change recorded in the Old Testament (Ex. 18:13–27) dealt with what we call today a *loosely coupled system*. In fact, it was too loosely coupled, and that was the problem. Moses was the client. Having escaped from the tyranny of the Egyptian pharaoh with thousands of Israelites as his followers, Moses had to deal with a daunting number of social system issues. Thousands of his followers had direct access to him. Moses was leader, counselor, judge, and minister to all. His father-in-law, Jethro, no doubt because he was concerned for his son-in-law's mental health, suggested what amounted to a reorganization. He proposed that Moses select a few good men to be rulers of thousands. They would have direct access to him and would bring to him only the problems they could not solve. Each of these rulers, in turn, would have lieutenants who would be rulers of hundreds and would have direct access to the rulers of thousands and would bring to them only the problems they could not handle, and so on, down to the lowest, the rulers of 10 persons. This was the birth of one of the first pyramidal organizations. It is possible, of course, that this idea of organization did not originate with Jethro; before Moses's deliverance, the Hebrews had been enslaved by the Egyptians, who had a highly organized society. In any case, changing organizations is not exactly new. What is comparatively new, however, is the *study* of organization change: what systematically seems to facilitate and enhance effective change (*effective* meaning the accomplishment of *planned* change goals) and what leads to failed attempts at organization change. Note the emphasis on *planned* change. Organization change can be unplanned, of course, and more often is. This distinction will be covered in more detail later.

Jethro, along with his client, Moses, were early organization change agents. Since that earlier time, there have been many others we could cite, such as Machiavelli and his client, the prince. In keeping with the promise in the chapter title of being brief, however, a leap to the 20th century will now be made. Besides, our primary perspective and purpose is to consider the study of organization change, and it has been only recently that organization change has become an interest of scholars. What follows, then, is a tracing of the important forerunners of the modern study of organization change:

Scientific management

The Hawthorne studies

Industrial psychology

Survey feedback

Sensitivity training

Sociotechnical systems

Organization development (OD)

The managerial grid and OD

Coercion and confrontation

Management consulting

An appropriate starting point is the first decade of the 20th century and the work of Frederick Winslow Taylor, the father of scientific management.

Scientific Management

To understand and appreciate Frederick Taylor's approach to organization change, we need to consider the historical time and content of his work. The time was the late 1800s and early 1900s—his famous book, *The Principles of Scientific Management*, was first published in 1912 (Taylor, 1915). Regarding the broader context, we need to recall that (1) the Industrial Revolution was in full swing, (2) the predominant type of organization experiencing considerable growth was manufacturing, and (3) the primary disciplines providing a strong foundation for (1) and (2) were economics and engineering. It is not surprising, then, that Taylor's conception of an organization was that of a *machine*. An organization, particularly a manufacturing one, should therefore be studied in scientific terms: What is cause, and what is effect? And in terms of operating principles, the machine may be thought of as being based on the idea of a physical entity with movable and replaceable parts.

Taylor's (1980) "scientific management," as he labeled it, was based on four principles:

Data gathering: amassing "traditional" knowledge about the way work has been done in the past, through discussions with workers and observations of their work; recording the knowledge; tabulating it; and reducing it to rules, laws, and, if possible, mathematical formulas. In addition to talks with the workers themselves, Taylor used time-and-motion-study methods. These consequent rules, laws, and formulas were then applied to the workplace by management, and if applied properly, greater efficiencies were typically realized.

Worker selection and development: paying considerable attention to selecting and placing the worker in a job that was as good a match as possible of human skills and ability with the requirements of the job, in other words, the nature of the work itself. Furthermore, Taylor was a strong advocate of training and helping the worker do the best job he or she (mostly "he" during those times) was capable of performing.

Integration of the science and the trained worker: bringing together scientific management and the trained worker to "make" the worker and science come together. What Taylor meant was that one could have the best-trained workers humanly possible, but if they did not use and apply the new methods of work, the entire effort would fail. To "make" this integration, to use Taylor's word, he argued that workers needed to be treated well, taking into consideration their wishes and allowing them "to express their wants freely" (Taylor, 1980, p. 21). Moreover, he was a proponent of incentive pay. He added, however, that if a worker refused to perform the new modes of work, then moving that person out (to another job in the company or severing the worker from the company) was the proper step to take. Scientific management did not mean mollycoddling the workers, Taylor pointed out. He also stated that "nine-tenths of our trouble comes with men on the management side in making them do their new duties" (Taylor, 1980, p. 21). Obviously, Taylor believed that changing managers was far more difficult than changing workers. For scientific management to succeed, *management must assume new modes of work,* which is essentially Taylor's fourth principle.

Redivision of the work of the business: dividing the work of the company into two large parts. The job of the worker was to perform the work itself (shoveling coal, operating a machine, hauling pig iron, and so on), and the job of management was to plan and monitor the work, *not* to actually *do* the work. Managers were to act like scientists, constantly collecting and analyzing data and then planning the next segment of the company's work accordingly. Managers were also responsible for providing the requisite resources for the workers to do their jobs. Taylor stressed the importance of cooperation between workers and managers for this division of labor to succeed.

Taylor demonstrated on a number of occasions that his approach worked; it reduced costs and improved profits. Yet not all was bliss. Frequently, Taylor's scientific management process did not succeed. Executives who used Taylor's methods were too often desirous of quick gains and either only partially or entirely inappropriately applied the methods. Workers resisted methods that appeared to them to be "speedups," used for no other apparent reason than to make more money faster, at their expense.

It is not surprising that Taylor became controversial. Some supported him strongly; others vilified him. There were, during Taylor's lifetime and still to some extent today, *two* Frederick Taylors (Weisbord, 1987):

Few men ever were such powerful magnets for both admiration and revulsion. [There were] two Taylors. One a mechanistic engineer, dedicated to counting, rigid control, and the rationalization of work, an unfeeling authoritarian who turned his own neurosis into repressive methods anathema to working people. . . . The other was a humanitarian social reformer, who believed workers could produce more with less stress, achieve greater equity in their output, and cooperate with management for the good of society. This [latter] Taylor has hardly been recognized publicly since 1925. (pp. 25–26)

Taylor was probably the first industrial engineering consultant, and, as an organization change agent, he believed deeply that taking a rational, "scientific" approach would provide the best opportunity for change. He recognized that workers were "feeling animals," to use his words, and that they should be treated humanely. Data collected systematically, analyzed carefully, and applied rigorously, if not rigidly, would in the end be the primary set of methods that would achieve the greatest efficiencies and have the most powerful and lasting effect on the organization.

Taylor's impact on organizational work, especially those enterprises that rely predominantly on technology and engineering, should not be underestimated. Some would argue that he is not only the father of scientific management but also the father of the whole field of industrial engineering. Initiatives that today we call *reengineering* and *business process engineering*, for example, have evolved from Taylor. Other related activities of today include ISO 9000, six sigma, and total quality management. These days, it may not be politically correct to claim to be a devotee of Frederick Taylor, but to be involved in any of the techniques and methods just mentioned is to live in his long shadow.

The Hawthorne Studies

Whereas Taylor's work was steeped in the disciplines of economics and engineering, the Hawthorne studies, as they turned out, were significant contributors to psychology and sociology. "As they turned out" is the operative phrase here, because the studies at the outset were not unlike Taylor's, for example, investigating the effects of lighting changes on worker productivity. In the early stages of their investigation, the research team was dumbfounded by the results. The assumed cause-effect linkage between illumination and productivity did not exist. Something else was clearly going on.

Beginning in 1924 and continuing into 1933, the Western Electric Company sponsored a series of experiments for studying worker productivity and morale at its Hawthorne Works, in Chicago. The researchers, from the Harvard Business School, were led by Fritz Roethlisberger, T. N. Whitehead, Elton Mayo, and George Homans and by W. J. Dickson of Western Electric. Full discussion of these studies is presented in Roethlisberger and Dickson (1939).

The studies can be categorized according to types of experiments, types of workers studied, and time period. The four categories of experiments, listed chronologically, were as follows:

The illumination experiments

The relay assembly group experiments

The interviewing program

The bank-wiring group studies

The intent of the investigators was to determine the effect of working conditions on productivity and morale. In the illumination experiments, lighting was changed in a variety of ways for a test group consisting of women. A control group was also studied. As lighting was increased, productivity increased, but, to the surprise of the investigators, productivity continued to increase even when lighting was subsequently decreased to significantly less than it had been originally. Other variations were tried. In some cases, even when the researchers pretended to change the illumination, the women responded positively and productivity increased. Throughout these experiments, regardless of whether the workers were in the test group or the control group, production either increased or did not change significantly. The researchers concluded that if light was a factor with respect to employee output, it was only one among many. They further hypothesized that worker attitude was a significant factor.

The next series of studies, the relay assembly group experiments, were conducted with a group of six women who assembled part of the standard telephone. The variables studied were shorter working periods, incentive pay, personal health, and supervision. The conditions of the study were that (1) the women worked in a special, separate area, (2) they were continuously observed by a researcher, (3) they were consulted by the researcher-observer prior to any change, and (4) although the observer served as a supervisor of sorts, it was clear to the women workers that he was not a formal part of management. Over a period of 2½ years, in spite of many changes, productivity steadily increased to a level 30% higher than it had been before the experiments, and morale among the six women had improved steadily. Their absentee record was superior to that of the other regular workers, and there was no turnover. Also, regardless of the direction of the change the researchers made, output continued to increase over time. The conclusion was that there is no cause-and-effect relationship between working conditions and productivity. The women themselves told the researchers that the primary factors contributing to the increase in productivity were as follows:

More freedom on the job

No boss

Setting their own work pace

Smaller group (Their pay was based on their performance as a small group, as opposed to the usually larger one of 30 or more; thus, they had more control over the relationship between their performance and pay.)

The way they were treated

This series of experiments had clearly shown the researchers the importance of worker *attitude* and provided information about factors other than physical working conditions that contribute to positive worker attitude. Managers at Western Electric were impressed with these studies, particularly with what they perceived to be a considerable amount of latent energy and willing cooperation that could be tapped under the right conditions.

In an attempt to investigate attitude more thoroughly, a third set of studies was launched in 1928. This program began as a vast data-collection process using individual interviews. Some 21,000 interviews were conducted by 1930. The interviews tended to become counseling sessions, and the researchers learned a great deal about employee attitudes, particularly those relating to supervision, worker relationships, and the importance of perceived status. A major outcome of these interview studies was learning how to teach supervisors about handling employee complaints: teaching them that an employee's complaint frequently is a symptom of some underlying problem, one that exists either on the job, at home, or in the person's past.

The researchers' desire, however, was to investigate social relations on the job more extensively. Thus, the final set of studies was conducted with a bank-wiring group of 14 men. This group's job was to wire and solder banks of equipment for central connecting services. Again, the group was separated for study, and data were collected by observers. The findings of this study concerned the importance of group norms and standards and the informal organization. For example, a group norm for rate of productivity significantly influenced the level of individual performance, and informal authority from influential group members often overrode formal authority from the supervisor.

The Hawthorne studies are significant as a precursor to our understanding of organization change for the following reasons:

They demonstrated the important influence of psychological or human factors on worker productivity and morale.

They signaled the criticality of certain variables for worker satisfaction: autonomy on the job (workers being able to set their own work pace), the relative lack of a need for close supervision of people who know their jobs, the importance of receiving feedback on the direct relationship between performance and reward, and having choices and some influence over change.

They ushered in more humanistic treatment of workers on the job.

They provided evidence for later theory, such as Herzberg's motivation-hygiene notion. The hygiene portion of Herzberg's theory is that there is no direct cause-effect relationship between working conditions and productivity (Herzberg, Mausner, & Snyderman, 1959).

They provided the stimulus and data for much of what we now know about group dynamics, especially in a work context. The bank-wiring group was analyzed thoroughly by Homans, and this study, plus others in the series, resulted in his theory about work groups, his leading-edge thinking about group norms, and his now classic book, *The Human Group*. (Homans, 1950)

A quotation from Roethlisberger (1980) is a fitting conclusion for this discussion:

What all their experiments had dramatically and conclusively demonstrated was the importance of employee attitudes and sentiments.

It was clear that the responses of workers to what was happening about them were dependent on the significance these events had for them. In most work situations the meaning of a change is likely to be as important, if not more so, than the change itself. This was the great *éclaircissement*, the new illumination, that came from the research. It was an illumination quite different from what they had expected from the illumination. (p. 33)

Industrial Psychology

Industrial psychology is now called *industrial and organizational psychology*, and the expanded label reflects changes in the field. In earlier days prior to, during, and immediately after World War II, industrial psychology was largely limited to business, industrial, and military organizations. Its primary thrust was testing, along with studies of morale and efficiency. Questionnaires for selection and screening were created by the hundreds and then tested for reliability and validity. As a result of the war effort, psychological testing came into its own. Industrial psychologists were also involved in training and development, especially supervisory and management training, during and after the war.

A research project conducted at the International Harvester Company by Edwin A. Fleishman (1953) during the late 1940s and early 1950s was typical of this era of industrial psychology. It combined supervisory training and the development of a psychological test. This series of studies, conducted over a period of more than three years, was highly significant for another reason; however, it provided useful background for our current understanding of organization change.

Fleishman (1953) was interested in the study of leadership and in the consequences of supervisory training: whether supervisors' attitudes and behavior would change as a result of a 2-week training program on leadership principles and techniques. Using several questionnaires, Fleishman took measures before the training and immediately after the program. Measures were also taken from a control group of supervisors and from the bosses and subordinates of both groups, the trained and untrained supervisors. In addition to measures taken right after the training, the same tests were administered at various intervals, ranging from 2 to 39 months later.

These tests reflected two primary functions of leadership: (1) *initiation of structure*, the provision of task direction and conditions for effective performance, and (2) *consideration*, the leader's sensitivity to and consideration of subordinates' needs and feelings. Prior testing had shown that first-line supervisors at International Harvester were strong in initiation of structure but were rarely considerate of their subordinates as people. The training program focused on increasing the consideration function.

Measures taken immediately after the training showed that the supervisors who had received the training scored significantly higher on consideration in comparison with both their own previous scores and the scores of the control group. Further measures taken over time with the trained group, however, revealed a startling outcome. These supervisors not only gradually reverted to their original behavior (not being very considerate) but, in a number of cases, they ended up being *less* considerate than the control group.

On further investigation, Fleishman (1953) found that the bosses of the trained supervisors also scored high on initiation of structure and low on consideration. The few supervisors who had considerate bosses continued to score high over time on consideration. There was a direct relationship between the attitudes and the behavior of the supervisors and those of their bosses. Moreover, this relationship was stronger than the effects of training.

Schein (1972) explains the outcome of Fleishman's research directly and succinctly,

> The effects of training were immediately related to the culture, or climate, of the department from which the men came. These climates had as much of an effect on the trainee as did the training. Consequently, the training was effective, in terms of its own goals, only in those departments in which the climate from the outset supported the training goals. (p. 44)

As early as 1953, therefore, the knowledge was available that organization change was not likely to occur as a result of an individual change strategy unless the objective of the training was in the same direction as the desired overall organization change.

One final point for this section: There have been many other contributions to our understanding of organization change from industrial psychologists during World War II and the decades that followed. The Fleishman study was singled out because it illustrated a critical point about organization change: the difference between focusing on the individual and focusing on contextual variables (such as group norms and organizational culture) and systemic factors (such as structure). These broader issues of organization change will be addressed in the next and later chapters.

Survey Feedback

As the previous section noted, psychologists rely rather extensively on questionnaires for data collection and for diagnosis and assessment. Leadership questionnaires typically have been associated with a group of psychologists at Ohio State University in the 1950s. Questionnaires for organizational diagnosis, however, are more likely to be associated with the psychologists of the 1950s and 1960s at the Institute for Social Research of the University of Michigan. Rensis Likert, the first director of the institute, started by founding the Survey Research Center in 1946. Kurt Lewin founded the Research Center for Group Dynamics at the Massachusetts Institute of Technology (MIT). With his untimely death in 1947, the center moved to the University of Michigan later that year. These two centers initially constituted Likert's institute. The two main thrusts of these centers, questionnaire surveys for organization diagnosis and for group dynamics, combined to give birth to the *organizational survey feedback method*. As early as 1947, questionnaires were being used to systematically assess employee morale and attitudes in organizations.

One of the first of these studies, initiated and guided by Likert and conducted by Floyd Mann, was done with the Detroit Edison Company. From working on the problem of how best to use the survey data for organization improvement, the method we now know as survey feedback evolved. Mann (1957) was important for the development of this method. He noted that when a manager was given the survey results, any resulting improvement depended on what the manager did with the information. If the manager discussed the survey results with subordinates, particularly through group discussion, positive change typically occurred. If the manager did not share the survey results with subordinates, however, and failed to plan certain changes for improvement jointly with them, nothing happened—except, perhaps, an increase in employee frustration over the ambiguity of having answered a questionnaire and never hearing anything further.

First, the survey feedback method involves the *survey*, data collection by questionnaire to determine employees' perceptions of a variety of factors, focusing mainly on the management of the organization. Second is the *feedback*, in which results of the survey are reported back systematically in summary form to all people who answered the questionnaire. *Systematically*, in this case, means that the feedback occurs in phases, starting with the top team of the organization and flowing downward according to the formal hierarchy and within functional units or teams. Mann (1957) referred to this flowing-downward process as the "interlocking chain of conferences." The chief executive officer, the division general manager, or the bureau chief—the highest officer in the organization or subunit surveyed—and his or her immediate group of subordinates receive and discuss feedback from the survey first. Next, the subordinates and their respective groups of immediate subordinates do the same, and so forth, downward, until all members of the organization who have been surveyed (1) hear a summary of the survey and then (2) participate in a discussion of the meaning of the data and the implications. Each functional unit of the organization receives general feedback on the overall organization and specific feedback on its particular group. After a discussion of the meaning of the survey results for their particular group, the boss and his or her subordinates then jointly plan action steps for improvement. Usually, a consultant meets with each of the groups to help with data analysis, group discussion, and plans for improvement.

Later, Rensis Likert (1967) took the survey feedback approach a step further by developing his "Profile of Organizational Characteristics," a questionnaire and model consisting of six sections: leadership, motivation, communication, decisions, goals, and control. These six were surveyed within an overall framework of four organizational categories or systems. Likert labeled System 1 *autocratic*, System 2 *benevolent autocracy*, System 3 *consultative* (employees are consulted about matters, but management, in the end, makes the decisions), and System 4 *participative and consensus management*. Likert argued that System 4 was the most desirable and that most employees felt the same way. Likert thus was able to *profile* an organization according to the four system types along the six organizational dimensions mentioned above.

Thus, survey feedback, this rather orderly and systematic way of understanding an organization from the standpoint of employee perceptions and processing this understanding back into the organization so that change can occur, is a primary method of leveraging organization change. Unless applied appropriately, survey feedback will work no better than any other change mechanism. Used properly, however, survey feedback can be powerful for the following reasons:

- It is based on data.
- It involves organization members directly.
- It provides information about what to change and according to which priority.
- It focuses change on the larger system, not on individuals per se.
- In later chapters, the survey feedback method will be explored in more depth with reference to certain more current sources, such as Kraut (1996).

Sensitivity Training

From a historical viewpoint, it would be interesting to know how many events, inventions, or innovations that occurred in 1946 had lasting impact through the subsequent decades. Apparently, once the war was over, people were somehow free to pursue a variety of creative endeavors. One such innovative event occurred in the summer of 1946, in New Britain, Connecticut. Kurt Lewin, at the time a member of the faculty of MIT and director of the Research Center for Group Dynamics, was asked by the director of the Connecticut State Interracial Commission to conduct a training workshop that would help to improve community leadership in general and interracial relationships in particular. Lewin brought together a group of colleagues and students to serve as trainers (Leland Bradford, Ronald Lippitt, and Kenneth Benne) and researchers (Morton Deutsch, Murray Horwitz, Arnold Meier, and Melvin Seeman) for the workshop. The training consisted of lectures, role play, and general group discussion. In the evenings, most researchers and trainers met to evaluate the training to that point by discussing participant behavior as they had observed it during the day. A few of the participants who were far enough from their homes to stay in the dormitory rooms at the college in New Britain asked whether they could observe the evening staff discussions. The trainers and researchers were reluctant, but Lewin saw no reason to keep them away and thought that, as participants, they might learn even more.

The results were impactful and far-reaching. In the course of the staff's discussion of the behavior of one participant, who happened to be present and observing, the participant intervened and said that she disagreed with their interpretation of her behavior. She then described the event from her point of view. Lewin immediately recognized that this intrusion provided a richness to the data collection and analysis that was otherwise unavailable. The next evening, many more participants stayed to observe the staff discussions. Observation alone did not last, of course, and three-way discussions occurred among the researchers, trainers, and participants. Gradually, the staff and participants discovered that the feedback the participants were receiving about their daytime behavior was teaching them as much as or more than the daytime activities were. The participants were becoming more sensitive to how they were being perceived by others and the impact their behavior was having on others. This serendipitous and innovative mode of learning, which had its beginning that summer in Connecticut, has become what Carl Rogers (1968) labeled "perhaps the most significant social invention of the century" (p. 265).

Sensitivity training, T-groups, and *laboratory training* are all labels for the same process, consisting of small-group discussions in which the primary, almost exclusive source of information for learning is the behavior of the group members themselves. Participants receive feedback from one another on their behavior in the group, and this feedback becomes the learning source for personal insight and development. Participants also have an opportunity to learn more about group behavior and intergroup relationships.

T-groups (T is for training) are educational vehicles for change, in this case, individual change. When this form of education began to be applied in industrial settings for organization change during the late 1950s, the T-group became one of the earliest interventions in what became known as *organization development.* See, for example, the classic article "T-Groups for Organizational Effectiveness," by Chris Argyris (1964).

Sociotechnical Systems

As mentioned previously, the period immediately after World War II was a productive time for innovation and creativity. While in the United States the serendipitous birth of the T-group was occurring, across the Atlantic, in the United Kingdom, a parallel and highly significant set of social developments was under way. The United Kingdom work emanated from the Tavistock Institute, based in London. There were two action research projects at the institute in the late 1940s. One studied group relations (like the T-group but different in the role of the group trainer, called a *consultant).* The other project studied the diffusion of innovative work practices and organizational arrangements. The former emphasized individual learning about oneself and group and inter-group dynamics, and the latter emphasized organizational matters, especially organization change. Eric Trist was the leader of this latter project. He and his associates began their work at the time in the British coal industry.

The newly nationalized coal industry, then the major source of power in the United Kingdom, was not doing well. There were problems with productivity, turnover, the union, and adaptation to new technology. One exception occurred in the South Yorkshire coalfield. Trist and his colleague, Ken Bamforth, a former miner himself, went to take a look. They found that the work organization consisted of the following (Trist, 1993):

> Relatively autonomous groups interchanging roles and shifts and regulating their affairs with a minimum of supervision. Cooperation between task groups was everywhere in evidence, personal commitment obvious, absenteeism low, accidents infrequent, productivity high. . . . The men told us that in order to adapt with best advantage to the technical conditions in the new seam, they had evolved a form of work organization based on practices common in the unmechanized days when small groups, who took responsibility for the entire cycle, had worked autonomously. These practices had disappeared as the pits became progressively more mechanized in relation to the introduction of "longwall" working. This method had enlarged the scale of operations and led to aggregates of men of considerable size having their jobs broken down into one-man/one-task roles, while coordination and control were externalized in supervision, which became coercive. Now they had found a way, at a higher level of mechanization, of recovering the group cohesion and self-regulation they had lost and of advancing their power to participate in decisions concerning their work arrangements. . . . It was not true that the only way of designing work organizations must conform to Tayloristic and bureaucratic principles. (pp. 37–38)

What Trist (1993) had discovered was a new paradigm of work and, what is interesting, the coal miners had designed it themselves. Trist went on to conceptualize and further develop the new paradigm, and it became known as *sociotechnical systems*, a new field of inquiry and approach to organization change. Some of the primary principles of sociotechnical systems are as follows (Trist, 1993):

Work organizations consist of two *interdependent* systems: the technical system (equipment, machinery, chemical processes, etc.) and the social system (individual workers and groups of workers).

The *work system* is the basic unit, comprising a set of activities that make up a functioning whole, rather than single jobs and tasks.

The *work group,* rather than the individual jobholder, is central.

Regulation of the system is performed by the group itself, instead of by supervisors (completely counter to Taylor's scientific management notions).

An individual worker is *complementary* to the machine, rather than an extension of it.

There is more to the sociotechnical systems field than these principles; however, those presented are designed to provide a flavor of sociotechnical systems thinking.

Considering organization change through a sociotechnical lens means that one would gather data about both the social and technical systems but would then consider and act with the perspective that the two are *interdependent:* A change in one system will directly affect the other, and this effect must be treated as another leverage in the change process. For example, changing a piece of software in an organization's information system (the technical) will directly affect how employees who use the software interact with one another in the future.

A final point: Sociotechnical studies need to be conducted at three broad levels, from micro to macro, according to Trist (1993). All three levels are interrelated. The first is *primary work systems,* identifiable and bounded subsystems of a whole organization, such as a department or a business unit. The second is *whole organization systems,* the entire company or institution; they persist, as Trist points out, by maintaining a reasonably steady state within their environment. And the third is *macrosocial systems,* organizations within communities and industrial sectors, as well as institutions operating at a societal level, such as national government.

The sociotechnical approach insists that systems are interdependent. Moreover, this approach "has also developed in terms of open system theory [the subject of the next chapter] since it is concerned with the environment in which an organization must actively maintain a steady state" (Trist, 1993, p. 41). For more on sociotechnical thinking, especially on the design of effective organizations, see Pasmore (1988).

Organization Development

Both sensitivity training and sociotechnical systems set the stage for the emergence of organization development (OD). As the T-group method of learning and change began to proliferate in the 1950s, it gradually gravitated to organizational life. Sensitivity training began to be used as an intervention for organization change; in this application, the training was conducted inside a single organization, and members of the small T-groups were either organizational "cousins," from the same overall organization but not within the same vertical chain of the organization's hierarchy, or members of the same organizational team, so-called family groups.

As French and Bell (1995) have reported, one of the first events to improve organization effectiveness by sensitivity training took place with managers at some of the major refineries of Exxon (then known as Esso) in Louisiana and southeast Texas. Herbert Shepard, of the corporate employee relations department, and Harry Kolb, of the refineries division, used interviews followed by three-day training laboratories for all managers in an attempt to move management in a more participative direction. Outside trainers were used, many of them the major names of the National Training Laboratories at the time, such as Leland Bradford and Robert R. Blake. Paul Buchanan conducted similar activities while he was with the Naval Ordnance Test Station at China Lake, California. He later joined Shepard at Esso.

At about the same time, Douglas McGregor, of the Sloan School of Management at MIT, was conducting similar training sessions at Union Carbide. These events at Esso and Union Carbide represented the early characteristics of OD, which usually took the form of what we now call *team building* (Burck, 1965; McGregor, 1967).

Also during that period, the late 1950s, McGregor and Richard Beckhard were consulting with General Mills. They were working on what we now call a *sociotechnical systems change effort.* They helped to change some of the work structures at the various plants so that more teamwork and increased decision making took place on the shop floor; more "bottoms-up" management began to occur. They did not want to call what they were doing "bottoms-up," nor were they satisfied with "sociotechnical systems" or "organization improvement," so they eventually labeled their effort "organization development" (Beckhard, 1997). This label also became, apparently independently, the name for the work Shepard, Kolb, Blake, and others were doing at the Humble refineries of Esso.

The first sustained long-term OD efforts were conducted with TRW Systems, the aerospace division of TRW, Inc. (Davis, 1967), and with the Harwood-Weldon Manufacturing Corporation (Marrow, Bowers, & Seashore, 1967). During the early 1960s, Herbert Shepard, who had left Esso for the academic world at Case Western Reserve, consulted with TRW Systems and worked particularly with internal employee relations managers James Dunlap and Sheldon Davis. Team building was the primary intervention used in those early days. Later, as OD practitioners became more sophisticated and diversified, TRW Systems began to use a variety of methods. In fact, the external and internal consultants at TRW during the 1960s helped to invent much of the OD technology we use today—such as the organization mirror, "reflecting" back to members of a work unit how they see themselves in comparison with how others see them—and other quick techniques for team diagnosis (Fordyce & Weil, 1979).

The primary method at Harwood-Weldon started with an *action research approach* (Coch & French, 1948), conducting a study for the purpose of application and corrective action to some problem, rather than as research that serves the primary purpose of contributing to a body of literature and scholarship; it then gradually incorporated the method of survey feedback developed at the University of Michigan.

OD, then, is an approach to organization change based on applied behavioral science and is reliant on the action research approach. It is steeped in the theoretical tradition of applied social psychology, especially the work of Kurt Lewin. In other words, the methodological model for OD is action research: Data on the nature of certain problems are systematically collected (the research aspect), and then action is taken as a function of what the analyzed data indicate. The specific techniques used within this overall methodological model (few of which are unique to OD) are (1) diagnosis, interviews with both individuals and groups and perhaps the use of a questionnaire and observation, followed by analysis and organization of the data collected; (2) feedback, reporting back to those from whom the data were obtained on the collective sense of the organizational problems; (3) discussion of what these data mean and planning the steps that should be taken as a consequence;

and (4) taking those steps. In OD language, taking a step is making an *intervention* into the routine way in which the organization operates. And finally, the field of OD is imbued with a strong humanistic value system, making certain that organization members are involved in the change decisions that will directly affect them and that interventions are frequently focused on change in the organization's culture. For coverage of this field, one may refer to the Addison-Wesley series on OD; the volume in that series that provides an overview is Burke (1994). Also, a more recent book series on OD and organization change is now provided by the publishers Jossey-Bass/Pfeiffer of Wiley.

The Managerial Grid and Organization Development

What might be characterized as a special case of OD, a comparatively highly structured approach to change, both individual and organizational, is Blake and Mouton's managerial grid. First, a brief overview of their model relating to the individual manager will be presented, followed by coverage of their approach to change at the organizational level.

Building on the earlier work of Fleishman and his colleagues at Ohio State University in the 1950s (see earlier Industrial Psychology section), Blake and Mouton (1964) took the two dimensions of leadership—initiation of structure and consideration—relabeled them *production* and *people,* respectively, and specified that the typical leader or manager had different concerns about each, some being more concerned with getting the job done than about the people involved, and vice versa for others. They arranged these two concerns on a graph, using 9-point scales to represent the *degree* of concern (Burke, 1997).

The juxtaposition on a graph resulted in what they called the "managerial grid," a two-dimensional model that describes managerial style (Blake & Mouton, 1964). How these two concerns combine for a given manager determines his or her style of management. The greater the concern for production, the more autocratic the manager's style tends to be; the greater the concern with people, the more permissive the management style. Blake and Mouton argue that a manager who has a simultaneously high concern for both production and people (what they label a "9,9 style") is likely to be the most effective (p. 5).

A few years later, Blake and Mouton (1968) applied the grid model to organization change, calling their approach "grid organization development."

Based on a large, cross-sectional study, Blake and Mouton began with an organizational diagnosis that they claimed generalizes to most organizations. Their study showed that managers consider the most common barriers to organizational effectiveness to be (1) communication problems and (2) a lack of planning. Blake and Mouton contended that these two barriers were at the top of managers' lists, regardless of country, company, or characteristics of the managers reporting. They went on to argue that communication and planning as barriers to effectiveness were *symptoms* and not causes of less than optimal performance. Poor planning or the lack of planning stem from senior management's not having a strategy or having a faulty one. Communication problems come from poor supervision and management.

To address these two causes, Blake and Mouton (1968) developed a six-phase approach that addressed the organization's strategic plan and, of course, the style and approach to supervision and management.

The first phase in the grid OD approach was to train all managers in how to become a 9,9, or participative, manager. This usually required five days. Phase 2 was teamwork development, in a sense, applying what had occurred in Phase 1 with "cousin" groups to "family" units. In addition, group norms and working characteristics of the team were identified. Phase 3 was intergroup development, which characterized cooperative behavior, as opposed to competition between groups in the organization. Today, this process is often referred to as *cross-functional group work*. Phase 4 consisted of developing an ideal strategic corporate model. Phase 5 was the implementation of Phase 4, and Phase 6 was a systematic critique of the previous five phases, with a particular focus on specific barriers to change that still existed and needed to be overcome. In summary, Phases 1, 2, and 3 were designed to deal with communication problems, and the remaining phases were to address the planning barriers. In addition:

> Blake and Mouton never state it, but they apparently assume that, unless an organization learns how to communicate more effectively (practice 9,9 management) and plan more logically and systematically (build an ideal strategic model and begin to implement it), its management will never be able to deal optimally with the specifics of running a business. Phase 6 in the grid OD sequence [is designed to get to] the specifics. (Burke, 1994, p. 121)

Ten years later, Blake and Mouton (1978) claimed success for their approach, but outside their own reporting, there is scant documentation. This is not to argue that grid OD fails. Following Blake and Mouton's approach can lead to successful organization change. It is more a matter of senior management's tolerance for a lock-step approach that is based on one best way to manage, participative, which goes against the grain of many organizational managers. On this final point, it should be noted that there is considerable evidence, despite the beliefs of many senior managers, that participative management is more likely than most other approaches to lead to higher unit and organization performance. See, for example, Chapter 5 in Druckman, Singer, and Van Cott (1997).

Coercion and Confrontation

Although coercion in the form of both nonviolent and violent strategies and techniques may not at first appear to be related to organization change, these kinds of social interventions have indeed been used. Disputes between labor and management have on occasion contained violent actions as well as nonviolent protests, such as company or plant entries being blocked by union members to prevent nonstriking employees from going to work. During the late 1960s, especially at the height of protests against the Vietnam War, attempts were made by students to change their universities. Their tactics were for the most part nonviolent yet highly intrusive, such as occupying the university president's office for several weeks.

Examining these coercive and confrontational strategies and techniques will not occupy a large space in this book (see Hornstein, Bunker, Burke, Gindes, & Lewicki, 1971, for more comprehensive coverage), but certain relevant points pertinent to our study of organization change should not be ignored. Two examples may help to make the point.

Groups, such as unions, minorities, and the disabled, who feel disenfranchised by the organization that employs them and confront or attempt to coerce management for changes may be understood to some degree by considering *in-group* and *out-group* theory and research. The pioneering experiments of Muzafer Sherif (Sherif, 1966; Sherif, Harvey, White, Hood, & Sherif, 1961; Sherif & Sherif, 1953, 1969) and the work of other scholars, such as Coser (1967) and Deutsch (1969), have helped not only to clarify and provide useful conceptualization in such situations but also to generate further ideas for dealing with such conflict. For example, the idea of a superordinate goal or common enemy is proposed to focus attention more on cooperation and less on competition and confrontation. Practical applications of such ideas for organization change may be found in publications such as Blake, Shepard, and Mouton (1964); Burke (1974); and Burke and Biggart (1997).

In the arena of community organizing and change, arguably the preeminent reflective practitioner was Saul Alinsky. His book *Reveille for Radicals* (Alinsky, 1946) became a handbook for how to organize and challenge accepted authority. Many of his targets were organizations that he attempted to change through coercion and confrontation. The relevance of his work to the dominant view of organization change presented in this book is, as Peabody (1971) has pointed out, that Alinsky's model for building a community organization contains most of the same phases described by Lippitt, Watson, and Westley (1958) in their book on planned change. In other words, even though the underlying value systems and tactics differ, the overall framework for how to conceptualize the main phases of change is essentially the same. The phases of Alinsky's model were *entry, data collection, goal setting,* and *organizing,* which correspond closely to Lippitt and his colleagues' phases of planned change. To quote Peabody (1971), "The parallels are no coincidence; the study of power requires the keenest observation of social dynamics. Whether or not he read any of these behavioral scientists, Alinsky made similar observations years ago, and applied them to his own imaginative manner" (p. 524).

It can therefore be useful to understand more about change strategies and techniques that do not normally constitute chapters in books for students in psychology, sociology, organizational behavior, and management. Such learning can help either to undermine coercive techniques or to support, say, a disenfranchised group that one values.

Management Consulting

Jethro, of the Old Testament, may have been one of the earliest management consultants, if not the original one. One of the first management consultants of modern times was Frederick Taylor. From the standpoint of establishing a professional service firm devoted to management consulting, the first, at least in the United States, was James O. McKinsey. (According to Drucker [1974], the first in the United Kingdom was Lyndall F. Urwick, born in 1891.) Born in 1889, McKinsey was younger than Taylor but knew of his work and was influenced by it, especially Taylor's strong emphasis on data collection and deep analysis. He started his consulting company around 1923 in Chicago. Unlike Taylor, McKinsey was not an engineer. He was educated in law and accounting (he was a CPA) and eventually became a professor in the Graduate School of Business at the University of Chicago. McKinsey was impressed with the rigor of Taylor's approach and stressed the importance of engineering principles for helping organizations improve and change. In fact, an early name of his firm, around 1938, was James O. McKinsey and Company, Accountants and Engineers.

Whereas Taylor stressed a scientific approach, McKinsey emphasized professionalism. McKinsey and Company was, and remains in emphasis to this day, a firm of professional practice, not a business per se. McKinsey believed that three ingredients were critical to establishing a professional practice (Bower, 1979):

> Unquestioned respectability: McKinsey spent much of his early life getting himself educated and had a goal of becoming a professor of business.

> Professional exposure: He wrote books devoted particularly to accounting and budgeting and gave numerous speeches and lectures.

> Reputation: McKinsey wanted to make certain that he had a strong reputation for special competence in an area of concern to management, in his case, accounting, budget control, and business strategy and policy in general.

To say that McKinsey was successful is an understatement. The firm that bears his name today is considered to be one of the most prestigious of its kind.

The McKinsey way of consulting, as it is for most management consulting firms, is to employ a strict problem-solving process (Rasiel, 1999). First, the consultant gathers as much factual information about the client organization's problem as possible. For example, the client's presenting problem (the presenting problem may not be the real problem, as most experienced consultants know) may be a sudden drop in sales. Although this presenting problem is real, it is a symptom of something. Finding that "something" is the task. The consultant uses interviews, particularly with people from the sales force; company records that reflect, for example, sales and marketing strategies and tactics; survey data from customers; and accounting and financial information to collect as many facts as possible. Experienced management consultants believe that "facts are friendly" and that being fact-based is the same as being a credible, competent consultant.

Second, after a thorough analysis of the facts, an initial hypothesis is formulated, to be tested with the client. A third facet of this problem-solving process is to be highly structured. This means (1) limiting the recommendations for solving the problem to what can realistically be done with the client's resources, the consulting firm's resources, and amount of time required; (2) proposing a reasonable number of recommended actions (McKinsey, for example, often limits recommendations to three, no more, no less; see Rasiel, 1999); and (3) establishing milestones that can be met with targets that can be achieved, along with the verbal assurance that the client will be satisfied.

The roots of management consulting, as mentioned previously, come from Taylor. Thus, applying the scientific method of data gathering, analysis, hypothesis generation, testing the hypothesis, and action, basing remedies for the problem on these facts and the hypothesis, is the modus operandi. McKinsey and Company adopted Taylor's approach and added their own structured way of problem solving. Most management consulting firms conduct their business similarly. For more detail on the "McKinsey way," see the book by Rasiel (1999).

Today, management consulting is a huge industry and continues to grow around the globe. Moreover, major firms today include as part of their practice what has been referred to as *change management*. Even a major accounting firm such as Deloitte conduct a significant practice in change management, which they call "Organization and Strategic Change Services." Change management, then, is an attempt to integrate some of the standard aspects of management consulting (e.g., changing a client's business strategy, modifying its information technology systems, or changing the organizational design and structure) with organization change methods that are based on applied behavioral science, particularly organizational psychology.

Summary

Although the length of this chapter may not deliver the "brief" history of its title, the coverage provided is only the tip of the iceberg. A full chapter could easily be devoted to each of the 10 forerunners that were summarized. For the purpose of this book, the coverage provided should suffice. It is important to remember the following 10 points:

1. Scientific management set the stage for a systematic approach to organization change; prior to Taylor, such rigor had not existed.

2. The Hawthorne studies demonstrated the importance of the human dimension of organization change and contributed significantly to the future of applied behavioral science.

3. Industrial psychology, with the fuller integration of the individual and the organization, has provided, and continues to provide today, the research and theory required for the growth and development of our understanding of organization change.

4. Survey feedback may not be the most important tool for diagnosing and implementing organization change, but it is certainly in the top tray of our tool kit.

5. Even though controversial to this day and not used as prevalently as it was in the 1960s, sensitivity training has provided an unsurpassed mode for learning about group dynamics, interpersonal behavior, and oneself.

6. Sociotechnical systems furnished what seems today the obvious and yet overlooked critical nature of the interdependence of people and the organizational tools with which they work.

7. OD has given us a systematic approach to organization change with its emphasis on the total system, clear steps and phases of organization change, and an underlying set of humanistic values to guide the entire process.

8. Although highly structured, grid OD has stressed the importance of priorities in organization change and which primary organizational issues need to be addressed.

9. Although unconventional for what we usually think of when considering organization change, much can nevertheless be learned from coercive and confrontational techniques of trying to change an organization or institution.

10. Greater integration of the standard forms of management with those from the behavioral sciences should strengthen our understanding and effectiveness of organization change methodologies and processes.

FOUR

Theoretical Foundations of Organizations and Organization Change

To understand organization change, we must begin with some basics about organizations. This understanding will be grounded in two somewhat different but overlapping theoretical domains:

- Open-system theory, which stems from the discipline of biology, especially cell biology
- A theoretical synthesis of recent thinking on shifts from physics to the life sciences as the predominant explanatory discipline

The study of organizations offers a choice of theories. We could include theory from sociology and political science, for example, but as the preface noted, the standard literature for organization theory, based in part on sociology and related disciplines, emphasizes stability and not organization change. So, an additional choice is to rely on disciplines aligned with open-system theory, which is rooted in the life sciences.

Open-System Theory

Any human organization is best understood as an open system. An organization is open because of its dependence on and continual interaction with the environment in which it resides. Closed systems exist only in the world of nonliving matter. Even a biological cell is an open system because it depends on its environment for survival, for taking in oxygen, for example.

For survival, an organization takes in energy from its environment. Energy is broadly defined and may include money, raw materials, or the work of people. This energy is then transformed into a product or service and returned to the environment. The output may encompass the same segments of the environment or others that were used as energetic inputs. One critical element of input for a business organization is money, which may take the form of a bank loan or the sale of ownership shares. After transformation into a product that is sold in the marketplace (another aspect of the organization's environment), the income from those sales provides additional input. For a profit-making organization to survive in the long term, sales income must become the primary input. The sales income then reactivates the system. This cyclical process is input-throughput-(transformation)-output, a feedback loop that connects output to input. Thus, for example, a bank loan (input) provides money to purchase raw materials (more input) so that a product can be made (transformation) and then sold (output) to consumers, and their payments provide money for further input, reactivating the cycle.

To identify the boundaries of an organization, therefore, it is not necessary to consider its name, location, or purpose (though these may add to the definition), but rather to follow, according to Katz and Kahn (1978), "the energic and informational transactions as they relate to the cycle of activities of input, throughput, and output. Behavior not tied to these functions lies outside the system. . . . Open systems [therefore] maintain themselves through constant commerce with their environment, that is, a continuous inflow and outflow of energy through permeable boundaries" (pp. 21–22).

Although their boundaries are permeable and open, organizations are also entities with internal elements or parts that are easy to identify: physical and technological parts, such as buildings, machines, desks, and paper (typically, piles of paper!); task- or work-related elements, such as specific jobs, roles (boss, subordinate), or functions (accounting, manufacturing); and suborganizations or subsystems, such as departments, divisions, or business units. Most important, there are the people: male or female, African American or

Irish American, skilled or semiskilled, old or young, and so on. All these parts compose a whole, a total organization that represents an entity different from the simple sum of its elements and dimensions, which is a basic tenet of Gestalt psychology. General Motors is more than the sum of Chevrolet, GMAC, Saturn, and the other subsystems. Similarly, a hospital is something more than the operating room and its staff, the various units, beds, nurses, doctors, patients, and so on, put together.

To consider organization change, it is important to take a total system perspective. Although one rarely tackles the entire system at once, one works diligently to keep the total in mind as one goes about changing parts, because the change of one part will affect other parts, perhaps all parts eventually.

Characteristics of Open Systems

Using as an intellectual source the general systems theory of biologist Von Bertalanffy (1950), Katz and Kahn (1978) delineate 10 characteristics that distinguish open systems.

1. *Importation of Energy.* No human organization is self-contained or self-sufficient; thus, it must draw energy from outside to ensure survival. Take the case of a consulting firm that specializes in conducting employee opinion surveys for client organizations. The energy that the firm draws from its environment comes from various sources, such as a line of credit from a nearby bank; the purchase of raw materials to produce the firm's product and services, for example, paper, high-speed color duplicating machines and services, three-ring binders, or computer disks for online processing; revenues from previous client work; and perhaps some temporary workers to help meet peak demands.

2. *Throughput.* The employees of the firm take these raw materials and other sources from the environment and use them to develop an employee-opinion survey questionnaire, administer the survey in their client organization, collect and analyze the survey data, and prepare a report for the client.

3. *Output.* Deliver the report, work with the client organization to take appropriate action according to the survey data, and finally, collect a fee from the client organization for the services rendered.

4. Systems Are Cycles of Events. Providing an excellent survey instrument and high-quality service with the delivery of the product will help to ensure that the consulting firm will stay in business, if not result in increased business and ensure that the input-throughput-output cycle will continue. Katz and Kahn (1978) used the term *events* (after F. Allport, 1962) to explain the nature of an organization's structure and boundaries. An organization does not have a physical boundary as a human being does (skin that encloses bones, muscles, organs, and so on) to identify it as a system. An organization's building does not suffice as the identifying feature of structure and boundary, although the TransAmerica Tower in San Francisco comes to mind as an attempt to erect a structure that at least symbolizes the company. Nevertheless, events, for the most part, rather than things, provide identity. Social structures, the chain of events between and among people, establish boundaries. For our consulting organization, the identifying and boundary-setting events were contracting; purchasing; hiring a workforce; preparing the survey and providing the service associated with it; collecting monies from the client to purchase more raw materials and to pay employees; and, eventually, contracting again with the client for additional work or moving on to a new client. Such a cycle of events is what establishes and identifies an open system—for our purposes, an organization.

5. Negative Entropy. According to general systems theory (Katz & Kahn, 1978), the "entropic process is a universal law of nature in which all forms of organization move toward disorganization or death . . . [but] by importing more energy from its environment than it expends, the open system can store energy and acquire negative entropy" (p. 25).

When an organization is losing money, the managers do not typically ask, "How can we stop this terrible entropic process?" but they do understand that, unless positive action is taken, they and all their employee colleagues may be out of jobs, for the organization will cease to exist under such a condition. For a profit-making organization, storing energy consists in part of having capital and lines of credit. For a private university, it is having a healthy endowment. For the consulting firm that is in the survey business, it is, for example, having the goodwill of clients, money in the bank, good relations with other members of the firm's profession so that referrals for future business will occur, and a solid reputation for high-quality products and services.

The point is that organizations are not self-sufficient; they are unstable and will not survive or grow unless active and deliberate effort is expended. The process of interpersonal trust serves as an analogy. Trust between people is a very unstable process that must be maintained constantly. When one party to the relationship behaves at all strangely or suspiciously, the trust in the relationship is automatically in jeopardy, and deliberate action must be taken for the trusting quality to be regained and maintained. Similarly, constant effort must be expended not only for the maintenance of an organization but for its very survival.

6. Information Input, Negative Feedback, and the Coding Process. If an organization obtains feedback on how well its output is being received, it can respond to its customers or clients more effectively in the future. This is especially true when the feedback is negative; then, corrective action can be planned and taken. When customers or clients complain about the service they are receiving, the firm's leaders can take action to change some elements within the input-throughput-output and feedback set of events. It is rare for all information in an organization's environment that could be used as feedback to be tapped. Some kind of coding occurs as organizational members are selective and try to simplify all the possibilities into fundamental categories that seem to be most relevant for a given system. The consulting firm would probably pay more attention to negative feedback from clients (good clients especially) than from professional peers. Although professional peers may influence the firm's reputation by what they say in public forums, the clients, after all, provide the firm's income (i.e., input), which is more directly linked to survival.

7. Steady-State and Dynamic Homeostasis. Organizations that survive are typically considered in steady state, but this does not mean that little activity is occurring. As Katz and Kahn (1978) depict it, "A steady state is not a motionless or true equilibrium. There is a continuous flow of energy from the external environment and a continuous export of the products of the system, but the character of the system, the ratio of the energy exchanges and the relations between parts, remains the same" (p. 26).

Lewin's (1947) concept of quasi-stationary equilibrium is relevant here. An organization's *apparent* equilibrium is actually up at one moment (during one event in the cycle) and down at another, but the overall averaging of these ups and downs gives the appearance of a stationary or steady-state situation.

To counteract entropy, organizations need to grow and to control more and more of their environment—that is, expand the original system. This counteracting process implies change. In Lewin's (1958) concept of equilibrium, the average of an organization's ups and downs does not always remain at the same level. Even so, the basic character of an organization tends to remain the same. To say that J P Morgan Chase or the Bank of America is now a financial intermediary institution, for example, is to reflect the organization's movement into a broader field of services, not necessarily to state that it is getting out of the banking business.

8. Differentiation. As an organization continues to offset the entropic process and therefore grows (not always meaning expansion but sometimes creating new businesses and eliminating old ones), differentiation and elaboration occur; that is, specialization and division of labor evolve. In our consulting firm example, this could be a division of labor consisting of those who work directly with the clients and others who conduct the data processing and analyses.

9. Integration and Coordination. In the effort to maintain stability, too much differentiation can occur. A certain degree of unification and coordination is then necessary. According to Katz and Kahn (1978), integration is accomplished through shared norms and values. Organization structure, roles, and authority are the social-system vehicles that managers use to achieve integration and coordination. The current hue and cry about the "silo effect" in many corporations is an outcome of too much differentiation and inadequate integration and coordination.

10. Equifinality. According to Von Bertalanffy's (1950) principle, an organization can attain the same goal from different starting points and by a variety of paths. To increase sales, a clear and specific goal, our consulting firm in the survey business may, for example, concentrate on referrals from current and past clients rather than, say, advertising via direct mail with follow-up phone calls. Either path might achieve the goal of increased sales.

An organization's success and effectiveness in a systems sense is contingent on two processes—openness and selectivity. The organization's managers must operate according to the foregoing 10 open-system characteristics, but they should be selective in their inputs and outputs, especially with respect to the feedback they obtain from the environment.

To summarize, open-system theory begins with the cyclical process of input (importation of energy)-throughput-output, that is, transforming input into a usable product or service. The output into the external environment (a customer, for example) creates the potential for feedback, which in turn generates another form of input so that the organization can correct its throughput to improve its future output, thus helping to ensure long-term survival. So systems are composed of cycles of events. Within these cycles, it is critical that organizational managers make sure that they store more energy from the external environment than they produce as output. In theoretical terms, this is referred to as *thwarting the natural process of entropy*. In practical business language, it is ensuring that sales are greater than costs. A primary mode of fighting entropy is to obtain feedback regularly about how well the organization is performing so that corrective action can be taken and the organization can remain adaptive (i.e., have a strong capacity to fight equilibrium and change itself).

As organizations do well in offsetting the entropic processes, they tend to grow and develop, which results in greater differentiation of products and services along with the congruent need for integration and coordination. A final characteristic of organization according to open-system theory is the principle of *equifinality*, which essentially means that for any given goal, there are multiple paths that organizational members can take to achieve it. In short, it should be clear that managers of organizations need to be constantly aware that they are managing a system that has permeable boundaries, is dependent on its environment for survival, and will go out of existence unless it is actively attended to (managed).

Organization Change Is Systemic

The objective for change is systemic; that is, some aspect of the system, such as the organization's managerial structure or the reward system, is selected for change. Usually, this selection is made as a result of a previous diagnosis and in collaboration with the relevant people within the organization.

The change objective should be systemic for at least three reasons. First, when some aspect of the system is changed, other aspects eventually will be affected, thus calling for a total system approach. If the leader or change agent works in one part of the organization and does not consider this impact and plan for the consequences of his or her actions for other parts of the system, the effort is likely to fail eventually (Burke, 1980).

The second reason for an organization change effort to be systemic is based on our knowledge of how to bring about change in an organization.

One of the precursors of organization change research and theory is sensitivity training (see Chapter 3), which is educational and individually focused on the objective for change, improvement, and learning. Sensitivity training was a primary intervention for organizational change in the 1960s. As we discovered through experience and research, however, although training may lead to individual change (Bunker & Knowles, 1967; Dunnette, 1969; Rubin, 1967) and, in some cases, to small-group change (Hall & Williams, 1966, 1970), there is scant evidence that attempting to change individuals will in turn change the organization (Campbell & Dunnette, 1968). The Fleishman (1953) research of the 1950s at International Harvester, mentioned in Chapter 3, is further evidence that individual training alone does not affect the total organization for purposes of change.

The target for change, then, is the system, not the individual (Burke & Schmidt, 1971). This systemic target is often the organization's culture, especially the group and organizational norms to which members conform. This approach is based in part on the original work of Kurt Lewin. His theories and research led him to conclude the following (Lewin, 1958): "As long as group standards are unchanged, the individual will resist change more strongly the further he is expected to depart from group standards. If the group standard itself is changed, the resistance which is due to the relation between individual and group standards is eliminated" (p. 210).

Others since Lewin also have shown in their research that work performance and satisfaction are greater when workers perceive that they influence the formulation of work group norms (Bachman, Smith, & Slesinger, 1966; Bowers, 1964; Hornstein, Callahan, Fisch, & Benedict, 1968; Likert, 1961; Tannenbaum & Kahn, 1957, 1958). Recall also the Hawthorne studies described in Chapter 3. The classic study by Coch and French (1948), based on Lewinian theory, clearly demonstrated this relationship of commitment, norms, and change. Because individual and group behavior in an organization are largely determined by group norms (fundamental to the organization's culture), the changing of certain of these norms and their accompanying values that are integral to culture needs to be a major focus of an organization change effort.

The third reason an organizational change effort should be systemic relates to the open-system characteristics of importation of energy and negative entropy. For an organization to survive, energy must be taken into the organization in a variety of forms and transformed into products or services that add value to the consumer, and the entropic process must be reversed. According to Katz and Kahn (1978), "By importing more energy from its environment than it expends, the open system can store energy and acquire negative entropy" (p. 25). It is therefore highly important to pay particular attention to how human energy is used in the organization. Are employees' efforts thwarted because of excessive bureaucracy? Is energy bottled up because of an overly centralized control and authority structure? Are people's efforts dissipated because power and authority are so diffused in the organization that people work at cross-purposes?

Paying considerable attention to the use of human energy can help the organization's leaders change things (norms, rewards, or authority structure) so that this energy can be focused more appropriately toward accomplishment of the organization's goals. Thus, negative entropy is more effectively established.

Open-system theory is highly relevant and even expedient for our understanding of organization change. Although it is necessary to our understanding of organization change, it is not sufficient.

Toward a Deeper
Understanding of Organization Change

Open-system theory is but a part of a much larger set of theories that constitute a paradigmatic shift from physics—which Kurt Lewin and many others have relied on as *the* explanatory discipline for understanding reality—to the life sciences, or as Capra (1996) refers to the new paradigm, "deep ecology." To use Capra's words,

> The new paradigm may be called a holistic worldview, seeing the world as an integrated whole rather than a dissociated collection of parts. It may also be called an ecological view [in a broader sense recognizing] the fundamental interdependence of all phenomena and the fact that, as individuals and societies, we are all embedded in— and ultimately dependent on—the cyclical processes of nature. (p. 6)

This section relies on the work of Fritjof Capra, the theoretical physicist who has written extensively and clearly for us nonphysicists. His books *The Tao of Physics* (1991; first published in 1975) and *The Turning Point* (1982) are prime examples of his ability to span disciplines, to integrate them, and to help us achieve a deeper understanding of science in particular and life in general. His latest contribution, *The Web of Life* (1996), brings us closer to a comprehensive theory of life that has relevance to organizations and organization change.

To continue with the transition from physics to the life sciences and from open-system theory to broader and more comprehensive modes of thinking, it was evident that by the 1930s, as Capra (1996) points out, the basis for systems thinking had been derived by biologists, Gestalt psychologists, and ecologists:

> In all these fields the exploration of living systems—organisms, parts of organisms, and communities of organisms—had led scientists to the same new way of thinking in terms of connectedness, relationships and context. This new thinking was also supported by the revolutionary discoveries in quantum physics in the realm of atoms and subatomic particles. (p. 36)

The primary criteria for systems thinking, such as the following, are now well-known and accepted:

> Living systems are integrated wholes with properties that none of their parts have.

> Living systems nest within other systems.

> A part of a system is actually "a pattern in an inseparable web of relationships" (Capra, 1996, p. 37).

> "None of the properties of any part of this web is fundamental; they all follow from the properties of the other parts, and the overall consistency of their interrelations determines the structure of the entire web" (Capra, 1996, p. 39).

But as it turned out, systems theory was not sufficient to achieve Von Bertalanffy's goal of its becoming a mathematical discipline. Mathematical techniques for dealing with the complexities of living systems were not available until decades later. According to Capra (1996):

> Instead of a formal *systems theory* the decade of the 1980s saw the development of a series of successful *systemic models* that describe various aspects of the phenomenon of life. From those models the outlines of a coherent theory of living systems, together with the proper mathematical language, are now finally emerging. (p. 79)

What follows is a brief summary of these emerging theories and models, with an attempt to relate this more comprehensive way of thinking to organization change.

Capra's Three Criteria for Understanding Life

The three concepts that Capra (1996) uses as criteria for understanding life are *pattern, structure,* and *process,* common words that are quite complicated when applied to an explanation of life and living systems. These three criteria are totally interdependent and therefore together form what Capra calls "a new synthesis": a deeper and more comprehensive theory based on certain commonalities that exist across all living systems, from a cell to a human being. It seems useful to learn more about this way of theorizing in order to determine the feasibility of generalizing this understanding to organizations and organization change.

Pattern

The pattern of organization for a living system is "the configuration of relationships that determine the system's essential characteristics" (Capra, 1996, p. 161). This configuration further determines how a living system will be recognized: a normal cell versus a cancerous one, a rose versus a gardenia, a dog versus a cat, and so on. To understand pattern more thoroughly, Capra relies on the work of Maturana and Varela (1987) and their theory of *autopoiesis,* or self-making. Using cell biology as their foundation, Maturana and Varela point out that the key characteristic of a living system, or living "network," as Capra (1996) often calls it, is that it continually produces itself. The function of each component of a plant or human cell is to participate in the production of other components in the network so that the network continually makes itself. A primary component of any cell is its membrane, which is the cell's boundary and which maintains the flow of external matter into the cell and dissipates waste into the cell's external environment: in other words, the input-throughput-output mechanism or process of a living system. Other cell components are its nucleus—the location for DNA and the cell's production center containing RNA molecules—enzymes, proteins, oxygen, and so on.

Even though cells interact with their environments exchanging energy and matter through their membranes, the entire system is closed organizationally. According to Maturana and Varela (1987), the cell (and any larger living system) is self-organizing in that its pattern is not determined by the external environment but is established by the system itself. Thus, living systems are autonomous. They interact with their environments to survive, taking in oxygen, for example, but their internal network or pattern of component relationships is not *determined* by the environment. In particular, the environment does not change the DNA. "Autopoiesis, then, is seen as the pattern underlying the phenomenon of self-organization, or autonomy, that is so characteristic of all living systems. . . . Moreover, the continual self-making also includes the ability to form new structures and new patterns of behavior" (Capra, 1996, p. 168). It should be noted, however, that an exception to the cell's independence of its external environment and autopoiesis is that carcinogens (from the external environment) can cause cancer, an altering of the cell's patterns.

It is not too much of a stretch to point out that business corporations are at least to some extent autopoietic networks. Two business organizations may be manufacturing and selling the same kinds of products to the same set of customers or marketplaces and yet, internally, be organized very differently and have highly distinctive cultures—both of which define the unique pattern of relationships for each of the respective organizations. Volvo and Toyota illustrate this point.

In summary, autopoiesis means that living systems continually change their structures, renewing themselves while preserving their *patterns* of organization. Components of the system "continually produce and transform one another with cells breaking down and building up structures, tissues and organs replacing their cells in continuous cycles. In spite of this ongoing change, the organism maintains its overall identity, or pattern of organization" (Capra, 1996, p. 218). A fascinating tidbit of Capra's is that "our skin replaces its cells at the rate of one hundred thousand cells per minute. In fact, most of the dust in our homes consists of dead skin cells" (Capra, 1996, p. 219).

Structure

The structure of a living network is the embodiment of the system's *physical* components: their shapes, chemical compositions, size, and the like. Capra's (1996) major source here is the work of Ilya Prigogine (Prigogine & Stengers, 1984) and his theory of dissipative structures.

Whereas Maturana and Varela (1987) focused on the closed nature of living systems, Prigogine and Stengers (1984) emphasized the openness of a system's structure to input and output. Capra (1996) then pointed out that living systems are both open and closed—open structurally and closed organizationally. *Open structurally* is what is meant by autopoiesis, and *closed organizationally* means that the system's overall pattern remains the same. This seeming paradox is the simultaneous existence of change and stability, which Prigogine and Stengers (1984) refer to as "dissipative structures."

Structure for us human beings is our physical body and its components: skin, bones, muscles, and organs. How we look to ourselves and to others is the particular pattern of these components. The same pattern, "human being," can, of course, be embodied in a great many individual structures. This example, however, though perhaps explanatory, oversimplifies the theory of dissipative structures.

From their research with physical and chemical systems, heat convection, for example, Prigogine and Stengers (1984) discovered that phenomena "far from equilibrium" that produced noise, nonlinearity, and other apparently chaotic conditions, when observed more carefully, closely, and over time gradually revealed new, unique structures and patterns—that is, a new order out of chaos. This back and forth quality of order to chaos to a new order is what Prigogine and Stengers (1984) meant by dissipative structures. (Note the similarity to Lewin's ideas of change.) The structure of a living system, its physical nature, is therefore open to considerable change, but the form or pattern of its components remains the same. As Capra (1996) notes, dissipative structures are not always living systems, even though he uses the idea to understand living systems more clearly. The example that Capra provides of water flowing through a bathtub drain is an interesting image of dissipative structures: That is, water flowing through the drain forms a stable state with self-balancing feedback loops, despite the fact that the water is constantly changing.

The stimulus for structure change in a living system comes from its external environment and triggers reactions and new events within the system. Given a strong enough stimulus of new matter and energy creating consequent reactions followed by feedback loops—from input to output back to input again—one can create conditions far from equilibrium: turmoil, even chaos. For the system, a new order may eventually be reached, a new structure may form, and another phase of evolution begin, perhaps, but the change occurs dissipatively, resulting in equilibrium again, but a different form of equilibrium. The *way* the system deals with this strong stimulus from the external environment, that is, the system's pattern of components, its process of input-output, and its feedback loops, remains the same.

The two criteria of Capra's (1996) synthesis theory of living systems that have been briefly described, pattern and structure, represent different perspectives or aspects but, in reality, are inseparable and interdependent. The way a system deals with input from the external environment depends on its internal component relationships, and the nature of the structure that houses this pattern depends on its interaction with both the external and internal environments of the overall system. If a new structure forms, its form will be a function of the network, or web characteristics, of the system.

These ideas of pattern and structure from the life sciences help to explain what Foster and Kaplan (2001; see Chapter 2) mean by *culture lock-in*, or the inability to change the culture (or to do so rapidly enough) even in the face of threats to survival from the marketplace. In other words, the way the organization deals with external threats remains the same and, according to Foster and Kaplan, is ineffective. Their argument is that the organization's culture (pattern of behavior) must change.

Process

Capra defines his third criterion of a living system as "the activity involved in the continual embodiment of the system's pattern of organization" (1996, p. 161). In this brief definition, he incorporates the previous two criteria: structure (i.e., embodiment) and of course, the term itself, pattern. Remember that structure and pattern are interdependent. *Process*, then, serves as the connection or link between pattern and the reinforcer of our support for the independent structure. The next logical question is, what does Capra mean by "activity"? He then introduces the term *cognition* as meaning the process of life. Thus, the activity is cognitive, that is, a way of knowing. We psychologists cannot assume that cognition has exactly the same meaning as the way these physical scientists use the term. With this third criterion, Capra relies on the work of Gregory Bateson (1979), who introduced cognition as a concept for understanding life, and again on the theorizing of Maturana and Varela (1987).

Next, Capra (1996) introduces the term *mind*. (As we proceed, it is helpful to our understanding to consider these terms and others already used as both literal and metaphorical, that is, to go back and forth in our thinking.) And it is key to our understanding to distinguish between mind (cognition) and *brain*. Our brain is a physical thing, but our mind is not: It is a process. For us, as higher levels of living systems, the brain is the structure through which the process of cognition or mental activity operates. "The relationship between mind and brain, therefore, is one between process and structure" (Capra, 1996, p. 175). Electrical and chemical activities in the brain that form connections for thought and emotions are analogous to what is meant by *process*. But what about lower levels of life that have no brains or central nervous systems? According to Maturana and Varela (1987), the brain is not necessary for mind or cognition or mental activity to exist. The simplest organism, a bacterium, can *perceive* its environment, can perceive changes, differences between light and dark, hot and cold, higher or lower levels of some chemical, and so on. This process of knowing is much broader than thinking that involves emotion, action, and perception. With humans, of course, cognition also involves thinking, language, and other aspects of consciousness. The concept of mind, as used by these theorists, is more comprehensive than thinking, incorporating emotion, context, and so on. This way of theorizing is not unlike Gardner's (1983) earlier work on multiple intelligences encompassing *emotional intelligence*. This work by Gardner challenges the Cartesian notions of a mind-body split, which is that feelings are not separate from thought and that emotional intelligence is an integral part of overall intelligence.

Cognition, or the process of knowing, can be understood only in terms of the living system's interaction with its environment. The living system does not process information the way a computer does, but instead brings its entire being to the interaction. This interacting is what Maturana and Varela (1987) refer to as "structural coupling." With autopoiesis, or self-making, the system goes through continuous structural changes yet maintains its pattern of organization. These recurrent interactions stimulate structural changes in the living system, but the system, remember, is autonomous. According to Capra (1996):

> The environment only triggers the structural changes, it does not specify or direct them. . . . The structural changes in the system

constitute acts of cognition . . . and by specifying which perturbations from the environment trigger its changes, the system "brings
forth a world" as Maturana and Varela put it. (p. 267)

Specifying which perturbation is important means that the living system does not react to everything in its environment but rather selects.
Thus, each living system is distinct, with its own mode of environmental
interaction. Moreover, the interaction is not a linear cause and effect. The
system "*responds* with structural changes in its nonlinear, organizationally
closed, autopoietic network [which] enables the organism to continue its
autopoietic organization and thus to continue living in its environment"
(Capra, 1996, p. 269).

Building on the works of scientists and theorists such as Prigogine,
Maturana and Varela, and Bateson, Capra (1996) presents us with his
synthesis by way of the three criteria for defining and understanding
life. While it is extremely complicated, and therefore overly simplified
in the summary provided previously, we can nevertheless speculate
about the larger meaning for organizations and organization change.

Let us consider a rough approximation of how these ideas from Capra
and others are applicable. Effective organizations and, particularly, successful corporations constantly monitor their external environments, but
because these environments are so complex and rapidly changing, organizational leaders have to be selective about what they monitor. These leaders
then attempt to adapt their organizations to the changes in the environment (the marketplace, for example). Successful adaptation is a function of
how congruent the selection made is with the internal organization
change. In part, the success of the merger of SmithKline Pharmaceuticals,
of Philadelphia, and Beecham, Ltd., of London, may be attributed to the
deliberate decision on the part of the top executives to monitor and focus
predominantly on the global marketplace—not at the expense of domestic
markets but a shift of emphasis, nevertheless. Internal organization change
at the newly merged SmithKline Beecham, especially in its business strategy, structure, and corporate culture, was therefore based on this selective
external environment focus. For more detail about this successful merger,
see Bauman, Jackson, and Lawrence (1997), Burke and Trahant (2000), and
Chapter 14 in this volume.

The following and final section of this chapter is a further attempt to
apply the ideas of Capra and other scientists he cites.

Implications for Organizations and Organization Change

Capra (1996) provides a sweeping summary and then raises an intriguing question:

> All living systems are networks of smaller components and the web of life as a whole is a multilayered structure of living systems nesting within other living systems—networks within networks. Organisms are aggregates of autonomous but closely coupled cells; populations are networks of autonomous organisms belonging to a single species; and ecosystems are webs of organisms, both single celled and multicellular, belonging to many different species. . . . Common to all these living systems is that their smallest living components are always cells. . . . thus autopoietic. (pp. 209–210)

Are larger systems, organizations and human societies, autopoietic (self-making) networks?

Maturana and Varela (1987) state that our current knowledge is not sufficient to give a definitive answer. Moreover, they point out, as a consequence of language and abstract thinking, human societies are distinct from "lower levels" of organisms and ecosystems. It is interesting that they further state that ants, for example, communicate with one another with chemical exchange; humans communicate with language.

Components of organisms exist to serve the larger whole, whereas societies exist for their components, that is, individual human beings. Furthermore, the laws of nature are not the same as the laws of a society; the latter can be broken, but the former cannot. Humans can choose to interact or not; molecules cannot choose to interact—they *must*.

Even with these caveats and critically important distinctions, one can still see numerous parallels and analogies. For example, organizations and societies have boundaries (membranes); these boundaries are largely social, of course, but can be defined nevertheless. See the previous open-system section of this chapter and the work of Katz and Kahn (1978). It is clear that organization change typically is initiated by some "perturbation" in the external environment, but the organization responds in its own unique manner and, in fact, may not respond at all—often to its peril. And although the organization may respond to the disturbances in its environment with some internal changes, say, to its strategy and structure, the organization's pattern of operations among its components may remain essentially the same (e.g., organizational culture). What rarely, if ever, changes is its *pattern*, or as we will see in the next chapter, its *deep structure*.

Additional examples from Capra and others that parallel or help to explain organizations and organization change are as follows:

- Organizations interact with their external environments in a back-and-forth manner, influencing and being influenced and "bringing their whole being" to the process in much the same way as Maturana and Varela (1987) describe. Recall how Katz and Kahn (1978) state it: "Systems . . . maintain themselves through constant commerce with their environment, that is, a continuous inflow and outflow of energy through permeable boundaries" (p. 22).

- Cells take in energy, matter, and the like and dispose of waste; organizations take in energy and "dispose" of products and services and excess human resources at times.

- Although cells are autopoietic, they, like human organizations, are not self-sufficient and depend for survival on the external environment.

- A cell does not respond to all elements or disturbances in its environment; selectivity occurs. So it is with organizations.

- Cells continuously reproduce themselves; organizations continually deal with entropy and in the process produce themselves.

- A cell's pattern is not determined by the external environment (except for carcinogens, as noted earlier) but by the system itself. For an organization, the same is largely true but not entirely. Organizational members are also members of a larger society and culture and therefore bring these patterns into the organization's pattern. This statement is consistent with Capra's (1996) point about networks being nested within networks.

- Cells have differentiated components, yet these components exist to support one another in the interest of the whole. This statement corresponds with the open-system concepts of differentiation and integration defined earlier in the chapter. This weblike quality of cells is totally congruent with open-system thinking and supports the ideas underlying the Burke–Litwin model of organizational performance and change described in Chapter 10. The components of this model are designed to support the organizational whole.

Capra's (1996) third criterion, process, is the living system's mind, cognition, or mental activity. This means that living systems perceive, sort through, and select for internal use certain but not all elements from the external environment. This implies that some form of information processing occurs. Do human organizations learn? Apparently so, but what is not clear is *how* they learn. At the present time, organizational learning is a growing area of interest for scholars and practitioners.

Other examples could be suggested and parallels drawn. And although Capra's new synthesis and the associated theories are not completely and uniformly applicable to human organizations and organization change, this way of thinking nevertheless provides plenty of thought-provoking ideas to warrant our attention and consideration.

One last point: Capra's synthesis takes us a step beyond open-system theory. For example, the latter calls to our attention the interdependence between an organization and its external environment—dependent for survival yet influential on that environment by means of its output (organizational performance, products, and services). Capra's synthesis helps us to more broadly understand executive organizational actions such as an organization's selective response to perturbations in the environment, and because the organization's pattern (or culture; recall cultural lock-in from Chapter 2) is unique and employs an autopoietic (self-making) process, the response to the perturbation may be inadequate to the task of reaching a stationary or steady-state situation, not to mention inadequate for long-term survival.

FIVE

The Nature of
Organization Change

As prime minister of Great Britain, Margaret Thatcher was hardly a shrinking violet. "Change agent" would be a more apt descriptor. She worked hard to move her country from a socialist economic system to a more capitalistic one. She believed strongly in a free-market system. As part of this overall political and economic change effort, she declared that many government-supported organizations, for example, public-sector water and electric utilities, would become private enterprises. Prominent among these changing organizations was British Airways (BA). About 1983, she declared that BA would become a publicly owned company, with shares of the company being traded on both the City of London and the New York stock exchanges. For its entire prior existence, BA had been a government-supported organization, and in essence, Thatcher stated that even though it had been the nation's flagship airline, it would now have to survive on its own in a global free-market system. The British government would no longer, year in and year out, bail it out financially. BA was therefore faced with a need to change itself rather radically if it wished to remain an organization—in this case, a commercial enterprise. An example of a successful transformational organization change effort, the BA story will be summarized later in Chapter 11, which focuses on culture change.

During the late 1980s, the general manager of a chemical division within a large, global pharmaceutical-chemical company was concerned about customer service. Customer orders were often delivered late, and as might be expected, the customers were complaining. The cause of this problem was not immediately apparent to the general manager, but he quite naturally assumed that it resided somewhere in the way customer orders were handled inside his division. He hired a consultant to tackle the problem. The consultant started with the end state, that is, with the customers' receptions of their ordered products, and then traced the process back through the chemical division's sales and delivery systems. The consultant recommended some structural organizational changes that would result in a more streamlined process. The general manager made these changes in his organization, and customer service improved, as well as overall customer satisfaction.

The two cases briefly described here both illustrate organization change, but as can readily be understood, they are very different in the scope and depth of the change efforts. The first, BA, represented a *revolutionary* change, and the second, an *evolutionary* one.

It is interesting to note that Darwin's theory of evolution has been characterized for many years as a slow, incremental process of change, but more recently, scholars have challenged this view, stating that changes in living organisms actually occur in spurts, or leaps, as perturbations. In other words, a species may live for many hundreds, if not thousands, of years with no significant change, that is, in a state of equilibrium. But eventually, an entirely new species will emerge, replacing the previous one as if overnight. Natural historian Stephen Jay Gould (1977) has been a primary challenger of the idea that change is merely gradual, and he has proposed a new way of thinking and theorizing called "punctuated equilibrium": a steady state for a period of time, then a sudden (punctuated) change, followed by equilibrium again.

Important for our understanding, then, is that change occurs both incrementally and radically. This is true for individuals, groups, and organizations, as well as for even broader domains, such as fields of science and biological species. First we will consider revolutionary change, then evolutionary.

Revolutionary Change

When scholars independently derive similar, if not the same, theoretical ideas (even though different words may be used), especially if these scholars represent different disciplines, it is time to sit up and take notice. Connie Gersick (1991) took notice of how the punctuated equilibrium idea had emerged in six distinct domains to explain change as revolutionary. In her study, she found commonality of thinking in the following:

Daniel Levinson's (1978) theory of individual change: We live our lives through a relatively orderly sequence, but at times, many of us, especially around 40 years of age, dramatically change that sequence.

Gersick's (1988) group change: Groups do not develop in a linear set of stages; rather, they proceed with not much happening and then recognize (almost suddenly) a need to move forward rapidly in a new way.

Organization change (e.g., Tushman & Romanelli, 1985): Organizations do not evolve but are more likely to change in strategic reorientations that demand significantly different patterns of operations.

Scientific fields (Kuhn, 1970): Truth is probably not discovered through the accumulation of individual findings, but more likely in paradigmatic shifts, that is, breaks in the prevailing mode of thinking.

Biological species (Gould, 1980): Change occurs after long periods of equilibrium and then in "rapid and episodic events of speciation" (p. 184).

Grand theory (Prigogine & Stengers, 1984): Systems vacillate between some kind of transition and the status quo, or equilibrium. At times of transition, that is, punctuated equilibriums, there is no end state that is a given, because during times of transition, system parts interact unpredictably. The change, therefore, becomes revolutionary.

The commonality of thinking across these six theories is in three domains, according to Gersick (1991).

1. Deep Structure. Gersick's (1991) definition is as follows:

> A network of fundamental, interdependent choices about the basic configuration into which a system's units are organized and the activities that maintain both this configuration and the system's resource exchange with the environment. Deep structure in human systems is largely implicit. (p. 15)

For individuals, it is the underlying pattern of a person's life at a given time (D. Levinson, 1986). For groups, it is the structure and process a group chooses to accomplish its task (Gersick, 1988). For organizations, it is the underlying culture—the structure itself, that is, organizational design for decision making, accountability, control, and distribution of power, and the *way* the organization monitors, reacts to, and, in general, relates to its external environment (Tushman & Romanelli, 1985). For scientific fields, it is the paradigm, that is, the pattern and set of standards for how a discipline develops and is maintained or sustained over time through scientific achievements (Kuhn, 1970). Change in scientific fields occurs through a break from the pattern, a paradigmatic shift. For biological species, it is a network of circular and interdependent interactions with feedback loops; thus, no single unit or part can interact with the environment independently (Gould, 1977, 1980; Wake, Roth, & Wake, 1983). This network of interacting parts helps to create resistance to change. A perturbation, then, brings about change; change will not occur as a result of life as usual within the species, that is, it will not occur in a linear, evolutionary manner. And, finally, for grand theory, collective modes and parameters determine order for the overall system (Haken, 1981).

2. *Equilibrium Periods.* Gersick's (1991) analogy is helpful here: "If deep structure may be thought of as the design of the playing field and the rules of the game, then equilibrium periods might be compared loosely to a game in play" (p. 16). Specifics of play vary, but the structure and rules remain fixed. The equilibrium period consists of (1) maintenance of the system and (2) choosing of activities, "calling the plays," but within an overall pattern of rules, standards, mores, and circular processes. Because part and parcel of equilibrium periods is inertia, one can begin to understand why it is so difficult for systems to change. O'Toole (1995), for example, lists 33 hypotheses for why organizations are resistant to change, for example, *homeostasis*—"Continual change is not a natural condition of life; hence resistance . . . is a healthy human instinct" (p. 161)—and the *rectitude of the powerful*—"The best and the brightest have set us on the current course. Who are we to question the wisdom of our leaders?" (p. 164).

Gersick (1991), after reviewing this literature, narrowed the resistance list to three albeit quite powerful barriers to change: (1) cognition, (2) motivation, and (3) obligation. These three are variations of the same phenomenon: resistance. Cognitive frameworks shape our awareness and thinking, how we interpret reality, and how we consider choices for action. In other words, cognitive frameworks, models of reality, and so forth, are useful for understanding reality; yet at the same time, they limit our awareness of other ways to look at reality.

With respect to motivation, change is accompanied by loss of some kind and by uncertainty. Resistance to loss and uncertainty are easy to understand; that is, one is motivated to reduce the loss and uncertainty. Regarding obligation, Gersick (1991) cites D. Levinson, Tushman and Romanelli, and Kuhn by pointing out "the inertial constraints of obligations among stakeholders inside and outside a system" (p. 18). Stakeholders hold expectations of and assumptions about how the system is supposed to operate. When this equilibrium is disturbed, they put pressure on the system to "get back into line."

3. *Revolutionary Periods.* As Gersick (1991) clarifies:

> Incremental changes in a system's parts [will] not alter the whole. As long as the deep structure is intact, it generates a strong inertia, first to prevent the system from generating alternatives outside its own boundaries, then to pull any deviations that do occur back into line. (p. 19)

So, how do revolutions occur? By (a) internal disruptions that pull subsystems and activities out of alignment with each other or the environment, for example, intrusion of a "foreign body" from an acquisition or merger and (b) changes in the system's environment that threaten its ability to obtain resources, for example, creation of new technology or severe consolidation of an industry via huge mergers. It is important to note that these internal changes or external ones do not in and of themselves bring about revolution. They simply create the need for change.

Revolutionary change, by definition, can be seen as a jolt (perturbation) to the system. As a result, nothing will ever be the same again. Organizations that change their missions exemplify revolutionary change—as in the BA case of focusing on the marketplace, after years of insularity and focusing on the most negative aspects of bureaucracy. Although the overall mission for BA remained transportation, the specifics changed significantly, for example, new goals of customer satisfaction and profitability, neither of which had ever been emphasized before. The change of mission affects all other primary dimensions of an organization: leadership, strategy, structure, culture, and systems. In Gersick's (1991) language, the *deep structure* has been affected significantly.

It should be reiterated that the fundamental mission of an organization is to survive. Most of the time, organizations survive by continuously fixing problems and trying to improve the way things are done. Sometimes, however, survival depends on an entirely new raison d'être with completely different products or services or both. The BA case is such an example and will be described in more detail later in Chapter 11. The Dime Bancorp case, a merger, will be used as the revolutionary change example for this chapter.

Evolutionary Change

No doubt, more than 95% of organizational changes are evolutionary. As noted previously, the resistances to revolutionary change are indeed strong. The second case vignette, at the beginning of this chapter (improvement in customer service at the pharmaceutical-chemical company), is illustrative of evolutionary change. Most organizational change consists of improvements, incremental steps to fix a problem or change a part of the larger system. Most organizational change in Japan, for example, is referred to as *kaizen*, meaning continual improvement: changing the way a product is packaged before shipment to the customer, instituting a new form of commission on sales for how salespeople will be compensated, developing a new set of products or services for an emerging market on the basis of demographic shifts, acquiring a smaller company to augment current business lines, and installing a new leadership development program for the top 300 executives in the organization, to name only a few examples. These examples illustrate evolutionary changes. Any one of these examples, however, could be part of a larger change effort that might be revolutionary. But if any one of these partial changes does not affect the whole and the deep structure of the organization is not fundamentally modified, then the change is evolutionary.

In an attempt to further clarify the meaning of evolutionary change in organizations, let us consider the writings of Orlikowski (1996) and Weick and Quinn (1999). In place of *evolutionary*, these scholars refer to *continuous change*. The meaning is the same, nevertheless. For Weick and Quinn, continuous change means "the idea that small continuous adjustments created simultaneously across units, can cumulate and create substantial change. That scenario presumes tightly coupled interdependencies" (p. 375).

The "looser" these interdependencies, the less likely that overall organization change will occur. The change is more likely to remain primarily within subunits of the organizations—although not necessarily exclusively. Ultimate organization change could occur if consistent with managers' abilities and desires to diffuse innovation from one unit to other units.

Orlikowski (1996), as cited in Weick and Quinn (1999), has also helped with definition and clarification. She had noted the following:

> Each variation of a given form is not an abrupt or discrete event, neither is it, by itself discontinuous. Rather, through a series of ongoing and situated accommodations, adaptations, and alterations (that draw on previous variations and mediate future ones), sufficient modifications may be enacted over time that fundamental changes are achieved. There is no deliberate orchestration of change here, no technological inevitability, no dramatic discontinuity, just recurrent and reciprocal variations in practice over time. Each shift in practice creates the conditions for further breakdowns, unanticipated outcomes, and innovations, which in turn are met with more variations. Such variations are ongoing; there is no beginning or end point in this change process. (p. 66)

I would question Orlikowski's assumption that "sufficient modifications may be enacted over time that fundamental changes are achieved." Although possible, it is unlikely. Overcoming inertia and equilibrium, as Pascale, Milleman, and Gioja (2000) emphasized, is difficult, if not impossible, without a discontinuous jolt to the system. Organization change does occur with continuous attention and effort, but it is unlikely that fundamental change in the deep structure (Gersick, 1991) of the organization would happen.

Another example of continuous change is the relatively new field of organizational learning (Argyris & Schön, 1978). Watkins and Marsick (1993) define organization learning as in the following.

Advocates may differ about specific details, but in general, they agree that the learning organization

1. Is not just a collection of individuals who are learning—instead, learning also occurs simultaneously at various collective levels within business units and sometimes within an entire company

2. Demonstrates organizational capacity for change

3. Accelerates individual learning capacity but also redefines organizational structure, culture, job design, and mental models (assumptions about the way things are; Senge, 1990)

4. Involves widespread participation of employees and often customers in decision making, dialogue, and information sharing

5. Promotes systemic thinking and building of organizational memory

Further examples of summaries of organization learning include Easterby-Smith (1997), Huber (1991), Lundberg (1989), D. Miller (1996), and Mirvis (1996).

In concluding this section, it should be noted, of course, that not all organizational changes lead to improvement, just as revolutionary change is not always good and does not always produce a significantly better organization. The following two cases do represent successful change, the first revolutionary, the second evolutionary.

Revolutionary Change: Case Example

This chapter began with a brief illustration of radical change, albeit over time. BA in the 1980s experienced significant organization change, a fundamental modification of its deep structure. The case to follow, Dime Bancorp, is another example of change in the organization's deep structure. The "jolt" to the system was a merger of two savings banks.

Dime Bancorp, Inc.

Dime Bancorp was the holding company for the Dime Savings Bank of New York, a regional financial enterprise serving customers and businesses through 120 branches or more, primarily in the greater New York City metropolitan area. Due to an acquisition in 1997, Dime also provided financial services and mortgage banking via more than 260 offices throughout the United States. The Dime case to be described was the result of a merger between the Dime Savings Bank and Anchor Savings Bank in January 1995. Our case begins with this merger. First, a little history.

Background

Dime was founded in 1859 as the Dime Savings Bank of Brooklyn. With a minimum deposit of a dime, the founder, William Edwards, encouraged all New Yorkers, even the most humble, to save. In 1862, the Dime was the first bank to offer banking by mail, permitting depositors fighting in the Civil War to send money to their families in the North.

It is interesting that Anchor was founded at about the same time, also in Brooklyn. Anchor also encouraged savings and focused on the local community as its primary market. Over the years, both Anchor and Dime grew by way of mergers and acquisitions that led to regional expansion and a broader range of services to individual customers and businesses.

With the merger of Dime and Anchor, a "merger of equals" as the deal was called in January 1995, it seemed at the time that with such similar histories and resemblances in size, revenues, customer base, and so on, one might assume that the two organizational cultures would be alike. In fact, the opposite was true: The two cultures were highly *dissimilar!* This conundrum was in part explained, however, by the idea of *attractors,* referred to later in the brief coverage of nonlinear complex system theory in Chapter 7. Attractors are patterns of behavior with the dual characteristics of "sensitivity to initial conditions" and "stability." The former characteristic suggests that the early history and founding of an organization is highly significant; that is, initial behaviors in the organization's start-up phase that receive positive feedback become reinforced and stabilize quickly. These initial behaviors are quite specific, if not unique, to the situation at the time, therefore they are distinct in nature, are likely to be undetectable at the time, and become entrenched over time as a consequence of consistent reinforcement. These small, undetectable behaviors loom large later and account for highly differentiated cultures, even though on the surface, judging on more macro similarities, one would assume likeness, not dissimilarity. Apparently, early in the development and growth of the Anchor Bank, attention to detail was rewarded. Their culture some 150 years later reflected this emphasis. Dime, on the other hand, was more concerned with the bigger picture and becoming a presence in the greater New York City area. This difference between the two banks, though perhaps minor over a century ago, was highly significant at the time of the merger.

The respective CEOs of Dime and Anchor were quite aware of the differences in culture and therefore sought consultative help with the merger. The merger occurred because the two CEOs and their respective boards of directors realized that their pieces of the financial services pie were shrinking and that proceeding alone, as in the past, was probably not wise to ensure a successful future for their businesses and for their stakeholders. Commercial banks were dominant (and still are), whereas savings banks were fighting hard for new business. Thus, an intent of the merger was to become less savings and more commercial.

Once the merger became official and the two companies were one enterprise, three major initiatives were undertaken. First, a strategic planning process was launched to better understand how the resources of the two former companies could now be deployed to gain market share rather than losing share, which had been true for each of the two prior to the merger. Second, an organizationwide opinion survey was conducted (1) to determine the state of morale, (2) to assess employee understanding of the company's strategy, its new culture, leadership, organizational structure, and so on, and (3) to establish an internal benchmark for future survey comparisons and to track trends and progress. The third early initiative was to draft a new mission statement for the merged organization. Each of the two companies had a mission statement, but these were discarded, and a task force consisting of 15 employees who represented the two merged banks and composed a cross-section of the organization was formed to draft the new mission statement. This task force tapped another 100 or so employees to get opinions and suggestions about what the mission content should be. After many drafts, they presented their statement to the top executive team and got further feedback and suggestions. The final version was then presented to the board of directors and was unanimously approved. This third initiative highly involved of many people in the organization and consequently led to strong commitment to the new mission statement. Moreover, when the task force presented their final draft of the mission statement, they were given a standing ovation by the board.

Organizational Survey

The initial organizational survey, designed according to the Burke–Litwin model (see Chapter 10), revealed that most employees at all levels were positive about the merger, supported leaders at the very top of the organization, believed in the mission statement, and understood the overall business strategy, but they were not very clear about the newly merged organizational culture and structure and were critical in general of several system elements (such as information systems and compensation) and of leadership and management. As a consequence of these survey outcomes, a number of actions were taken. Changes were made to strengthen the information system (new management, updated software, etc.), the reward system was improved, some of the organization's structure was changed, and a major initiative was launched to improve leadership and management, starting with the top 125 executives and managers.

The CEO was highly supportive of these change efforts deriving from the survey and served as a role model for leadership and change. Working closely with an external consultant who had been involved from the beginning, the CEO and the head of human resources authorized, planned, and implemented a major effort to clarify the organization's culture and to develop and train managers in both leadership and management skills. Using the mission statement as a primary source, five values were extracted that seemed to represent the desired culture. In other words, corporate values were implicit within the mission statement. These values were then tested throughout the organization and eventually, a sixth one was added. The six values served as content guides for determining a set of practices that were behavioral manifestations of these values. These 36 practices, 6 per value, were then used in a questionnaire for the purpose of providing feedback for the top 125 people in the company. A 2½-day leadership program was conducted for these top managers, and this feedback was the central element. Before the program, each participant rated themselves on the 36 practices and simultaneously were rated by their respective bosses, peers, and subordinates. Other questionnaires were used as prework as well. During the program, all participants received this multirater feedback and could compare how they viewed themselves with how the other three rating sources perceived them on the same set of behavioral practices, the primary content of which was leadership. Six months later, these 125 top people participated in another 2½-day program, but this time the focus was on performance and project management. Multirater feedback was integral to this second program as well, coupled with a "Time 2" assessment of the earlier 36 leadership practices to see how these top managers were doing. The 125 also received intensive coaching on the feedback they received.

At about the same time that the leadership development program was launched, a second organizationwide survey was conducted using approximately 90% of the questions asked at Time 1, so that comparisons could be made and trends determined. The ratings via a 5-point Likert-type scale showed that out of 125 questions asked at both Time 1 and Time 2 (about 2 years later), except for two items, which remained about the same, all ratings were higher at Time 2. Significant improvements had been made over the 2-year period, at least in the eyes of the employees (see Figure 5.1).

Figure 5.1   1996/1998 Burke–Litwin Model Summary Scores for Dime

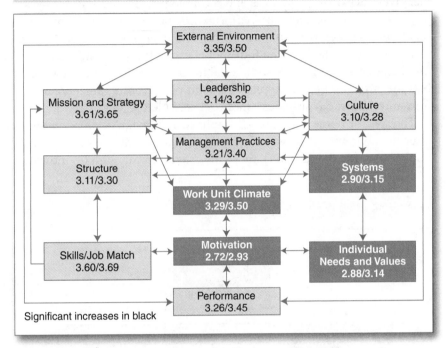

Combining data from the second survey and these multirater norms in summary form—that is, no individual was identified—trends and further problem areas could be discerned. For example, it became clear from these data that further work had to be done with helping managers do a better job in coaching and developing their subordinates. A further next step in this organizational change effort was to cascade down to the next levels of management in the 2½-day programs on leadership and management.

As can be seen from Figure 5.1, the survey items of both Time 1 and Time 2 and the results reported to the managers and employees of the bank were organized according to the Burke–Litwin model. Further statistical analyses within the framework of the model were conducted. For example, a regression analysis performed using the Time 2 results (1998) appeared to be associated with the respondents' perceptions of organization performance. To be clear, the performance category was assessed by survey questions such as "To what extent does the bank provide high quality customer service?" and "To what extent is the bank currently achieving the highest level of employee performance of which it is capable, given its existing resources and technology?" So, their responses are *perceptions* of organizational performance, not performance measurements per se. Referring to Figure 5.2, it can be seen that employees' responses to questions in the four model categories of business environment, mission and strategy, individual needs and values, and motivation had the strongest statistical relations with perceived organizational performance. Figure 5.3 provides a more detailed picture.

The specific items in Figure 5.3 that have a plus sign (+) in parentheses after the abbreviated survey statement indicate an above-average score on the survey (3.5 or greater); those that have a minus sign (−) indicate a

Figure 5.2   1998 Predictive Model for Dime

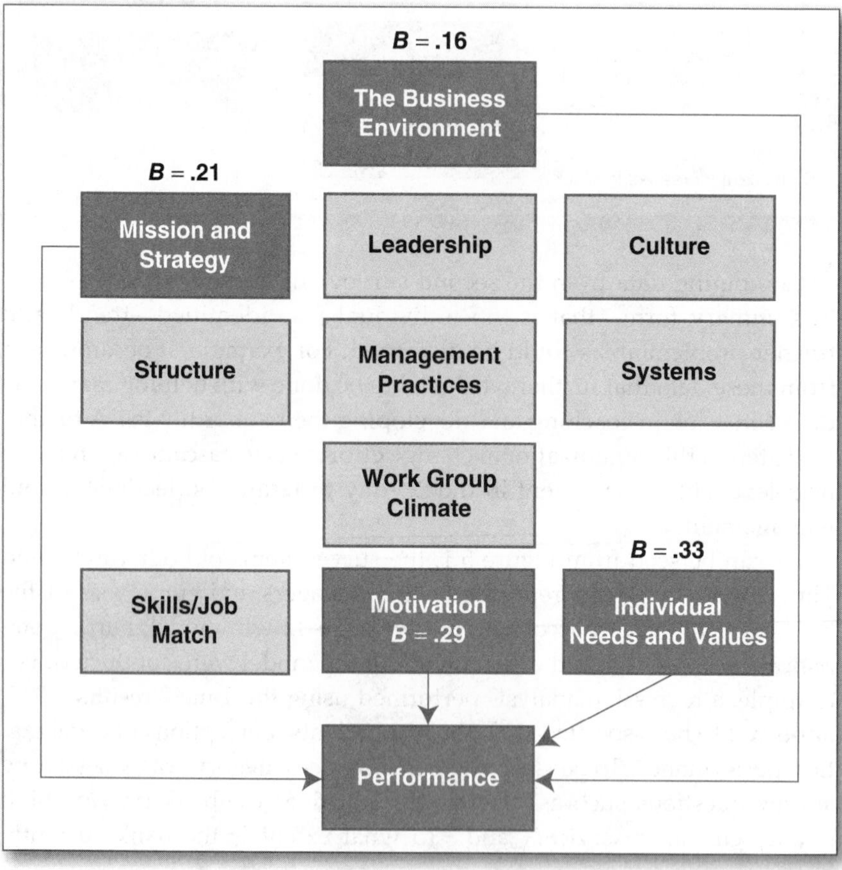

Figure 5.3   Detailed Scores, 1998 Predictive Model for Dime

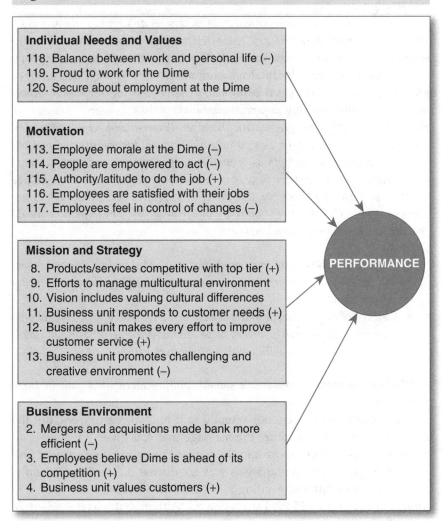

below-average score (2.9 or less). All items listed in each of the four boxes (individual needs and values, motivation, mission and strategy, and the business environment) were positively correlated with perceived performance.

The message to the client went something like this: *The parts of the model that appear to be most positively related to employees' perceptions of how well the Dime is performing include their views of the bank's external business*

*environment and their understanding of and commitment to the bank's mission
and strategy.*

In other words, these transformational factors relate significantly and positively to perceived performance. These related perceptions could perhaps be reinforced even more, so that a self-fulfilling prophecy could have more effect; that is, assuming that clarity about environment and mission and strategy relates positively to perceived performance, strengthening these perceptions might eventually influence organizational performance positively. The categories related to morale are problematic, however. Lower-than-average ratings on individual needs and values, especially work–personal life balance and motivation (e.g., employees' perceptions of morale, empowerment, and control), may be contributing to a negative view of organizational performance and could be affecting performance adversely. It is therefore suggested that a thorough examination of people's jobs in the bank be undertaken. This examination would include consideration of the following:

- *Degree of workload: Are some employees overloaded in their jobs and others not, or is it true that most people are overworked and an increase in hiring is warranted?*
- *Feelings of empowerment and a related sense of having little control over changes in the bank: These need to be examined further; that is, do people have too much responsibility with too little authority?*

Working on these morale issues should improve motivation and, in turn, performance.

These exact words were not actually said to Dime employees, but the above statement does capture the message that was given. Of course, all the other items in the survey and the model categories were covered and explained. The regression analysis was conducted on the Time 2 results only. The important and exciting news was the increase from Time 1 to Time 2 in 123 of the 125 total survey items. Although it was not scientific proof that the desired changes at Dime were successful, the executives, managers, and employees believed nevertheless that positive change had occurred.

What has been briefly described, that is, from the original merger to these later action steps, spanned a period of more than four years. The financial services company continued to focus on organizational change and improvement and sought growth of market share primarily by acquiring other, similar businesses.

In summary, it should be clear that this case represents organization change that is more revolutionary than evolutionary in nature, because the emphasis of change was mission and strategy and culture. A compelling case for change as a consequence of the merger was made by the respective leaders of both companies, and a disruption ensued as a consequence. The organization's initial and continuing change process had been effective because of many factors; the main ones are as follows:

- The CEO's leadership, support for change, and modeling behavior
- Change initiatives carefully planned and driven by data
- An enlightened human resource leader and staff
- Strategic change expertise provided by external consultants
- Key changes made among the top 20 executives
- Significant acquisitions of additional businesses

Significant change over the four-plus years described in this case had clearly been made. The fundamental nature of the business changed somewhat in that the organization made a deliberate effort to become more of a commercial and less of a savings bank. The merged culture was a bit more representative of one of the previous organizations than of the other, but it became a new culture nevertheless. Systems were significantly improved with the introduction of new technology. Moreover, shifting demographics caused changes in managers' behavior, that is, to becoming more attuned and sensitive to individual differences.

The main objective of presenting the Dime case was to demonstrate how revolutionary change can be implemented and managed. Another objective was to provide an overview of the entire change effort at Dime so that our major theme of organization change can be continued. In the case of Dime, the initial change was transformational, and as shown by the survey data, the transformational factors in the model were the primary levers for change: external environment, mission and strategy, leadership, and more gradually, culture. A business strategy for Dime at the time was to expand its business beyond the New York City metropolitan area. This expansion was to be via an acquisition either by Dime or by acquisition of Dime by a larger company. The latter occurred in 2002 when Washington Mutual acquired Dime. A few years later Washington Mutual unfortunately experienced serious business problems and was gobbled up by bigger players. Perhaps if it had adopted more of Dime's culture, leadership, and ways of doing business it would have survived.

Evolutionary Change: Case Example

This case concerns a comparatively small professional services partnership that was close to a century old. The partnership consists of about 50 partners, with approximately the same number of associates, plus administrative and technical staff. The firm is relatively small, deliberately. It is a specialty house providing highly individualized services, to corporations primarily. Its mission is to remain specialized, not to provide a broad array of general services for clients. It serves more than half the Fortune 500 corporations, and more than half its revenue comes from clients it has served consistently for more than 20 years. The firm serves clients in 400 U.S. cities and in 15 foreign countries. Although growth of the firm is a goal, the partners do not favor "rapid growth, mergers, and branch offices." In fact, the firm is located in only one building in a large metropolitan area in the eastern United States.

The structure of this professional services firm is rather simple and straightforward. At the top is the managing partner (the CEO equivalent), and working closely with him is a small executive committee consisting primarily of department heads, or as they prefer to call them, "practice group chairs." Following the managing partner and the executive committee are the senior partners, then the junior partners (recent entrants into the partner status), followed by the associates (most of whom have partner aspirations), and the staff.

The organizational consultants working with this firm were initially asked to meet with the managing partner and some of his executive committee members to explore ways of evaluating the performance of their senior and junior partners and, eventually, to cascade the process down to include the associates. The managing partner had heard about something called a "360-degree feedback process" and wondered whether this kind of procedure could be used to measure and reward performance. The consultants who were asked to meet with the managing partner and his colleagues had considerable expertise in this type of feedback process, as well as in the broader arena of organization change and development.

Briefly, a 360-degree feedback process gets its name from a "full circle" procedure of rated behavioral practices. The behaviors rated are usually in the domains of management and leadership. The central person rates himself or herself on a set of behavioral practices that are employed in leadership or management, and three other categories of raters rate the person on the same set of behavioral practices (examples will be provided later in this case presentation). The three other categories of raters are the central person's supervisor, the person's peers, and the person's direct reports or subordinates. The self and three other sets of raters compose the full circle, or 360 degrees, as it is often called. Incidentally, instead of the overly popularized and metaphorical label, a more accurate description would be *multirater* or *multisource feedback,* because other raters may be included, such as clients or customers.

The feedback process consists of the comparison between his or her self-ratings and those of the others (one or sometimes two supervisors and a minimum of three peers and three direct reports). The degree of congruence or divergence in the ratings is, of course, the main focus of attention.

In the exploratory discussion with the managing partner and his colleagues, the consultants quite naturally asked many questions and, in due course, offered opinions and suggestions. In addition to finding a way to evaluate partner performance, the managing partner also stressed the need for more leadership especially from among the senior partners, the need for identifying potential leaders among the junior partners, and the need for more teamwork. The consultants explained in detail how a multirater feedback process works and then offered the opinion (actually the expression of a value that the consultants hold) that using this kind of procedure as a measure of performance for certain organizational purposes was not wise. That is, to employ multirater feedback in the service of performance appraisal and then to base organizational rewards (incentive compensation, promotion, etc.) accordingly would create the strong possibility of rater bias. To base evaluations and rewards on the rating procedure would mean that one's ratings become somewhat public, that is, known to those who make decisions about performance evaluation and rewards, certainly to the managing partner and his executive committee. In other words, what would likely drive the process would be the rewards to be obtained, not so much one's desire to be a more effective leader or team player. Moreover, when one knows that his or her ratings of someone, especially one's supervisor, will be used for evaluative purposes, rather than for the purpose of individual and organization development, the ratings are likely to differ. It is not necessarily a matter of using multirater feedback for organizational administrative purposes (for example, performance appraisal) versus using the process solely for individual and organization development.

As London (2001) has pointed out in his coverage of the "debate," it does not have to be one or the other:

> [The feedback process] can be used for both development and administrative purposes, but this takes time. The organization may need to start by using MSF (multisource feedback) for development alone to establish a culture of interpersonal trust and attention to development. (p. 383)

With respect to the professional services firm, this multirater feedback process was a first for them. For more coverage of using this process for individual and organization development, see Bracken (1996) and Church, Waclawski, and Burke (2001).

The consultants therefore urged the managing partner and his executive committee colleagues to use the multirater process for individual and organization development. Individually, the purposes would be to increase one's self-awareness in particular (studies have shown a positive link between self-awareness and performance, e.g., Church, 1997) and to increase personal and professional development in general. Organizationally, the purposes would be to (1) select behavioral practices related to functioning as a leader and manager and to teamwork that fit with the managing partner's objectives and (2) encourage partners through the feedback process (that is, coaching by the external consultant) to work on improving their leadership qualities and to improve them so as to enhance teamwork in the firm. Furthermore, the consultants urged the firm's leaders to authorize that the multirater feedback process be confidential, so that only the person being rated and the external consultant directing the overall process and providing the feedback and coaching would have access to and knowledge about the individual's ratings. Finally, the consultants assured the managing partner that when a sufficient number of feedback sessions with partners had been conducted, an overall summary of all the ratings would be provided.

The consultants then recommended that the behavioral practices be as tailored as possible to the firm's change needs, mission, and values. *Not* recommended were off-the-shelf or "general purpose" practices but, instead, the process of identifying and selecting behaviors that they, as the firm's leaders, thought made the most sense, that is, in terms of aligning partner behavior more closely with desired values and change directions for the firm.

At the end of the discussion of almost three hours, the managing partner and his colleagues told the consultants that they would talk further among themselves about what was being recommended and let the consultants know within a week or two. There was no expectation by the consultants that a decision by the firm's leadership would be made that day. Rarely do potential client organizations make a decision to move forward that quickly. Besides, in this case, the consultants had attempted to persuade the managing partner and his executive committee members to move in a different direction from what had been asked for in the first place, namely, a change from an administrative appraisal to a developmental one.

The firm's leadership did decide to move forward with the consultant's recommendation (otherwise there would be no story to tell!), and the process began.

The Tools for Assessment and Ratings

To start, the consultants asked for certain materials and documents from the firm, such as their mission statement, strategic plan, statement of values, and any other information that addressed their desired future state. Because the firm's leadership were rather conservative and careful about organization change, requesting these materials from the firm suggested a course of action consistent with continuous improvement, rather than a significant and sweeping change of mission—the firm wished, you will recall, to remain relatively small and specialized. Although they wanted to expand their services to new clients and broaden their base, the range and nature of these services would continue as they were. They considered themselves among the best at their specialty and wanted to remain so. They had good reason to believe that they were among the best—they still are—because their clients list was indeed desirable, and more than half their clients stayed with them for long periods of time, more than two decades.

Behavioral Practices

On the basis of these documents and some selected interviews, the consultants, from their data bank of hundreds of behavioral practices that had proved to be effective in other organizations, developed a working list of behavioral practices that were as relevant to the firm as possible. These behavioral statements were categorized according to the firm's list of values, for example, promoting a courteous, collegial, and trusting culture. Through a collaborative, back-and-forth, iterative process with the client firm that required about three months, the consultants and the firm's leadership agreed on a final list of 59 behavioral practices. In the end, at least half these behavioral statements were written "from scratch," that is, expressly for the firm. Much debate about the right phrases and proper wording had ensued.

The 59 practices were then arranged into a rating questionnaire using a 5-point Likert-type scale. Each of the behavioral statements was rated twice—first, according to the extent to which the person being rated practiced that specific behavior, and second, according to how important the behavior was to the part of the firm represented by the partner being rated. Comparing the behavior in terms of how much it is practiced with how important it is viewed to be helps the individual being rated decide how much change in the given behavior may be needed. If the behavior is not seen as very important, little, if any, change may be required. If there is a gap—the behavior is perceived to be highly important, but the person is rated as practicing it very little—then behavior change may be needed. The 59 practices were categorized according to the firm's 12 primary values. An example of a practice for six of these values used in this multirater feedback process is shown in Table 5.1.

In addition to the 59 behavioral practices, three other rating instruments were used in this feedback process. These additional three were

Table 5.1   Main Values of Professional Services Firm With Behavioral Practice Example

Value	Behavioral Practice
• Solidifying and maintaining close client relationships	• Solicits and responds to client feedback on the quality of service provided.
• Promoting a courteous, collegial, and trusting culture	• Relates in a courteous and professional manner, regardless of the level of the person with whom he or she is dealing.

Value	Behavioral Practice
• Working effectively in teams	• Promotes an atmosphere of teamwork, cooperation, and coordinated effort among people.
• Developing, mentoring, and training others	• Plans and reviews personal development goals jointly with associates.
• Developing the business	• Effectively manages and balances priorities among many projects, relationships, and clients.
• Leading and managing	• Provides a vision of the future that captures the commitment of people.

related more to one's personality than to specific behaviors. There were two primary reasons for adding these three questionnaires.

First is the matter of context. One's day-to-day behavior is in part a function of the situation and in part due to a person's temperament or personality. In a sense, one's behavior is foreground and the personality underlying the behavior is background. Thus, in providing feedback to a person about behavior, that form of feedback can be understood more thoroughly if one can also see the rated behavior in the context of one's nature, that is, personality and temperament. An introverted individual behaves differently from one who is extroverted. Linking this dimension of personality to behavior can help one more clearly understand feedback from others.

Second, the firm's leaders wanted to encourage their partners to assume more leadership, and they wanted to understand more about the potential for leadership in the firm, especially from among the junior partners.

It should be noted that providing leadership and management in a professional services firm is not exactly easy. There are clearly exceptions, but professionals—lawyers, accountants, and consultants—do not as a rule join firms to be managers or leaders. They join because they want to practice law, consult with clients, or analyze a company's financial situation. They do not want to lead and certainly do not want to manage other professionals. They definitely do not want to have to be concerned with such mundane matters as budgeting, hiring other professionals, generating a business plan, providing performance feedback to others, determining compensation, and so on.

So, the managing partner wanted to know whether he could count on more help with leadership for the firm—or was his firm like most other professional service enterprises in this regard?

What follows is a brief description of the three other instruments of assessment that were used in this feedback study.

Myers-Briggs Type Indicator

Based on Carl Jung's theoretical notions about individual differences, the Myers-Briggs Type Indicator (MBTI) assesses a person's degree of strength of preference along four continua of personality dimensions (Briggs & Myers, 1943). Briefly defined, these dimensions are as follows:

- Extroversion-introversion: the degree to which individuals differ with respect to sociability and being energized while around others, as compared with introversion, which stresses keeping more to oneself and being energized more while alone than with others.
- Intuition-sensing: the degree to which individuals depend more on intuitiveness and hunches for assimilating information, as compared with a preference for concrete, fact-based information, that is, more a function of what a person sees, touches, hears, smells, and so on.
- Thinking-feeling: the degree to which individuals differ with respect to what they do with information once they take it in, that is, whether one (1) uses primarily thought processes such as logic, analysis, and objectivity or (2) prefers instead to rely more on emotional consideration when making decisions, for example, feeling domains such as interpersonal relationships, values, and certain internal, personal standards.
- Judging-perceiving: the degree to which individuals prefer order, planning, achieving closure, and decisiveness, rather than keeping one's options open and "going with the flow," or spontaneity.

A person's results on the MBTI become eight preference scores that represent comparisons with norms based on many thousands of others' scores on the continua of thinking to feeling, judging to perceiving, extro-version to introversion, and intuition to sensing.

Although it would be possible to have others answer the MBTI as a rat-ing of the central person, this other-rating is not typical. The MBTI is lengthy, well over 200 questions, and has strengths of reliability and valid-ity; thus, it serves the feedback process well only with self-ratings.

NEO-Personality Inventory (NEO-PI)

Also a self-rating instrument only, the NEO-PI provides measures that are linked to the "Big Five" factors of personality (Costa & McCrae, 1985). The NEO-PI is also lengthy, with 240 items, and is based on extensive research and practice. NEO stands for three of the five factors, briefly defined below:

- Neuroticism: the higher the score, the more one tends to be anxious, depressed, and angry.
- Extroversion: very similar to the same measure on the MBTI; that is, the higher one's score, the more the individual tends to be gregari-ous, warm toward others, and outgoing.
- Openness: primarily meaning open to ideas and new learning; the high-scorer's behavior is likely characterized by curiosity, a love of intelligence, and creativity.
- Agreeableness: the higher the score, the more one tends to be coop-erative, trustworthy, kind, and sympathetic toward others.
- Conscientiousness: high scorers on this factor tend to be reliable, well organized, responsible, and disciplined.

There is some overlap with the MBTI, and the feedback to a person needs to highlight convergence where it exists, such as the obvious extro-version dimension and intuition with openness and perhaps judging with conscientiousness. Consistency across instruments helps convince the person receiving the feedback that his or her responses are credible.

Leadership Assessment Inventory (LAI)

This instrument was included to determine the extent to which part-ners in the firm preferred leadership to management. It is possible, as noted previously, that many of the partners preferred neither. If neither, a person's scores would be relatively low on a large set of norms. The LAI consists of 18 items that measure an individual's preference for leader-ship over management. It is based on the thinking of Burke (1986), Burns (1978), and Zaleznik (1977). See Chapters 10 and 12 for more coverage of this kind of thinking. The LAI is a multirater instrument including rat-ings by oneself, one's supervisor, and one's subordinates but not one's peers. The content of the 18 items does not lend itself to peer ratings. Peer ratings in this case are not as relevant or as reliable as those from supervi-sor and subordinates. In addition to an overall preference score for lead-ership compared with management, individuals receive ratings on five subfactors, namely, determining direction (5 items), influencing follow-ers (5 items), establishing purpose (3 items), inspiring followers (3 items), and making things happen (2 items). For more information on the LAI, see Sashkin and Burke (1990) and Van Eron and Burke (1992).

Data Summary of the Firm's Partners

The 50 partners in the firm were rated the highest on practices catego-rized as "Solidifying and Maintaining Close Client Relationships" and "Promoting a Courteous, Collegial, and Trusting Culture." Their "Team-work" ratings were fairly strong, but "Developing the Business" resulted in so-so ratings, and the lowest were "Leading and Managing." In fact, the lowest-rated practice of all was "Provide a Vision of the Future that Captures the Commitment of People." Moreover, the ratings on the LAI reflected little desire for service as a leader. Management activities were not exactly popular, either.

The MBTI pattern of the firm did not fit norms for the United States very closely. Whereas 25% of the overall U.S. population scored as intro-verts, 56% of the partners did so. On intuition, the partners scored 68% compared with 25% for U.S. norms; thinking was at 72% for the partners, compared with about 50% for U.S. norms; and 62% scored as judging com-pared with approximately 50% for U.S. norms. The overall combination of traits among the partners, among the 16 possibilities for the MBTI of intro-version, intuition, thinking, and judging, occurs in less than 2% of the U.S. population. This firm's partners may not be like most American personali-ties, but they may not be that different from other professional service firm populations. Although some research has indicated that perceived leaders in organizations are likely to be higher on intuition and a bit higher on per-ceiving rather than judging (Van Eron & Burke, 1992), the only dimension conducive for leadership in our professional services firm is intuition. So, there may be some potential in the firm for leadership but, in the main, not a clear, strong profile for it.

The results on the NEO-PI were well within the normal range for neuroticism—no problems here—and showed consistent scores on extroversion (rather low), with openness and conscientiousness being strong. Agreeableness was in the average range.

Conclusion

The lead consultant in this case made the following points and recommendations to the managing partner and executive committee of the firm:

- This professional services firm is indeed highly professional, showing a strong emphasis on serving clients promptly and effectively; internal firm norms of courtesy, respect, and collegiality; and a clarity about mission and the identity within the larger professional community, that is, strong specialization.
- Although a reasonable amount of teamwork in the firm seems to exist, there is insufficient attention being paid to mentoring and providing professional development for junior partners and associates.
- The leadership picture is rather bleak. Although there may be leader ability among the partners, there is little motivation.

The latter two points overlap. Mentoring is a form of leadership.

Approximately halfway into this consultant-client relationship of about three years, the managing partner hired a senior partner from another firm to help with leading and managing. This seasoned outsider enjoys leadership and appears to be quite good at it. The consultant discussed this decision with the managing partner and suggested these options for the future: This method of providing further leadership for the firm could be followed and focus could be made on changing the firm's reward system in such a way that internal leadership could be reinforced more strongly and be recognized to the same degree as effective client work.

Much more could be stated about the interesting culture of this firm and the issues facing it. However, the point of providing this case example is this: Organization change for this firm comes slowly; it is clearly evolutionary in nature. Future work is on leadership development, whether internally or externally by means of new hires. The firm needs to do a much better job of (1) mentoring, (2) considering the firm more as a business and less as a professional club, and (3) learning how to improve from the kind of process it has spent considerable time and money on, its multirater feedback program.

This professional service firm was not in trouble. There had been no need for a sea change. Evolutionary change was therefore quite appropriate. Continuous improvement was its slogan.

Summary

The primary purpose of this chapter was to make clear that not all organization changes are the same. An important distinction is the difference between revolutionary (later to be referred to as transformational) and evolutionary (later to be referred to as transactional) change. The inclusion of the two case examples was intended to clarify the distinction between the two.

Revolutionary change, perhaps by definition, occurs in leaps, spurts, and disruptions, not in an incremental, linear fashion. Our understanding of revolutionary change has been enhanced and emboldened by similar findings across disciplines and multiple levels of analyses. These similarities are quite remarkable. Deep structure, as explained by Gersick (1991), is perhaps the key concept for understanding the nature of revolutionary change more fully.

Evolutionary change is characteristic of most organization change. Evolutionary change is typically an attempt to improve aspects of the organization that will lead to higher performance. The fundamental nature, or deep structure, of the organization, its culture, for example, remains undisturbed. The primary mission of the organization remains the same, and the primary rationale for its strategy to implement the mission also remains intact. Yet major organizational changes can occur, such as modifications of the structure, installing a new system of information technology, or launching a new line of businesses. These kinds of changes are simply evolutionary when it comes to a comprehensive understanding of organization change.

SIX

Levels of Organization Change

Individual, Group, and Larger System

W e now know the importance of considering organization change in systems terms (Chapter 4). An organization is a totality, a whole with interacting parts or components. To change a part may be a change in the organization, but it is not organization change. To change a part of the component does not constitute a change in the system. To understand organization change as thoroughly as we can, however, it is useful to analyze, to examine the various pieces and parts and how they affect and are affected by each other and by the whole. Also, to understand organization change as thoroughly as we can, particularly in light of the fact that the process is so complex, it is critical to consider multiple perspectives. The previous chapter attempted to distinguish between revolutionary and evolutionary change. Although definitions of the two types of change overlap, separating them helps us understand more clearly that organization change occurs quite differently when the change goal is to improve operations and when the goal is to turn the organization in an entirely new direction.

This chapter examines change at three different yet overlapping organizational levels and focuses on the internal organization. Not only does evolutionary organization change differ from revolutionary change, but change differs at different levels in the organization.

Our analysis in this chapter examines three levels: the individual, the group, and the total system. There is more to an organization than these three broad levels, of course. The prefix *inter* comes to mind. Individuals in organizations relate with one another, so there is the interpersonal level. Groups in organizations relate with one another, so there is the intergroup level. And organizations relate with other organizations, so there is the interorganizational level. We will touch on these other, "inter" levels, but our main focus will be on the three broad ones.

Organizational behavior and change can be at least partially understood according to the three broad levels that form the focus of this chapter, but we must constantly bear in mind that individuals in organizations always behave in context. The context is at the interfaces, that is, relations with others, or as Capra (1996) would put it, "networks within networks."

With this caveat in mind, let us now proceed with an analysis of organization change at the level of the person.

Change in Organizations at the Individual Level

First, an assumption: An important pretext for addressing any level of change is to decide an overall direction for organization change. Changes at the individual level are therefore designed and implemented to help the organization to move in its new direction. This assumption is critical to our understanding. Many, perhaps most, changes at the individual level in organizations are not in the service of moving the total system in a new direction. Training programs, for example, are often conducted because another competitor in the industry is doing it, and "to remain competitive, we had better do it, too." This "keeping up with the Joneses" mentality accounts for many changes at an individual level that rarely, if ever, affect the whole.

Now let us consider three primary change examples for individuals that can be in the service of helping to implement organization change.

Recruitment, Selection, Replacement, and Displacement

This category of individual change concerns getting, placing, and keeping the right people in the right roles and jobs to facilitate the larger change effort. For example, almost three decades ago, General Foods, now a part of the Phillip Morris Corporation, decided to try an experiment with a new plant start-up that, if successful, would be disseminated throughout the company in the interest of its becoming more competitive in the food industry. As reported by King (1972), the plan was to design this new manufacturing organization, a food-processing plant, according to the criteria of Likert's (1967) System 4. This meant that major tasks would be accomplished by teams and that first-line supervisors would be team leaders rather than operate more traditionally as supervisors by giving close individual supervision. Status differences among all employees were to be minimized. There would be no executive dining room, for example, but one cafeteria for all, and a participative approach to management was to be practiced. The top management group for the plant, the general manager and three operating managers (operations service, manufacturing, and technical) had been selected by corporate headquarters according to the new plant design criteria; that is, these individuals were compatible with and committed to managing their organization according to the participative management premises of System 4. The objective of the selection process, therefore, was to find people who were also compatible with a participative approach. Team leaders would be expected to manage participatively.

The selection process was managed by the top team with the assistance of an organization development consultant. The principles that guided their work were as follows:

1. All selection decisions would be made by the people who were to work with those selected.

2. Decisions would be based on how applicants behaved in collaborative and conflicting group situations.

3. All applicants would receive feedback from the decision makers on why they did or did not receive job offers.

4. The selection process would reflect as much as possible the types of tasks and relationships that would be characteristic of work in the

plant; that is, status differences were minimized; the process was personalized; there was a growth and development emphasis for all employees; communication was two way; and considerable activity took place in small groups.

5. Psychological tests would be used but only as secondary information, and the results would not become a part of an individual's employee file.

6. Contact between those who were already members of the organization and those who were strong prospects would gradually become more extensive and open as the selection process progressed.

King has described in detail the two-day process for the selection of team leaders. The process included a plant visit, a detailed description of the new organization, role-playing exercises, a battery of psychological tests, group decision-making tasks, and simulation exercises of plant work. As King (1972) pointed out,

> The selection decision makers must obtain an accurate indication of whether or not the candidate is likely to function well in a participative organization. At the same time, prospective employees need accurate information to assist them in deciding whether or not it is advisable for them to join such a new system. (p. 201)

King's report was written about nine months after the start-up of the plant. During that time, only two people had left the organization, absenteeism was less than 1%, and productivity had exceeded original expectations. This early success was sustained (Walton, 1975), but the managerial and change process associated with it did not spread to the overall parent company. Walton (1975) has hypothesized several reasons for this lack of diffusion within General Foods and in six similar cases in organizations in the United States, Canada, the United Kingdom, and Norway. Some of the reasons were an inadequate pilot project, a poor model for change, confusion over what was to be diffused, and deficient implementation. An eighth organization, Volvo, of Sweden, was an exception. The success of an initial pilot effort there was effectively diffused into other parts of the overall organization (Gyllenhammar, 1977). This more effective diffusion was due to an effective pilot project, a better model for change, less confusion about what to diffuse, and better implementation than the other organizational examples. Also, as work by Levine (1980) has shown, innovative enclaves in organizations that are incompatible with the over-all culture and are unprofitable remain isolated and do not diffuse what-ever innovation they develop.

The opportunity to select people for a new organization in a planned, systematic way is rare. The advantages of such an opportunity are clear (King, 1972):

> Many difficult problems in overcoming resistance to change are obviated. New norms, different from traditional norms in industry, can be developed. Rather than the problem of changing established roles and role expectations about how supervisors or employees "should" act, roles are established anew. The newness of the physi-cal setting and technology is congruent with the institution of a new approach to organization and interpersonal relationships. (p. 201)

Although still relatively rare today, selecting employees in this deliber-ate, planned way does occur. The Saturn automobile division of General Motors was started and has continued to operate according to many of these more participative ways of selecting and working with people. Procter & Gamble has used similar practices, and some of the newer high-tech companies like those in Silicon Valley do the same.

Replacement and displacement in the interest of organization change also occurs. The brief story of revolutionary change at British Airways (BA) related in Chapter 5 began in part with reducing the workforce by more than 20,000 people. This displacement occurred over some period of time, because early retirements and other forms of natural attrition were predominantly used. The main objective, nevertheless, on the part of the CEO at the time, Colin Marshall (today Lord Marshall), was to reduce bureaucracy and move BA toward a more market-oriented, customer ser-vice enterprise. In other words, this huge reduction in the workforce was in support of the overall organization direction and change effort.

Finally, a key replacement tactic in many organization changes is to recruit a new leader from inside the organization, but more often from the outside. Marshall, the change leader of BA, was recruited from an outside yet similar industry, Avis car rentals, a service organization in the broader travel industry. Lou Gerstner was recruited from outside the computer industry to change IBM (and he did). Many other examples could be given.

The point is that frequently, a deliberate tactic for organization change at the individual level is to infuse the system with new leadership, especially at the top.

Training and Development

Again assuming that a training program is designed and conducted to help bring about organization change, most of the time the effort is directed toward individuals in managerial positions. How this approach to training was implemented was described in Chapter 5 with the brief story of the change at BA. Let us now consider another example also conducted by a service organization, a global bank.

Citicorp, now known as Citi, launched a unique training program, "Managing People," early in 1977. The corporation's top management was concerned that, along with its rapid growth in the late 1960s and 1970s, the increasing strain on managers to continue to produce profits and adapt to rapid change had caused mounting "people problems" in the organization. More and more people were feeling like cogs in a (money) machine. Because it was accepted by top management that people were the organization's most important resource, particular attention had to be paid to managing this resource more effectively. William Spencer, president of the corporation at that time, publicly stated in a filmed introduction to Citicorp's program, "The management of people is probably a greater skill mandated than individual brilliance. Even the most brilliant person, if there is little or no ability to manage people, is a lost cause in our operation" (Burke, 1982, p. 244). He was talking about what Daniel Goleman (1995) today calls *emotional intelligence.*

To begin the process, a study was conducted (1) to identify the best management talent within the organization, (2) to determine the specific set of management practices that seemed to distinguish the best from average managers, and (3) to design a training program based on these superior practices. A criterion group of managers was thus established by asking senior executives to identify subordinate managers within their respective groups who were outstanding and would most likely be taking their places as senior executives within the next decade. They indentified 39 such managers. The researchers then asked these same senior executives to identify 39 additional managers within their groups who were satisfactory managers but not as effective as the first group. The researchers next arranged for 353 subordinates of these 78 managers (39 in the "A" group [outstanding] and 39 in the "B" group [satisfactory]) to rate their bosses on 59 management practices culled from a list of hundreds. The ratings were done with 5-point Likert-type scales. Some of the practices rated were as follows:

- Your manager communicates high personal standards informally—in conversation, personal appearance, and so forth.
- Your manager tries to make the best use of staff members' skills and abilities when making assignments.
- Your manager works with staff members (subordinates) to reach mutual agreement on their performance appraisals.
- Your manager uses recognition and praise—aside from pay—to reward excellent performance.
- The work group meetings your manager conducts serve to increase trust and mutual respect among the work group members.

The A group was rated significantly higher than the B group on 22 of the 59 practices, regardless of their management situation in the corporation. Another eight practices differentiated between the two groups but only under structured conditions of management, such as in a back-office operation of check processing. The A-group practices were then used as the basis for design of the training program. Because this group had been identified as outstanding managers, and subordinate ratings had further identified some of the specific practices that these managers did exceptionally well, it followed (to Citicorp's top management) that the larger population of managers should be trained to adopt this special set of people-management practices. Before the program began, managers were rated by their subordinates on the selected practices.

The 5-day program then consisted of training in clusters of these practices, with each training day devoted to one cluster. The five clusters were (1) getting commitment to goals and standards, (2) coaching, (3) appraising performance, (4) compensating and rewarding, and (5) building a team for continuity of performance. Training techniques included case method, role practice, group problem-solving and decision-making exercises, and occasional short lectures. For each day of the program, the managers received a computer printout of their ratings by their subordinates on that day's cluster of practices. This feedback for the manager was the most powerful part of the training program, because managers focused their learning and improvement objectives on the practices that received the lowest ratings. In its first three years, about 2,000 Citicorp managers went through the program. It continued to be popular and highly valued among Citicorp managers for at least another 15 years.

This Managing People program of Citicorp's was designed to change the management of the organization from an insensitive and results-only mentality to a management group that focused more on people, with a better blend of getting results and managing subordinates in a more participatory and caring fashion. Although some qualitative studies were done over the years to determine the degree of success of the Managing People program, its ultimate payoff is not clear. The fact that the program continued for almost two decades supports the belief that it had value for Citicorp. In any case, the value was primarily individual in nature and its value for the organization as a whole is unclear. Assuming that change did occur, it was certainly evolutionary, not revolutionary.

Coaching and Counseling

Counseling in an organizational work setting, or as we prefer to call it today, coaching, is not exactly new. Counseling was recognized as a tool for individual development and organizational improvement at least 70 years ago, when the Hawthorne studies were conducted (Dickson & Roethlisberger, 1966). When counseling/coaching is used for purposes of furthering organizational change, we have the problem of integrating individual needs and organizational goals. This is not an easy problem to solve (Beer, 1980),

> since the requirements of system-wide change may not be in the interest of the individual, and vice-versa. However, if the counselor [coach] can relate equally to the demands of organization change and to the needs of the individual, he is in a unique position to help the individual and the organization renegotiate a new psychological contract. (p. 190)

The new psychological contract, then, is an attempt to integrate individual improvement objectives with organization change goals.

Most of the time, coaching or counseling occurs informally with internal organizational professionals, usually in the human resource function, serving in the helping role. These informal encounters may be carried out during lunch conversations, brief and spontaneous talks with a manager before or after an intense meeting, phone conversations with a manager about scheduling the next time together in which a current problem is discussed incidentally, and so forth. One of the most important times is when the coach is helping his or her client (usually a manager) deal with feedback that the client experiences as negative (Crockett, 1970). Defensive feelings are the most common ones, and the more the coach can help the client talk about those feelings, the more the client will be able to move on to a problem-solving mode of behavior.

More recently, the term *executive coaching* has become incorporated into our language. Actually, coaching today occurs at all levels of management in an organization, but *executive coaching* has more panache as a term. In any case, this form of coaching currently consists of providing help to a manager or executive in much the same way an athletic coach works. Witherspoon and White (1998) have specified at least four roles that executive coaches play:

1. Coaching for *skills:* The focus is on tasks that a person has to accomplish and the skills and competencies required. An example might be a highly important speech that the executive has to deliver, and the help needed concerns how best to "win over" the audience.

2. Coaching for *performance:* The focus here is broader and encompasses the executive's entire job, and the help needed is how to perform the overall job effectively. An example would be an executive's job change from operations or line responsibility to staff; in the former job, success would be defined more in terms of supervision, whereas with the latter, job success would be defined more in terms of how well one can influence others to accomplish tasks when formal authority is minimal.

3. Coaching for *development:* Here, the focus is on the future; it is more about helping the executive with career choices and about the next job.

4. Coaching for the *executive's agenda:* In this case, the executive decides what is needed. An example would be to help with a forthcoming meeting that the executive must lead; the help provided might be designing the meeting, how the executive could share leadership, how certain difficult subordinates could be managed in the meeting, and so on.

Determining at the outset the need that the executive has for coaching more clearly defines the particular role the coach will play. In other words, distinguishing among these four possibilities helps the coach respond more directly and precisely to what the executive may require.

It is also useful to think about the coaching sequence:

- Gaining *commitment* to the coaching process with an agreement or contract between the coach and the executive about the work to be done
- *Assessing* the problem presented by the executive, which determines for the coach which of the four roles to play
- *Action* to be taken by the executive after a given coaching session
- *Follow-up* by the coach after the executive's action(s), in which the coach helps the executive learn from his or her experience

This synopsis of what constitutes executive coaching helps illustrate how change at an individual level can facilitate organization change. More specifically and also currently, coaching is frequently conducted as part of multirater feedback in which help is provided in understanding the feedback more clearly and in planning changes in one's behavior accordingly. Moreover, research is beginning to show that multirater feedback by itself does not seem to lead to positive change in performance. Coaching appears to make a helpful and positive difference (Luthans & Peterson, 2003; Seifert, Yukl, & McDonald, 2003; Smither, London, Flautt, Vargas, & Kucine, 2003). In any case, if the content of the feedback is congruent with organization change goals, then this individual process helps to leverage the change. We will return to this type of leverage for organization change in Chapter 11 and, by implication, in Chapter 12, which is about leading organization change.

Individual Responses to Organization Change

Individuals' reactions to significant change in organizations, change that directly affects them, has been likened to the psychiatrist Elizabeth Kubler-Ross's (1969) description of the five stages that most people go through when they are faced with a terminal illness. The struggle begins with (1) shock and denial, (2) moves to anger, (3) to bargaining, or attempts to postpone the inevitable, on to (4) depression, and finally to (5) acceptance. Not everyone moves through all these stages; some never move beyond denial. And so it is with organizational behavior. Some organizational members fight the change "to the death," constantly denying that the change is necessary. Others embrace the change readily and move with it. Most people are somewhere in between and move through all stages.

H. Levinson (1976) has argued that whether change is resisted or embraced, all change is nevertheless a loss experience, particularly a loss of familiar routines. And the more psychologically important the loss, the more likely one's behavior will take the form of resistance. Levinson further argued that all loss needs to be mourned (a bachelor party on the eve of a groom's wedding, most often a joyful change, could be thought of as a mourning ritual) and that people should have an opportunity to discuss and deal with their feelings if they are again going to be able to perform effectively on the job. He went on to state:

> Most organizational change flounders because the experience of loss is not taken into account. When the threats of loss are so severe as to increase people's sense of helplessness, their ability to master themselves and their environments decreases. To undertake successful organizational change, an executive must anticipate and provide means of working through that loss. (p. 83)

Resistance

The phenomenon of resistance to change is not necessarily that of resisting the change per se but is more accurately a resistance to losing something of value to the person—loss of the known and tried in the face of being asked, if not forced, to move into the unknown and untried. Feelings of anxiety associated with such change are quite normal.

Another form of loss that leads to resistance can come from one's experiencing a lack of choice, that is, the imposition of change, or being forced to move to some new state of being and acting. That is, people are not simply and naturally resistant to change. What comes closer to a universal truth about human behavior is that people resist the imposition of change. Brehm's (1966) research and his theory of *psychological reactance* help to explain this human phenomenon. When one's feeling of freedom is in jeopardy, the immediate reaction is likely to be an attempt to regain the feeling of freedom. This reaction is so strong, in fact, that people frequently will not bother to defend their beliefs and may even change them to oppose others' attempts at changing them. In some cases, the issues of advantage and change are in conflict, leading to a situation in which people may prefer to continue on a path that is not in their best interests rather than to give up the feeling of free choice.

Research shows, for example, that when a smoker is *told* to stop smoking, his or her typical reaction is either to continue as usual or increase the rate. Brehm's (1966) theory is that when people believe themselves free to behave in a certain way, they will experience psychological reactance (that is, they will resist) if that freedom is threatened or eliminated. The degree of ease and success with which an organization change is introduced is therefore directly proportional to the amount of choice that people feel they have in determining and implementing the change.

It is also important and useful to consider the *kind* of resistance that is being manifested. Hambrick and Cannella's (1989) distinctions are helpful in this regard. In other words, diagnostically, one should determine whether the resistance is blind, political, or ideological:

Blind Resistance. Some people, no doubt a small minority, are simply afraid and intolerant of change—any change. Two kinds of response may be useful here. One is to provide as much reassurance as possible: Moving into something unknown is always discomforting, at least for a while, but things rarely turn out as dire as we imagine. Second, allow time to pass. Some people in this category merely need time to get used to the new idea; it is just their nature to react defensively at first, like a reflex, but not necessarily forever.

Political Resistance. Persons engaged in political resistance believe that they stand to lose something of value if the change is implemented, such as loss of one's power base, status, job, income, and or the like. With this kind of resistance, one needs to counter with negotiation, trading something of value with something else of value. Also, one might argue long-term gain versus short-term loss: Yes, for a while we will be losing some things, but over the long haul, we stand to gain much more.

Ideological Resistance. Some people may genuinely believe that the planned change is ill fated (it simply will not work, and here are reasons why) or in violation of deeply held values (this change is the wrong thing to do, and here are reasons why I feel this way). In other words, the resistance comes from honest, intellectual differences or genuine beliefs, feelings, or philosophies that are different. Under these circumstances, it can be useful to counter with strong persuasion based as much as possible on data, facts, and substance. Mere opinion will not be persuasive. Careful prediction from and linkage to this information is absolutely necessary.

It also should be noted that resistance to change is not necessarily a bad thing. Apathy is worse. At least with resistance, there is energy, and the person cares about something. Moreover, resistance is a natural human response and, like one's defense mechanisms, should be respected. There are reasons for defenses to be in place. As the previous paragraphs have attempted to explain, there are likewise reasons for resistance. Understanding these reasons is important if the organizational change agent wishes to be successful.

To summarize, change usually involves a shift away from a known situation, with all its familiarity, comfort, and advantages. The people affected are exchanging the known for the unknown, certainty for uncertainty, existing patterns of behavior and adaptation for new patterns, or tried rewards for untested ones. In addition to the uncertainty of the satisfactions to be gained from the new situation, the people being asked to make the change are required to spend a great deal of effort and psychological energy in getting to know the new situation and in tolerating and coping with frustration until they can evolve new work or living patterns. In psychological terms, newness and the need to cope with it constitute stress. If the long-term rewards to be gained from the change are no greater than those enjoyed formerly, the stress cost outweighs the future advantage. If the new advantages outweigh the old but are not well understood by those undergoing the change, again the effort will not seem worthwhile. Only if the advantages are greater and are desired sufficiently to outweigh the efforts required to make the transition are people likely to embrace change willingly.

Finally, it should be clear that resistance is not a universal human phenomenon. Individuals do indeed differ in their responses to organization change. Oreg (2003), for example, has demonstrated that people's responses to change differ in four primary ways—in the extent to which they (1) seek routine, (2) react emotionally (particularly common when the change is imposed), (3) take a short-term focus, and (4) react in a cognitively rigid way. And Wanberg and Banas (2000) found that the more organizational members tended to be optimistic, possessed high self-esteem, or had high internal locus of control, the more open to and supportive of organization change they were.

Most people, therefore, do not easily fall into an either/or category of resistance versus acceptance of change. In fact, most of us when confronted with the possibility of change are likely to be ambivalent—the change, or some aspect of it, might be good, yet there may also be some adverse consequences. As Piderit (2000) has noted, responses to change are "neither consistently negative nor consistently positive" (p. 783).

Individuals Coping With Change

There are at least three ways to help organizational members deal with change: conceptually, by achieving closure, and through participation.

Frequently, giving people a way of thinking about what they are experiencing can be useful. The framework developed by William Bridges (1986) is an example. First, he distinguishes between change and transition. Change, he states, is something that "starts and stops, or when something that used to happen in one way starts happening in another" (Bridges, 1986, p. 25). Transition is a psychological process extending over a long period of time that cannot be managed in a rational way, whereas change can be. People in transition, Bridges (1986) contends, move through three phases of ending and letting go. People must let go and stop identifying with the old before they can embrace the new:

1. Surrender: People must give up who they were (role, position, title, etc.) and where they have been if they are to make a successful transition. A great deal of what we call resistance to change is really difficulty with the first phase of transition.

2. The "no man's land": People in this second phase experience ambiguity, confusion, and perhaps despair and a sense of meaninglessness. It is also a time of reorientation, and gradually, a new psychological place can be attained.

3. A new beginning: People may begin to learn new skills and competencies, make new relationships, and develop a new vision for the future.

In managing people's transition, Jick's (1990) caution and perspective need to be heeded:

These basically optimistic theories about how people eventually embrace change, while psychologically accurate, are somewhat simplistic. Most people will work through the emotional phases they delineate; some will do so more quickly than others. But others will get stuck, often in the first stages, which encompass the most keen and jagged emotions. . . . People get stuck for two basic and obvious reasons: "Change" is not some monolithic event that has neat and tidy beginnings and ends; and people's subjective experiences of change vary considerably as a result of individual circumstance. [Moreover,] frameworks that presume periods of psychological sorting out while the change is being digested are somewhat flimsy in helping us deal with multiple changes. How are we to be in "defensive retreat" with one change, in the "neutral zone" with another, while adapting to a third? If these changes are also rapid-fire, a fairly common situation in these upheaving days in the political and economic arenas, it becomes clearer why some people "resist." (p. 5)

Achieving closure is most relevant to the surrender or disengagement phase, letting go of the past. As Jick (1990) implies, this is easier said than done. Although there are individual differences, most, if not all, people have some need to complete "unfinished business" and, at some level, energy will be spent in an attempt to "finish the thing." For example, when one has an argument with someone that stops, for one reason or another, short of resolution, one tends to continue the argument mentally, even though the other party is no longer present. People spend mental and emotional energy in an attempt to finish, resolve, or complete the argument. So it is with organizational change. When newness is thrust on organization members, replacing, say, formal ways of doing things, with no time to disengage and "finish the business" of the former way, they will spend energy trying to deal with the incompleteness. This energy may take the form of simply continuing to talk about the former ways or, even more resistantly, sabotaging the new ways. What is referred to as "resistance to change" often amounts to attempts to gain closure. Providing ways for organization members to disengage from the past, at least to some extent, helps them focus on the change and the future.

A case of achieving a reasonable degree of closure occurred at one of the centers of the National Aeronautics and Space Administration (NASA). Because certain technology was obsolete, the center director had to terminate a certain rocket program as part of a larger change effort. Several hundred scientists, engineers, and technicians were affected. The center director held a brief ceremony for all these people that symbolized the "death and burial" of the program. He also made a toast to the group commemorating the fine work that had been done on this program in the past. Follow-up interviews indicated that this NASA executive achieved closure for his part of the agency. (For more detail about this closure experience, see Burke, 1994, pp. 147–148.)

Finally, getting people involved, or participating in making the change work, can go a long way toward resolving resistance. A principle of behavior that is central to effective management in general and managing change in particular is "involvement leads to commitment." Stated a bit more elaborately, the degree to which people will be committed to an act is a function of the degree to which they have been involved in determining what the act will be. This is a commonsense principle of human behavior that is corroborated by considerable research. This principle helped to explain why so many elegantly and appropriately designed plans never get implemented. When a single person or small group of people plan a change that will involve a much larger group of other people and fail to involve the others in the planning, the likelihood of successful implementation is diminished. The larger group is likely to perceive the plan as something imposed on them, and their reactance is aroused. Although they may agree that the plan is intrinsically logical and appropriate, there will be no *psychological commitment* to it if they have not been involved in the planning itself and have had no influence on its content or choice in whether to contribute to it. This lack of psychological commitment does not necessarily cause complete resistance to implementation, but the best that can be expected (unless organizational loyalty is extraordinarily high) is slow, reluctant compliance. Getting people involved, then, can not only mitigate resistance but can also contribute to a more effective overall change process.

Change in Organizations at the Group Level

The primary work group, whether it is a top management team, a packaging unit at plant level, or a district sales team, is the most important subsystem within an organization. The work group serves as the context and locus for (1) the interface between the individual and the organization, (2) the primary social relationships and support of the individual employee, whether or not he or she is a manager, and (3) a determination of the employee's sense of organizational reality. The extent to which members of a group work well together and the extent to which they, as a group, work well with other groups in the organization will determine in part the overall effectiveness of the organization.

Work groups have always been important for organizational effectiveness. We first recognized this systematic importance in the Hawthorne studies (see Chapter 3). This importance is increasing. The single individual who knows many of the functions and specialties within an organization is becoming more and more a rarity. Groups of various specialists attempting to produce something that is greater than the total of their individual specialties are becoming more the rule than the exception. Newer organizational structures, such as the matrix design and networks, require an increase in group activities.

Team Building

Organization change efforts typically rely heavily on the use of work groups. These family units within the organization have to make changes in the way they conduct their work. Their unit goals may need to be entirely different, their roles within the unit may need to be modified, and so forth. Conducting team-building activities often supports the larger organization change. And the more the work unit has at least one goal that is common to all group members and the accomplishment of that goal (or goals) requires cooperative interdependent behavior on the part of all members, the more likely a team-building activity is in order. Dyer (1987) has developed criteria to help determine whether team building is needed, for example, in the case of difficulty between the team leader and members or difficulty among team members; Beckhard (1972) has provided a set of four purposes for team building:

1. To set goals or priorities

2. To analyze or allocate the way work is performed according to team members' roles and responsibilities

3. To examine the way the group is working—its processes, such as norms, decision making, and communications

4. To examine interpersonal relationships among members

Beckhard (1972) pointed out that all these purposes are likely to be operating in a team-building effort, "but unless *one* purpose is defined as *the* primary purpose, there tends to be considerable misuse of energy. People then operate from their own hierarchy of purposes and, predictably, these are not always the same for all members" (p. 24). Thus, Beckhard's order for the four purposes is important. The reason for this ordering of the purposes is as follows: *Interpersonal* problems could be a consequence of group members' lack of clarity on team goals, roles and responsibilities, or procedures and processes; problems with *procedures* and *processes* could be a consequence of group members' lack of clarity on team goals or roles and responsibilities; and problems with *roles* and *responsibilities* may be a result of group members' lack of clarity about team goals. To begin a team-building effort with work on interpersonal relationships may be a misuse of time and energy because it is possible that problems in this area are a result of misunderstanding in one of the other three domains. Clarifying goals, roles and responsibilities, or team procedures and processes may eliminate certain interpersonal problems among team members; clarifying roles and responsibilities may in itself eliminate some of the problems with the team's working procedures and processes; and clarifying team goals and priorities may in itself eliminate certain problems team members have with their roles and responsibilities.

A smoothly operating group of people in a work unit, or in a temporary task force, for that matter, can be highly beneficial to an overall organization change effort, particularly if the group is the top management team of the organization. To have everyone pulling in the same direction is critical to the success of an organization change effort.

A well-honed, highly cohesive, smoothly operating work unit or task force can have adverse consequences for the overall good of the organization, however. Kanter (1982), for example, has addressed the importance of linking teams with their environments. She points out that this linking has six dilemmas:

1. Suboptimization: Too much team spirit can cause insularity, with members losing sight of their team's role and function in the larger organization.

2. Turnover: A highly cohesive team has a difficult time accepting new members.

3. Problem of fixed decisions: Norms and ground rules can become rigid, and prior decisions may become immutable.

4. Stepping on toes and territories: A highly cohesive team can feel powerful and believe that no one else can understand what they know; their expertise should therefore have great influence in the larger system.

5. NIH: "Not invented here" is the problem of ownership and transfer, a reluctance to share and to be influenced by other individuals and groups.

6. As Kanter (1982) put it, "A time to live and a time to die" (p. 22): Groups have life cycles and, after a high of effectiveness, may then dip to ineffectiveness.

Self-Directed Groups

It may be that as part of a larger change effort, management has decided to "flatten" the organization's hierarchy, that is, to eliminate several layers of supervision. Usually, with such changes, the span of control for a given manager or supervisor broadens from, say, 1:9 to 1:20 or more. Organizational members need to learn more about how to manage themselves individually and in work units. So-called self-directed or self-managed groups have become much more prevalent in organizations of late. With many organizations downsizing and delayering to become more nimble and adaptable to rapid changes in their marketplaces, the growth of self-management, particularly in groups, has significantly increased.

Hackman (1992) has (a) delineated the key features of self-directed groups, paying particular attention to the authority and leadership issues, (b) specified the behaviors that distinguish self-directing from the more traditional modes of operating, for example, taking personal responsibility, mentoring and managing one's own performance, actively seeking guidance when needed, and helping others in the group, and (c) suggested conditions that foster and support the kinds of self-direction that will contribute both to personal satisfaction and to group achievements, such as having clear and engaging goals, a supportive structure for the unit, expert coaching and consultation, and adequate material resources. Paying attention to Hackman's criteria and conditions should lead to greater team effectiveness for self-directed groups. In any case, evidence is beginning to emerge that self-directed groups can indeed be successful. In a comprehensive meta-analysis of 70 studies, Goodman, Devadas, and Griffith-Hughson (1988) concluded that self-directed groups had a positive impact on productivity. In another study by Pearson (1992), attitudes on the job were favorably influenced as well.

As one might expect, there are problems to overcome for self-directed groups to be effective:

- Group members must learn to share power and leadership.
- Effectively managing differences and conflicts within the group is critical to success.
- Not all group members are equal with respect to skill and ability, experience, knowledge, and expertise. Managing these differences is key to success, that is, deploying the human resources of the group toward task accomplishment in an efficient and effective manner.

It is likely that for overall organization change to be successful now and in the future, there will need to be more and more reliance on self-directed groups. Why? Because of the demand for organizations to be as flexible and adaptable as possible for future survival. A part of this greater adaptability is a flatter hierarchy with more rapid decision making and less bureaucracy.

Intergroup

Work units or groups in organizations that normally depend on one another—such as marketing people working with operations people, research and development with manufacturing, or headquarters with field as they exchange information, hand off one aspect of the production process to another unit, and so on—will from time to time experience problems and issues with one another. Each group has its own mission, but for that mission to be accomplished, each group occasionally must rely on the other. This mutual dependence, or interdependence, is a natural setting for conflict.

The original research in intergroup conflict, which set the stage for how we deal with it in practice today, was conducted by Sherif and his colleagues in the late 1940s and early 1950s (Sherif, Harvey, White, Hood, & Sherif, 1961). In a series of studies with groups of boys at summer camp,

Sherif and his colleagues demonstrated how to develop strong in-group feelings with two separate groups by creating opportunities for success and enhancing pride and then showing how these feelings translated into competitive behavior when the two groups were placed in a win-lose situation. Experiments were also conducted in reducing conflict and in establishing a cooperative attitude between the two groups by focusing on a superordinate goal, that is, a goal that could only be accomplished with cooperative efforts between the two groups. These experiments were also conducted over a period of years with adults in industrial organizations (Sherif & Sherif, 1953). Blake, Shepard, and Mouton (1964) summarized Sherif's work and demonstrated refinements of the processes in work done with actual groups in conflict, such as staff and line, headquarters and field, sales and operations, and management and union. Alderfer (1977a) has provided an overview and summary of intergroup relations, as has Schein (1980).

It is important to distinguish between real conflict between groups and what Harvey (1977) referred to as "phony conflict." Otherwise, what action to take remains unclear. According to Harvey, the difference is that real conflict involves substantive differences. One party says, "The research project is technologically feasible," and the other says, "Not according to my understanding of the data." Phony conflict, however, consists of negative, even hostile blaming behavior that occurs when *agreement is mismanaged*. One party says, "I told you the project couldn't work. Look at the mess you've got us in," and the other says, "Don't blame me. It would have worked if you had done your job." Harvey argued that such conflict is a symptom, not a condition in itself. As a symptom, conflict may reflect real differences, or it may be symptomatic of agreement that people are not willing to acknowledge: For example, all members of a team believe that a project is doomed to fail, but no member will voice this agreement because they also may believe, perhaps incorrectly, that the team leader is fully behind the project.

Harvey (1977) further argued that when managers and consultants fail "to distinguish between real and phony conflict they collude with maintaining the problem they are attempting to solve" (p. 166). In a phony conflict, all members—regardless of group—know what the problem is and what solution is required. They are reluctant to act because of action anxiety, negative fantasies, fear of separation, real risk, or psychological reversal of risk and certainty (Harvey, 1974). Confronting reality and recognizing and acting on the implicit agreement may require more risk than people in the situation feel like taking. Thus, there is an underlying agreement not to discuss the implicit agreement, but it is not being exposed and managed. According to Harvey (1977), it is highly important to bring this agreement to the surface and help manage it toward action.

Real conflict between groups involves substantive issues, and the two (or more) groups express competitive behavior, not merely blaming one another. Within each group, we are likely to find that members are close and loyal to one another. Their internal differences are submerged; group climate is formal, serious, and task oriented, rather than informal, playful, and oriented toward members' psychological needs; the group leader is more directive and less participative; activities are structured and organized; strong norms exist that demand loyalty to the group from each member; and there is considerable energy to resist the other group.

Once it has been determined that real conflict exists and that there is motivation within both groups to work on the problems, action to resolve the conflict is warranted. As the earlier coverage of experiments about intergroup conflict by Sherif and others suggested, the first action step for resolving conflict among groups is to establish a superordinate goal. For a description of action that is based on the theoretical foundations briefly described previously and on the earlier work of Sherif and colleagues, see Burke (2006).

Group Responses to Organization Change

The more that work units in the organization are involved in helping to plan and implement change, the more they are likely to embrace rather than resist the organization change effort. Resistance by organizational groups, on the other hand, can take at least four forms (listed in no particular order):

"Turf" Protection and Competition. "To change our unit is to endanger a central and core competence of the organization" is an expression often heard during organization change. The work group, function, department, or business unit is fighting for survival and will muster every rationale, fact, and guilt-inducing behavior to justify its continuation.

Closing Ranks. "Circle the wagons"; "One for all and all for one." In a recent structural change at a university, the anthropologists were asked to divide themselves among two or three new academic departments. They refused, declaring that they must remain as a group and join only one department, none of which they liked, incidentally. Their arguments and feelings were that the president was attempting to destroy their identity and function in the university by dividing them.

Changing Allegiances or Ownership. To avoid having to deal with the organization change, a group may opt for becoming a separate entity, that is, formally departing from the parent organization. The group can be "spun off " as a separate business and go its merry way. Leveraged buy-out (LBO) is one form of separation. The group may join another division within the organization but remain intact. The group may become a "wholly owned" subsidiary and have to survive on its own but remain intact and maintain its autonomy. A spin-off, LBO, or subsidiary may be a carefully planned and deliberate action as part of an overall change effort for the organization. Just as likely, these kinds of actions are ways of avoiding conflict and having to deal with difficult change issues.

The Demand for New Leadership. Analogous to distinguishing between real and phony conflict, there are times and circumstances in which the group leader is simply not capable of dealing with and leading a change effort. Under these conditions, perhaps the leader should be replaced. There are times, on the other hand, when the leader is quite capable, but the followers in the group revolt as a way of resisting the change. In other words, they collude with one another to resist their change leader by suggesting, if not outright averring, that their leader is incompetent. This form of resistance is a deeper psychological process and may reside more in the collective unconscious of the group than in its consciousness. Bion's (1961) theoretical distinction between a work group (conscious of its task and the passing of time) and what he calls a "basic assumption" group (colluding to destroy the leader, that is, assuming that the leader is no longer a leader) is useful for more thoroughly understanding this form of resistance. After all, organization change generates strong emotions for organizational members; feelings may "run high," as the expression goes. People may be aware of their feelings but may not always be conscious of what is causing them.

Ways of dealing with change for individuals—conceptually, achieving closure, and participation—apply to groups as well. A few additional points on group action are worth our consideration.

Achieving closure at a group level, for example, conducting a brief "funeral" for a former program or the past ways of operating and then celebrating the new way or program, may be more beneficial than closure at an individual level. Sharing feelings, that is, having an opportunity to discuss these feelings with people who are going through the same experience, is often valuable, a worthwhile expenditure of human energy.

Conducting group problem-solving meetings off-site, where members can participate in determining the specific change actions that will directly affect them, may be highly beneficial.

Finally, it may make sense to recompose a group, not changing its function necessarily, but changing its membership. It may be that new skills and technology are needed for a particular work unit to go forward in support of the larger organization change effort. Or it may be that the members are so resistant to the change, for whatever reasons, that they need to be reassigned—as Kanter (1982) noted, a "time to die." In other words, for the overall common good, the local group must be recomposed.

Change in Organizations at the Larger-System Level

An organization change effort rarely, if ever, begins all at once with the total system, especially in a large organization. Beginnings typically involve an individual, a group, or a program, such as management training, or an already recognized need to make a significant change—in the organization's structure, for example. The previous sections in this chapter have dealt with much of the groundwork that either leads to large-system change or facilitates it. In this section, we shall consider some of these previously described interventions in attempts to change a large organization, a system composed of multiple groups, functions, and processes. In examining large-system change, we shall briefly consider the orders or levels of change, the phases of large-system change, the change focus (mission or structure), some examples of change processes at the larger-system level, and finally, change at the interorganizational level.

Orders of Change

Because change at the larger-system level is so complex, it is useful to think strategically about different orders of change. Kimberly and Nielsen

(1975) have suggested three orders of change. (*Order* refers to the level of the ultimate target for change.) For *first-order* changes, the initial focus is some subsystem of the organization. The change would occur as a result of an intervention in a particular unit or division (subsystem) within the organization. The unit may be a relatively autonomous business line or the top management team, and the intervention could be team building, with a change objective of developing more collaborative, consensual decision-making behavior. First-order change, then, is within a subsystem, and although change in that unit will have some consequences for the larger system, the likelihood is that, unless other complementary and supplementary changes are also occurring in related parts of the total system, the change within the initial subsystem will be short lived. For an excellent and classic example of this point, see the Hovey and Beard case (Whyte, 1955).

Second-order change means that the target is a subsystem or process that is beyond the initial focus but that will be affected if the initial effort is successful. The focus is frequently a category or a particular set of subsystems within the organization. An intervention may take place with one group of employees, first-line supervisors, for example, when the ultimate objective for the change effort is to affect all workers below these supervisors in the organizational hierarchy. If we want to decrease absenteeism and turnover among the workers who are accountable to these supervisors, our initial effort may be a training program for the supervisors in which they would have the opportunity to learn more about human motivation, the consequences of certain kinds of rewards and punishment, and effective ways of providing feedback on worker performance. With proper application of this learning, the supervisors would help reduce absenteeism and turnover, our ultimate target for change.

Third-order change eventually influences some organizational process or outcome that is affected by multiple factors. Third-order change, therefore, means the involvement of multiple factors in some causal sequence toward an ultimate goal. Wherever the interventions or series of interventions are made, the ultimate objective of the change effort is larger, to increase productivity, for example. Staying with this example, because multiple factors affect productivity, no single first-order or even second-order change is likely to be successful. Also, for third-order change, there is likely to be a chain or sequence of factors that eventually leads to higher productivity. We may begin with changing how to treat their subordinates, for example, by getting them to manage more participatively. This change in turn will affect work climate and subordinate motivation, which then may lead to greater individual and group performance and finally, to increased productivity.

Documenting change at the first order is fairly straightforward; at the second level, it is more difficult; and at the third, very difficult, as we shall see in the next chapter. Nevertheless, we must understand that changing the entire system is a third-order change.

Change Phases

One of the first psychologists to help us understand organization change at the larger-system level was Kurt Lewin. His rather simple three-phase model set the stage for the more elaborate and comprehensive models we embrace today. These more recent models are explained in a later chapter. For now, let us briefly examine what is meant by these three phases.

Although applicable to the larger system, Lewin (1958) explained his three-phase model for change at the group level. The term *step* is often used in describing Lewin's model, but *phase* is a better word because the steps are not discrete; they overlap.

Lewin (1958) argued that in Phase 1, we must *unfreeze* the system. This unfreezing phase may take a variety of forms: creating a sense of urgency about the need for change, educating managers to behave differently, merging with another organization, and so on; but the underlying notion is that the system must be shaken up, must be confronted with a compelling need to do business differently, and must be thawed from its present way of doing things so that in a new, more malleable, perhaps even vulnerable state or condition, the system is accessible and amenable to change interventions.

The second phase, then, is *movement*, or changing the organization: moving in new directions with different technologies and ways of operating. Lewin's (1958) point was that the system will *not* move or change in any meaningful way unless and until an unfrozen condition has been achieved.

Once change, or movement, is under way, the third phase, *refreeze*, must be initiated (Lewin, 1958). The change that has occurred cannot be allowed to dissipate or drift away. The new, changed condition or state therefore needs to be reinforced, or undergirded, with a process and infrastructure in place to maintain the new system. This means, for example, having a different reward system that reinforces the behaviors that are congruent with the new, changed organization. In other words, organizational members see a clear and direct relationship between what the organization's mission and strategy are and their individual roles and responsibilities. Other examples could be noted, such as organizational structure and information systems. The point is that as the new state is "frozen" in the early stages of change, it is delicate, somewhat vulnerable, and, until jelled, is subject to further change that may not be desired. Thus, reinforcing the new state is just as important in the change process as shaking up the old one was in Phase 1. Chapter 13 will provide more about sustaining a change effort.

We examine in more depth this phased way of thinking about, planning, and implementing organization change in Chapter 8.

Change Focus

In a sense, the question here is, where do we start with our change effort, what comes next, and then where do we focus? The answer to "Where do we start?" depends on what is initiating the change in the first place, particularly from the organization's external environment, and how deep the change should be. Are we talking about revolutionary or evolutionary change? If revolutionary, then the focus is on deep issues such as the raison d'être of the organization, its purpose, its mission, and related matters, for example, strategy. We will also focus on issues of leadership and organizational culture. If, on the other hand, the changes needed are not as fundamental or transformational in nature—that is, what seems to be required is some fine tuning, improvements here and there, or changing some important parts of the organization but not the entire system—then we are talking about evolutionary, or transactional, change. The focus, therefore, is on matters such as organizational design and structure, the information system, or perhaps management practices.

Staying with our theme, larger-system change, implying more transformational than transactional change, we start with a focus on the bigger picture—mission, leadership, and culture—followed by a focus on the more transactional dimensions. The focus of change in the latter case is on the support and infrastructural aspects of the organization that will reinforce the transformational changes: organizational structure (*after* the new strategy has been determined), the reward system (to reinforce new behaviors), information technology (to align with and support new operations), new roles and jobs for people, improving the climate of groups and teams, and so on.

Change Processes

In general, *process* here refers to mechanisms that facilitate the overall change effort, such as communication systems (newsletters that tell stories about successful changes that support the overall effort, videos of the CEOs championing the cause, etc.) and training programs that focus on the new skills and behaviors needed to make the change work. More specifically, process refers to certain interventions meant to significantly implement the change effort, as in the following two examples.

Large-Group Intervention. Large-group intervention involves bringing together a large, key group of organizational members (e.g., the top 100 executives or all 500 first-line supervisors) into one room for a day or two to address a significant organization change issue, for example, determining the new mission and set of guiding values for the organization or responding to an organizationwide survey with action plans. This kind of intervention requires a significant amount of design and logistical planning, yet it can be powerful for moving the organization (a huge step) toward the change goals. For more information about this kind of large-scale intervention, see the book by Bunker and Alban (1997) and the article by Burke, Javitch, Waclawski, and Church (1997).

Survey Feedback. The historical development and brief description of what this kind of intervention entails is provided in Chapter 3.

Suffice it to say here that in support of an overall change effort, an organizationwide survey helps to achieve the following:

- Establish data points at a particular time that can serve as milestones or benchmarks for how well the change is progressing; further value is provided when a Time 1 assessment is compared with a Time 2 measure, say, a year later.
- Establish priorities about which aspects of the organization to emphasize for change and in what order to address them.
- Send messages, by the content of the questions that are asked, to organizational members about what is important in the change process.

- Keep the change effort based on data.
- Involve a large number of people in the organization change effort through feedback and action planning.

For more information on this kind of organizational intervention, see Kraut (1996).

Interorganizational

Currently and probably for some time yet to come, larger-system change comes about by way of mergers and acquisitions, strategic alliances, joint ventures, and the like. There are a number of reasons for these joinings, two in particular: (1) the opportunity to share resources that neither organization by itself has and (2) the opportunity to improve cost-effectiveness by reducing redundancies. By their very nature, these decisions and occurrences force organization change. This is particularly true of a merger in which two organizations of relatively equal size and scope come together as one. But most of these joinings fail, especially mergers and acquisitions. Using the criteria of what is promised by the leaders of merged and acquiring companies and the objectives of the decision to join ("achieving synergies" is a phrase often bandied about), there are many more failures than successes. Burke and Biggart (1997) conducted a study of interorganizational relations and found that this majority of failures could be attributed to the following primary reasons or conditions:

- Insufficient clarity about goals and how to measure progress toward the goals
- Imbalance of power and control between the two organizations when they merged or, say, established a strategic alliance or joint venture
- Imbalance of expertise, status, or prestige between the two parties
- Overconfident and unrealistic notions about future success of the relationship, that is, holding an erroneous belief of having sufficient control over key variables
- Lack of a contingency plan (as Chapter 2 notes, organization change, including these joinings, never unfolds as foreseen)
- Lack of perceived equity, for example, in distributions of key jobs and roles

Conditions for success in organizations' coming together are the opposite of those on the failure list. To clarify, here are a few examples:

- Having a superordinate goal, that is, a goal or goals that can be accomplished *only* through the cooperative efforts of the two parties. (See the section "Coercion and Confrontations" in Chapter 3 for the original research in this domain, the work of Sherif and Sherif [1969] and Blake et al. [1964].)
- Having a balance of power, expertise, and status
- Creating mutual gain
- Having a committed leader
- Aligning of rewards—in the early stages of a merger or acquisition, it is important to consolidate various compensation systems into one
- Having respect for differences
- Achieving equity
- Having realistic assumptions about what can be accomplished and in what time frame
- Having good luck

In an informal discussion with senior executives who had recently been through an acquisition (some the acquirers and some the acquired) and were about to go through yet another one, I asked them what they had learned from their previous experiences. The following is a quick summary of what these executives said:

1. They emphasized the importance of having a vision for the future (sound familiar?).

2. They noted that having a rationale behind the joining and explaining this carefully to all those affected is critical.

3. They stressed the importance of being open and honest about the change.

4. They pointed out how important it is in the early stages to have informal relations between the two parties, such as going to a ball game together, having meals together, and so on.

5. These executives argued that rapid decision making was imperative even if some of the decisions would have to be changed later. They pointed out that people cry for structure and order and this need should be addressed.

6. The executives emphasized the importance of what they referred to as "walking the talk," meaning matching words with actions, or the absence of hypocrisy. (Chapter 13 elaborates on this aspect of leading change.)

7. They stated that in midst of this kind of organization change, typically the customer is forgotten. With so much time and energy being focused inwardly, conducting the business and serving customers suffers.

Although these executives made some interesting and unique points, as can be seen, there is considerable overlap with the findings from the study by Burke and Biggart (1997).

To see how a successful merger changed two organizations, SmithKline Beckman of Philadelphia and Beecham of London, into a new, single organization that required the coming together of two companies as well as two nationalities, see Bauman, Jackson, and Lawrence (1997) and Burke and Jackson (1991). And to see how a strategic alliance that cut across three companies and three nationalities (United Kingdom, France, and Germany) affected the internal organization change effort of British Aerospace, see Evans and Price (1999). Finally, as already cited, for an overview and analysis of interorganizational relations in general, see Burke and Biggart (1997).

System Responses to Organization Change

Again, with strong efforts at following a planned process to bring about large-scale organization change, including heavy use of involvement and participatory activities as well as clarity of direction with strong leadership, successful organization change can occur. The change at BA and the successful merger of SmithKline Beecham are good cases in point. Yet even with successful changes, resistance occurs along the way, and when success is not achieved, the resistance dominates and lingers. We will touch on six examples of resistance to larger-scale change.

Revolution Becomes, at Best, Evolution. When a transformational change is attempted, in the end, only some components of the organization are changed or perhaps just some fine-tuning occurs. The old culture is simply too powerful, the bureaucracy too pervasive. Even though the perturbation(s) from the external environment may have been strong—say, a significant technological change in the industry (such as going from analog to digital in the communications industry)—the organization's response to this external shift is insufficient, and the deep structure (pattern) does not change.

Insufficient Sense of Urgency. In this instance, which happens often, the case for change is simply not compelling. The question is obvious: "Why change?" Many people in the organization lack the motivation to tackle an organization change process and program because they harbor disbelief about the need, serious skepticism, a lackadaisical attitude, or a combination of these responses. For whatever reasons, not enough organizational members are convinced that change is required, and there is not a critical mass to move the organization in another direction.

"This Too Shall Pass." This response is typically a function of history. Time and again, management has tried this and tried that, taking on the latest fad for improving the organization, or the "flavor of the month," as this process is sometimes called. And people believe the cliché "the more things change, the more they stay the same." So, organizational members' response is to "wait 'em out." The response shows more apathy than it does active resistance.

Diversionary Tactics. This category of response is indeed resistance and reflects a strong desire on the part of organizational members to sabotage the effort in one way or another. One way is to create a crisis that must be addressed before any change can get under way. Sales may drop all of a sudden, a technological glitch may pop up, or some waste products may be declared to be toxic. There are many possibilities. Another more common form is to argue that the *timing* for such a change is wrong. There are far too many other things "on the plate," as the expression goes. "We have residual problems from last year that still need fixing." "People are stretched to the limits, too much stress, we simply cannot afford to pile yet another organizational initiative onto their agenda." "This kind of effort will divert us from the *real* work, manufacturing and selling our products, or attending to customer needs." The point is that people will grab at anything in order to avoid, if not sidetrack, the change.

Lack of Followership. "Well, the platform may be burning, but if you think I'm going to follow this CEO into the flames, you're out of your mind!" This response is, of course, similar to if not the same as the one mentioned earlier in the group-level section. Followers, or more accurately, potential followers, collude or even conspire with one another to find fault with the leader. And if there is no followership, by definition, there is no leadership. Without leadership, *intended* change will not occur.

Coping With Responses to Change at the Larger-System Level. Many of the coping mechanisms at the individual and group level are applicable at the larger-system level: achieving closure on the previous way of doing things, providing conceptual frameworks to help people understand more clearly what is happening to them, and involving organizational members in the process of planning and implementing the change.

In addition, we can easily point to the list of responses and resistances and then suggest antidotes. First and foremost is the issue of making a compelling case for the need to change. A clear example is the change at British Aerospace. The top 100 executives were complying with the CEO's desire to bring about change, but a deep commitment on their part was lacking. A senior and highly respected executive in the company was given the assignment of making the case for change. He conducted an environmental scan and showed conditions in the past and in the present, and—"if things continue as they are"—what the future would look like. These conditions were in the categories of sales, technological shifts, what and how their competitors were doing, and likely scenarios for the future with respect to the aerospace industry, which currently can be described as a shrinking marketplace. British Aerospace is, of course, loaded with engineers. The senior executive's presentation to the company therefore was, quite appropriately, in the form of many bar charts, line graphs, and statistics. An engineer himself, he argued that if they remained as they were at the time, within a decade or less, they would be out of business. Critical to this senior executive's success in getting the message across was his knowledge of the audience. Although he was a senior executive, he was nevertheless one of them, an engineer, and therefore knew how to talk to them, using appropriate language, supporting documentation, and the proper medium (charts with data). From that time to the present, there has been a significantly stronger commitment to the overall organization change effort (Burke & Trahant, 2000; Evans & Price, 1999).

To combat apathy and responses such as "this too shall pass," the change leaders must demonstrate as clearly and strongly as possible that

(1) this time, the change initiative is different (because of a compelling and pervasive need) and (2) we are in this for the long haul, that is, showing at the outset that persistence will prevail. The British Airways story of change had both these qualities.

With respect to diversionary tactics, it is incumbent on the part of change leaders to be as clear and committed as possible to the organization change goals and objectives and to establish a set of priorities—to address strategy first and then to tackle structure, and so on. And although it may not be desired, for the change to be successful may mean that certain saboteurs must be dealt with by job changes, early retirements, or outright severance from the organization.

Finally, two points: (1) Described briefly previously are examples of the kind of leadership that will attract followers, and (2) if revolutionary change is called for, the deep structure of the organization must be changed. This means changing the culture particularly, perhaps new leadership with a different mission and strategy, followed by addressing the more transactional aspects of the organization, such as structure, with respect to decision making and accountability, teamwork, and so on.

Summary

We have considered organization change in this chapter from the perspective of levels: individual (including interpersonal), group (including intergroup), and the larger system (including interorganizational). The point of the parentheses following each of the three is to emphasize that taking this perspective is somewhat limited. Organizations are far more complex than merely three levels. In fact, the interactions across these levels are very important. As we proceed with additional chapters, these interactions will become more salient.

Considering organization change according to these three levels, although limited, is useful nevertheless. As noted, organization change must start somewhere, and understanding how it can start at each of these levels helps us to more clearly understand how to plan and how to lead and manage the overall change. This chapter was intended to deepen this understanding by addressing the nature of change at each level, the likely responses in general and resistances in particular that occur at each level, and some examples of coping mechanisms at each level. Moreover, these three levels of understanding are not discrete. Individuals reside within groups and groups within the larger organization. And although our analysis, taking the organization apart by level, is helpful, we must remain highly cognizant of the fact that we are dealing with totalities, wholes, and systems.

This chapter covered a lot of ground. Tables 6.1 and 6.2 are therefore attempts at further summary. Also, in Table 6.1, the intent is to connect with Chapter 5, that is, by including examples at the three organizational levels that show both evolutionary change and revolutionary change.

In Chapter 7, we take a closer look at research on organizational change and at further theory, in this case, theory that is more closely related to the research.

Table 6.1 Summary of Levels of Organization Change According to Primary Change Example and Whether Evolutionary or Revolutionary Change

Organizational Level	Primary Organization Change Example	Evolutionary Change	Revolutionary Change
Individual	• Recruitment, selection, replacement, and displacement	Operational: Place people in positions as a consequence of changes that are under way.	Strategic: Place people in positions that are key to the overall change effort (King, 1972).
	• Training and development	Facilitate targeted change (e.g., people management skills, as in the Citicorp example).	Facilitate large-scale culture change, as in the British Airways example.
	• Coaching and counseling	Conduct at all levels in the organization for purposes of general improvement.	Conduct primarily with change leaders to enhance overall change effort.
Group	• Team building	Conduct team-building activities throughout the organization to improve teamwork and cooperative behavior.	Conduct team building with top executive group initially to model behavior desired for overall change effort.
	• Self-directed groups	Promote the adoption of self-directed groups due to structure change (i.e., eliminating some layers of management in the hierarchy).	Promote the adoption of self-directed groups to enhance culture change in the direction of values that encourage participation, involvement, autonomy, and greater teamwork.

Organizational Level	Primary Organization Change Example	Evolutionary Change	Revolutionary Change
	• Intergroup	Use conflict resolution techniques to reduce inappropriate intergroup competition.	Use conflict resolution techniques to promote cross-functional and interunit cooperation to reduce "silo effects" that in turn serve to change organization culture.
Organization	• Orders of change	First order	Second and third order
	• Change phases	Lewin's three phases	Lewin's three phases
	• Change focus	Issues such as systems, work unit climate, motivation, and performance management	Deep issues such as purpose, mission, strategy, culture, and leadership
	• Change processes	Those that promote problem solving and continuous improvement	Those that facilitate large-scale change, such as large-group interventions and survey feedback
	• Interorganizational	Acquisitions, strategic alliance, consortia	Mergers, large-scale acquisitions, strategic alliances, partnerships

Table 6.2 Summary of Responses to Organization Change According to Organizational Level

Organizational Level	Resistance	Coping With Change
Individual	• Has to do with losing something of value to the person	• Transitioning: ending and letting go, going through the neutral zone, making a new beginning
	• Forms: blind, political, and ideological (Hambrick & Cannella, 1989)	• Achieving closure: dealing with unfinished business
	• Apathy is worse; with resistance, there is energy, and the person cares about something	• Participation: helping to make the change work
Group	• "Turf" protection and competition	• The sense for individuals as listed above
	• Closing ranks: "circle the wagons"	• Conducting a closure ceremony (e.g., "funeral")
	• Changing allegiances or ownership	• Conducting group problem-solving sessions, preferably off-site
	• Demand for new leadership	• Recompose the membership of groups
Organization	• Revolution becomes, at best, evolution	• The above for individual and group are applicable for the organization level as well
	• Insufficient sense of urgency	• Ensuring that a compelling case for the change has been made
	• "This too shall pass"	• This time, the change initiative is different—we mean it, and we are in it for the long haul
	• Diversionary tactics: sabotage, timing is all wrong, too many initiatives and other things on our plate as it is, and the change is a way of avoiding our real work	• Strong, effective leadership

SEVEN

Organization Change

Research and Theory

T he objective of this chapter is to provide a guide through the mazes of both organization change research and organization change theory. Although we will review the compilations and summaries of research studies from the appropriate sources, for example, the *Annual Review of Psychology*, when it comes to theory, we will not rely on the "usual suspects," such as textbooks on organization theory, but will explore the less typical literature instead. Organization change theory barely exists, and we must therefore seek other theories that may begin to inform us in such a way that in a decade or so, a clearer and more definitive theory about organization change will emerge. For our theory bases, then, we will explore domains such as nonlinear complex systems theory, stemming from chaos and related theories, and some of the more fundamental psychological theories such as the one developed by William James and C. G. Lange, more than a century ago, known today as the James–Lange theory (James, 1890; Lange, 1885/1922). But first, let us see what research tells us about organization change by examining the literature of the past 30 years or so.

Reviews of Organization Change Research

One of the early reviews of organization change research was the *Annual Review of Psychology* chapter by Friedlander and Brown (1974). Writing under the banner of organization development (OD), these authors framed their review of research in the field in terms of "target of interventions" that led to outcomes. The two broad categories of interventions were (a) people and (b) technology, with the former emphasizing organizational processes, such as communication, decision making, and problem solving and the latter emphasizing organizational structures, such as task methods, job design, and organizational design. These two categories of interventions could lead to two outcomes: (a) human fulfillment and (b) task accomplishment (see Figure 7.1).

> These components interact in the techno-structural and human-processual [their term, not in the dictionary] systems on behalf of the objectives of human fulfillment and task accomplishment—and the environment obviously interacts with all these components in terms of input to and output from the organization. (Friedlander & Brown, 1974, p. 315)

Their framework is reflective of an open-system approach to conceptualizing organizations.

Figure 7.1   Approaches to Organization Development

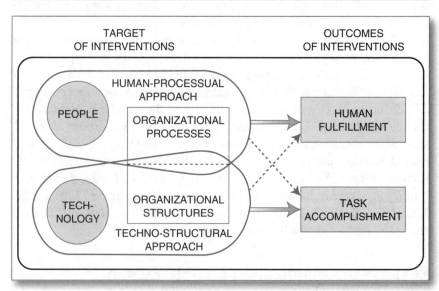

Friedlander and Brown's (1974) main conclusions from their review of the research literature at the time were as follows:

- Research showing change in the techno-structural category was clearer and more definitive than studies investigating the human-processual (their language, which essentially means interactions among organizational members, for example, group dynamics) approach. They attributed this difference to types of measurement tools, that is, techno-structural change is easier to measure than the more abstract and less objective human processes domain.
- "OD today is a long way from being the general theory and technology of planned social system we would like to see it become" (Friedlander & Brown, 1974, p. 335).

Although there was some evidence at the time that OD interventions had an effect on organizational performance, remembering the differences noted previously, the pervasiveness of the impact was not clear, and there was no overall guiding theory.

Three years later, Alderfer (1977b) provided a review of the research up to that time and concluded that "the overall quality of research ... is showing increasing signs of both rigor and vigor as more careful studies ... are being conducted and reported" (p. 197). Alderfer, unlike his two predecessors, did not use an overall framework or model to discuss his review of the literature.

In a subsequent summary of theory and research in organization change, three Europeans wrote a wide-ranging, cross-cultural review of the field (Faucheux, Amado, & Laurent, 1982). Their review differed somewhat from Alderfer's conclusions five years earlier. Citing the work of Porras (and his colleagues), one of our foremost researchers in OD and planned change, Faucheux and colleagues (1982) reported that there remained a "paucity of good research and particularly fundamental research" (p. 350). For example, there was even evidence to counter "that changed process caused changed outcome" (p. 350). In other words, part of Friedlander and Brown's (1974) model dealing with the outcomes of human processes (see Figure 7.1) was not substantiated. Faucheux and his colleagues called for a stronger linkage between the social and the technical approaches. This sociotechnical linkage (see Chapter 3) and the need to account for the broader context of organization change, such as understanding the relationship between a given organization and the society within which it resides, are critical. They contended that bringing about true organization change that is measurable and endurable requires such a linkage. This way of thinking is quite compatible with Capra's (1996) notion of networks (systems) embedded within networks (systems).

With the passage of another five years, the lament was similar: "Despite more sophisticated research methods, OD research results are still inconclusive. One can find support for many different conclusions, among the results reported in the studies" (Beer & Walton, 1987, p. 343). In sum, these reviewers raised an all-important question: "Why should this be so?" They stated that organization change research "suffers from problems," which are described as follows:

1. This kind of research attempts to determine causation. Most researchers rely on traditional scientific methods, working hard to identify the effects of some change intervention, such as team building, structure change, survey feedback, training, a shift in business strategy, installing a new information system or compensation plan, and so forth. What is overlooked is the larger system, the interconnectedness of the various parts (sound familiar?), and the context—changes that are occurring in the industry, for example. As Beer and Walton (1987) pointed out, "Exogenous variables and intervening events will always prevent any powerful conclusions. . . . Even worse, normal science methodology can damage the experiment itself" (p. 343). The authors then presented a very interesting example, a study by Blumberg and Pringle (1983). These researchers described an intervention that included job redesign and worker participation in managing a mine. Blumberg and Pringle had a control group and an experimental group, as normal science would dictate. In this case, however, the control group discovered what was going on with the experimental group and resented the latter's advantage. Moreover, the control group of miners then voted to stop the whole process, and no further changes occurred.

2. Most research on organization change is a snapshot, not a longitudinal view. Thus, it is difficult to determine how permanent a change may be.

3. Beer and Walton (1987) used the word *flat* to signal the third problem. What they meant is that much research methodology and

instrumentation is quite precise, but the meaning and interpretation of the data are anything but precise. History is often ignored, as is environmental context. The authors also pointed out that quantitative methods are not very useful for understanding an outcome that has multiple causes.

4. The research often does not fit the needs of the user. "Good science can be antithetical to good action" (Beer & Walton, 1987, p. 344). The use of highly technical, if not esoteric, statistical procedures can make research outcomes so complicated that managers and executives in organizations (users) end up with glassy eyes wondering what all this may mean. Also, researchers often equivocate about results and use phrases such as "on the other hand" and "this outcome can only be expected under these conditions." The researchers, certainly from their point of view, are using proper language for normal science. The users expect something quite different, such as simple declarative sentences.

Beer and Walton (1987) went on to state that organization research may be at a turning point—continuing as it was would lead only to studying isolated and episodic events. Going in another direction, namely "action science," as Argyris, Putnam, and Smith (1985) called it, may be the better choice. This means moving away from typical positivistic assumptions about research in organizations and toward a process that (a) involves the users in the study, (b) relies on self-corrective learning, say, trying certain assessment methods and then modifying them along the way as trial and error yields knowledge, and (c) occurs over time, not episodically. As Beer and Walton noted (1987), the literature about this kind of choice for organization change research has begun to grow. See, for example, Carnall (1982), Legge (1984), and Morgan (1983).

In addition to the four problems covered by Beer and Walton (1987), at least two more can be identified, (a) the researchers themselves and (b) determining *what*, if anything, changed:

1. Numerous studies have shown that the research can affect the outcome (Rosenthal, 1976). The degree to which the researcher is directly involved makes a difference: collecting data from organizational members, as a more distant observer, or not directly intervening in the organization at all and relying exclusively on archival information. Clarity must be sought, therefore, about the objective

of the organization change research. Is it for evaluative purposes, and are the organization's members the primary users? If so, then from the outset, these organizational members need to be involved, as Argyris (1970) has argued, in decisions about what data to collect and how to collect them. This increases the likelihood that appropriate data will be collected and analyzed with valid inferences being made. It further ensures that the data will be used. If, on the other hand, the primary user is the scientific community, then more objectivity with the process is necessary, with a greater reliance on data that are more likely to be objective, such as archival information, financial outcomes (although these need to be chosen carefully because "creative accounting," for example, is not dead), and independent assessments of the organization's effectiveness, such as Dun and Bradstreet ratings.

2.   With respect to a more complete understanding of what, if anything, changed, the work of Golembiewski, Billingsley, and Yeager (1976) is enlightening. They drew distinctions among three types of change, which they labeled alpha, beta, and gamma. Alpha change concerns a difference that occurs along some relatively stable dimension of reality. The change is typically a comparative measure before and after an intervention. If comparative measures of trust among team members showed an increase after a team-building intervention, for example, then we might conclude that our organizational intervention had made a difference. Golembiewski and colleagues (1976) asserted that most evaluation research designs consist of such "before" and "after" self-reports.

Suppose, however, that as a result of our team-building intervention, a *decrease* in trust occurred—or there was no change at all. One study has shown that, although no decrease in trust occurred, neither did a measurable increase occur as a consequence of a team-building intervention (Friedlander, 1970). Change may have occurred, however. The difference may be what Golembiewski and colleagues (1976) called a *beta* change, a recalibration of the intervals along some constant dimension of reality. As a result of a team-building intervention, team members may view trust very differently. Their basis for judging the nature of trust changed, rather than their perception of a simple increase or decrease in trust along some stable continuum. In other words, their *standard* for judging what trust is may have changed.

A *gamma* change "involves a redefinition or reconceptualization of some domain, a major change in the perspective or frame of reference within which phenomena are perceived and classified, in what is taken to be relevant in some slice of reality" (Golembiewski et al., 1976, p. 135). This involves change from one state to another. Staying with the example, after the intervention, team members might conclude that trust was not a relevant variable in their team-building experience. They might believe that the gain in their clarity about roles and responsibilities was the relevant factor and that their improvement as a team had nothing to do with trust.

Thus, selecting the appropriate dependent variable—determining specifically what might change—is not as simple as it might appear. This is especially important when self-report data are used.

Returning to reviews of organization change research and focusing on the latest work in this genre, we apparently can no longer rely on the *Annual Review of Psychology*. The last review article was published in the *Review* at the close of the 20th century and written by Weick and Quinn (1999). We will summarize this article at the end of this chapter because Weick and Quinn did not actually summarize research studies but instead provided interesting and somewhat new conceptual thinking. Thus, their coverage is more appropriate for the final section of the chapter.

Conducted by Oreg, Vakola, and Armenakis (2011), the most recent review of organization change research appears to be the extensive coverage of change recipients' reactions to change—that is, how people react to and feel about what is happening to them. Beginning in 1948, these researchers' coverage spanned about 60 years. The focus was on quantitative studies that measured organizational members' reactions to change—what they experienced. Over these six decades of organization change studies, they found about 700 published articles. Using standard criteria from "normal science"—that is, the scientific method, for evaluating the quality of a given study—Oreg and his colleagues narrowed their universe of 700 publications to a final group of 79. Based on these more rigorous studies, the researchers provided a framework consisting of three primary antecedents of organizational members' reactions to change: (a) change recipient individual characteristics—for example, style of coping; (b) change process—for example, degree of recipients' participation in the change process; and (c) change content—that is, what was the primary focus of the change—organizational structure, job design, information technology, etc. They linked these antecedents in a quantitative manner to explicit reactions—behavioral, affective, and cognitive—which in turn were associated with change consequence, for example, organizational performance, job satisfaction, personal well-being, etc. Oreg and his colleagues then concluded that their framework deals with inconsistencies of terms typically used in research, particularly with respect to change reactions. In other words, by clarifying the varieties of antecedents—that is, recipients' reactions and how they are linked to consequences, for example, resistance, and what affects what. They were careful to point out that determining what is cause and what is effect can be tricky. Variables such as organizational commitment and job satisfaction can be "antecedents as well as change consequences" (Oreg et al., 2011, p. 513).

Oreg and colleagues (2011) also provided a critique of the 79 studies that they reviewed. They did the following:

- Emphasized that when conducting organization change research it is critical to match variable definitions to measurement instruments (a validity issue)
- Pointed out that most of the 79 studies were based on self-reports from a single source
- Noted that many of the longitudinal studies were deficient regarding a Time 1–Time 2 linkage—that is, Time 2 recipients were not the same individuals who responded at Time 1; in other words, only overall trends could be reported not trends at the individual level
- Admitted disappointment that "the vast majority of studies explored change processes that occurred in a single organization (or department). This prevents the consideration of variables, e.g., antecedents, at the organizational level such as change content" (p. 514).

These researchers went further with their critique by arguing that executives are often incapable of predicting how change recipients will react to organization changes that contribute to ineffective leadership.

The consistent findings from Oreg and his colleagues' (2011) review of change recipients' reactions led these researchers to conclude that three aspects of organization change are critical—(a) trust, (b) involvement, and (c) selection—to lead a successful change effort to emphasize the following:

- Change recipients must trust their leaders and the process that they portray
- Involvement in decisions that directly affect change recipients leads to commitment to the change effort

- Selection of people to help lead and manage the change needs to have a personal disposition associated with positivism regarding change rather than with a negative and resistant disposition. After all, there are individual differences regarding resistance to change (Oreg, 2003).

These conclusions by Oreg and colleagues are not exactly a huge surprise. We have been clear for quite some time now that trust, involvement, and value congruence are indeed critical to success when it comes to leading change. It is comforting nevertheless to have empirical support and consistency for what we teach and practice.

Whereas the extensive review of research studies on organization change by Oreg and colleagues (2011) focused mainly on the recipients of change, another recent summary of organization change studies conducted by Ford and Ford (2012) targeted the other side of the relationship—the leadership of change. Ford and Ford began their article by referring to my statements regarding the question of whether leadership of change in organizations actually matters. The quote they cited was as follows:

What has not been clear from the literature is the impact of leadership on organization change . . . [and] there has been little evidence that scientifically demonstrates the leader's impact. It seems reasonable to assume, nevertheless, that because there is mounting evidence that leaders affect organizational performance in general, surely they have an impact on organization change in particular. We will proceed . . . with the assumption that leaders have significant influence on organization change. . . . (Burke, 2011, p. 249)

Ford and Ford tended to agree that my assumption was justified but they wanted to test this thinking by reviewing recent empirical evidence on the leadership of organization change. They did not have an easy time of it. As they pointed out, the literature is not clear-cut. The body of literature covered by Ford and Ford (2012) was empirical studies "dealing specifically with the leadership of change published in peer-reviewed academic business journals between 1990 and 2010" (p. 2). This approach yielded 27 empirical articles. But Ford and Ford wanted to be even more specific and limit their review to the leadership of change per se. This final criterion then narrowed their search to only 14 articles. Their summary and conclusions were therefore based on these few articles that met their criteria.

Initially Ford and Ford believed that it was critical to distinguish between different forms of leadership by pointing to the important difference of *focused* compared with distributed leadership. Citing the work of Gronn (2002), focused leadership refers to a single individual in a leadership position. The unit of analysis is therefore the "stand-alone leader." Most leadership research and writing has focused on this form that Yukl (1999) labeled as the "heroic leader paradigm." Distributed leadership, on the other hand, involves many people with their individualistic, and hopefully complementary, versions of leading. Distributed leadership has at least two subsets according to Gronn (2002): (a) collective and (b) co-performing. Collective distributed leadership means that leadership is dispersed among many organizational members at all levels and functions. "Senior management" might be a collective and therefore the unit of analysis. Co-performing distributed leadership is performed by a specific group of individuals who collaborate with one another. In other words, co-performing is more like deliberate team work, whereas collective distributed leadership is more dispersed. Ford and Ford (2012) classified their 14 studies into 7 that were focused, 2 that were distributed-collective, and the remaining 5 that were distributed-co-performing.

Ford and Ford (2012) also help us to understand leading change from the 14 studies they reviewed by addressing three ways of studying leadership: (1) *Approaches to change* such as directive, master, self-assembly, and emergent based on (a) whether the change effort is simple or complex and (b) whether the change can be driven from the top or from a more local, differentiated approach (Higgs & Rowland, 2005). Ford and Ford (2012) also pointed to the study of university mergers by Kavanagh and Ashkanasy (2006) and their three alternative approaches: (a) immediate (conducted quickly in a short period of time), (b) incremental, and (c) indifferent (no action taken over an extended period of time). Ford and Ford (2012) concluded this section on *approaches* by suggesting "that leaders who have a top-down approach to change may believe change is best done quickly, and those with a more local approach may take a more differentiated and delegated view of change" (p. 8). (2) *Leader behaviors*, a second way of studying leadership, rely on identifying specific behaviors of individuals in positions of authority. In the studies covered by Ford and Ford, the researchers either emphasized traditional leadership behaviors that are assumed to be stable over time and across situations, for example, transformational leadership, or as in the case of the study by

Higgs and Rowland (2005), identifying behaviors specifically related to change such as "shaping behavior, framing change and creating capacity." Ford and Ford (2012) summarized it this way:

> Shaping behaviors include leader communications and actions directly related to the change. Framing change behaviors include establishing starting points for the change, designing and managing the change journey, and communicating guiding principles. Creating capacity behaviors include developing individual and organizational capabilities and "communicating and creating connections. (p. 9)

(3) *Leader change activities* are Ford and Ford's (2012) third way of studying leadership of change. The emphasis is on particular change activities such as communicating a vision, coaching organizational members, engagement activities, and evaluating progress.

As Ford and Ford (2012) pointed out, one might assume that there are relationships among change approaches, leader behaviors, and leader change activities, but this apparently is not the case. They went on to raise important questions regarding this lack of relationships—that is, whether leaders of change efforts (a) stop doing things they usually do, (b) add new things while continuing what they usually do, (c) modifying the extent or degree to what they usually do, or (d) some combination of these (p. 12).

The primary analysis that Ford and Ford (2012) conducted with the 14 studies they reviewed concerned the question of whether leadership made a difference—and more particularly, a difference in what? In response to this question, researchers have considered two areas: (a) the personal reactions and experiences of change recipients—see, for example, the studies by Herold, Fedor, Caldwell, and Liu (2008) and by Oreg and colleagues (2011)—and (b) leader effectiveness in making change happen—for example, Gilley, McMillan, and Gilley (2009), one of the 14 studies that Ford and Ford reviewed. Moreover, in reviewing these 14 studies, Ford and Ford considered a third area of research: that is, the impact of leading on the leaders themselves—for example, see the study by Denis, Lamothe, and Langley (2001) among the Fords' 14 articles reviewed.

First, with respect to recipients' personal reactions and experiences of change, Ford and Ford (2012) concluded that there is some evidence that the way leaders approach change has an effect on recipients as measured by their commitment and readiness for change.

Second, regarding leader effectiveness in change implementation, the problem with attempting to draw conclusions from the studies was the fact that no study used an objective measure of effectiveness such as something as simple as percent of milestones attained. There was one exception among their 14 articles: The study by Kavanagh and Ashkanasy (2006) showed that with respect to university mergers, at least, a highly directive approach tended to be more successful although the recipients were not very happy about it.

Concerning the *third* area of leading change identified by Ford and Ford (2012) as the impact of change on the leaders themselves, they concluded that it was unlikely "that leaders can make it through a change unscathed by the process of which they are an integral part" (p. 21). Leaders of change do seem to alter their behavior—for example, communicate more rather than less, and choose certain activities over others, for example, organizing and deploying a special task force to help implement the change; however, the studies that Ford and Ford reviewed did not consider the psychophysiological costs of leading change. The Fords cited an article by Boyatzis, Smith, and Blaize (2006) that does address these costs for leaders of change.

In an attempt to summarize and integrate some of the main findings from the Ford and Ford (2012) review, the following points should help to clarify what they deem to be primary issues and tentative conclusions:

- The studies reviewed by the Fords used cross-sectional data where measures were taken at only a point either at some stage during the process of change or at the end. Organization change is by its very nature a longitudinal process. What is lost with snapshot measures is, for example, the dynamic interplay between leader behaviors and the activities of change over time.
- Although not completely clear from these 14 studies, it does seem that individuals in positions of leading change alter their behavior during the process, at least to some extent, perhaps, for example, becoming more transformational and at times more directive.
- Leadership effectiveness in a co-performing form appears to be based on the complementarity of behaviors among leaders rather than change outcomes being based on one person in a leadership position. Moreover, no single approach to change or particular set of leader behaviors, with the possible exception of communication, seem to dominate.

- Communication is the one behavioral category that apparently cuts across all of these studies. But what kind of communication? The language used in these studies were such phrases as "engaging communication," "communicating the need for change," "communicating appropriately," and "communicating and creating conditions," all of which, after all, do not tell us much about the actual content of communication, how much and how often, or which way—up or down, laterally.
- Measuring outcomes of organization change is quite problematical. The studies reviewed by Ford and Ford relied on assessments, ratings, and questionnaires capturing organizational members' perceptions, reactions, and opinions rather than factual data regarding success or failure based on the Fords' suggestions such as a priori specification of intended outcomes and objective measures necessary to determine their accomplishments and determining the impacts of actual activities and behaviors on objective outcomes.

These five points that were just listed may raise more questions than they answer regarding leading change, but at least the questions are likely to be in the right directions for improving and enhancing our understanding.

Finally, in concluding the Ford and Ford (2012) review article, we will use their language. First is their conclusion about research on leading change:

Research on the leadership of change appears to be challenged by four weaknesses:

1. an over-emphasis on the role of the individual leader in a position of authority,

2. the use of subjective assessments of change implementation and leadership without addressing the original intended outcomes for the leadership of a successful change,

3. the single-point data collection of many studies that does not include the temporality of change and its implications for the process and interactions of leadership, and

4. a vocabulary that adds confusion and vagueness to both the research and its conclusions. (pp. 31–32)

And then the Fords (Ford & Ford, 2012) ended their review article as they began—that is, referring to a certain assumption:

> With regard to Burke's assumption that leaders have a significant influence on organization change, we're willing to agree but unfortunately can't say what that influence is, what leader actions and interactions are responsible for it, or whether the influence is only on the subjective perceptions of people affected by the change or also impacts the objective outcomes of change. (p. 33)

This final statement by the authors seems fair to me, and in any case, it points the way for where future research needs to focus.

In summary, we have learned over the past three decades that measuring organization change is not simple. Following traditional methods of normal science may be straightforward, but the results may not be. Determining cause and effect in organizations is difficult because so many variables are involved and most cannot be controlled. In our attempts to measure organization change, we must also be clear about who the research is for. If the users are other researchers, then following normal science may be important. If the users are the members of the organization being studied, then they need to be involved and normal science is not necessarily appropriate. The emerging field of action science may need to be followed.

Recent Approaches to Research and Theory

The Shift From "Normal" Science

So-called normal science methods originated with the physical sciences and were adopted by the social and behavioral sciences. But the physical sciences have not stayed exclusively with "normal" methods. Chaos theory, nonlinear systems theory, and related concepts and theories, such as fractals, have precipitated changes in research methods. As Svyantek (1997) and his colleagues have pointed out (e.g., Svyantek & Brown, 2000; Svyantek & DeShon, 1993), organizational researchers need to move in similar directions. Svyantek and Brown (2000) referred to this kind of direction as a "complex-systems approach" to the study of organizations, meaning that organizational behavior can rarely be explained by analysis—that is, breaking down the system into its component parts:

> Explaining the behavior of a complex system requires understanding (a) the variables determining the system's behavior, (b) the patterns of interconnections among these variables, and (c) the fact that these patterns, and the strengths associated with each interconnection, may vary depending on the time scale relevant for the behaviors being studied. (p. 69)

With respect to their third point, (c), Svyantek and Brown (2000) cited an example by Koch and Laurent (1999) in which reaction time is the measure. With respect to light, sound, a machine, or the human nervous system, reaction-time differences may be measured in milliseconds, whereas for measurements of change in "corporate performance, the time scale might be in months or years" (Svyantek & Brown, 2000, p. 69).

Svyantek and Brown (2000) went on to point out some fundamental differences between traditional (normal science) approaches to the study of organizations—that is, the use of linear methods such as regression, and complex systems approaches that rely on nonlinear methods; with respect to the latter, the following applies:

> [The] data gathered consist of multiple measurements of both independent and dependent variables, and these data are then graphed. The predictions made are more molar and qualitative than the predictions in traditional approaches. The value of these predictions is based on the degree to which a consistent pattern of behavior is found in the system across the repeated measurements. The results of such an experiment are used to make predictions that are context-specific. (p. 69)

Relying on the work of Liebovitch (1998) and Richter (1986), Svyantek and Brown (2000) proposed two nonlinear concepts "that have explanatory value for understanding social systems . . . *phase space* and *attractor*" (p. 70).

Phase space consists of a depiction of multiple behavioral measurements over time (the phase aspect). The depiction can be a three-dimensional graph (the space aspect) that shows how a particular behavior can be affected by, say, three variables over time. Richter (1986) has provided examples of this phase-space method: how an individual's responses in a particular situation may be affected by his or her level of aggressiveness, fear, and guilt, all at the same time and over time. Patterns of behavior can then be traced.

Attractors are these patterns of behavior. They have two primary characteristics: (a) sensitivity to initial conditions and (b) stability.

Sensitivity to initial conditions means that an organization's history is highly important. (A number of years ago, a colleague of mine, also an organization change consultant, and I were working together. He kept saying to the client, "Spare me the history!" I thought it was a mistake then, and I am even more convinced today.) By way of positive feedback, early behaviors in an organization's developmental stages get reinforced and stabilized. Two organizations in the same domain (e.g., business) that originated at the same time under similar, if not identical, conditions can become very different from one another over time. Small differences at the beginning can lead to large differences years later, as a result of highly specific, even undetectable, behaviors consistently reinforced in the first year.

A personal consulting experience recently illustrated this attractor characteristic dramatically. After almost 150 years of independent existence, two banks in a large metropolitan area decided to merge. These two businesses were remarkably similar. Both were founded at about the same time, in the mid-19th century, in the same community of the larger metropolitan area, and 10 decades later, they were almost equal in size in number of employees, number of directors on their respective boards, annual revenues, and number of branches. Moreover, the announcement of the deal was touted as a "merger of equals." At the outset, the consulting project seemed easy. Such similarities would no doubt make the integration of the two banks quick and smooth. In reality, the merger was anything but quick and smooth. The corporate cultures of the two banks, despite all those similarities, were entirely different. The culture of Bank A was loose, risk taking, rather spendthrift, and led rather than managed, whereas Bank B could be characterized as tight, risk averse, highly cost conscious, and managed, not led. The descriptors of the two cultures are examples of multiple behaviors that represent the phase-space concept. A century earlier, small, undetectable but different behaviors in the two banks were positively reinforced (and became attractors), and decades later, these differences loomed large. It took more than two years for the merger to even be accepted, much less integrated. And these were not huge organizations in the first place—about 1,700 employees in each. This example is explained later in considerable detail in Chapter 11.

The second characteristic, *stability*, can best be understood analogously, as an organization's culture. One interesting point by Schein (1985) is the importance of a founder's behavior in shaping an organization's culture, especially through what he or she emphasizes and values.

This nonlinear approach helps us with a new way of thinking about the research process and phase spaces and gives a clearer focus on what to study: attractors.

In summary, the primary point is that measuring organization change is extremely complex and therefore requires extremely complex approaches and methods. Although still useful, "normal" and traditional approaches to research nevertheless are limited indeed.

The Organizational Change Research Theory of Porras and Colleagues

Although by no means exclusively, in the early 1990s, theory and research most closely associated with OD were reflected largely in the work of Jerry Porras and his colleagues. They have reviewed and to some extent consolidated the literature on organization change research and theory (Porras & Robertson, 1992; Porras & Silvers, 1991). To begin with, Porras and Robertson (1992) have provided some useful distinctions to help us understand organization change more thoroughly: planned versus unplanned change and first-order versus second-order change.

Planned change. This is a deliberate, conscious decision to improve the organization in some manner or perhaps to change the system in a deeper, more fundamental way.

Unplanned change. In this case, the organization has to respond to some unanticipated external change—for example, creation of a whole new technology that affects the very core of the business, as was true for Swiss watchmakers when the digital version came on the scene. In unplanned change, the response is adaptive and often spontaneous.

First-order change. This form involves what we today refer to as "continuous improvement" (the Japanese call it *kaizen*); that is, the change consists of alterations or modifications in existing system characteristics, such as eliminating a layer of management or administration in the organizational hierarchy, rather than a shift in some fundamental way, such as change of organizational mission. In Chapter 5, we referred to this first-order level of change as evolutionary.

Second-order change. This form is radical, more fundamental change. We earlier referred to this form as revolutionary, a change of the organization's deep structure (see Chapter 5). The change is paradigmatic.

Quite naturally, Porras and Robertson (1992) then placed these concepts into a 2 × 2 arrangement (see Table 7.1). Although this arrangement is rather neat and easy to grasp, it oversimplifies, unfortunately. Revolutionary change can be planned after all (see, for example, Goodstein & Burke, 1991), and so can evolutionary change (see Chapter 5).

In a related paper, Porras and Silvers (1991) distinguished between first order (they classified OD as first order; again, see Table 7.1) and second order, or what they referred to as "organization transformation" (OT). With respect to the former classification, OD, they concluded the following:

> Much of this research is fragmented and does not build on work done by other authors laboring in a similar arena. More effort should be directed at the development of a paradigm for OD, and thus researchers must build more consciously on each other's work. (pp. 69–70)

And concerning the latter, OT, Porras and Silvers (1991) stated the following:

> Although the broad outlines of the field may be sketched (e.g., a focus on vision, conscious change, etc.), there is still considerable

Table 7.1   Types of Organizational Change

Change Category		
Order of Change	**Planned**	**Unplanned**
First	Developmental	Evolutionary
Second	Transformational	Revolutionary

SOURCE: Dunnette and Hough (1992). Copyright ©1992 Nicholas Brealey Publishing. Used by permission.

diversity in this area and consequently many different directions for future development. It is therefore difficult to predict where the field will be in ten years. (p. 73)

Now, more than a decade and a half later, the designation *OT* itself has faded, but the distinctions have not. In fact, in the most recent review of the literature, Weick and Quinn (1999) organized their report according to *episodic* change (discontinuous, transformational, and revolutionary) and *continuous* change (continuous improvement, transactional, and evolutionary). We will return to their review later in this chapter.

Organization Models

As noted earlier, Friedlander and Brown (1974) provided a framework or approach for understanding organization change, or OD (see Figure 7.1). They referred to two primary approaches to organization change: (a) people, or human-processual, and (b) technology, or techno-structural. They were categorizing targets of intervention (people and technology) and two outcomes of these interventions, (a) human fulfillment and (b) task accomplishment.

Some years later, in a more elaborate attempt to diagram the way planned organization change occurs, Porras (1987) provided a model that is grounded in open-system theory—that is, environment (input), organization (throughput), organizational performance, and individual development (output), with a feedback loop connecting output back to input. The organization part of his model (throughput) consists of organizational members' behavior and the work setting (context).

Porras (1987) further delineated within the work setting part of his model's four components, what he calls "streams," or four basic dimensions: (a) organizing arrangements (e.g., goals, strategies, structure, and systems); (b) social factors (primarily culture but also including social patterns and networks and individual attributes); (c) technology (tools, equipment, machinery, job design, and technical systems); and (d) physical settings (space, ambiance, interior design, etc.). In the reviews of the literature that Porras and his colleagues provided (Porras & Robertson, 1992; Porras & Silvers, 1991), this model was used to organize their analytical summaries. See Figure 7.2 for a diagrammatic summary of the model.

Figure 7.2 A Change-Based Organizational Framework

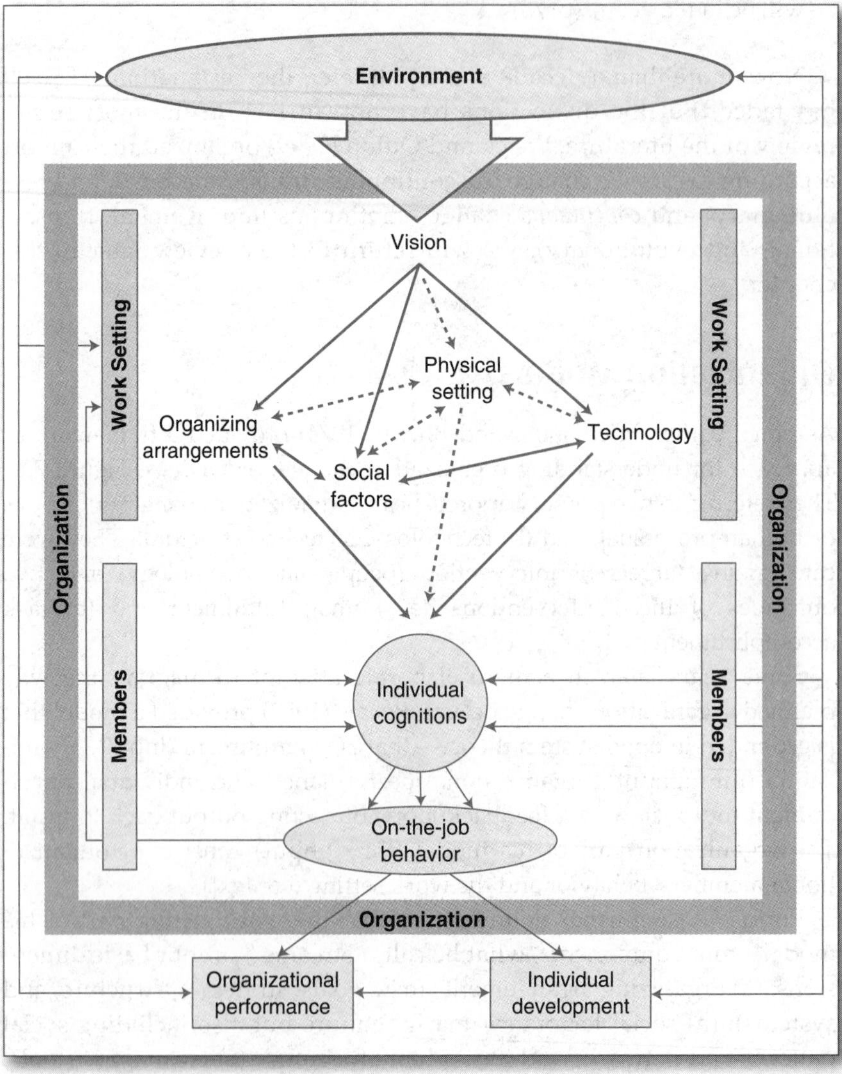

SOURCE: Dunnette and Hough (1992). Copyright ©1992 Nicholas Brealey Publishing. Used by permission.

Porras's (1987) model is essentially a description of how input from the external environment gets transformed into output—organizational performance and individual development. The model also highlights what, for Porras, are the primary elements and dimensions of an organization: the work setting elements (social factors, physical setting, etc.) and the member elements (cognitions and behaviors). With respect to output, he distinguished between the performance of the organization and individual development, as opposed to, say, individual performance. One could argue, however, that organizational performance includes both unit (group, team, and department) and individual performance. These in turn affect or produce organizational performance.

This model by Porras is a description of how organizations operate and what the key elements are in that operation. The model adds to the array of like models in the field of OD and change. See, for example, Burke (1994). The reason for coverage of the Porras model is to establish a backdrop or context for his thinking about how organization change occurs.

Organization Change Theory

Before plunging into the various change ideas and theories, let us consider what an adequate theory should include. Whetten (1989) proposed that a "complete" theory contains four elements:

1. *What* (constructs): factors that should logically be considered as explanatory parts of what is being considered—for example, if organizational, such factors as strategy, culture, and performance.

2. *How* (linkages): how the factors under *what* relate to one another, typically portrayed in the form of boxes and arrows—what comes before what (strategy before structure), and what causes what.

3. *Why* (conceptual assumptions): the logic underlying the theory or model. As Whetten put it, "The soundness of fundamental views of human nature, organizational requisites, or societal processes provide the basis for judging the reasonableness of the proposed conceptualization" (p. 491).

4. The fourth element in Whetten's criteria set includes the combination of *Who/where/when*: "These temporal and contextual factors set the boundaries of generalizability, and as such constitute the range of the theory" (p. 492).

These elements and criteria for what should be included in a complete theory can guide our review of the theories and models that follow.

In their review of the OD and change literature, Porras and Silvers (1991) stated at the outset, "Planned change that makes organizations more responsive to environmental shifts should be guided by generally accepted and unified theories of organizations and organizational change—neither of which currently exists" (p. 51).

They followed with a new model or theory of planned change that proposes a process of how organization change occurs. The framework begins with organizational interventions that are intended to affect certain variables, which in turn affect individual behavior and ultimately improve organizational performance and enhance individual development. This model (see Figure 7.3) relies on Porras's previous organizational model (see Figure 7.2) but is now cast in terms of change processes.

Porras elaborated further on his perspective about the change process in a slightly later work (Porras & Robertson, 1992). He was clearly on target when declaring that for organization change to occur, organizational members must "alter their on-the-job behavior in appropriate ways. This assumption is rooted in the belief that behavior is significantly influenced by the nature of the setting in which it occurs" (Porras & Robertson, 1992, p. 724). Moreover, the schema presented in Figure 7.3 is a straightforward and rather linear depiction of how organization change occurs. The process begins with some intervention that is intended to affect an organization's vision, purpose, and mission (an OT intervention) or an intervention that is aimed at changing aspects of the work setting (an OD intervention), if not both. These interventions in turn affect organizational members' thought processes or mental sets that may occur at any one level or at multiple levels—alpha, beta, or gamma changes—and thus, behavior is changed, which then leads to improved performance and enhanced individual development. This theoretical framework by Porras is fairly easy to understand and has a certain logical flow to it; that is, A leads to B, which in turn affects C, and so on.

Moreover, with this theory, Porras meets Whetten's (1989) criteria for completeness reasonably well. The *what* (constructs) is there (vision, work setting, performance, etc.); the *how* (linkages) is in place; and the *why* is explicated. Also, the boundaries of the theory are fairly clear: This addresses how change occurs within an organization.

It is not likely, however, that organization change occurs in this manner. First, assuming that organizational members, who are human beings, after all, plan (or simply react to events from the organization's external environment) and implement organization change, we must

Figure 7.3 Planned Process Model of Organizational Change

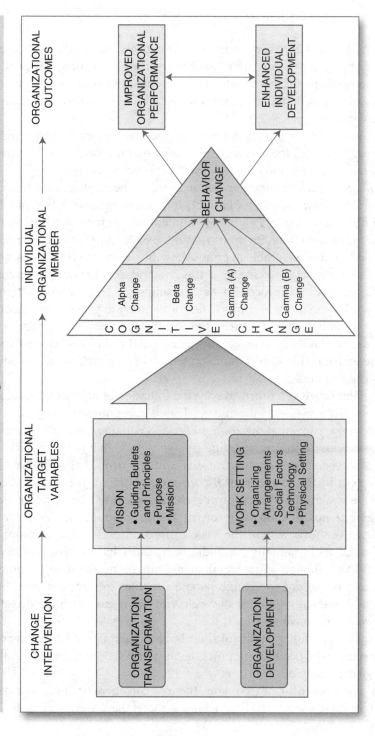

SOURCE: Porras and Silvers (1991). Reprinted with permission from the *Annual Review of Psychology*, Volume 42 ©1991 by Annual Reviews www .annualreviews.org.

account for how this very human process takes place. Although cognitive change can precede behavior change, most of the time, particularly the more emotional the situation is, it is the other way around; that is, behavior comes first, then cognition. We act and *then* attribute meaning to that action.

Second, we must account for what happens at the larger, more complex organization level, the social effect—how organizational members *collectively react* to events and how they interact with one another.

So, a problem here for organization change is being able to establish the causal links between vision (thought) and action (behavior). We want this attributed causation to ensure commitment and in turn, implementation of the new vision (mission, purpose, and goals). The argument now to be made is that it is preferable to promote, if not induce, the action desired to cause movement, for example, a training and development program, a multirater feedback process, a new business strategy, or installation of new work procedures and processes, rather than to provide an elaborate plan and rationale for change and expect the appropriate behavior to follow. Yes, one needs to have a change plan, but the implementation thereof is essential and should turn more on the desired behavior and less on the rationale and thoughts.

To summarize in a practical way, the initiation of organization change begins with a vision of the future. This is a cognitive process. But we should not assume that this thought process will then generate the necessary behavior for the organization change. Although it is a necessary first step, the vision, or cognition, is not sufficient for change. Behavioral movement in the direction of the vision is required. It is best to begin with the vision (it is difficult to get there if we don't know *where* we're going) but not to *concentrate* on it. We concentrate on the behavior needed. As movement in the vision direction occurs, the appropriate attribution will gradually be made to explain why the direction makes sense. Even though organizational executives make pronouncements such as "We've got to change people's mental sets around here!" the change in mental set comes *after* behavior has occurred in the direction desired for the new mental set.

It may be that this argument sounds a bit illogical, but let us now consider some evidence that supports the idea of behavior change first, then change in mental set.

In the area of research and theory, considerable evidence now strongly suggests that William James, more than a century ago, was largely correct. He stated that emotional behavior precedes emotional experience (James, 1890):

> Our natural way of thinking about these coarser emotions is that the mental perception of some facts excites the mental affection called the emotion, and that this latter state of mind gives rise to the bodily expression. My theory, on the contrary, is that the bodily changes follow directly the perception of the exciting fact, and that our feeling of the same changes as they occur IS the emotion. Common sense says, we lose our fortune, are sorry and weep; we meet a bear, are frightened and run; we are insulted by a rival, are angry and strike. The hypothesis here to be defended says that this order of sequence is incorrect. . . . and the more rational statement is that we feel sorry because we cry, angry because we strike, afraid because we tremble. (p. 449)

It should be noted that at about the same time, more than a century ago, Danish physiologist C. G. Lange (1885/1922) independently suggested much the same idea. And as we may recall from our introductory psychology course, this idea became known as the James–Lange theory. Is this idea mere speculation or illogical theory?

Approximately seven decades after the James–Lange theory had been proposed, the social psychologist Stanley Schachter decided to test the idea. The theory, at the time, was controversial, and many believed it to be wrong. In a series of ingenious studies with college students, Schachter (1959) put the theory to the test. He injected adrenaline in the arms of experimental group participants and a saline solution in the control group participants. Adrenaline causes a rise in emotional energy. But what is the emotion exactly? Schachter hypothesized that he could *determine* what the emotion would be. The further two conditions of the study were to "cause" either anger or euphoria with the experimental groups. His results provide considerable validation for the theory. Compared with the control groups, the experimental groups behaved significantly more as Schachter's hypothesis predicted. In other words, an emotion was induced, but the attribution as to which emotion the subject experienced came *after* the inducement and the enacted behavior. Since then, supportive evidence has mounted. See, for example, a summary article by Laird and Bresler (1990).

In the same vein as the James–Lange theory, there is also growing evidence to suggest that the actual causes of our behavior are rarely conscious to us. Causation stems far more from our unconscious. We, of course, attribute causation via a conscious process, but this process is perceptual. The real causes are a result of intricate mechanisms that occur in our brains, of which we are unaware. In a comprehensive article on this theoretical perspective and put in the context of challenging the notion of "conscious will," Wegner and Wheatley (1999) summarized their premise by stating the following:

> The experience of will is a result of the same mental processes that people use in the perception of causality more generally. Quite simply, it may be that *people experience conscious will when they interpret their own thoughts as the cause of their action.* This idea means that people can experience conscious will quite independent of any actual causal connection between their thoughts and actions. (p. 480)

In other words, we *perceive* a causal link between our thoughts and actions. Our "will is not a psychological force that causes action" (Wegner & Wheatley, 1999, p. 481).

To perceive a causal link, Wegner and Wheatley (1999) posited that three criteria must be met: (a) priority, (b) consistency, and (c) the lack of other possible attributed causes. First, we must have the thought shortly before the action. (Studies show that if 30 seconds or more elapse, the causal link is less likely.) Second, the thought should be compatible with the action.

> When people do what they think they are going to do, there exists consistency between thought and act, and the experience of will is enhanced. When they think of one thing and do another—and this inconsistency is observable to them—their action does not feel as willful. (Wegner & Wheatley, 1999, p. 485)

Third, the thought should be the only apparent cause of action. "A basic principle of causal inference is that we tend to discount the causal influence of one potential cause if there are others available" (Wegner & Wheatley, 1999, p. 486).

In related work by psychologist John Bargh and his colleagues, a strong case is made that the ability to control our behavior consciously and intentionally is of course possible but actually quite limited. Most of our daily psychological lives function through nonconscious means, via what has been referred to as "automaticity" (Bargh & Chartrand, 1999).

In summary, first, to account for how the linkage typically occurs for organizational members between vision or mission (concepts, cognitions) and action (behavior), we must not assume that it is primarily a conscious, deliberate, and rational process. It is primarily the opposite. With a set of values and goals declared, we then quickly move to action: behavior that enacts these values and implements these goals without assuming that organizational members have made the linkages. As appropriate movement (behavior) continues over time, the proper attributions can eventually be made, for example, "We are doing this because we believe it is the right (value) thing to do." Behavior is followed by cognition. It should also be noted that this manner of theorizing is not unlike the thinking of Karl Weick, a contemporary organizational scholar. See his award-winning book on "sensemaking" (Weick, 1995).

Second, to account for what happens at the larger, more complex organization level, we must rely on theory and concepts that are nonlinear, such as the work of Svyantek and others (e.g., Svyantek & Brown, 2000). Executives trying to bring about change often talk about how "messy" the process is or how little control they have ("Once we started this change effort, it seemed to take on a life of its own") and how difficult it is to sustain ("For every step forward we take, we seem next to fall back two—resistance is a very powerful thing!").

At the organization level, then, we must think in terms of attractors, the concept from nonlinear complexity theory, in terms of organizational culture (norms and values) and what gets systematically reinforced, so that we can strengthen some attractors and eliminate others. It is also useful to think of organization change as a series of "loops"—taking initiatives and then looping back to correct details missed on the first attempt or loop (see Chapter 2). It's messy and nonlinear but, at the same time, realistic. In fact, Beer, Eisenstat, and Spector (1990) identified a number of false starts in the change effort at General Products. As Weick and Quinn (1999) pointed out, "This suggests that change is not a linear movement through . . . stages, but a spiral pattern of contemplation, action, and relapse and then successive returns to contemplation, action, and relapse before entering . . . maintenance and then termination stages" (p. 373).

Current Thinking on Organization Change and Research

We will end this chapter in the same way that we began—that is, by considering the last review article on organization change and development in the *Annual Review of Psychology*. The first of this genre was the review by Friedlander and Brown (1974). Throughout this chapter, subsequent reviews have been highlighted. One of the more recent reviews is by Armenakis and Bedeian (1999) covering the organization change literature of the 1990s. They concluded "that the field is robust and that it continues to be responsive to contemporary organizational demands" (p. 313). The *Annual Review of Psychology* chapter by Weick and Quinn (1999) is not so much a summary of the research literature like the Porras and Silvers (1991) chapter—and like the one by Armenakis and Bedeian (1999). The Weick and Quinn (1999) review is more one of describing and commenting on recent thinking about the nature of organization change. Weick and Quinn (1999) organized their chapter according to what they consider to be the two primary categories of organization change: (a) episodic and (b) continuous. These two ways of conceptualizing organization change were addressed in the previous chapter—that is, (a) revolutionary versus (b) evolutionary change in organizations. Their definition of episodic change is clear and useful (Weick & Quinn, 1999):

> The phrase "episodic change" is used to group together organiza-
> tional changes that tend to be infrequent, discontinuous, and inten-
> tional. The presumption is that episodic change occurs during
> periods of divergence when organizations are moving away from
> their equilibrium conditions. Divergence is the result of a growing
> misalignment between an inertial deep structure and perceived
> environmental demands. This form of change is labeled "episodic"
> because it tends to occur in distinct periods during which shifts are
> precipitated by external events such as technology change or inter-
> nal events such as change in key personnel. (p. 365)

On the other hand, according to Weick and Quinn (1999), continuous change is "ongoing, evolving, and cumulative" (p. 375). They went on to clarify the following:

> The distinctive quality of continuous change is the idea that small
> continuous adjustments, created simultaneously across units, can

cumulate and create substantial change. That scenario presumes tightly coupled interdependencies. When interdependencies loosen, these same continuous adjustments, not confined to smaller units, remain important as pockets of innovation that may prove appropriate in future environments. (p. 375)

By gleaning ideas and research results from the literature, Weick and Quinn (1999) conclude that episodic change arises as a result of inertia (entropy in open system theory terms) and an organization's inability to respond to external environmental changes adequately. Continuous change is driven, they argue, "by alertness and the inability of organizations to remain stable" (p. 379), but as Pascale, Milleman, and Gioja (2000) pointed out, such alertness and tendency to disequilibrium is rare.

Weick and Quinn (1999) also provided a new way of applying Lewin's three-stage model of the change process. They state that episodic change follows (or should follow) the stages as Lewin (1958) originally conceptualized—that is, unfreeze–movement–refreeze, whereas continuous change, to be effective, is more like freeze–rebalance–unfreeze. To *freeze* continuous change is to find the patterns in day-to-day life in the organizations and to reinforce them. To *rebalance* is to change the patterns so that fewer restraints and barriers are present and the continuous change can flow more freely. To *unfreeze* after the rebalancing is to innovate and find new ways of ensuring continuous change. These new ways evolve from habits of continuing to look for means of improving the manner in which work gets done and of continuing to strengthen the critical interdependencies of organization members. An example of this notion about continuous change is provided in Chapter 5, in the case of the professional services firm.

This differentiated way of considering organization change is likely to endure. The mounting evidence is impressive that change in organizations does indeed take one, but rarely both, of these two paths.

Summary

This chapter has focused on reviewing the reviews of organization change research and theory over the past quarter century. Earlier, the lament was about not having enough or the right kind of research to draw any significant conclusions. Later, the argument was made that organization change research followed the wrong model—that is, normal science (Beer & Walton, 1987). Action science would be better. Then Porras argued, quite appropriately, that we had no adequate theory about how organization change actually works, and he proposed a framework and process (see Figure 7.3) as a remedy (Porras & Silvers, 1991). Two problems arise from Porras's proposed model or theory. One is its linearity and the other is his proposed sequence of the process—that is, cognition preceding behavior. Theory and research were cited as support for considering organization change more in terms of complex nonlinearity and in terms of behavior typically preceding thought, attribution, meaning, and related cognitive events.

Finally, it seems quite clear today that a highly useful way to understand, if not lead and manage, organization change more effectively is to consider whether the change is, or needs to be, episodic or continuous.

We will end on a pithy statement: To assume that change in organizations is or can be rational is irrational.

EIGHT

Conceptual Models for Understanding Organization Change

I n the previous chapter, organization change was considered as either discontinuous (revolutionary, or transformational) or continuous (evolutionary, or transactional). This kind of distinction can be useful in helping us understand and diagnose the nature of the required organization change. As a result, one is in a better position to know what types of action to take. If the required change is discontinuous ("a big leap"), then we need to concentrate on the organization's interface with its external environment, on the organization's mission, goals, and strategy, and probably on the organization's culture as targets for change. If, on the other hand, the required change is not as revolutionary and more resembles continuous improvement, then our focus may be on targets in the organization such as the reward system, information technology, workflow processes, or management practices.

The purpose of this chapter is to consider additional categorical concepts for understanding organization change more thoroughly, namely, content, or *what* to change, and process, or *how* to bring about the change. In Chapter 6, we considered the phenomenon of resistance to change. A link between the concepts and ideas presented there and in this chapter can be expressed as follows: The *content* of resistance is the threat of loss, and the threat of loss of control is *process*. In this chapter, we also consider (1) organizational change process frameworks in terms of both theory and practice and (2) a select group of 10 mini-theories about organizational behavior that are germane to organization change.

Content: What to Change

What to change usually (but not always) begins when the organization's leaders are confronted with some event or shift in the organization's external environment. Examples are an economic downturn; the bursting forth of a new technology (e.g., from analog to digital); an announcement of a merger between two competitor organizations; the passage of new legislation; or some new mandate by a political leader, as in the case of Prime Minister Thatcher's decision to change British Airways from a government-owned airline to a public-owned corporation. Such modifications in the organization's external environment then cause senior executives and their constituents to consider what to change about their organization to meet the new challenges and to survive as an organization. This may mean a change as significant as changing the organization's mission, purpose, and raison d'être or as straightforward and less complicated as discontinuing certain products or services without changing the overall mission and purpose.

A useful perspective on what to change comes from the management guru and business and organizational observer and philosopher Peter Drucker. In his 31st article written for the *Harvard Business Review*, Drucker (1994) argued that highly successful companies that do the right things often end up doing them "fruitlessly," and decline ensues. This "paradox," as Drucker called it, set the stage for his articulation of what he labeled "the theory of the business." This theory is a set of assumptions about how a given business can succeed in a particular environment and marketplace. According to Drucker, these assumptions "shape any organization's behavior, dictate its decisions about what to do and what not to do, and define what the organization considers meaningful results" (p. 96). Notice that in this quotation, he used the word *what* three times. In times of trouble for a business, Drucker was arguing that *what* to change is the theory of the business—the fundamental beliefs and assumptions about what causes what and how success is defined. Companies therefore get into trouble when "the assumptions on which the organization has been built and is being run no longer fit reality" (Drucker, 1994, p. 95). Drucker cited IBM, General Motors, and Deutsche Bank as examples.

According to Drucker (1994), a theory of the business has three parts:

1. Assumptions about the external environment of the organization, such as society and its structure, the market, the customer, and technology

2. Assumptions about the organization's mission, purpose, and raison d'être

3. Assumptions about the organization's core competencies, that is, the skills and abilities required to accomplish the mission

Drucker (1994) followed with his four specifications of, or criteria for, a valid theory of the business:

1. The three assumptions must fit reality.

2. All three assumptions must fit or be congruent with one another.

3. The theory of the business must be known and understood by all organizational members.

4. The theory needs to be tested constantly.

Although Drucker (1994) did not label his ideas as such, it should be clear that he was addressing transformational or discontinuous change. His argument was that tinkering with the organization when its theory of the business is out of sync with what is going on in the external environment will inevitably lead to business failure. Also implied in Drucker's thesis is that organizations that have experienced considerable success in the past (his examples of IBM and General Motors) tend to hold on to their assumptions and theory entirely too long, that is, persisting when reality has already changed.

A study by Audia, Locke, and Smith (2000) supports this implication quite dramatically. Moreover, the title of their article is "The Paradox of Success." Their research consisted of two studies. One was archival, based on data from the airline and trucking industries over a 10-year period, and the other was a laboratory experiment. Their studies showed that greater past success led to greater strategic persistence after a radical environmental change, and such persistence induced performance declines. The laboratory study also demonstrated that dysfunctional persistence is due to greater satisfaction with past performance, more confidence in the correctness of current strategies, higher goals and self-efficacy, and less seeking of information from critics. (p. 837)

In summary, the content of organization change can vary. It can be mission and strategy, culture, structure, or systems. We can apply the discontinuous–continuous change distinction to the content. With discontinuous change, our content concerns more transformational factors, such as the external environment, mission, purpose, and strategy—or, in Drucker's (1994) language, the fundamental assumptions or theory of the business. With continuous change, our content concerns more day-to-day operations and transactions, and we would therefore focus more on factors such as products and services, work-flow processes, organizational structure, and information technology. The model by Porras and Robertson (1992) presented in Chapter 7 provides examples of the content for organization change: vision, technology, physical setting, organizational arrangements (structure), and on-the-job behavior. The organizational models covered in Chapter 9 provide further examples of content: purposes, rewards, helpful mechanisms, leadership, tasks, informal organization (culture), mission, and strategy.

Finally, it is interesting to note that the more successful an organization has been in the past, the more senior managers seem to hold on to the business content that got them to their current level of success—in spite of radical changes in their organization's external environment. General Motors' insistence on business as usual when the Japanese were encroaching on their territory is a case in point. It is no doubt safe to conclude that change comes the hardest for organizations (and individuals, for that matter) that have experienced success in the past. The values of staying in touch with one's external environment and listening to criticism cannot be overemphasized when it comes to change that is needed for future success and survival.

Process: How to Change— A Theoretical Framework

In an attempt to integrate the diverse theories about organization change, Van de Ven and Poole (1995), using the key words *change* and *development,* conducted a computerized literature search across disciplines and turned up over 1 million articles. They reviewed about 200,000 titles and read about 200 of the articles. They identified 20 theories of development and change and clustered them into 4 ideal types of development theories, or 4 primary schools of thought. These 4 categories are useful in that they help us understand better, at least broadly, the primary ways to consider process: the *how*, and sometimes the *why* as well, of organization change. We will now briefly summarize the 4 primary theories or schools of thought that Van de Ven and Poole identified, that is, life-cycle, teleological, dialectical, and evolutionary theories.

Life-Cycle Theory

Life-cycle theory states that an organization "follows a single sequence of stages or phases, which is cumulative (characteristics acquired in earlier stages are retained in the later stages) and conjunctive (the stages are related such that they derive from a common underlying process)" (Van de Ven & Poole, 1995, p. 515). Change is inevitable; life-cycle theory rests on the metaphor of organic growth: In other words, an organization is like a living organism. Although an organization may undergo change as it passes through its phases, perhaps in both form and function, it nevertheless maintains its identity throughout the phases.

Although Van de Ven and Poole (1995) classified Greiner's (1972) model of organization development as both life-cycle and dialectical, his model is easy to understand in life-cycle terms. Greiner posited five stages in an organization's life cycle: creativity (the start-up phase), direction (more focus needed), delegation (as organization grows larger), coordination (with differentiation of functions, integration is then required), and collaboration (working together more effectively as a total entity). As Van de Ven and Poole (1995) described the other critical ingredient of the Greiner model, "Each of these stages culminates in a different dialectical crisis (of leadership, autonomy, control, red tape and '?' [Greiner's symbol for not knowing what this stage would be], which propels the organization into the next stage of growth" (p. 530).

Others have proposed life-cycle models of organization development and change, for example, Adizes (1979) and Kimberly, Miles, and Associates (1980), but Greiner's remains popular with managers because his framework is easily understood. The Greiner model is popular with managers also because it seems to correspond closely with their experiences.

Teleological Theory

Rooted in the philosophical doctrine of teleology, teleological theory assumes that an organization is purposeful and adaptive. Accordingly, an organization develops toward a goal or some end state. As Van de Ven and Poole (1995) pointed out, "Proponents of this theory view development as a repetitive sequence of goal formulation, implementation, evaluation, and modification of goals based on what was learned or intended by the entity" (p. 516). So, even though goals may be reached, new ones are set, usually as a function of changes in the external environment. Establishing an organizational mission statement, creating a new vision, planning a different strategy, or simply listing a set of goals are all examples of application of this school of thought. The point is this: Organizations change as goals and purposes change. The process is ongoing and iterative; in other words, an organization is never static or in permanent equilibrium.

Dialectical Theory

The basic assumption with dialectical theory is that organizations exist "in a pluralistic world of colliding events, forces, or contradictory values that compete with each other for domination and control" (Van de Ven & Poole, 1995, p. 517). Organization change occurs as two different points of view collide and some resolution is reached. The desired resolution is a creative synthesis of the two opposites, or at least the two sufficiently different positions. As Van de Ven and Poole (1995) stated, "There is no assurance that dialectical conflicts produce creative syntheses" (p. 517). In the business world, acquisitions and hostile takeovers often represent resolutions that are not necessarily creative. A creative synthesis is usually mutually beneficial, but this kind of outcome is quite rare. So, organization change that occurs as a consequence of a dialectical process may be good or bad.

Evolutionary Theory

As might be expected, evolutionary theory assumes that organization change proceeds, as in biological evolution, according to a continuing cycle of variation, selection, and retention among organizations competing for resources in a designated marketplace or environment. "Competition for scarce environmental resources between entities [organizations] inhabiting a population [particular environment] generates this evolutionary cycle" (Van de Ven & Poole, 1995, p. 521). Organization change, then, is explained in terms of an ongoing, evolving process. As in other theories, the organization is never static; there is no permanent equilibrium. It's as if organizations have no choice but to change. As in biological entities, evolution is constant. Again, a living organism is the primary metaphor for understanding an organization according to this theoretical perspective about process.

Borrowing a couple of dimensions (metaphor and event progression) from Van de Ven and Poole, we summarize these four process schools of thought in Table 8.1.

Van de Ven and Poole (1995) proceeded to argue quite logically and persuasively that although these four schools of thought may seem discrete, in reality, they are not. By considering interplay among these schools and examining underlying assumptions, the authors developed "a framework of 16 possible explanations of organization change and development" (Van de Ven & Poole, 1995, p. 534). Of these 16 explanations or theories, 4 are the original ones—life-cycle, teleological, dialectic, and evolutionary. The remaining 12 are combinations: 2 in combination might form, for example, an "organizational punctuated equilibrium theory" (Tushman & Romanelli, 1985); an example combining 3 would be

Table 8.1   Four Process Schools of Thought for Organization Change

	Life Cycle	Teleological	Dialectic	Evolutionary
Key metaphor	Organic growth	Purposeful cooperation	Opposition, conflict	Competitive survival
Event progression	Linear and irreversible sequence of prescribed stages	Recurrent, discontinuous sequence of goal setting, implementation, and adaptation of means to reach end state	Recurrent, discontinuous sequence of confrontation, conflict, and synthesis	Recurrent, cumulative, and probabilistic sequence of variation, selection, and retention

SOURCE: A. H. Van de Ven and M. S. Poole, "Explaining Development and Change in Organizations," 1995, *Academy of Management Review, 20,* p. 514.

Weick's (1979) *Social Psychology of Organizing*; a theory that uses all 4 is human development progressions (Riegel, 1976). Van de Ven and Poole further argued that these schools of thought, although historically important and helpful to our greater understanding of organization change and development, are largely linear in nature; and organizational researchers have treated unexplained patterns of change as "noise" and "error" distributions that "mess up" their experiments. Van de Ven and Poole conclude that a major extension of their framework of 16 explanations of organization change and development "is to develop and study nonlinear dynamics systems models . . . [and to examine] chaos as an alternative explanation" (p. 535). This conclusion, of course, relates to themes we address in Chapters 5 and 7.

Process: How to Change— Practice Frameworks

In this section, we move from a more macro, theoretical way of considering the change process to a more applied, practice-oriented way of considering the change process. In other words, we focus more specifically on the *how*, the actual steps involved, the sequence of these steps, and related interventions. The general flow of this section will be from simple to more complex.

Early in the process of initiating organization change, it is important to determine as clearly as possible how ready people in the organization are to accept and implement the change. Another way of expressing this question of degree of readiness for change is to consider if people directly affected by the proposed change will be resistant and how they will resist. A way of assessing this degree of readiness is to conceptualize the potential according to what the social and psychological costs may be. David Gleicher's formula for determining these costs is cited by Beckhard and Harris (1977) as follows:

$$C = (ABD) > X$$

Where C = change, A = level of dissatisfaction with the status quo, B = clear desired state, D = practical first steps toward the desired state, and X = the cost of change. In other words, there has to be enough dissatisfaction with the current state of affairs (A) for someone to be mobilized for the change. The various subsystems need to have clear enough goals

(B); otherwise the "cost" *(X)* is too high. For each subsystem, there needs to be some awareness of practical first steps *(D)* to move, if movement is to take place (pp. 25–26).

Both clarity of change direction and motivation are necessary for acceptance and commitment on the part of organizational members.

We will now proceed to discuss the process of change implementation more specifically.

Lewin's Three Steps

In the 1940s and 1950s, Kurt Lewin (see Chapters 3 and 4 for other references to his work) and his associates (Lewin, 1947) conducted a number of studies as part of a larger effort to change food habits to adapt to war needs at the time, that is, to influence people to eat less desirable but cheaper foods (whole wheat bread instead of white, beef briskets and organs instead of steak, etc.). After four years of studies and action research projects, Lewin concluded that to be successful, the change process needed to follow a three-step procedure: (1) unfreezing, (2) moving, and (3) freezing at a new level (or refreezing). The first step is to unfreeze the present level of behavior. This step, according to Lewin, can take many forms and needs to be tailored as much as possible to the particular situation. To reduce prejudice, for example, this first step of unfreezing might be catharsis (G. Allport, 1945) or participation in a series of sensitivity training sessions (Rubin, 1967). At the organizational level, the unfreezing step could be one of presenting data to organization members that show a sizable gap between where they are and where they need to be to meet growing demands in their marketplace, for example, where customer service is slipping dramatically. The second step is to move toward the new, desired level of behavior. In the organizational gap example, moving might take the form of (1) training managers to behave differently toward their subordinates in order to improve customer service (see Schneider, 1980, for research related to this example) or (2) implementing action plans for changing work processes or improving information systems. The refreezing step establishes ways to make the new level of behavior "relatively secure against change" (Lewin, 1947, p. 344). This step could include installing a new reward system to reinforce the new, desired behavior (Lawler, 1977) or restructuring certain aspects of the organization so that new accountability arrangements and new ways of measuring performance are put into place.

Lewin's Three Steps Expanded: Schein

Schein (1987) has appropriately pointed out that although Lewin's steps may convey discrete actions, the steps are not discrete. Schein states that the steps (he calls them *stages*) overlap and the process is more elaborate and complicated than a mere three steps. He kept the three stages, but within each one, he expanded and elaborated.

Stage 1: Unfreezing. Creating motivation and readiness to change. There are at least three ways of unfreezing an organization, according to Schein (1987):

- Disconfirmation or lack of confirmation: Demonstrate a need for change by, for example, surfacing organizational members' dissatisfaction by showing that the customer base is eroding and something must be done to stem the tide or by providing information about radical change in the organization's external environment that threatens the survival of the enterprise.
- Induction of guilt or anxiety: When organizational members are faced with data that show a gap between what is and what would be better, they are likely to be motivated by guilt feelings and general anxiety to reduce the gap and to take action toward goals that would make things better.
- Creation of psychological safety: Creating disconfirmation and inducing guilt and anxiety are not enough to accomplish the unfreezing stage, however. Schein contends that for people to move to the second stage and actually change, they must believe that doing so will not cause feelings of embarrassment, humiliation, or loss of face or self-esteem. Organizational members need to feel worthy and psychologically safe, that is, to have no fear of retribution or punishment for embracing the change.

Stage 2: Changing. Changing involves cognitive restructuring, according to Schein (1987). What he meant is that organizational members need to see things differently from how they saw them before and, as a result of this different view, must act differently. Two processes are necessary to accomplish this stage:

1. Identification with a new model, mentor, leader, or even a consultant to "begin to see things from that other person's point of view. If

we see another point of view operating in a person to whom we pay attention and respect, we can begin to imagine that point of view as something to consider for ourselves" (p. 105).

2. Scanning the environment for new, relevant information. Has this kind of change worked in other organizations? Are we in danger of reinventing the wheel? Can we learn from others' experiences? Action involved here may mean inviting outsiders with relevant experience to visit us and share their stories or a select group of organizational members attending relevant conferences to gain new information about this kind of change. Or it could take the form of sending the top executive team to Japan to study their experiences with quality improvement and related initiatives, as was the case with SmithKline Beecham in the early days of their merger (Bauman, Jackson, & Lawrence, 1997).

Stage 3: Refreezing. As indicated earlier, refreezing is the integration of the change for organizational members that, for Schein (1987), has two parts:

1. Personal and individual: helping the organizational member feel comfortable with the new behavior that is required to make the change succeed, that is, to link the new behavior with one's self-concept. Schein noted that this process requires considerable practice: trying out the new behavior, getting feedback, and then being rewarded when one gets it right.

2. Interpersonal: making sure that the new behavior fits well with others who are significant in the organization and that these other significant individuals (organizational members that one works with closely) are comfortable with the new behavior from the "changed" person. In other words, "If I change, you will also need to change if we are to work together effectively in the future."

Phases of Planned Change

Ronald Lippitt, a protégé of Lewin's, also elaborated on the three-stage procedure (Lippitt, Watson, & Westley, 1958). Working with his two colleagues, Lippitt expanded the three stages to five phases. Similar to Schein's point, some 30 years earlier, Lippitt and his colleagues thought that *phase* was a better term to use, because overlap occurs across the three stages. The five phases are as follows:

1. Development of a need for change (unfreezing)

2. Establishment of a change relationship between the change agent (consultant, usually external to the organization or perhaps an internal organizational member who is championing and leading the change effort) and the client organization

3. Working toward change (moving/changing)

4. Generalization and stabilization of change (refreezing)

5. Achieving a termination in the relationships, that is, ending the "change contract" between the consultant–change agent and the client organization

Lippitt and colleagues (1958) wrote an entire book about these five phases, and the simple list above gives only a flavor, not the depth, of their thinking. For more specifics on their five phases, see their original book, or summaries provided by Burke (1994) and by Hornstein, Bunker, Burke, Gindes, and Lewicki (1971).

Organization Change as a Transition

Many practitioners and scholars have written about the concept of transition as a way of understanding the process of organization change. For our purposes, that is, considering the more applied ways of thinking about change, we will briefly consider two models that are based on this idea of transition.

Beginning with what they call "demand system," meaning forces in the environment that initiate the process of organization change, Beckhard and Harris (1987) described their transition model as involving the following:

Three distinct conditions: the *future state*, where the leadership wants the organization to get to; the *present state*, where the organization currently is; and the *transition state*, the set of conditions and activities that the organization must go through to move from the present to the future. (p. 29)

These authors pointed out that organization change and the leading and managing thereof "is not a neat, sequential process" (Beckhard & Harris, 1987, p. 30). After the demand system has been delineated, the next step is to define the need for change and then to determine whether to change. If the choice is to change, Beckhard and Harris defined their process for bringing it about (identifying the future state, assessing the present state, and—where most time and energy is spent—working on getting from the present to the future) as the transition state. *Transition management,* as Beckhard and Harris labeled it, is a process of conducting activities such as planning a road map for the change effort. This involves determining where to intervene first, choosing transition technologies, such as pilot programs, educational interventions, and confrontation meetings (Beckhard, 1967) and creating transition management structures, for example, a parallel structure for change purposes that operates alongside the traditional structure. See, for example, E. Miller (1978).

A second transition model comes from the popular writings of William Bridges (1980). His model is an individual one, not one for organizations (see Chapter 6 for this perspective on Bridges), but can be easily applied to organization change. Moreover, his three phases are not unlike Lewin's three-step procedure. The first phase for Bridges is *endings,* the process of letting go of the past and of the previous ways of doing things. Bridges emphasized the need for people to achieve some closure about the past and to celebrate what was good about it. Bridges labeled the second phase the *neutral zone,* a period of time in which the individual is neither in the past nor in the new phase. This phase is experienced as a state of limbo and emotional disconnection and as ambiguous and often anxiety provoking. There are individual differences in the time it takes for people to let go of the past and embrace the new, but leaders of change need to be sensitive to this phase and should not rush people through it. Bridges calls the third and final phase *new beginnings,* the time when organizational members start to focus on new goals and priorities, begin to try the requisite new behaviors, and are psychologically prepared to move ahead. Again, patience on the part of change leaders is needed, because as people try new behaviors and skills, mistakes will be made and corrective action will be required.

Although simple in concept, the transition models of Beckhard and Harris and Bridges nevertheless illustrate the complexities of large-scale organization change. Together, these models help us to be clearer about the importance of understanding organization changes at multiple levels all at the same time.

In summary, it should be recognized that these process models of organization (and individual) change, beginning with Lewin in the 1940s, are sequential—steps, stages, or phases—and they are helpful for planning and managing a change effort. This sequential planning in linear and causal terms can be useful: If we do A, B is likely to follow; if Y happens, it will likely be a consequence of X. This mode of thinking helps us to make sense out of complex, seemingly unrelated organizational behavior. Taking this way of thinking too literally, however, will often result in errors of judgment and being blindsided by unanticipated outcomes. We must bear in mind, therefore, that as organization change actually occurs, it is not sequential and is far more complex, ambiguous, and even "messier" than the models convey. Recall the point in Chapter 2: The implementation of organization change is nonlinear and often unpredictable. Also, as Chapter 7 noted, it is useful for us to be as clear as possible about whether the change requires large-scale, radical, and discontinuous initiatives or whether instead, the change is more continuous, requiring partial improvements to the organization, not major surgery. Although we need to think and plan these sequential ways even for discontinuous change processes, these models may be more directly applicable to continuous improvement initiatives because the latter do not, as a rule, take the form of punctuated equilibrium, but move along in a smoother, linear way.

We now move from models to theories. The models we have covered have addressed process and, although somewhat simple, they were fairly comprehensive in scope. The theories we will now cover address change in more circumscribed or limited ways. These theories address both the content and process of organization change but are partial, not comprehensive, statements. These mini-theories do not in all cases concern organization change per se, but they do inform us about the what and the how, the content and the process.

Mini-Theories Related to Organization Change

The purpose of this section is to provide brief coverage of 10 theories from psychology and organizational behavior that are applicable to organization change and development. The choice of the theories presented is selective. Other theories could have been covered. The intent is to use these theories as examples of how to apply theory to organization change. The intent is not to attempt an exhaustive listing of theories that might be applicable. For a broader coverage of these theories, see Burke (1994).

We begin with theories that address primarily the individual, then cover those that are more interpersonal and focused on groups, and conclude with theories that emphasize the larger system.

Individual Emphasis

Need Theory: Maslow/Herzberg

Although both Maslow (1954) and Herzberg (1966) based their theories on individual needs, they differed in two primary ways. Maslow's hierarchy of needs addressed motivation per se, whereas Herzberg's focused more on job satisfaction. The second difference is that Maslow's hierarchy was represented as a single continuum, from basic, creature comfort needs to self-actualization, whereas Herzberg posited two continua—one addressing dissatisfaction, from high to low, and the other addressing job satisfaction, from low to high. Herzberg's two-factor theory stated that so-called hygiene or maintenance factors, adequate versus inadequate (e.g., fringe benefits, good supervision, etc.), contributed to dissatisfaction, and motivator factors (e.g., degree of autonomy on the job, recognition, opportunity to achieve) contributed to job satisfaction. The *content* for applying Maslow's theory would be extent of motivation, and for Herzberg, it would be degree of job satisfaction. The *process* focus for both theories would be enriching individuals' jobs, that is, providing more autonomy, recognition, and achievement opportunities and empowering employees by giving them more authority and decision-making responsibilities.

Expectancy Theory (Cognitive): Vroom/Lawler

The study of motivation from an expectancy perspective focuses more on extrinsic behavior and less on internal or intrinsic needs. The theory is based on three assumptions (Lawler, 1973; Vroom, 1964):

1. People believe that their behavior is related to certain outcomes—the performance-outcome expectancy.

2. Outcomes (rewards) have different values for different people; for example, some are more attracted to money than others are.

3. People relate their behavior to certain probabilities of success—the effort-performance expectancy. "If I try harder, will the increased effort pay off for me?"

Thus, as stated in Burke (1994),

People will be highly motivated when they believe that their behavior will lead to certain rewards, that these rewards are worthwhile and valuable and that they are able to perform at a level that will result in the attainment of the rewards. (p. 39)

The *content* for applying expectancy theory is both motivation and rewards, particularly the degree of effort put forth by organizational members, whether the reward system is the right one for most people and whether people see a strong link between their efforts and the rewards they receive. The *process* focus could be on changing both the way organizational members' performance is measured (i.e., attempting to ensure that people see the link between their behavior and how performance is measured) and the reward system, to ensure that organizational members (1) value the rewards they may receive and (2) see the link between their performance and the rewards they receive. To ensure that these processes work optimally, it is imperative that organizational members believe that the measuring and reward processes are administered in a fair and just manner.

Job Satisfaction: Hackman and Oldham

Grounded in both need and expectancy theories yet more specific and targeted, Hackman and Oldham's (1980) *content* emphasis is on three primary psychological states that affect employee satisfaction:

1. Experienced meaningfulness of the work itself

2. Experienced responsibility for the work and its outcomes

3. Had knowledge of results, that is, performance feedback

The *process* focus, therefore, is on work and job design, that is, designing jobs and roles for organizational members that enhance these three psychological states and, in doing so, increasing motivation and perhaps performance as well. *Perhaps* is inserted in this latter phrase because performance is often based more on ability than on motivation.

Positive Reinforcement: Skinner

B. F. Skinner was not exactly an organizational theorist, but he did address organizational issues and the application of his empirical theory when he wrote the book *Walden Two* (Skinner, 1948). Key to understanding Skinner and his work is to understand his emphasis on control, that is, control of one's environment. *Walden Two* describes a utopian community designed and operated strictly according to Skinner's principles of operant behavior and schedules of reinforcement. This book is fictional, of course, but is very clearly an application of Skinnerian theory and research. More recently and certainly not fictional, Skinner's principles were applied in a business setting, Emery Air Freight, in the early 1970s (see "At Emery Air Freight," 1973). His principles were applied carefully and as "close to the letter" as possible, and as a result, Emery realized an annual savings of $650,000.

The content for *change*, then, is the reward system, particularly the application of incentives in the form of partial positive reinforcement. The *process* focus is on the work environment, with the intent of controlling the conditions of how employees are rewarded. The initial determination is to clarify the performance behaviors desired and then to administer positive reinforcement accordingly.

Group Emphasis

The Group as the Focus of Change: Lewin

Field theory is the succinct way of labeling Lewin's contribution. Borrowing concepts from physics, Lewin (1951) explained individual behavior as an interaction between a person's needs and personality and the field of forces impinging on the individual from the external environment. The key in this explanation is the matter of perception, how the individual perceives these forces—especially in terms of whether the forces are perceived to be imposed or induced or whether they are "owned" by the person, that is, directly affecting his or her needs. Forces that are perceived to be induced are usually resisted, whereas those that are owned by the individual are embraced. Lewin (1958) also distinguished between driving forces and restraining forces: *drivers* push an individual toward new behavior (e.g., higher productivity), and *restraining forces* inhibit new behavior. A driving force toward greater productivity may be strong supervision, and a restraining one may be a group norm that expects organizational members to conform to a certain level of productivity and perform no higher.

Content, for application of Lewin's theory, would be an analysis of perceived forces in the work environment and what people perceive the norms and values to be. The nature and degree of conformity to group standards (norms) represent Lewinian content as well. The *process* focus would be on (1) changing group norms, (2) reducing restraining forces instead of increasing driving forces (the latter increases resistance, after all), and (3) increasing owned forces and decreasing imposed forces. And finally (Burke, 1994):

> Adherence to Lewinian theory involves viewing the organization as a social system, with many and varied subsystems, primarily groups. We look at the behavior of people in the organization in terms of (1) whether their needs jibe with the organization's directions, usually determined by their degree of commitment, (2) the norms to which people conform and the degree of that conformity, (3) how power is exercised (induced vs. own forces), and (4) the decision-making process (involvement leading to commitment). (p. 43)

Changing Values Through the Group: Argyris

The value base for Argyris (1971) is largely represented by McGregor's (1960) theory Y, as opposed to theory X. By theory X, McGregor meant certain assumptions that managers hold about people in work organizations: that they are inherently lazy and require structure and direction and, given too much freedom, they will not work responsibly. Theory Y assumptions, on the other hand, hold that people are not lazy, want to do a good job, do not require close supervision, and prefer work that is meaningful and challenging. Argyris contended that many managers and executives assert Y values but behave according to X beliefs. This inconsistency between words and actions, particularly on the part of organizational leaders, causes mistrust, lower commitment, and poor morale on the part of employees, Argyris argued. He has written widely on such topics as the relationship of individual personality and organizational dynamics, organizational intervention theory and method, and organizational learning, but a core, if not *the* core, of his work is the degree of congruence between what he calls *espoused theory* and *theory in action* (Argyris & Schön, 1982). Argyris has often worked with top organizational executive groups and attempts to apply many of Lewin's principles to such areas as induced versus owned forces. See the previous section on Lewin, "The Group as the Focus of Change."

The *content* for Argyris (1971) is values, at least espoused values in the organization, the substance of decisions, and whether these decisions, when enacted, are congruent with spoken beliefs and values on the part of the top executive group. Argyris's *process* focus is on the actual behavior of executives. The process may involve, for example, recording an executive group's meeting, analyzing the content of the meeting (problems discussed, decision debated and then made, etc.), and then reporting the analysis back to the group. This analysis often emphasizes the degree of congruence between statements and arguments made and subsequent action taken. Argyris used the theory Y versus theory X concepts and the values of McGregor as his frame of reference. The overall change goal, then, is to reduce the gap between words and deeds.

The Group Unconscious: Bion

Originally trained as a psychiatrist and then as a psychoanalyst, Bion (1961) held the theory that a group has an unconscious just as an individual does; this "collective unconscious," as he refers to it, operates parallel to the conscious group, or the work group. The work group has the purpose of task accomplishment, whereas the unconscious, or "basic assumption group," as he calls it, has the purpose of destroying the group leader. Bion's main issue, therefore, is authority: who has it and especially how it is exercised. The collective unconscious assumes that authority is to be resisted, destroyed, and then replaced with a new leader who will get it right—which according to Bion, never happens. The same dynamic continues regardless of the individual players. As long as the work group is dominant over the basic assumption group, productive outcomes can be realized. But if the group members wander from the task, frequently fight among themselves, form subgroups that are unintegrated with the total group, and overly defer to the leader instead of assuming task responsibility themselves, then the basic assumption mode has become dominant and the group will fail at task accomplishment.

The *content* for Bion is purely and simply the collective unconscious, that is, issues of authority. The *process* focus is to reduce the effect of the basic assumption mode and enhance the work-group mode by staying focused on the task and being aware of the passage of time.

The Larger-System Emphasis

Participative Management—The One Best Way: Likert

Likert's main contributions are his linking-pin idea of management hierarchy and his four-system model of organizations (Likert, 1967). The latter is more relevant to our coverage.

Likert, perhaps best known for his agree-disagree, 5-point scale, "the Likert scale," categorized organizations according to their management approach and declared four main categories (1967):

System 1   Autocratic management: Decisions flow from the top down, and power is exercised exploitatively.

System 2   Benevolent autocracy: not exploitative but still top-down. "We at the top know best, and we will take care of you as long as you do your job."

System 3   Consultative management: Managers ask their people for their opinions, ideas, and suggestions but reserve the right to make the final decisions.

System 4   Participative management: Decisions involving policy and affecting a large number of people are made in groups by consensus.

Likert (1967) then used seven behavioral functions within organizations to further describe and differentiate his four systems: leadership, motivation, communication, interaction and influence, decision making, goal setting, and control. The *content* for Likert was quite specific and clear: the four systems, or management approaches, and how they are manifested or practiced within each of the seven functions. Likert was just as specific and clear about *process*, which was the use of survey feedback methodology. The "Profile of Organizations" in Likert (1967), later called "Survey of Organizations," is a diagnostic questionnaire organized according to the seven functions across the four-system models (i.e., management approaches). Answers by organizational members are profiled according to the four systems in two ways: what the respondents perceive the current situation to be and what they believe their ideal responses would be. Usually, the respondents' current perceptions center on System 2 or 3, and their ideal typically clusters around System 4. In other words, a gap between what is and what should be is established. Organizational members' motivation, it is contended, is quite naturally a desire to reduce the gap.

Likert (1967) not only argued that there is one best way to manage—according to System 4—and established what he considered to be the relevant *content*, he also posited one best *process*, that is, survey feedback. In an organization change effort, then (Burke, 1994):

> Likert's approach is highly data-based, but the diagnosis is largely limited to the functions he deems important. Once the survey data are collected, they are given back in profile form to organizational family units—to a boss and his or her team. . . . Although organizational change agents may be uncomfortable with Likert's one best way and may prefer an approach that is more contingent and perhaps more flexible, they can be very sure of the direction and the objectives of the change effort. (p. 48)

It All Depends: Lawrence and Lorsch

Unlike Likert, Lawrence and Lorsch are contingency theorists: There is no one best way for management, for strategy, for structure, or for how to deal with systems and processes in the organization. It all depends. Depends on what? you might reasonably ask. The one word that captures their point of view is *interface*, and they focus primarily on three forms (Lawrence & Lorsch, 1967): (1) the organization's relationships with its external environment, (2) relationships of units within the organization, and (3) the relationship, or implicit contract, between the organizational member and the organization.

The main contribution that Lawrence and Lorsch (1967) have made is their replication in the United States of a study conducted by Burns and

Stalker (1961) in the United Kingdom. The respective studies showed that the most effective internal structure or organization design for a business-industrial enterprise depended on how stable or dynamic (rapidly changing) the organization's external environment or marketplace was. Moreover, how units within the organization should relate with one another, that is, the degree and nature of information exchange, cooperative behavior, and the way conflict should be handled again depended on the nature and characteristics of the organization-environment interface. These interfaces in turn affected the individual-organization relationship, for example, how permanent and secure one's job might be, as opposed to having to change jobs or having to learn new skills.

If an organization's environment is rapidly changing, as in a high-tech industry, then the internal structure needs to be more decentralized than centralized so that many more organizational members would be in a position to monitor and keep up with changes in technology, what customers want, and changes in government regulations. If the external environment is not as volatile, then a more centralized internal structure may be more effective, that is, decisions being made at the top more than unit by unit.

Lawrence and Lorsch (1967) further argued that highly differentiated organizations, those that are structured largely by function or by highly separate business units, are likely to experience considerable conflict between functions, such as marketing versus manufacturing or between separate business units (the so-called silo effect). In such cases, a premium is placed on managing and resolving conflict.

To summarize, the *content* for Lawrence and Lorsch (1967) consists of the interfaces and the nature and characteristics of these relationships, beginning with the environment-organization interface. The *process* would emphasize internal restructuring, conflict management and resolution, and how all of the above affect the relationship between management and the employee and the implicit set of expectations between these two parties within the organization.

The Organization as a Family: Levinson

Educated and trained originally as a clinical psychologist, with a lacing of Freudian psychoanalytic theory, it is not surprising that Levinson (1972) views an organization much like a nuclear family. His claim (H. Levinson, 1972) is that organizations replicate family dynamics with, for example, the CEO as father and ego-ideal, the head of human resources as mother, the nurturer, and the remaining executives who report directly to the CEO as siblings, with the requisite behavior of sibling rivalry. It is also not surprising to learn that much of H. Levinson's consulting experiences have been with family-owned businesses.

H. Levinson (1972) believes that an organization has a personality (we might call it culture), just as an individual has a personality, and that the health or effectiveness of an organization, not unlike that of a person, depends on how well the various parts of the personality (id, ego, and superego, in Freudian terms) are integrated. Levinson refers to this process as "maintaining equilibrium."

For organization change and improvement, the relevant *content* for H. Levinson (1972) consists of, first, the behavior of the top executive group, diagnosed according to family dynamics that are viewed through the lens of psychoanalytic theory; second, how the top-family dynamics affect and are replicated throughout the organization; and third, how integrated the various parts of the organization's personality are. H. Levinson (1975) also pays considerable attention to the levels of stress in an organization, especially among executives, and how stress is handled. Further content is what organizational members do with their energy, that is, the balance between energy directed toward goal accomplishment and energy directed toward dealing with stress.

Levinson's *process* would be to conduct a "clinical history" of the organization, much as a physician or therapist would do with a patient, and then work with the top executive team, especially the CEO, to ensure better integration of the organization's personality and to direct as much energy as possible toward the task and less toward dealing with stress.

Summary

The 10 theories from psychology and organizational behavior that were selected for this chapter are those most applicable for organization change and development. These mini-theories address only certain aspects of organization change, and none is truly comprehensive. It is likely that at some stage in the future, a more comprehensive theory will emerge from domains such as cell biology, chaos theory, or nonlinear complex systems theory. But until that day, we must rely on combinations of theories that alone are unsatisfactory, but together can enhance our understanding.

Table 8.2 is an attempt to succinctly summarize the 10 theories covered in this section of the chapter.

Table 8.2 Summary of Primary Psychological and Organizational Behavior Theorists According to Their Perspectives, Content, and Process/ Applications

Perspective	Theorist	Content Emphasis	Process/Application
Individual	Maslow; Herzberg	• Individual motivation • Job satisfaction	• Career development • Job enrichment
	Vroom; Lawler	• Individual expectancies and values • Individual motivation and rewards	• Performance measurement • Reward system design
	Hackman and Oldham	• Job satisfaction and psychological states regarding work	• Job and work redesign • Job enrichment
	Skinner	• Individual performance • Reward system	• Work environment • Incentive systems and reward system design
Group	Lewin	• Field of forces • Norms and values	• Reducing restraining forces • Changing conformity patterns • Increasing owned, decreasing imposed forces
	Argyris	• Espoused values • Decision substance • Congruence of words and actions • McGregor's theory X, theory Y	• Analyzing content of executive meetings • Changing executive behavior toward greater congruence

Perspective	Theorist	Content Emphasis	Process/Application
	Bion	• Group unconscious • Issues of authority	• Reducing the adverse effects of the group unconscious and enhancing the work group mode
Larger system	Likert	• Management style and approach • (four-system model)	• Survey feedback • Moving toward participative management (System 4)
	Lawrence and Lorsch	• Organizational interfaces, especially external environment and internal structure	• Changing structure • Conflict management and resolution between organizational units
	H. Levinson	• Behavior of top executive group from perspective of family dynamics and psychoanalytic theory • Organizational personality (culture)	• Clinical history of organization • Integrating disparate parts of organizational personality • Stress management

The Content and Process of Strategic Change in Organizations

At a more macro level of theory and research on organization change, Rajagopalan and Spreitzer (1997) reviewed the literature on strategic change and classified their findings into two schools of thought on the research domains and the methodologies that researchers used: the *content* school and the *process* school. The former refers to antecedents and consequences of strategic change, the *what*, and the latter focuses on the role of managers, or *how* they seemed to have implemented strategic change. Rajagopalan and Spreitzer (1997) went on to point out that although these two schools of thought are related, they "have evolved independently with little theoretical or empirical synergy, resulting in theoretical and practical gaps in researchers' understanding of strategic change" (p. 48). These authors further classified the 59 studies that they reviewed from the 1980s and 1990s into four research and theoretical perspectives. The four categories represented their attempt to reduce the theoretical and practical gaps in understanding. In other words, they found the content-process distinction to be overly simplified. They identified three distinct "theoretical lenses: the rational, learning, and cognitive lenses" (p. 50). Their fourth classification was various combinations of these three, which they appropriately labeled "multi-lens studies."

All three lenses, or perspectives, are alike in that they consider both content and process and are concerned with an organization's alignment with its external environment. In this regard, Rajagopalan and Spreitzer (1997) cast their perspectives well within the larger open system theory framework and stated, at least implicitly, that for survival, an organization is dependent on its external environment. Briefly defined, the three lenses, or perspectives, are as follows:

- Rational: This school of thought focuses more on content than on process and assumes that the external environment can be viewed objectively; that is, there are facts out there that can be obtained, classified, and acted on. Sequential planning and somewhat linear thinking also characterize this perspective.
- Learning: This perspective makes a different assumption about the external environment, that it is dynamic, changing, and uncertain. Objectivity is very difficult. Although the change process (emphasized more than content) takes the form of a series of iterative actions that are evolutionary, not discontinuous, these actions are not linear or sequential. Managers must take change steps, learn from the consequences of these steps, and then take the next change step according to what was learned from the preceding steps.
- Cognitive: Like the learning perspective, this school of thought focuses more on process than content and focuses on *managerial*

cognitions, such as core beliefs, causal maps, and knowledge structures. Managerial actions in pursuit of strategic change are studied through this lens. Then, retroactive attributions serve to deduce what managers were thinking to have caused such actions.

As part of the conclusions from their analysis of the 59 studies, Rajagopalan and Spreitzer (1997) stated:

> The rational lens perspective reflects a crucial aspect of the reality facing managers, namely, that changes in strategies must match the requirements of a firm's environmental and organizational contexts in order to be successful. . . . The learning and cognitive lens perspectives provide value to the rational lens perspective because they help researchers to understand (a) *why* different firms respond differently to a similar context (because of different cognitions and actions) and (b) *how* firms can maximize the effectiveness of their adaptive responses (through different managerial actions aimed at the environment and/or the organization). (p. 70)

This synopsis does not do justice to the depth of Rajagopalan and Spreitzer's (1997) work. Nevertheless, the point of the brief summary is twofold: First, their review of the strategic change literature demonstrated that content and process are intertwined. Discussing content as separate from process is like attempting to explain behavior as driven by either nature or nurture. It is not possible to explain causes of behavior as being one or the other. Conceptual distinction in this case may serve as an analytical and theoretical convenience but does not reflect reality. Second, a contribution that Rajagopalan and Spreitzer have made was to show us a little more clearly what the reality of strategic change is; in other words, strategic change in organizations is not exactly obvious, cannot be explained adequately from a single perspective, and is not a linear process (see Chapter 7).

Strategies for Effecting Change in Human Systems

In this final section of the chapter, we will consider, again briefly, broad strategies for change. In the previous section, with the summary of Rajagopalan and Spreitzer's (1997) work, the term *strategic* was used.

Strategic, for this review, referred to the organization's strategy, that is, how the organization implemented its mission. Strategic therefore concerned content, although most of the studies they reviewed addressed both content and process.

Strategies for change covered in this final section refer more exclusively to process, or how change is implemented. Our coverage relies on the classic work of Chin and Benne (1985), because their thinking represents a broader and more comprehensive perspective than we have considered thus far and because it is an appropriate way to conclude and integrate the wide-ranging content of this chapter.

It should be noted initially that Chin and Benne (1985) discussed strategies for change genotypically and in the context of *planned* change: a conscious, deliberate attempt to change an individual, a group, an organization, or a community. They grouped their strategies into three categories. The first one, and, they argued, the one most frequently used, was what they called *empirical-rational* strategies. They labeled the second *normative-reeducative* and designated the third group of strategies *power-coercive*. What follows is a definition of each of these three groups of strategies for effecting change.

Empirical-Rational Strategies

The fundamental assumption underlying this group of strategies is that people are rational and that they will follow their rational self-interest once it is made apparent to them. As Chin and Benne (1985) put it:

> A change is proposed by some person or group which knows of a situation that is desirable, effective, and in line with the self-interest of the person or group, organization, or community which will be affected by the change. Because the person (or group) is assumed to be rational and moved by self-interest, it is assumed that he (or they) will adopt the proposed change if it can be rationally justified and if it can be shown by the proposer(s) that he (or they) will gain by the change. (p. 23)

There are six strategies within this empirical-rational group, according to Chin and Benne (1985):

1. Basic research and dissemination of knowledge through general education: the strategy of knowledge building and general education to

widely spread the results of studies so that thinking people will understand, approve, and act in accordance.

2. Personnel selection and replacement: The difficulty of getting knowledge into practice may be due to certain people occupying positions of responsibility who do not take appropriate action. In other words, the wrong people are in these positions and need to be replaced. This strategy comes from industrial psychology.

3. Systems analysts as staff and consultants: In this case, we have experts who deliver knowledge in a rational and systematic manner (often by computers, which are even more rational), the assumption being that their expertise is unique, highly technical, and specialized; therefore, they know best. This strategy is represented by traditional management consulting.

4. Applied research and linkage systems for diffusion of research results: Chin and Benne (1985) used the words *applied research*; we could also use *action research*. In any case, what is meant here is the use of sound research methodology, data gathering, and analysis in the service of promoting change. The research conducted is highly targeted, and the changes are driven by data. The assumption is that these kinds of data will be accepted for change because the methodology is steeped in the scientific method.

5. Utopian thinking as a strategy of changing: Perhaps the best example of this strategy has already been mentioned in this chapter, that is, Skinner's *Walden Two* (1948). The point is that utopian thinking is an effort to extrapolate from science to a future and better vision for society, a community, or an organization.

6. Perceptual and conceptual reorganization through the classification of language: Enemies of a rational-empirical strategy are superstitions and myths. One way to counter this type of enemy is to purify language. Experts here are people disciplined in semantics. The assumption is that experts in semantics can "see more correctly, communicate more adequately and reason more effectively and thus lay a realistic common basis for action and changing" (Chin & Benne, 1985, p. 31). For example, Hayakawa (1941), a prominent semanticist of his time, sought ways of clarifying and correcting the names of things and processes, according to Chin and Benne (1985).

Names associated with this group of strategies include Thomas Jefferson, Horace Mann, Henry Murray, E. L. Thorndike, Frederick Taylor, B. F. Skinner, and S. I. Hayakawa.

Normative-Reeducative Strategies

Change agents adopting this group of strategies would accept the premise that human beings are rational and intelligent. But as important—if not more so—is the assumption that people conform and are committed to sociocultural norms. Undergirding these norms are individual beliefs, attitudes, and values. Thus (Chin & Benne, 1985):

> Change in a pattern of practice or action, according to this view, will occur only as the persons involved are brought to change their normative orientations to old patterns and develop commitments to new ones. And changes in normative orientations involve changes in attitudes, values, skills, and significant relationships, not just changes in knowledge, information, or intellectual rationales for action and practice. (p. 23)

An application of this strategy would be the T-group, or sensitivity training. Further assumptions are that people are more active than passive in their attempts to satisfy needs and that our interaction with the environment is transactional, that is, we seek information and gratification from the environment and attempt to influence the interactive process.

There are two primary strategies within this normative-reeducative group, and they have the following in common:

- The client system is heavily involved in the change process—change is *not* imposed.
- The problem the client is facing is not assumed to be a technical one since it may have more to do with norms, values, and attitudes, thus requiring reeducation.
- Nonconscious factors may need to be surfaced.
- Applying methods and concepts from the behavioral sciences is primary.

These are the two main strategies within this group:

1. Improving the problem-solving capabilities of a system. Chin and Benne (1985) stated that organization development, as based on the thinking and practice of Kurt Lewin, was the major representation of this strategy. Also, later, the work of Argyris and Schön (1978) introduced the concept of organizational learning with their ideas of *single-loop learning,* or fixing problems, and *double-loop learning,* or fixing problems plus learning more about the problem-solving process. Double-loop learning, then, is much like what Chin and Benne were describing with this change strategy.

2. Releasing and fostering growth in the persons who make up the system to be changed. Those who promote this strategy tend to view the individual as the basic unit within an organization, a group, or a community. That individual's growth and development take precedence. The work of Maslow, summarized earlier in this chapter, and McGregor's theory Y and theory X have been highly influential. Also, the sensitivity training (T-group) movement has been a significant lever for their strategy of change. In addition to Maslow and McGregor, other names associated with the normative-reeducative strategy are John Dewey, Sigmund Freud, Kurt Lewin, Warren Bennis, Eric Trist, Carl Rogers, Rensis Likert, Chris Argyris, and Leland Bradford, Kenneth Benne, and Ronald Lippitt of the National Training Laboratories sensitivity-training era.

Power-Coercive Strategies

This group of strategies is based on the use of power in whatever form it may take: political, nonviolent resistance, and so on (Chin & Benne, 1985):

> The influence process involved is basically that of compliance of those with less power. . . . Often the power to be applied is legitimate . . . thus the strategy may involve getting the authority of law or administrative policy behind the change to be effected. (p. 23)

The source of power in the rational-empirical approach is knowledge, but here, the sources are more likely to be political and economic sanctions for lack of compliance to the proposed change. Chin and Benne (1985) describe three strategies within this group:

1. Nonviolence: Names that immediately spring to mind are Mohandas Gandhi and Martin Luther King Jr. Coercion is the prime lever, but conducted nonviolently, often dividing the opposition via moral conviction, perhaps combined with economic sanctions (e.g., boycotting certain commercial enterprises).

2. Use of political institutions: Coercion here does not necessarily involve oppression, provided a democratic process can be sustained. A recent example of this strategy was the use of both state (Florida) and federal courts to decide the Bush versus Gore presidential election. This form of change, even though enacted in law and resolved by legal means, can nevertheless feel oppressive to those being affected.

3. Changing by the recomposition and manipulation of power elites: Chin and Benne (1985) cite Karl Marx as a classic example of this strategy, in that he believed strongly in a classless society and in overcoming the power of the ruling class. This strategy depends largely on economic action and on a large number of people organizing, as in a union, to become a power of production in society.

In addition to Marx, representative others within the power-coercive group of strategies are C. Wright Mills, Bayard Rustin, and Saul Alinsky. For more specific coverage of these three broad strategies of change by Chin and Benne, see the volume by Hornstein et al. (1971).

Some evidence has arisen showing that effective organization change begins with sudden bursts of a radical nature followed by comparatively "sedate progress"—transactional processes—toward the change goal, and that *sequence* is highly important. Changing first "high-impact elements"—transformational factors—"sends a clear message that the changes being implemented will be substantive and enduring" (Amis, Slack, & Hinings, 2004).

Summary

The theme of this chapter has been the content-process distinction in analyses of organization change, with *content* referring to the *what*, or substantive, aspects of change (we found Drucker's [1994], "theory of the business" instructive) and *process* referring to the *how*, or ways that change occurs or can occur. With respect to the latter, Van de Ven and Poole (1995) discussed four theories of the change process. Their coverage discussed how organization change happens through the lenses of life-cycle, teleological, dialectical, and evolutionary theories or schools of thought, whether or not the change is deliberate and planned. They noted that although these four theories are useful to our understanding, they overlap, and in reality, organization change more often than not is explained through multiple theoretical lenses.

We then moved from theory to practice and considered different (but again overlapping) frameworks for understanding how change can occur. These frameworks, beginning with Lewin's (1958) three steps and the elaborations of Schein (1987) and Lippitt et al. (1958), address *planned* change, or deliberate initiatives.

Returning to theory again, this time summarizing mini-theories from the behavioral sciences that are relevant to but not necessarily directed toward organization change, we considered the 10 theories from both the content elements of each one and the process for change advocated, or at least implied.

The work of Rajagopalan and Spreitzer (1997) addressed both content and process, but they argued that the distinction, although useful for helping us understand strategic organization change more thoroughly, was, after all, not reflective of reality. They discussed three theoretical perspectives—rational, learning, and cognitive—and showed how these distinctions can be integrated for a deeper understanding of strategic change.

Finally, to help integrate much of the chapter, we considered the broad conceptual framework on process and planned change developed by Chin and Benne (1985). It is not obvious as to how Van de Ven and Poole's (1995) four developmental theories fit within Chin and Benne's framework. The former, though theoretical, is largely descriptive and explanatory, whereas the latter, which is also descriptive, is, however, about planned change and therefore has an advocacy component to the explanations. In a sense, both the Van de Ven and Poole and the Rajagopalan and Spreitzer contributions explain and enrich our understanding. Chin and Benne also seek explanation and understanding, but their understanding has more to do with the choices of change agentry when the objective is to deliberately bring about change in an organization, group, or community. With regard to the broad strategies of Chin and Benne, the practice frameworks of Lewin and others fit largely within the normative-reeducative group of strategies. Rajagopalan and Spreitzer's rational school of thought is similar to the rational-empirical group of strategies; their learning school of thought is similar to the normative-reeducative group of strategies, and their cognitive school of thought is similar to some combination of rational-empirical and normative-reeducative strategies.

NINE

Integrated Models for Understanding Organizations and for Leading and Managing Change

I n the previous chapter, we considered organization change from a *content* perspective, *what* to change, and from a *process* perspective, *how* to bring about the change. These perspectives were addressed both theoretically, for example, Van de Ven and Poole (1995), and from the standpoint of what research has to tell us, for example, Rajagopalan and Spreitzer (1997).

An additional perspective on content and process can be taken by returning briefly to a comparison of management consulting, as it is described at the end of Chapter 3, with the kind of organization change consulting implied so far in this book. (What has been implied will become much more explicit in the remaining chapters.) The point to be made here is that management consulting tends to focus on content—on *what* needs to be changed. The process of *how* to bring about the change is either ignored or left to others, especially the client, to implement. Effective consulting for organization change must focus on *both* content and process. The organizational frameworks examined in this chapter help to integrate content and process as we consider organization change in a more applied manner. The title for Chapter 8 used the term *model*, meaning conceptual model, in other words, frameworks and ways of thinking that emanate from theory.

A brief recap: In Chapter 7, we reviewed the organization change literature and, in so doing, began to introduce the notion of an organizational model with the framework provided by Porras and Robertson (1992). In Chapter 8, we considered conceptual frameworks about organization change in terms of content and process. And now in the present chapter, we address organizational models per se.

In this chapter, the notion of a model is considered more in terms of "a representation of," that is, a graphic depiction of an organization. Theoretical concepts help us understand organization change in a more profound way, for example, Gersick's (1991) use of *deep structure* as a means of distinguishing between fundamental and superficial changes in an organization. Organizational models as used in this chapter help us map and choreograph organization change in both content, or what to emphasize, such as organizational mission and purpose (see coverage of Drucker's theory of the business in the beginning section of Chapter 8), and process, or how to think through a planned change effort (see Lewin's three steps in Chapter 8, for example).

With the present chapter, we are gradually shifting from how to think about organization change to how to think about doing it. Referring once again to chapter titles, this time the modifier *integrated* is used. The organization models covered in this chapter address content explicitly and process either explicitly or implicitly. Our primary purpose is to present integrated models that help us to know more about what to change and how to do it. Application of theory and concepts is the raison d'être of this chapter and chapters that follow.

What Is an Organizational Model?

The first definition of *model* in dictionaries is something like a "standard to emulate, to imitate, or with which to compare." Additional definitions often include a "copy" or a "subject for an artist." But the usual second definition is the one meant here, that is, a "representation, to show the construction or appearance of something." By model, then, we mean a representation of an organization that more often than not is metaphorical in nature. One of the most commonly used metaphors is an organism, in which any organization is depicted as an open system (see Chapter 4) that, like an organism, has input and output. The throughput is what the organization (organism) does with the input to produce an output, transforming input to output. With the organism, input is oxygen and other ingredients from the external environment, which the organism uses and transforms into energy as well as waste. With the organization, it is money, people, and materials from the external environment that are used and transformed into products and services that are thrust back into the external environment. Other metaphors for organizations have been a machine, brain, culture, political system, and psychic prison (Morgan, 1997).

Organization and organization change models were discussed in Chapter 7. A brief recap should remind us. With respect to the latter, early work by Friedlander and Brown (1974) provided a framework for understanding organization change that was based on two primary approaches: human-processual and techno-structural. Integrating these two approaches was the challenge, according to Friedlander and Brown.

Porras (1987) has provided an example of the former, an organization model grounded in open-system theory and metaphorically based on an organism (see Chapter 7). Porras's model consists of four components: organizing arrangements, such as goals; social factors, such as culture; technology, such as tools; and physical settings, such as space. These four components plus organizational members' behavior form the throughput dimensions of his model.

The remainder of this chapter will be devoted to examining models like the one by Porras, that is, organizational models that integrate content and process and either imply or explicitly address ways of implementing change.

Why Use an Organizational Model?

An organizational model can be useful in a number of ways (Burke, 1994):

- *An organizational model can help to categorize.* When observing or collecting data about activities and behavior in an organization, we are faced with informational bits in the thousands, if not millions. Because we cannot deal with everything, what should we select out or pay attention to? A model can help to "chunk" and categorize the bits and pieces into a more manageable set of, say, 10 or 12 components instead of thousands.

- *An organizational model can help to enhance our understanding.* If we find that serious organizational problems exist with our model in, say, three of the categories but not in the remaining components, then we know more readily where we should take action than we might otherwise have.
- *An organizational model can help to interpret data about the organization.* Assume that, in our model, we have the two categories of strategy and structure. As it turns out, most organizational models do include these two components. Suppose further that from data we have about the organization, we recognize that a serious problem exists with the structure, such as the hierarchical arrangement or decision-making authority, and we need to do something soon about this problem. We know from research (Chandler, 1962) that for optimum organizational effectiveness, there must be a strong link between the organization's strategy (i.e., how the mission and purposes are to be accomplished) and the structure. First, we must achieve clarity about strategy and then let this clarity help us to determine what the structure should be. Borrowing from the world of architecture, it means that form (structure) should follow function (strategy). So, we would not attempt to correct the structure until we were clear about what the organization's strategy would be for now and into the future. To concentrate only on the structure without due consideration initially of the strategy would fix nothing; in fact, it would make matters worse. An organizational model with these two components that are linked and in the proper order—strategy before structure—can help us to interpret our data appropriately and make the right decisions.
- *An organizational model can help to provide a common, shorthand language.* Instead of making statements such as "Well, it's the way we do things here; it's our beliefs and values," and so on, we can simply say "culture," and we will quickly know what we mean. A model, therefore, can help us to be more efficient with language.
- *An organizational model can help to guide action for change.* If an organizational model is arranged in such a way that (1) certain dimensions under certain conditions are more important or carry more leverage or weight than other dimensions and (2) an order or sequence of dimensions or organizational elements and functions is at least implicit, if not obvious, then the direction of change can become

clear. That is, priorities about what to tackle first and what comes next, and so on, can establish a road map and implementation strategy for the overall change effort. The model described in the next chapter provides this kind of help.

An organizational model can indeed be useful, but there are at least two important caveats:

1. A model is only as good as the components selected and the arrangement of these components, that is, how each part relates to each of the others. As we know, organizations consist of many components. We need to categorize thousands of parts into a workable number and decide which components are the most important.

2. Gareth Morgan (1997) stated the second caveat eloquently: "Metaphor is inherently paradoxical. It can create powerful insights that also become distortions as the way of seeing created through a metaphor becomes a way of *not* seeing" (p. 5).

Organizational Models and Organization Change

By way of introduction to this main body of the chapter, it should be noted that many organization models exist. Most organizational theory textbooks provide one or more models. Mintzberg (1989), for example, like Morgan (1997), describes a variety of approaches: the entrepreneurial, machine, diversified, professional, and innovative organizations, and he has his own version (see Mintzberg's chapter on "Deriving Configurations"). Most of these models are descriptive and do not address organization change as such.

Many current models are based on the earlier thinking of Harold Leavitt (1965). His diamond-shaped organizational systems model helped to set the stage for thinking about organizations as interdependent *multivariate systems* (see Figure 9.1).

Although Leavitt's (1965) model was primarily descriptive, he did consider change by noting first that the four major components, *task* (the organization's purpose, e.g., to provide a service, to manufacture a product), *people* (those who carry out the task), *technology* (tools, computers, etc.), and *structure* (work flow, decision-making authority, communications, etc.) all interacted and were interdependent with one another. Second, Leavitt pointed out that change in any one of the components would result in change among the other three.

Figure 9.1   Leavitt's Organizational Systems Model

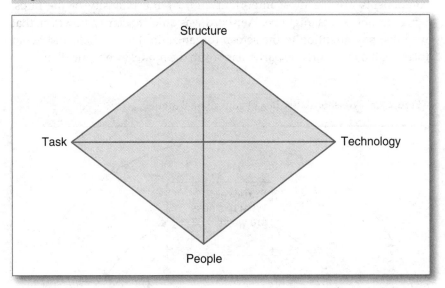

Leavitt's (1965) early version, although grounded in systems thinking—describing four interdependent components, each affecting the other three—was not based on *open*-system theory, at least not in its entirety. The model represents only throughput, or the transformation process, with no accounting for input or output.

The following three models are based on open-system theory and come from the world of organization development, meaning that they address *what* to diagnose for change and consider, at least to some degree, how to intervene so that organization change can be implemented. These models represent an integration of content and process and have evolved from both practice and theory. Each author of these models has spent time and energy as an organizational consultant, and most have also taught graduate students in business schools and therefore have spent time and energy as academics. Thus, the models are grounded in both research and change-consulting practice.

Weisbord's Six-Box Model

Marvin Weisbord (1976) must be more intuitive than most people, because he preferred a visual way of presenting his model. He relied on the organism metaphor as well as another one—the air traffic controller's radar screen. The six "blips" on the screen tell us which organizational components are the most important and, by the intensity of the blips, where trouble spots might be. Weisbord was quick to clarify, however, that we must pay attention to the screen (organization) as a whole and avoid focusing too much on one particular box in the model (see Figure 9.2).

Figure 9.2   Weisbord's Six-Box Organizational Model

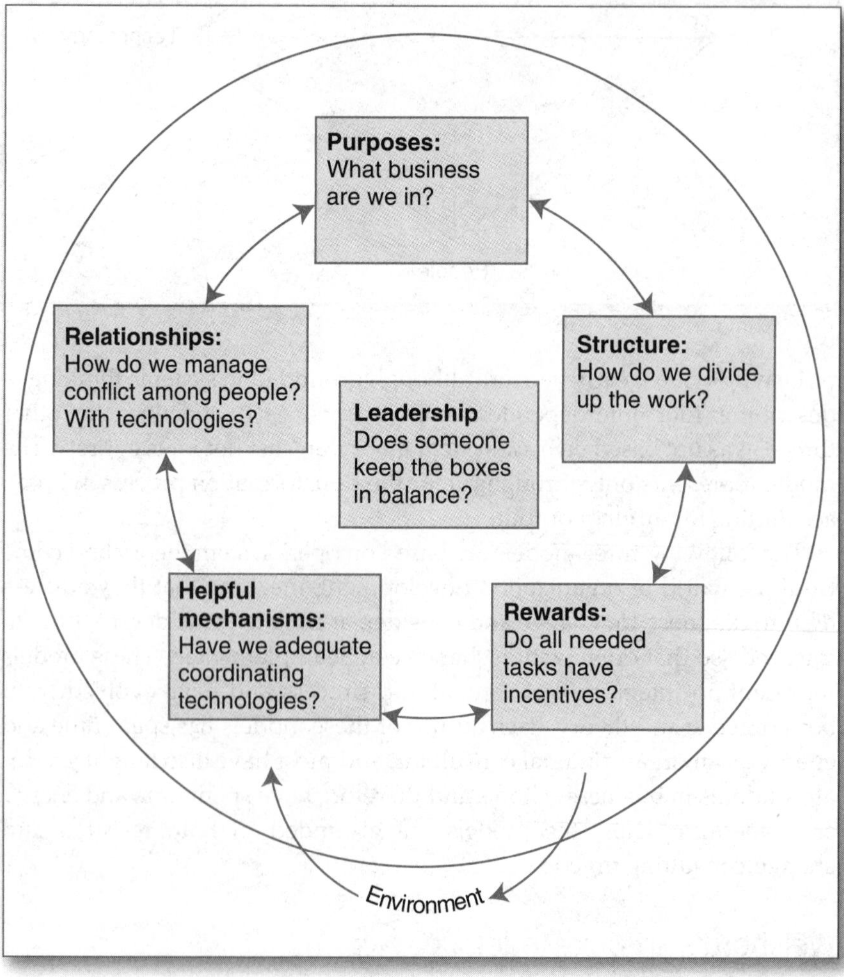

SOURCE: M. R. Weisbord, "Organizational Diagnosis: Six Places to Look for Trouble With or Without a Theory," 1976, *Group and Organization Studies*, 1, pp. 430–447. Reprinted with permission of Sage Publications.

As Figure 9.2 shows, the boxes are surrounded by a circle that represents the external environment, with arrows pointing in both directions, that is, the input and output representations. Weisbord (1976) is a proponent of understanding organizations from both the formal and the informal perspective. In other words, there is the formal system—represented by, say, the structure—and the informal system embedded in the organizational culture. But Weisbord stated that there are informal and formal aspects to each of the six boxes. So, for example, the structure box has its formal dimensions, in that the organization chart depicts lines of authority and accountability, and also has its informal dimensions, its unspoken rules about how authority is actually exercised. Diagnostically, Weisbord argued, the extent of the gap between the formal and informal is highly important, and the action to be taken (the process side) is that of reducing the gap. Otherwise, the organization will remain more ineffective than effective.

To understand more clearly what Weisbord meant by or how he defined each box, it is instructive to consider the primary questions he asked about each one. The boxed questions in Figure 9.2 give us the general idea for each organizational component in the model. More specifically, Weisbord's (1976) primary question(s) for each box are as follows:

- Purposes: How clear are organizational members about the organization's purpose and mission? How supportive are they of the organization's purpose and mission?
- Structure: How adequate is the fit between the organization's purpose and mission and the internal structure that is designed to serve that purpose? (This question is similar to the strategy-structure link mentioned earlier.)
- Rewards: What are the similarities and differences between what the organization formally rewards and punishes and what organizational members actually believe they are rewarded or punished for doing?
- Helpful mechanisms: Which processes and procedures in the organization (planning, budgeting, information systems, etc.) actually help organizational members do their work, and which of them hinder more than help?
- Relationships: For this box, Weisbord was concerned with three categories: between individuals; between and among groups, units, and departments, and so forth; and between the person and the requirements of his or her job. He argued that, diagnostically, first, one should consider the quality of these relationships, and then one

should consider the adequacy of the models for managing and dealing with conflict.
- Leadership: This box is at the center of the model because Weisbord
  believed that organizational leaders' jobs are to watch for blips in
  each of the other five boxes on the radar screen and to make sure
  that they are in alignment.

To summarize, Weisbord (1976) believed that regardless of the wording
for these organizationally diagnostic questions, they need to be asked on
two levels:

1. How large is the gap between the formal and informal dimensions
   of the organization, that is, the degree of fit between the individual
   and the organization?

2. What degree of discrepancy is there between what is and what
   ought to be, that is, the congruence between the organization and
   its external environment?

Some of the strengths of Weisbord's six-box model are simultaneously
its weaknesses: Although categorizing the many organizational dimensions into six boxes helps to simplify and provide quick understanding,
organizations are far too complicated to be represented by only six categories. A strength of the model is the prominent position of the *leadership* box
in the middle, signifying the coordinating function. If there are negative
blips on this part of the radar screen, we know that we have serious
issues. It is also clear that the *purposes* box links most directly with both
the *relationship* and *structure* categories, but how does *purposes* link to the
other boxes? The *leadership* box does imply a causal linkage with all the
other five boxes, but no other causal linkages are suggested.

Weisbord's six-box model can be helpful for rapid and simple diagnostic purposes. It is also useful for client organizations that have little
sophistication about systems thinking and the larger complexities of organizational dynamics. But when a deeper and more complicated diagnosis
is required, these six boxes are simply not sufficient.

The Nadler-Tushman Congruence Model

Nadler and Tushman (1977) developed their model at about the same
time Weisbord was creating his, and they made the same assumptions: that

an organization is an open system and therefore is influenced by its environment (inputs) and also shapes its environment, at least to some extent, by its outputs. The Nadler-Tushman model will be presented according to the open system framework, starting with inputs, then outputs, and finally, the bulk of the model, which they refer to as the transformation process, or the throughput (see Figure 9.3 for a depiction of the model).

Inputs

Nadler and Tushman (1977) viewed inputs to the system as relatively fixed. The four they cited are the *environment*, the *resources* available to the organization, the organization's *history*, and *strategies* that are developed and then evolve over time. These inputs help define how people in the organization behave, and they serve as constraints on behavior as well as opportunities for action.

As we know from the works of Burns and Stalker (1961) and Lawrence and Lorsch (1967), the extent to which an organization's environment is

Figure 9.3   The Nadler-Tushman Congruence Model for Diagnosing Organizational Behavior

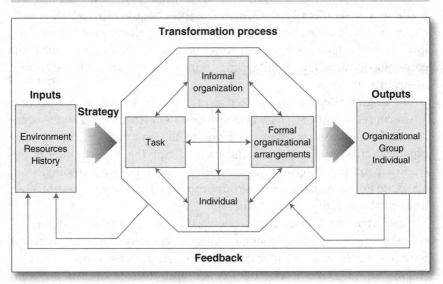

SOURCE: D. A. Nadler and M. L. Tushman, "A Diagnostic Model for Organization Behavior," 1977, in *Perspectives on Behavior in Organizations*, edited by J. R. Hackman, E. E. Lawler III, and L. W. Porter, pp. 85–100, New York: McGraw-Hill. Reproduced by permission of the McGraw-Hill Companies.

relatively stable or dynamic significantly affects internal operations, structure, and policy (see Chapter 8). For many organizations, a very important aspect of environment is the parent system and its directives. Many organizations are subsidiaries or divisional profit centers of larger corporations, such as colleges within a university or hospitals within a larger health care delivery system. These subordinate organizations may operate relatively autonomously with respect to the outside world (having their own purchasing operations, for example), but because of corporate policy, they may be fairly restricted in how much money they can spend. Thus, for many organizations, we must think of their environments in at least two categories: the larger parent system and the rest of the outside world—government regulations, competitors, and the marketplace in general.

Resources within the Nadler-Tushman model include capital (money, property, equipment, and so on), raw materials, technologies, people, and various intangibles, such as company name, logo, or brand, which may have a high value in the company's market.

An organization's history is also input to the system. The history determines, for example, patterns of employee behavior, policy, the types of people the organization attracts and recruits, and even how decisions are made in a crisis. Recall from Chapter 7 the example of two banks with highly similar backgrounds. When they merged after some 150 years of independence, their respective histories had shaped two entirely different corporate cultures. History is an important variable in the understanding of any organization.

Although strategy is categorized as an input in the model, Nadler and Tushman set it apart. Strategy is the process of determining how the organization's resources are best used within the environment for optimal organizational functioning. It is the act of identifying opportunities in the environment and determining whether the organization's resources are adequate for capitalizing on these opportunities. History plays a subtle but influential role in the strategic process.

Some organizations are very strategic; they plan, for example, the rational perspective regarding strategic change delineated by Rajagopalan and Spreitzer (1997; see Chapter 8). Other organizations simply react to changes in their environments or act opportunistically, rather than according to a long-range plan that determines which opportunities will be seized and which will be allowed to pass, similar to the learning perspective described by Rajagopalan and Spreitzer. As Nadler and Tushman

(1977) pointed out, however, all organizations have strategies whether they are deliberate and formal or unintentional and informal. Rajagopalan and Spreitzer made the same point.

Outputs

Shifting to the right side of the model (Figure 9.3), we will consider outputs before covering the transformation process. Thus, we shall examine the organization's environment from the standpoint of both how it influences the system and how it becomes influenced by the system's outputs.

For diagnostic purposes, Nadler and Tushman (1977) presented four key categories of outputs: system functioning, group behavior, intergroup relations, and individual behavior and effect. With respect to the effectiveness of the system's functioning as a whole, the following three questions should elicit the necessary information:

1. How well is the organization attaining its desired goals of production, service, return on investment, and so on?

2. How well is the organization using its resources?

3. How well is the organization coping with changes in its environment over time?

The remaining three outputs are more directly behavioral: how well groups or units within the organization are performing; how effectively these units communicate with one another, resolve differences, and collaborate when necessary; and how individuals behave. For the last output, individual behavior, we are interested in matters such as turnover, absenteeism, and, of course, individual job performance.

The Transformation Process

The components of the transformation process and their interactions are what we normally think of when we consider an organization: the people, the various tasks and jobs, the organization's managerial structure (the organization chart), and all relationships of individuals, groups, and subsystems. As Figure 9.3 shows, four interactive major components compose the transformation process, changing inputs into outputs.

The *task component* consists of jobs to be done and the inherent characteristics of the work itself. The primary task dimensions are the extent and nature of the required interdependence between and among task performers, the level of skill needed, and the kinds of information required to perform the tasks adequately.

The *individual component* consists of all the differences and similarities among employees, particularly demographic data, skill and professional levels, and personality-attitudinal variables.

Organizational arrangements include the managerial and operational structure of the organization, work flow and design, the reward system, management information systems, and the like. These arrangements are the formal mechanisms used by management to direct and control behavior and to organize and accomplish the work to be done.

The fourth component, *informal organizational,* is the social structure within the organization, including the grapevine, the organization's internal politics, and the informal authority-information structure—whom you see for what.

Congruence as the Concept of Fit

As Nadler and Tushman (1977) pointed out, a mere listing and description of these system inputs, outputs, and components is insufficient for modeling an organization. An organization is dynamic, never static, and the model must represent this reality, as the arrows in Figure 9.3 do. Nadler and Tushman went beyond depicting relationships, however. Their term *fit* is a measure of the congruence between pairs of inputs and especially between the components of the transformation process. They contend that inconsistent fits between any pair will result in less than optimal organizational and individual performance. If, for example, an organization's strategy is to become a global corporation, but one of the "formal organizational arrangements" (structure) is a division of international operations, and international emphasis is not a structural aspect of all units within the organization, then we have a lack of fit, or incongruence. Nadler and Tushman's hypothesis, therefore, was that the better the fit, the more effective the organization will be.

Nadler and Tushman (1977) recommended three steps for diagnosis:

1. Identify the system: Is the system for diagnosis an autonomous organization, a subsidiary, a division, or a unit of some larger system? What are the boundaries of the system, its membership, its tasks, and—if it is part of a larger organization—its relationships with other units?

2. Determine the nature of the key variables: What are the dimensions of the inputs and components? What are the desired outputs?

3. Diagnose the state of fit. This is the most important step, involving two related activities: determining fits between components and diagnosing the link between the fits and organization outputs.

For their model, then, Nadler and Tushman (1977) argued that one must concentrate on the degree to which the key components are congruent with one another. It should be noted that measuring these degrees of congruence is no easy undertaking. The process requires considerable data gathering and analysis.

For diagnosing the link between fits and outputs, the organizational change agent must focus the outcome of the diagnoses of the various component fits and their behavioral consequences on the set of behaviors associated with system outputs: goal attainment, resource usage, and overall system performance. Considering the component fits, or lack thereof, in light of system outputs helps identify critical problems of the organization. As these problems are addressed and changes are made, the system is then monitored for purposes of evaluation through the feedback loop.

In summary, the Nadler-Tushman model is comprehensive and sophisticated—which is the reason that so much space is devoted to the framework. Although mostly descriptive, the model does suggest certain cause-effect linkages, that is, the idea of congruence. Little or no congruence between, for example, strategy and structure would produce poor organizational performance. Moreover, incongruence between the external environment and strategy would also suggest a causal relationship with performance. The point is that many other congruencies or incongruencies could be emphasized. There are many possibilities. What would help, but are not provided in the Nadler-Tushman model, are ideas for determining which organizational dimensions are more central or "weightier" than which other dimensions. Their category "formal organizational arrangements" consists of quite a number of components, such as structure, job design, formal policies and systems, and goals or objectives. Some of these, such as goals, for example, might be more central than others. Finally, no means are suggested for determining when congruence is in place or for determining what levels of congruence or incongruence produce desirable or undesirable effects.

Perhaps it is chaos and nonlinear complex systems theory (see Chapters 4 and 7) that has influenced Nadler and Tushman (1989) more recently to question their own congruence position. To use their words:

> While our model implies that congruence of organizational components is a desirable state, it is, in fact, a double-edged sword. In the short term, congruence seems to be related to effectiveness and performance. A system with high congruence, however, can be resistant to change. It develops ways of insulating itself from outside influences and may be unable to respond to new situations. (p. 195)

Tichy's TPC (Technical, Political, Cultural) Framework

Although similar to the other two models, particularly the Nadler-Tushman framework, Tichy (1983) focused much more explicitly on organization change. In fact, his nine components should be seen less as boxes in a model and more as change levers. Figure 9.4 displays these levers in a certain order that Tichy considered important for organization change.

Briefly, the nine change levers are as follows:

1. External interface, or the organization's external environment (input)

2. Mission

3. Strategy (Tichy combined mission and strategy in the model, but he considered them distinct levers)

4. Managing organizational mission and strategy processes (that is, realistically engaging the relevant interest groups)

5. Task (change often requires new tasks)

6. Prescribed networks (more or less, the formal organizational structure)

7. Organizational processes (communicating, problem solving, and decision making)

8. People

9. Emergent networks (more or less, the informal organization)

Figure 9.4   Tichy's Framework

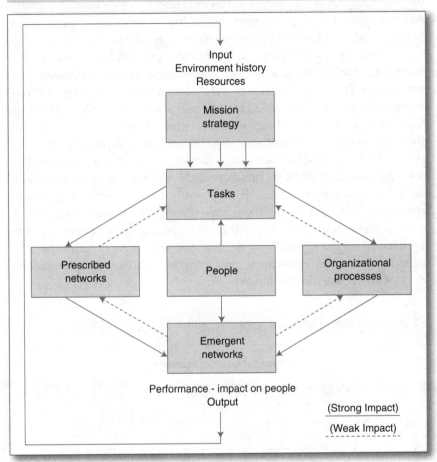

SOURCE: N. M. Tichy. *Managing Strategic Change: Technical, Political, and Cultural Dynamics.* © 1983. Reprinted by permission of John Wiley & Sons, Inc., New York, p. 73.

Managing as such is not shown in the model. Tichy considered management as pervading the entire framework. He assumed "that organizational effectiveness (or output) is a function of the characteristics of each of the components of the model, as well as a function of how the components interrelate and align into a functioning system" (Tichy, 1983, p. 72).

The TPC in Tichy's (1983) thinking provides the more unique aspect of his framework. Technical, political, and cultural represent the three primary systems that cut across the nine levers. Tichy considered these three systems to be the dominant ones for understanding organizations in general and organization change in particular. The technical system is based on science and hard data and therefore represents a highly rational perspective. The political system is based on power dynamics and the fact that in organizations, some groups and individuals are more powerful than others. With respect to change, the primary behavior representing this perspective is negotiation. The cultural system concerns shared values and norms, or "cognitive schemes," as Tichy called them. These schemes are what link people together and constitute the organization's culture. Consistent with Lewinian thinking (see Chapter 8), culture change occurs, according to Tichy, by developing new norms and perhaps values. Dealing with only one or two of these systems instead of all three simultaneously will lead to ineffectiveness in organizational performance. All three must be realigned for successful change. Tichy, therefore, saw these three systems as intertwined metaphorically as three strands of a rope. The three systems or perspectives can be understood separately, but for effective change to occur, all must be managed together. Overlaying these three systems with the change levers produces a matrix like the one shown in Figure 9.5.

Figure 9.5 Tichy's Technical, Political, Cultural Matrix

								Amount of
Core Systems		Mission Strategy	Tasks	Prescribed network	People	Processes	Emergent networks	within-system alignment
	Technical system							____
	Political system							____
	Cultural system							____
Amount of required organizational component change		____	____	____	____	____	____	Total Alignment Score = (Min. 0 – 36 Max.)

SOURCE: N. M. Tichy. *Managing Strategic Change: Technical, Political, and Cultural Dynamics.* ©1983. Reprinted by permission of John Wiley & Sons, Inc., New York, p. 19.

Tichy (1983) argued that these systems must be aligned with levers and each with every other one for effective change to occur. For diagnostic purposes, data must be collected for each cell of the matrix. These data need to be informative about the degree of change required for proper alignment. Across the matrix, the alignment is *within* a system, and down the matrix, the alignment is *between* systems. An illustration of the former, within, might be a case of new technology arising in the external environment and the organization's holding on too long to its own technology, which may be rapidly reaching obsolescence. An illustration of the latter, between, might be a case of attempting cultural change toward a more trusting set of values when the political system in the organization is based in part on "information is power," and it is best to share this form of power very sparingly.

To summarize, Tichy's model includes most of the variables that are critical to understanding and especially changing organizations. The TPC rope is a unique feature of his framework and adds to our understanding of what to consider in and how to think through the implementation of a large-scale change effort in an organization.

There are some limitations, however. The *people* component in Tichy's model is barely mentioned. Moreover, issues at the individual level of organizational analysis have a lower priority than at group and organizational levels. To be fair, Tichy (1983) did admit this omission in his book by stating that he skimmed over the psychological aspects of change. Also to be fair, the cultural and political strands of the TPC rope do address people issues, but at a more macro level than at the level of, say, job-person match (congruence) or local work unit activities, such as self-directed work group dynamics and teamwork. Finally, the previous criticism that too much emphasis on congruence could have an adverse or dampening effect on organization change could also be true for Tichy's argument that alignments are very important.

A Comparison of the Three Models

The models by Weisbord, Nadler-Tushman, and Tichy are more alike than unlike. All three are based on the open system theoretical way of thinking and consequently include the external environment (input), the bulk of each model being the throughput (or transformation process) and performance (outputs). With Weisbord (1976), the output was accounted for merely by an arrow pointing outside the circle; Nadler and Tushman

(1977) actually used the term *outputs* and referred to them at three levels, individual, group, and organization; and Tichy (1983) used both terms, *performance* and *output*. All three models refer to organizational direction in one way or the other—purpose, mission, or strategy—and all three account for structure and people. Tichy is unique with his systems rope metaphor, and Weisbord is the only one to make leadership and rewards explicit. Culture looms large in Tichy's model, Nadler-Tushman included an informal organizational component, and Weisbord used relationships, which he would probably argue accounts for culture. Tichy was simply much more explicit about it because he considers culture to be critical to organization change. And finally, as noted before (Burke, 1994):

> With regard to explanation, Weisbord argues that leadership is criti-
> cal, Nadler and Tushman advocate congruence (but not too much of
> it), and Tichy espouses alignment. The Weisbord and Nadler-
> Tushman models present more of a contingency viewpoint, whereas
> Tichy takes a strong normative stance. Tichy's strategic rope, con-
> sisting of technical, political, and cultural strands, must indeed be a
> braided rope; that is, the strands must be aligned, the three systems,
> as he labels them, must be aligned with his key levers (organiza-
> tional components), and the levers themselves must be aligned with
> one another. (p. 70)

Summary

Organizational models can be useful in helping us to understand the dynamics of action taken and organizational members' behavior in organizations. Because actions and behavior cover such a wide array of data, categorizing this enormous universe into more manageable chunks helps us to transform the data into useful information. Models, then, help us to be more efficient and to be more rational as we attempt to understand and change an organization.

But any organizational model has its limitations. How can we be certain that the categories of our model are the primary and correct ones? And even if our components make sense and are widely accepted, what is missing and perhaps overlooked?

The models covered in this chapter and the one by Porras described in Chapter 7 were all born from a combination of practice, theory, and research.

Thus, from the standpoint of organization change, these models do provide our best guesses so far about what is important to consider. Nevertheless, they are selective; that is, they are all based on the same organism metaphor (as noted, there are other useful metaphors), and they conform more to Chin and Benne's (1985) normative-reeducative strategy for change than to either their empirical-rational or power-coercive strategies (see Chapter 8). Recall that a primary example of a normative-reeducative strategy for change is organization development (OD). The models covered in this chapter as well as the one by Porras and Robertson (1992) from Chapter 7 all evolved from the field of OD.

This chapter does not complete our coverage of organizational models. After all, as the author of this book, I have not had my say! The next chapter is my statement about organizational modeling and change. The Burke–Litwin model (Burke & Litwin, 1992) is presented next and represents an attempt not only to provide a descriptive model of what is important to consider in understanding an organization but also to take a position about organizational performance and change. The Burke–Litwin model is therefore a statement about cause and effect, and the perspective taken is a normative rather than a contingent one.

TEN

The Burke–Litwin Causal Model of Organization Performance and Change

T he organization models we have considered thus far, the one by
Porras covered in Chapter 7, and by Weisbord, Nadler-Tushman,
and Tichy in Chapter 9, integrate content and process, at least implicitly, but they are more about organizational functioning than about
change. The exception is Tichy's technical, political, cultural (TPC)
framework. His model addresses change: the importance of alignment
for organization change to be effective. But Tichy is not explicit about
cause and effect and neither are the authors of the other organization
models. How does the political system in Tichy's TPC affect or influence
the cultural system and vice versa? How does the alignment of the
technical system with the lever of mission and strategy affect performance, and more particularly, how does it shape change? These questions
are not addressed.

The purpose of this chapter is to respond to some of these kinds of questions by first explaining the Burke–Litwin model and, second, by attempting to validate the framework with brief coverage of related research and theory.

Background

My colleague in the derivation of the Burke–Litwin model, George Litwin, conducted research in the 1960s on organizational climate (Litwin & Stringer, 1968; Tagiuri & Litwin, 1968) that established the groundwork for what later became our overall organizational framework (Burke & Litwin, 1992).

In graduate school at the University of Michigan and later as a professor at the Harvard Business School, Litwin was influenced by the works of Atkinson (1958) and David McClelland (1961), respectively.

McClelland was a need theorist and believed that human needs could be aroused by manipulating the environment. Although we all may have some degree of need to achieve, McClelland (1961) showed from his research that such a need could be increased and enhanced. Litwin wanted to demonstrate this phenomenon organizationally and from the standpoint of leadership. He hypothesized that different styles of leadership could create different organizational climates (environment) that would appeal to (arouse) different motives or needs. Working with MBA students in a laboratory setting, Litwin created three separate organizations led by distinctly different leaders, one being a power-oriented leader to arouse followers' need for power, a second being an achievement-oriented leader having a strong task focus with challenging goals, and a third being an affiliation-oriented leader to arouse relationship and interdependence needs. His study showed that performance and morale differed significantly across the three laboratory organizations, with the achievement leader having both the highest performance and the highest morale (Litwin & Stringer, 1968).

Based on this early work, Litwin (Litwin, Humphrey, & Wilson, 1978) developed an abbreviated organizational model with climate as the centerpiece. He defined organizational climate as a set of psychological priorities of a given (usually) work environment that are based on the collective perceptions of the people in that environment. The nature of a climate is determined by a number of organizational variables, not just management or leadership approach. These other variables for Litwin et al. (1978) included norms and values (culture) and management systems (policies and procedures). Figure 10.1 depicts this early version of Litwin's model.

Figure 10.1   Organizational-Climate System

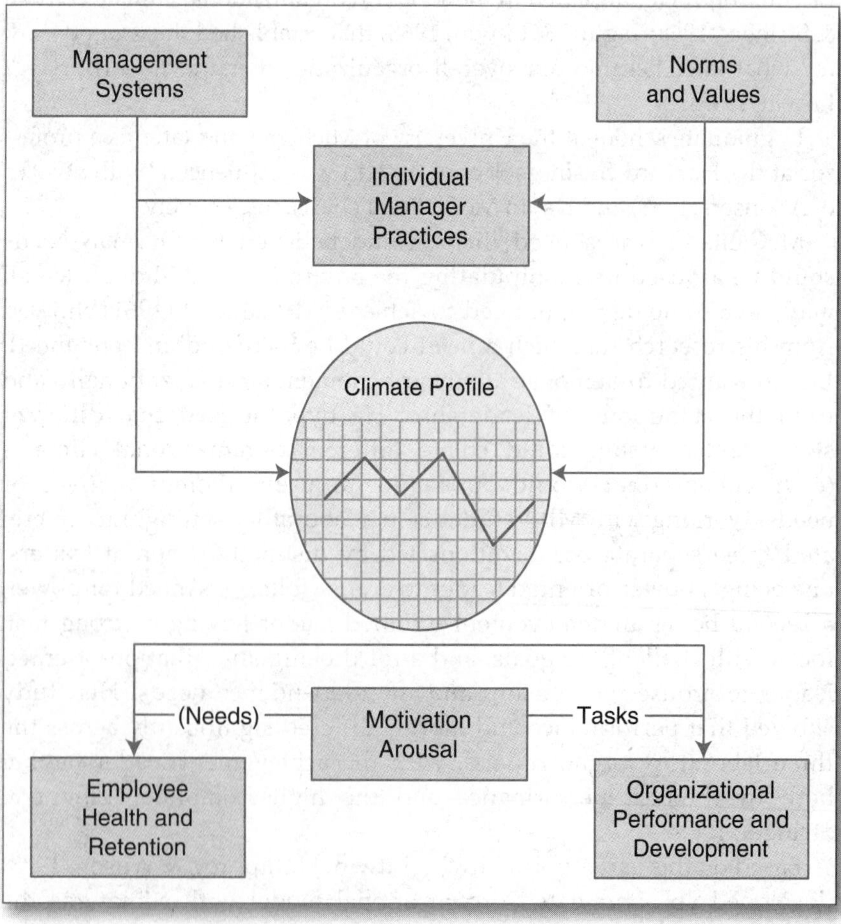

SOURCE: G. H. Litwin, J. W. Humphrey, and T. B. Wilson, "Organizational Climate: A Proven Tool for Improving Performance," 1978, in *The Cutting Edge: Current Theory and Practice in Organization Development*, edited by W. W. Burke (p.190), La Jolla, CA: University Associates.

Note that Litwin et al. (1978), in addition to modeling climate as affecting motivation, also included the outcome variables of organizational performance and employee health and retention. Also, it should be noted that the importance of this early research and theory development on organizational climate was the cause-effect position that Litwin took, that is, the linkage of psychological and organizational variables. His empirically testable claim was that the better the work unit climate, the greater the likelihood of high organizational performance.

In other words, this kind of thinking and research set the stage for how we developed the Burke–Litwin model. One final point before we proceed to a description of the model: Although there is overlap between climate and culture (in any organization, rarely, if ever, is a single variable discrete), we do make a distinction (Burke & Litwin, 1992):

> Climate is defined in terms of perceptions that individuals have of how their local work unit is managed and how effectively they and their day-to-day colleagues work together on the job. The level of analysis, therefore, is the group, the work unit. Climate is much more in the foreground of organizational members' perceptions, whereas culture is more background and defined by beliefs and values. The level of analysis for culture is the organization. Climate is, of course, affected by culture, and people's perceptions define both, but at different levels. (pp. 526–527)

Schneider (1985) has made similar distinctions between climate and culture in organizations. Moreover, although there are similarities, understanding the differences between culture and climate is one of the keys to understanding organization change more thoroughly.

The remainder of this chapter is devoted to, first, a description of the model and then to coverage of research and theory that supports the primary tenets of the model.

The Model

As noted earlier, the Burke–Litwin model has its roots in the organizational climate studies conducted by Litwin and his colleagues during the latter part of the 1960s. Further development of the model did not occur until the late 1970s and 1980s, when Burke and Litwin began their collaborative work in the arena of organizational change consulting, first with Citibank, as the financial enterprise was known back then, and later with British Airways (BA), beginning in 1985.

The model as conceived today actually emerged from practice, that is, as a consequence of trying to understand more about how to bring about change at BA. This case is introduced in Chapter 5. The organization change of BA at the time was initiated by a decree from the prime minister of Great Britain, Margaret Thatcher. BA, the nation's flagship airline, (1) was not exactly efficiently run, (2) had evolved from the Royal Air Force of World War II and was therefore managed rather bureaucratically and in a top-down military manner, and (3) ended each year financially in the red, with the government having to make up the deficit. Thatcher decided to put a stop to this way of doing business and declared that BA would have to survive on its own as a private corporation, publicly owned, with stock traded on both the City of London and the New York stock exchanges. The decree was finally enacted in February 1987. Thus, BA, in order to survive, had to change. Every nook and cranny of the organization was affected, especially, at the outset, BA's mission, business strategy, leadership, and organizational culture. The theory of the business (Drucker, 1994; see Chapter 8) had to be altered significantly, primarily from conceiving of BA as *the* national airline with all the requisite rights and privileges to a commercial enterprise that must serve customers to survive. This story of change at BA, with all its complexities, could easily take up many additional pages. The change, after all, took time (about five years), was quite dramatic and dynamic, and was deemed successful by a variety of measures and independent sources. For more, see Burke (1994), Burke and Trahant (2000), Georgiades and Macdonell (1998), Goodstein and Burke (1991), and Litwin, Bray, and Brooke (1996).

As we proceed with a description of the model, the influence of the change at BA and our consequent learning can easily be discerned. The criticality of an organization's external environment, for example, cannot be overestimated. For BA, at the time, the external forces impinging on the enterprise were in no small way represented by the persona of Margaret Thatcher. For most organizations, the external environment is not as dramatic, but just as important nevertheless for understanding organization change. The overall model is depicted in Figure 10.2.

As can be seen, the model conforms to the open-system way of thinking, in which the external environment box serves as the input dimension and the individual and organizational performance box

Figure 10.2   The Burke–Litwin Model of Organizational Performance and Change

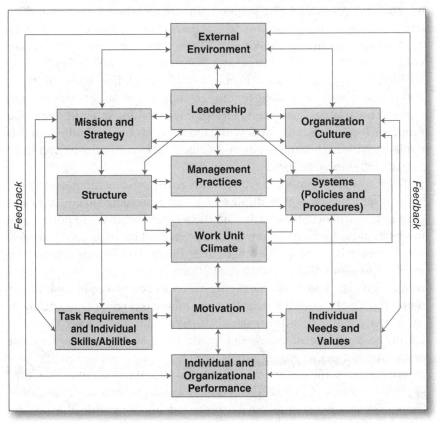

serves as the output dimension. The remaining boxes represent what we consider to be the primary throughput dimensions. To complete the picture (metaphor), the feedback loop connects the input with the output. Note that the arrows for the feedback loop go in both directions, meaning that organizational outcomes—products and services—affect the external environment, for example, customer satisfaction, and that forces in the external environment can affect performance directly (depending on how performance is defined and measured), for example, when Wall Street trends affect a change in government regulations or company stock price.

As noted, the 12 boxes that compose the model represent our choices of what we consider to be primary for organizational understanding and analysis. Although we made our own choices, we have definitely been influenced by the thinking of others. One can easily see overlap with the Weisbord (1976), Porras and Robertson (1987, 1992), Nadler and Tushman (1977), and Tichy (1983) models. And like some of these authors, we have accounted for dimensions at the larger-system level with such variables as mission, strategy, leadership, and culture; at the group or local work unit level with climate; and, finally, at the individual level with individual needs and values, task requirements and individual skills, and motivation.

The arrows that connect the boxes and go in both directions signify the open-system principle of multiple effect, that is, a change in any one category or box will eventually affect all the remaining boxes. To portray the model as close to reality as possible, there would be arrows, or linkages, between each box and all the other boxes. Figure 10.2 depicts some of the more important linkages rather than attempting to show every possible connection. The clutter of displaying all connections would look rather daunting, if not messy. But daunting and messy is no doubt closer to reality. Moreover, our two-dimensional display is limited. Closer to reality would be a display of the model in the form of a hologram. Circular arrows would depict reality much more accurately. Yet our model predicts cause, so some directions are more important or weightier than others when it comes to planning and implementing successful organization change. A quick example can be provided by comparing the linkage between the culture and systems boxes. Although the arrow connecting the two is bilateral, culture probably has a stronger influence on systems than the other way around. Evidence for a strong linkage between the two boxes has been provided by Kerr and Slocum (1987). Their research showed that an organization's reward system (a subdimension of the larger systems box) is a manifestation of its culture and that the reward system can be used, perhaps should be used, to facilitate change in an organization's culture. In other words, their study supports the notion of linkage and its bidirectional nature. With our display of culture above the systems box (and therefore carrying more "weight," or influence), we are going farther than the Kerr and Slocum study, that is, beyond mere linkage, and stating that culture, especially the aspects of beliefs and values, helps to *determine* the type of reward system senior managers deem appropriate. Therefore:

> Displaying the model the way we have is meant to make a statement about organizational change. Organizational change, especially an overhaul of the company business strategy, stems more from environmental impact than from any other factor. Moreover, in large scale or total organizational change, mission, strategy, leadership and culture have more "weight" than structure, management practices, and systems: That is, having organizational leaders communicate the new strategy is not sufficient for effective change. Culture change must be planned as well and aligned with strategy and leader behavior. These variables carry more weight, because changes in them (e.g., organizational mission) affect the total system. Changing structure, on the other hand, may or may not affect the total system. It depends on where in the organization a structural change might occur.
>
> We are not necessarily discussing at this stage where one could *start* the change, only the relative weighting of change dynamics. When we think of the model in terms of change, then, the weighted order displayed in the model is key. (Burke & Litwin, 1992, p. 529)

Transformational and Transactional Dimensions

Key to understanding change according to the model is the top half compared with the bottom half. Borrowing language and concepts from James McGregor Burns (1978) and his distinction between two primary forms of leadership—transformational and transactional—we have conceived of the model similarly. Burns classified *transformational leaders* as being those who bring about change; they never leave a situation the way they found it, and the "situation" (organization, community, nation, etc.) will be different as a consequence of this kind of leader being in charge. He classified as *transactional leaders* those who see the leader-follower relationship as just that, a transaction: "If you do such and such for me, I'll see that you (follower) get rewarded" (promotion, bonus, time off, etc.). This latter form of leadership may involve change, but not change that is sweeping or transformational in nature (change in the *deep structure* of the system; see Chapter 5). Transactional leaders are more interested in maintaining the status quo, but if change is necessary, they would argue that it should be gradual and evolutionary, not sudden and revolutionary.

The categories or boxes in the top half of the model—external environment, mission and strategy, leadership, and culture—are referred to as the *transformational factors*. Changes in these boxes are likely to be caused by direct interaction with external environmental forces and will as a consequence require significantly new behavior from organizational members. Figure 10.3 is a display of these transformational factors. It is similar to Burns's conception of transformational leadership, but, of course, in an organization context, a change in any of these boxes or organizational dimensions means that the entire organization or system is affected and that the change is discontinuous and revolutionary in nature (see Chapter 5), that is, affecting the deep structure of the system and requiring visionary leadership.

The remaining boxes or organizational dimensions in the lower half of the model are what we refer to as the *transactional factors*. These dimensions build on the original thinking and climate research of Litwin and his colleagues (1978; see Figure 10.1). These factors concern more of the day-to-day operations (transactions) of the organization, and for any change there we would use terms such as *continuous improvement, evolutionary,*

Figure 10.3   The Transformational Factors

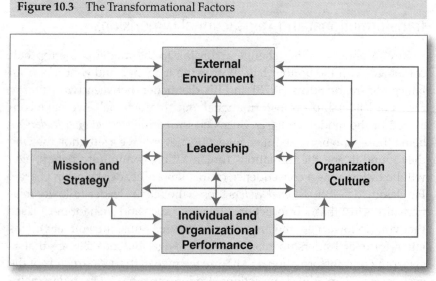

SOURCE: From "A Causal Model of Organizational Performance and Change," by Burke, W. W., & Litwin, G. H., in *Journal of Management, 18,* pp. 523–545. Reprinted with permission from Sage Publications, Inc.

Figure 10.4   The Transactional Factors

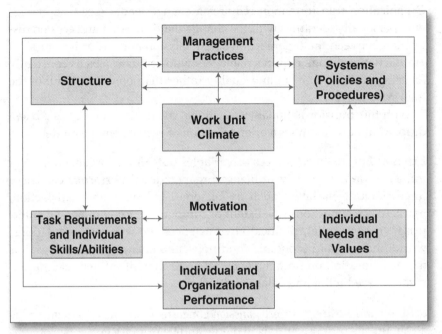

SOURCE: From "A Causal Model of Organizational Performance and Change," by Burke, W. W., & Litwin, G. H., in *Journal of Management, 18*, pp. 523–545. Reprinted with permission from Sage Publications, Inc.

and *selective*, rather than *sweeping*. Figure 10.4 is a depiction of the transactional factors in the model.

As noted previously, the transformational-transactional distinction in organization modeling and change comes from theory about leadership. This theory has several sources, perhaps the first being Zaleznik's (1977) distinction between a leader and a manager, and one year later, Burns's (1978) similar distinction, though phrased differently. Transformational (Burns) is very much the same as Zaleznik's *leader*, and transactional (Burns) is very similar to Zaleznik's *manager*. Burke (1986) combined these two ideas about leadership and hypothesized that each leader (transformational) or manager (transactional) could empower others effectively, but the behaviors would differ when one was acting as a leader and when as a manager. With respect to our organizational model and staying with the transformational (leader) and transactional (manager) distinctions, transformational change is more closely linked with leadership and transactional change is more closely associated with management. Organization transformation requires a change leader (see Chapter 12) who personally identifies with the change that is needed and sees no distinction between the organization's new mission and his or her mission. Transactional change requires managers who see their jobs as constantly focusing on improvement and quality rather than on an overhaul of the total system.

With this transformational-transactional distinction serving as a backdrop, what now follows is a brief definition of each box in the model.

External Environment. Forces or variables outside the organization that influence or will shortly influence organizational performance. These forces include variables such as customer behavior and satisfaction, marketplace conditions (the extent of competition for commercial enterprises, for example), political circumstances, government regulations, world financial and economic conditions, and changing technology. For more elaboration on how the external environment influences an organization, see Pfeffer and Salancik (1978).

Mission and Strategy. Briefly, *mission* concerns what the organization "is all about," its purpose, its raison d'être, and its primary goals. The organization's *strategy* concerns the *how,* or implementation, that is, how the mission is to be accomplished. Of late, the term *vision* has emerged as a popular organizational and leadership concept. Vision is more associated with the leadership category in the model, but a quick word of distinction here between mission and vision is warranted.

Mission is current, or the present, and concerns ultimate purpose. It is cerebral, meaning that the statement of mission is carefully and logically crafted, with key words carrying significant weight, for example, "to serve." Mission is tied directly to the core competencies of the organization and provides an answer to the question "If this organization did not exist, what difference would it make?" Vision addresses the future and concerns aspirations and desired outcomes. Though not irrational, vision nevertheless is emotional and often reflects passion that organizational members feel, especially leaders. Vision statements can be lofty and imply challenge and a "stretch" for the organization over the next three to five years. Vision, therefore, is more about leadership, and mission is more about purpose.

Part of the following chapter is devoted to the Dime Bank's change story. As an example of an organizational vision, their statement follows (Dime Savings Bank, 1997):

Our Vision

The Dime will be the preeminent super-community bank in the greater New York area and a high-performance mortgage banking and consumer financial services company in select markets through-out the United States. We will be a leading provider of diversified financial products and services to individuals, families, and busi-nesses, creating profitable relationships with our customers and communities. Extraordinary customer service and the highest ethi-cal standards will be our defining characteristics. We are committed to delivering customer satisfaction, achieving employee partner-ship, and demonstrating superior financial performance.

For research on the nature and importance of corporate mission state-ments, see Pearce and David (1987), and for an in-depth treatment on how strategy links to the external environment, internal structure, and corpo-rate culture, see Porter (1985).

Leadership. Although this category is usually associated with the behavior of senior executives—and appropriately so—leadership is, after all, exercised throughout an organization. In any case, the primary association here is with providing *direction,* whether it comes from the chief executive officer or from a first-line supervisor. Also by leadership, we mean persua-sion, influence, serving followers, and acting as a role model, and we do not mean command and control, domination, and serving edicts instead of followers. As the model shows (Figure 10.2), leadership and management practices are in separate boxes. Although there is definitely overlap between the two (thus, the boxes are juxtaposed), we believe that there are sufficient differences to warrant separateness. Leadership is about vision; change; using one's intuition, influence, persuasive and presentation skills; and rewarding people with personal praise and providing opportunities to learn new skills. Management is about role, task accomplishments, setting objectives, using the organization's resources (for example, budget or information systems) efficiently and effectively, and rewarding people with extrinsic factors such as money, titles, and promotions. For more specifics on this distinction, see, for example, Bennis and Nanus (1985), Burke (1986), Burns (1978), and Zaleznik (1977).

Culture. Although not very scholarly sounding, the popular definition, namely, "the way we do things around here and the manner in which these norms and values are communicated" (Deal & Kennedy, 1982) is quite appropriate for quickly describing what organization culture actually means. The *way* means the norms we conform to and the values we believe in. *Culture,* then, embodies rules that we follow, both explicit and implicit. *Explicit* rules (norms), for example, are what the human resource manual states about issues such as mode of dress and hours of work. *Implicit* rules are followed but never discussed, informal rules of behavior or codes of conduct that are not written down but govern much, if not most, behavior in organizations, for example, when subordinates conform to an implicit norm by telling their boss what they believe he or she wants to hear, rather than telling the truth. The history of an organization is also important for understanding culture, particularly knowing about the values and customs of the founder(s) (Schein, 1983). For one of the more definitive sources for understanding organization culture, see Schein (1992).

Structure. We normally think of structure as the "organization chart," the diagram of boxes with titles and people's names in them, with lines that connect them—solid lines of connection, with the occasional addition of dotted lines to complicate matters even further. With respect to definitional words, *structure* refers to the arrangement of organizational functions (e.g., accounting, manufacturing, human resource management) and operational units (e.g., the western region, customer service for product group X, Goddard Space Flight Center within NASA) that signify levels of responsibility, decision-making authority, and lines of communication and relationships that lead to implementation of the organization's mission, goals, and strategy. For one of the classic articles about structure, see Duncan (1979), and for more current coverage see Galbraith (1995).

Management Practices. This category addresses what managers do each workday to carry out the organization's strategy. *Practices,* in this case, refer to a particular set of specific behaviors. An example of a management practice might be "to encourage direct reports and associates to take initiative with innovative approaches to various tasks and projects." In practice, two different managers may "encourage direct reports and associates" to the same degree, but how each one does it behaviorally and specifically may differ. One manager may challenge; the other may use highly positive remarks and "pats on the back." Although he used the term *competency* instead of *practice*, Boyatzis (1982) is an early contributor to this line of research and thinking; for additional examples, see Burke and Coruzzi (1987) and Luthans (1988).

Systems. We are concerned here with policies and procedures that are designed to help and support organizational members with their jobs and role responsibilities. This category in the model is akin to one of Weisbord's (1976) six boxes, the one labeled *helpful mechanisms.* Included within this *systems* box are subcategories such as information systems and technology, sometimes referred to as MIS (management information systems), the organization's reward system, and a variety of control systems: performance appraisal, the setting of goals and the budget process, and human resource allocation. In other words, the systems category within the model covers a lot of territory. Sources that help explain what is meant by some of these subcategories include Lawler (1990) on reward systems; Flamholtz (1979) on control systems; Beer, Spector, Lawrence, Mills, and Walton (1984) on managing human resource assets; and Kraemer, King, Dunkle, and Lane (1989) on MIS.

Climate. *Climate* is the collective perceptions of members within the same work unit. These perceptions include the following:

- How well they are managed, in general
- How clear they are about what is expected of them in the workplace
- How they feel their performance is recognized
- How involved they are in decision making
- Whether they believe they are managed according to standards that are challenging and fair
- How much support they feel from fellow work unit members
- How effectively they believe they work with other units in the organization

For more on climate, see the works by Litwin and the book edited by Ashkanasy, Wilderom, and Peterson (2000).

Task Requirements and Individual Skills/Abilities. The short version of this category is job-person match: the degree to which there is congruence between the requirements of one's job, role, and responsibilities and the knowledge, skills, and abilities (competence or talent) of the individual holding the job. For more on what we mean by this category and its importance to individual motivation and productivity, see M. Burke and Pearlman (1988).

Individual Needs and Values. This is the category on the other side of the *motivation* box from *task requirements and individual skills/abilities,* meaning that these two categories influence motivation significantly.

Both boxes have to do with congruence. In this latter case, *needs and values* concern the extent to which one's needs are met on the job: for example, the need for security or achievement and the degree to which there is congruence between what the individual organizational member believes is important, worthwhile, and valuable and what the organization stands for, such as its purpose, values, and how people in and out of the organization (including customers) are treated. The arrow connecting *culture* with this box represents this linkage and potential for congruence between the individual and the organization. Moreover:

> [Most] behavioral scientists believe that enriched jobs enhance motivation and there is evidence to support this belief, yet as Hackman and Oldham (1980) have appropriately noted, not everyone has a desire for his or her job to be enriched. For some members of the workforce, their idea of enrichment concerns activities off the job, not on the job. As the American workforce continues to become even more diverse, the ability to understand differences among people regarding their needs and values with respect to work and job satisfaction increases in importance. (Burke & Litwin, 1992, p. 533)

For more about individual needs and values in organizations, see Meglino and Ravlin (1998) and Sagie and Elizur (1996).

Motivation. For all living humans (and for animals as well), being motivated is a natural state. If Freud is correct about dreams, we are constantly motivated, even while asleep. With respect to the workplace, however, we must be more specific, and in this context, we are concerned with certain needs being aroused—in the language of McClelland (1961), the need to achieve, to affiliate with others, and perhaps to have power. These aroused feelings are not random but are directed toward goals that, when reached, will help to satisfy our needs, and these needs will persist until some degree of satisfaction has been attained. A primary function of organizational leaders and managers, therefore, is to establish the proper goals, that is, goals that are organizationally important and will respond to individual needs for ends such as achievement, meaningful work, reasonable autonomy on the job, and recognition.

As noted previously, job-person match and congruence between the goals and values of the organization and the individual's needs and values contribute significantly to workplace motivation. For brief summaries of relevant theory and research on workplace motivation, see Chapter 8 and the section on mini-theories related to organization change with individual emphasis. And finally, for a definitive statement on the nature of work motivation with supportive theory and research, see Katzell and Thompson (1990).

Individual and Organizational Performance. To be more complete, we should note that *group*, or work unit, should be added to the description of this category in the model; *output*, in the language of open-system theory, refers to the outcomes and results of all the throughput activities that in turn are responses to the external environment (input). Also, as indicated by the feedback loop directly connecting the external environment with performance, the external environment may directly affect performance in its broadest sense, for example, stock price in the case of a publicly owned corporation. In general, however, performance is defined and measured by indices such as productivity, customer satisfaction, quality of product or service, and profit or earnings per share. A deeper understanding of performance, especially at the organizational level, can be found in the writings of Cameron and Whetten; see, for example, Cameron (1980) and Cameron and Whetten (1981, 1982).

More recent work that reflects a unique approach to measuring performance and one that has caught the imagination of many corporations now using them is Kaplan and Norton (1996). Their "balanced scorecard" concept and related measurements have broadened the corporate notion of the bottom line from merely financial indices to measures of customer satisfaction, innovation, and internal business practices.

Now that a definitional overview has been provided, we will consider evidence in support of our normative stance, that is, the causal assumption underlying the model.

Support for the Model's Validity

Recall that a fundamental premise of the model is that planned change should follow the flow from top, or external environment, to bottom, or performance. Although the arrows connecting the boxes travel in all directions—down, up, and laterally, to reflect open system theory fundamentals—those pointing downward are presumed to carry more causal weight. The earlier example of culture influencing systems is a case in point. The following coverage of research and theory in support of the premise of the model is therefore selective, that is, it emphasizes studies that demonstrate the downward weighting. Thus, concerning organization change, the premise is that external environment has the greatest impact. Then, inside the organization, the transformational factors (mission/strategy, leadership, and culture) have the greatest impact. Next in importance come the transactional factors as they are serially portrayed in the model.

The Influence of the External Environment

First, it should be noted that two excellent sources for defining the *texture*, describing the causal nature of and understanding the linkage between the external environment and organizations, are Emery and Trist (1965) and Katz and Kahn (1978, Chap. 4). Second, the Burke–Litwin model is an attempt to represent reality; it is not reality itself, however. After all, human beings in the organization are the reality, with their decisions and daily activities. To put things in boxes is only a depiction and an overly simplified one at that.

The immediate box in the model affected by the external environment is leadership, the senior executives and primary decision makers for the organization. These executives in turn determine the mission and strategy, or at least change these variables. These executives also shape the organization's culture—but not entirely. The work of Hofstede (1991) shows that organizational culture is influenced by societal norms and values. In any case, much of reality can be described as what influences the thinking and feelings of senior executives, and their consequent decisions in turn help shape the two boxes on either side of leadership in the model (see Figure 10.2). Collins (2001), for example, has shown with his concept of "Levels 1 to 5" of leadership, particularly Levels 4 and 5, how a CEO can significantly influence the ultimate performance of a corporation. So, with respect to organization performance and change, leadership does indeed matter. For more evidence, see the comprehensive article by Hogan, Curphy, and Hogan (1994).

Prescott (1986) provided evidence for the way external environment influences strategy, which in turn influences performance. Executives' perceptions of their organization's external environment have been shown to directly and causally affect their strategy decisions (Miles & Snow, 1978). For the effect of environment on organizational culture, we can once again refer to Hofstede's (1991) research, which demonstrated the powerful influence of national origin, with its customs and mores, on individual behavior. And if we consider a more limited perspective, that is, industry group, as representing environment, then Gordon's (1985) study of utility companies and financial institutions showed that corporate culture is directly affected by industry category.

The Transformational Factors

Mission and strategy, leadership, and culture are the transformational factors that most immediately and directly respond to external environmental dynamics. Mission and strategy are together because both concepts concern direction, goals, and objectives for the organization and its various units, with mission being the *what* and strategy the *how*. The order (mission, then strategy) is important for reasons of common sense. (How could strategy be implemented effectively if the mission were not articulated?) Furthermore, at least one study indicates that mission does influence strategic decisions that in turn affect performance (Pearce & David, 1987). Moreover, although Figure 10.3 does not reflect it, an arrow should directly connect mission and strategy with culture (yet leadership is the most important conduit between the two boxes) because mission statements usually either explicitly or implicitly include values and philosophy. These statements represent and reflect the organization's culture (Wilkens, 1989).

For the influence of strategy, three additional studies are worthy of note. First, Chandler's (1962) classic study demonstrated the importance of strategy *preceding* structure; that is, the more successful companies in a given industry determined strategy *before* designing or changing the internal organizational structure. Chandler's criterion for success was a company's financial performance. In the model, therefore, strategy carries more weight than structure.

More recently, an analysis of 262 large companies over a span of 28 years showed the "reciprocal relationship between strategy and structure. However, our results support the original conception of a hierarchical relationship between the two—strategy is a more important determinant of structure than structure is of strategy" (Amburgey & Dacin, 1994, p. 1427). A third study, a meta-analysis by Miller and Cardinal (1994) of 26 previously published studies, suggested that strategic planning positively affects performance. What is interesting about this analysis is the link between strategy and performance and the speculation about the mediating variables between the two. Of course, the underlying assumption of the Burke–Litwin model is that those mediating variables are the transactional factors that lead to climate, to motivation, and so on, and finally to performance.

As already noted in discussing leadership, there is ample evidence that senior executives in leadership positions influence organizational performance. Also, an early study by Fleishman (1953) showed how supervisors are influenced by their managers' approaches and styles. Thus, the leadership box precedes the management practices category in the model. Finally, two studies about 30 years later showed that leadership accounted for more variance in organizational performance than did other variables (Weiner & Mahoney, 1981) and that leadership was significantly related to improved organizational performance over time (Smith, Carson, & Alexander, 1984).

The Transactional Factors

The remaining categories (boxes) in the model leading to performance and change are in the transactional domain. These categories—structure, systems, management practices, work unit climate, individual needs and values, task requirements and individual skills and abilities, and motivation—represent organizational dimensions and activities that are more day-to-day operations than the transformational factors, and more incremental in making changes. They also are more related to foreground (work unit climate) than to background (culture).

Joyce and Slocum (1984) showed that structure, the next category in the model, had a direct impact on climate, as did management practices, another primary variable in the study. In an earlier study, Schneider and Snyder (1975) essentially demonstrated the same outcome. Lawrence and Lorsch (1967, 1969) have shown that structure influences management practices, and Galbraith (1973, 1977) has demonstrated that structure directly affects task requirements as we depict them in the model. As noted before:

> Regarding the impact of *systems,* perhaps the most important subsystem of the policy and procedures (systems) box is the organization's reward system. The belief that "people do what they are rewarded for doing" is practically a cliché. Demonstrating this relationship of rewards and behavior in the workplace is not as obvious and straightforward as one might presume, however. Witness the pay-for-performance controversy for a case in point. There is evidence, nevertheless. (Burke & Litwin, 1992, p. 537)

Bullock and Lawler (1984), for example, have shown linkages down the middle of the model between management practices, climate, motivation, and performance in their research on gain sharing (a participative incentive process). Deutsch (1985) has shown a linkage between reward systems and individual needs and values, as has Jordan (1986).

Another subsystem of the policy and procedures box is human resource management (HRM), or the HR system. In a large-scale study of 293 U.S. firms, Huselid, Jackson, and Schuler (1997) showed that at least for large companies, HRM effectiveness had a positive impact on performance. Multiple measures of performance were used by these researchers, including indices of finance, productivity, and market value. It is interesting that they compared technical HRM effectiveness—for example, strong capabilities in recruiting, selection, performance measurement, training, and compensation and benefits administration—with strategic HRM effectiveness, capabilities, and activities, that is, "designing and implementing a set of internally consistent policies and practices that ensure a firm's human capital contributes to the achievement of its business objectives" (Huselid et al., 1997, p. 172). This means, for example, strategic use of compensation for purposes of organization change instead of simply administering compensation to remain competitive in the labor marketplace. Huselid et al. (1997) further found that, although it was less commonly practiced among the organizations they studied, strategic HRM was a stronger predictor of positive organizational performance than was technical HRM effectiveness.

And finally, another major subsystem in the policy and procedures box is the MIS, or sometimes simply referred to as IT (information technology) or IS (information system). One of the leading experts in this arena is Zuboff (1988). Her work has demonstrated rather dramatically the impact that IT has on worker behavior in general and on motivation and performance in particular.

Directly in line between leadership and climate is the category of management practices. Even though it was defined earlier, for more comprehensive coverage of what we mean by management practices, including numerous examples, see Burke, Richley, and DeAngelis (1985). With respect to research, the work of Schneider is the most relevant here. In a series of studies, he has shown a clear and direct connection between management practices and climate (Schneider, 1980; Schneider, 1990b; Schneider & Bowen, 1985, 1995).

While covering the history and background of the Burke–Litwin model earlier in the chapter, we noted that the work of Litwin and his colleagues has demonstrated the impact of climate on motivation and in turn on performance. Independent of this earlier work, Rosenberg and Rosenstein (1980) have also shown that climate, with particular emphasis on participation, influences productivity positively.

Motivation in the model can perhaps best be understood as an intervening or mediating variable, because in research studies, motivation is sometimes treated as an independent variable (for example, the hypothesis might be that highly motivated workers are more productive) and at other times as a dependent variable (for example, when job satisfaction or morale is used as a surrogate). In any case, what is important from the perspective of the model are the two categories (boxes) on both sides of motivation, *task requirements and individual skills/abilities* and *individual needs and values*. With this perspective, we are considering motivation as an intervening category, with performance as the ultimate dependent variable or outcome. A premise of the model is that these two boxes significantly influence motivation: If the job and the person do not match well, motivation will suffer; if individuals' needs on the job and values about work and the workplace are incongruent with the organization's culture, areas such as the reward system and motivation will suffer. With respect to research on the effect of job-person match (task requirements and individual skills/abilities), M. Burke and Pearlman's (1988) chapter provides considerable evidence for this aspect of the model, as does the research by Hunter and Schmidt (1982). Hackman and Oldham's (1980) work provides some of the clearest support for the impact of individual needs and values on motivation and so do the research outcomes in the study by Guzzo, Jette, and Katzell (1985).

Referring again to the work on organizational climate by Schneider (Schneider, 1980, 1990a; Schneider & Bowen, 1985, 1995), support for the hierarchical relationship of climate, motivation, and performance in the middle of the Burke–Litwin model comes from their research with front-line people in service businesses, such as tellers and loan officers in banks or ticket agents and cabin crews at an airline (regarding the latter, see Burke, 1994, and Goodstein & Burke, 1991, for the BA case example). How these front-line employees are treated by their supervisors has a direct effect on customer satisfaction. In bank branches, for example, where these service employees were managed more participatively as opposed to bureaucratically (following procedures strictly), customer satisfaction was significantly higher. In other words, the managers' practices of participation created a climate that positively influenced motivation and in turn performance, which then had a positive effect on customer satisfaction.

Finally, recall that when changing the transformational factors in the model (external environment, mission/strategy, leadership, and culture), the consequent organization change is more likely to be discontinuous (episodic and revolutionary) and affect the deep structure (Gersick, 1991) of the total system. Changing the transactional factors (structure, systems, and climate) is more likely to result in continuous improvement: incremental and evolutionary organization change.

Summary

The goal of this chapter was to provide an organizational model or framework that would help to explain open system theory in action and to provide a way of thinking about planned organization change. Background about and a brief descriptive overview of the model was covered, followed by the section on support for the model's validity. It should be noted that the studies cited in this latter chapter section were selective. Other studies could have been included that both support and call into question some of the underlying assumptions of the model.

However, the main point is that evidence exists to support the model's validity. To be fair, it should be noted that the evidence cited comes from a variety of sources and, as it relates to the model, is somewhat piecemeal. An ideal test of the model's validity would be research that simultaneously examines the effect of all boxes in the model across an array of organizations.

Although not always a test of the entire model, some "simultaneous examinations" have been approximated. A study by Bernstein and Burke (1989) demonstrated support for parts of the model, and Fox's (1990) research in a hospital "demonstrated that leadership, culture, and management practices predicted significant variances in employees' perceptions of work unit climate and organizational performance [with] leadership and culture [being] clearly the two strongest indicators" (Burke & Litwin, 1992, p. 540). A longitudinal study of a large British corporation by Anderson-Rudolf (1996) and a more recent employee survey analysis within a major global corporation (Alexander, 2002) have both demonstrated support for the model's assumptions. We can therefore conclude that the model represents organizational reality to some degree and that practitioners can apply it with a reasonable amount of confidence. Moreover, the proof of any organizational model is its degree of usefulness for (1) adequately understanding current organizational dynamics (diagnosis) and (2) helping to steer change in such a way that performance of an organization will be improved. In other words, a useful model should help us understand and guide the process that it models, in this case, organization change.

ELEVEN

Organizational Culture Change

A s the title suggests, the purpose of this chapter is to continue our process of exploring and explaining the nature of organization change but, in this case, focus on changing an organization's *culture*— "the way we do things"—the most difficult aspect of organization change. In the previous chapter covering the Burke–Litwin model, recall that culture is a transformational factor meaning (a) systemwide (every organizational component and activity in one way or the other reflects the organization's culture), (b) directly related to the external environment, and (c) with respect to change requires revolutionary rather than evolutionary interventions.

First, using examples, we will explain in more depth than we have covered so far and more precisely just what organizational culture is. Most useful for this explanation are Edgar Schein's three concepts: artifacts, espoused beliefs and values, and basic underlying assumptions (Schein, 2004).

Second, we will use the story of British Airways (BA) as our primary example of culture change—that organization's journey from being a government-owned airline to becoming a private, stockholder-owned enterprise competing on its own in the marketplace of global airline companies.

Finally, we will refer to a previous theory covered in earlier chapters to help explain the culture change at BA.

Experiencing Organizational Culture

Early in my career I was involved with an organization that operated in the world of law enforcement and corrections. It was known as the National Parole Institute, which was funded by the federal government to train parole board officers nationwide in group decision making. As a part of my indoctrination, I visited a new federal prison, in Minnesota as I recall, with the director of the parole institute. As we entered the new facility, I noticed that he was observing everything he saw quickly yet intensely. The facility was brand new with all of the latest architecture and technology. Cameras and TV monitors were everywhere. The floors, walls, and windows (what few there were) sparkled with cleanliness, and everyone from the warden all the way down the hierarchy to the officer in charge of a cellblock was dressed impeccably. Within only a few minutes of observation, the parole institute director in an aside to me said, "This is the 'tightest' prison I have ever seen. No one here will be unruly much less escape from this place." I marveled at how quickly he could size up the joint by only looking around. We had not yet interviewed anyone much less collected any further data.

Although I did not pursue a career in law enforcement, several decades later, I had the opportunity to visit a county jail in upstate New York. It was entirely different from the federal prison. The warden dressed in "civilian" clothes, had a doctoral degree in criminology, and knew each prisoner personally. The prisoners spent their days in a community room, not in cells; had access to sports equipment, books, magazines, board games, and so forth; and interacted freely and informally with one another and with the jailers and other staff members. In the few hours that I was there, I never felt in danger. This facility may have been the "loosest" jail that my colleague of long ago had ever seen.

The descriptive terms *tight* and *loose* suggest something about each of these two facilities' cultures. Even though the terms may have been accurate reflections of the organizations' cultures, they barely scratch the surface of an in-depth diagnosis of culture. The "surface" was the extent of the diagnosis at the time—that is, what was seen, heard, touched, and smelled. These surface observations are what Schein (2004) referred to as *artifacts*, the visible manifestations such as the ones previously described and technology, products, language, mode of dress, manners of human interactions, rituals, ceremonies, and so forth. Artifacts are but one level of understanding culture, and though they are obvious to see and sense, determining the meaning behind them is not all that obvious. For example, one might infer that the federal prison was very efficient, using its resources frugally, whereas the "looser" county jail was inefficient and perhaps wasteful. But the opposite could be true. Efficiency is inferred from artifacts but for the observer is an *interpretation* of what one sees. The interpretation can be wrong. Schein went on to argue that understanding two additional levels are absolutely necessary to comprehend and diagnose more thoroughly an organization's culture. To address Schein's second level, let us consider another brief consultant anecdote of mine.

As I recall, it was a day in the late 1960s that I spent time with the internal organization development (OD) group at the Cincinnati headquarters of Procter and Gamble (P&G). In those days, P&G was heavily involved in OD work, and considerable innovation about organization change was under way. Most of the day involved discussion between the P&G OD folks and me regarding what was going on in other organizations. I was executive director of the OD network at the time. At one stage during our discussion, especially about organizational culture, the head of the OD group made a provocative statement. He said that if there were 100% turnover of the entire P&G population within a 24-hour period, the new workforce would behave and operate the company exactly the same as they had been doing. I said something to the effect of "You've got to be kidding!" He then said, "Come with me for a short walk." We left the meeting room and walked down the hallway to a large open space. We stopped before two large oil portraits. My friend then said, "These two paintings are of Mr. Procter and Mr. Gamble, founders of the company and long since dead. But they watch us constantly to make sure that we present-day employees continue to live the values of the company that they instilled long ago, so the new employees would conform to these values and behave just the way we do because that's the way Mr. P and Mr. G would want it."

The second level for understanding an organization's culture is what Schein (2004) referred to as *espoused beliefs and values*. When a group is first formed to solve a problem, perhaps to initiate an enterprise, to deal with a major issue, and so forth, an individual or two will emerge as a leader, or leaders, and propose a solution, suggest ideas, and so forth. What the leader proposes might work, but it is only what the leader wants to do. Until the group has taken some joint action and that action turns out to be successful will the members believe that what they did actually works. This common belief and acting on it is what Schein called *social validation*, meaning

> that certain values are confirmed only by the shared social experi-
> ence of a group. For example, any given culture cannot prove that its
> religion and moral system are superior to another culture's religion
> and moral system, but if the members reinforce each other's beliefs
> and values, they come to be taken for granted. Those who fail to
> accept such beliefs and values run the risk of "excommunication"—
> of being thrown out of the group . . . the group learns that certain
> beliefs and values as initially promulgated to prophets, founders,
> and leaders, "work" in the sense of reducing uncertainty in critical
> areas of the group's functioning. (Schein, 2004, p. 29)

Examples of statements promulgating beliefs and values for the organization include Hewlett-Packard's (2013) *The HP Way* and Johnson &
Johnson's (2013) *Credo*.

Schein (2004) referred to this second level of culture diagnosis as
espoused beliefs and values for a reason. When organizational members,
particularly at the executive level, say what the beliefs and values are but
rarely behave consistently with those statements, then the espoused
words become limited in helping us to understand fully the culture. This
second level can be useful for helping us to understand organizational
members' intentions, but if actions do not always match the espoused
beliefs and values, we know that some important ingredient of the culture
is unavailable to us. It is below the conscious, overt level of artifacts and
what people espouse. It is that below-the-surface level, the third dimension, that Schein (2004) labeled *basic underlying assumptions*.

For the better part of 25 years I was a consultant to the National
Aeronautics and Space Administration (NASA). I helped establish their
Management Education Center and conducted many development programs there. I also helped to create an annual employee opinion survey
system and provided executive coaching from time to time. The span of
time for my involvement was from the late 1970s to about 2000. Thus, I
was involved at the time of the tragic *Challenger* accident in 1986 and the
O-ring seals problem located primarily at the Marshall Space Flight Center in Hunstville, Alabama. An important aspect of NASA's culture at the
time was the espoused value of openness, candor, and honesty. In other
words, it was a "tell-it-like-it-is" culture. Sometimes NASA engineers and

scientists could be quite blunt and confrontational with one another. Yet prior to the accident it was known that there was an O-ring problem and that in subfreezing conditions the rings could become brittle and break. This knowledge was concentrated at lower, technical levels in NASA's hierarchy but not at higher executive levels. In other words, there was a reluctance to deliver bad news to one's boss. The problem did not reach high-enough levels in the system to influence decision making in a timely manner. Although the espoused value of openness may have held for peer interactions and top-down relationships, it did not hold for bottom-up interactions. In fact in an analysis of data following the accident, we found that in our 40-item multirater feedback system, the one practice that was rated the lowest by peer, boss, subordinate, and self-ratings was "You present bad news in a constructive manner."

It looked as though whether constructive or not, bad news was simply not communicated especially upward in the hierarchy. And that was particularly true at the Marshall Center. So there was an exception to the "can-do" attitude and the espoused value of openness lying beneath the surface—the basic assumption of openness *except* with your boss. This assumption was deeply buried in the culture—not discussed—and probably emanated from the first center director at Marshall, Wernher von Braun, who was known as a top-down executive and a rather intimidating personality.

Basic assumptions, then, consist of behaviors that are (a) rarely if ever discussed, (b) taken for granted, and (c) based on repeated successes— these behaviors "work" for us whether "work" means to be embraced or avoided. Basic assumptions according to Schein (2004) "tend to be non-confrontable and non-debatable, and hence are extremely difficult to change" (p. 31). To change a basic assumption requires a reexamination of dearly held beliefs and therefore can destabilize a system, whether an individual or a group, and consequently cause considerable anxiety. Schein went on to state that

> culture as a set of basic assumptions defines for us what to pay attention to, what things mean, how to react emotionally to what is going on, and what actions to take in various kinds of situations. (p. 32)

Moving on to changing culture, Schein (2004) argued that

> the two keys to successful culture change are (1) the management of the large amounts of anxiety that accompany any relearning at this

level and (2) the assessment of whether the genetic potential for the new learning is even present. (p. 32)

In summary, an organization's culture can be understood at three levels—its artifacts, its espoused beliefs and values, and its basic underlying assumptions. To fully understand culture, one must reach the third level because we can only interpret the meaning of artifacts and give credence to espoused beliefs and values by knowing, at least to some extent, the pattern of basic underlying assumptions.

With Schein's fundamentals of culture as background, and keeping in mind his warning that culture change is difficult, we will now consider a large-scale case of organization change with a primary focus on culture that was successful and took well over five years to accomplish.

The British Airways Story: A Case of Culture Change

In the 1980s, BA experienced significant organization change and with considerable and focused effort over a number of years gradually realized a fundamental modification of its deep structure, the concept explained earlier in Chapter 5. Described briefly at the beginning of that chapter were the external forces threatening BA's survival—the edict handed down by Prime Minister Margaret Thatcher and the growing deregulation of international air traffic—that is, many fares were no longer being set by governments but instead were being determined by the marketplace. Recall that Thatcher believed strongly in a free-market society, and accordingly, her actions were to change public sector organizations supported by the government to private enterprises. One of the first of these changes was to consolidate a number of disparate government organizations in the aerospace and aviation area into one "free-market" company, British Aerospace. Following soon thereafter was Thatcher's declaration that BA would become a publicly owned enterprise with company stock being traded on the stock exchanges of London and New York. As a government-supported organization, BA had been the country's flagship airline but now had to survive on its own. Employees wanted BA to remain the flagship, but they realized that they would have to do so competitively in the world marketplace. In the mid-1980s, the pressure to survive and to develop a more competitive strategy quickly was intense. Things had to change.

In an attempt to become more competitive and cost conscious, an early decision made by the CEO, Colin Marshall, was to reduce the workforce from about 59,000 to 37,000. This act got everyone's attention and, as might be expected, drew lots of criticism. Marshall stayed the course, however, and went on to emphasize a mission of providing superior service and to focus on a strategy that would increase market share and customer satisfaction.

These changes of mission and strategy began to affect the deep structure of BA but were not sufficient to complete the change. Marshall knew that he had to change the BA culture. Historically, BA was formed from the former pilots and staff of the Royal Air Force of World War II and early on was actually two airlines: British Overseas Airline Company (BOAC) and British-European Airline (BEA). Flying all over the world, BOAC was the more glamorous airline with royal blue uniforms with large airplanes for long trips, and BEA flew short trips and the crew wore brown uniforms. These artifacts—as Schein would call them—became a problem when the two airlines later merged and formed what we now know as BA. The former BOAC staff held more status, of course, and even with common uniforms as a result of the merger one could still tell who were the glamorous ones and who were the "brown suits." Becoming one airline took a long time, but by the 1980s, they were essentially and finally one company but now had to change again. Yet a vestige of the past remained, a part of BA's deep structure, and that was the military influence from World War II, which had quite naturally evolved over time into a command-and-control culture that was engineering rather than market driven. BA had a terrific maintenance and safety record, but passengers seemed to be incidental to the whole process. It was a question of what to change in the culture while keeping those aspects that could continue to support the superb maintenance and safety records.

Let us pause here for a moment and consider two important points. One concerns the second of Schein's (2004) three levels of organizational culture: espoused beliefs and values. BA employees, particularly those in the engineering and maintenance functions, believed strongly in the emphasis on solid engineering and maintenance of their aircraft. After all, these activities, done well, resulted in the closely held value of safety. BA has been known for its safety record, and their maintenance staff has enjoyed an excellent reputation in the industry. In fact, a significant source of income for BA is providing maintenance services for other airlines.

The second point concerns a fundamental principle of managing organization change. The principle is this: In an organization change effort, communicating what will remain the same is as important as communicating what will be different. Wisdom from the world of counseling and clinical psychology is relevant and can be applied to leading and managing change at an organizational level. To help individuals cope with and manage change in their lives, the wisdom is that of keeping something stable in one's life while changing other aspects. It is not wise to change one's career, quit one's job, and get a divorce all at the same time. Holding on to something that is not changing in one's life—having an anchor, as it were—helps one immeasurably to deal with the complexity of change in other parts.

The same is true at an organizational level. People can more adequately deal with and manage what may be considerable chaos and complexity with respect to an organizational change effort if they know that some aspects of the organization will remain stable—at least for the time being. We can more easily handle, say, a major overhaul of the organization's structure and even accompanying changes in our jobs if we can at the same time be assured that, for example, our compensation will not change—that is, the organization's reward system will remain intact.

In the case of BA it was, of course, a matter of keeping intact, that is, largely as it had been, the engineering and maintenance functions. Marshall, the CEO, was clear about what needed to change (i.e., to become market and customer driven), and he was just as clear about keeping the technical standards at the highest levels (where they had always been) regarding the flying and maintaining of their aircraft.

To be more specific about the culture change, a series of programs and activities were launched to move BA from a bureaucracy laced with military residue to a service business in which passengers were treated as human beings rather than as another form of baggage. The initial programmatic effort was a 2-day orientation to the new culture called "Putting People First." The program challenged the prevailing wisdom about how things were to be done at BA. This initiative served as one of the action steps to launch the "unfreezing" stage of Lewin's three stages—unfreeze, movement, and refreeze.

The next activities were to focus even more intensely and directly on the culture. Nick Georgiades, the head of human resources at the time, conceptualized this aspect of the change effort in terms of a "three-legged

stool." The "seat" was the new, desired culture—one that was more customer focused—and the three legs of the stool were

1. "Managing People First" (MPF) programs that were a 5-day resi-
   dential set of activities to help managers learn how to (a) communicate more openly and build trust, (b) manage their people more
   participatively, (c) manage their direct reports more as a team and
   less in a one-on-one manner, and (d) provide constructive feedback
   in performance appraisal sessions with their people. Considerable
   time and energy during the program was devoted to providing
   feedback to the managers via a multirater process that was based
   on specific behaviors that represented (a) through (d).

2. The second leg of the stool concerned performance appraisal for all
   managers. Previously BA managers were evaluated according to
   results accomplishment—and results only. Now half of a manager's
   evaluation would be based on results, and the other half was to be
   based on *how* they got the results—in other words, the rated behaviors from the MPF program. This rating process became an annual
   activity—that is, the behaviors from the program became a formal
   part of a manager's annual performance appraisal.

3. And the third leg was pay for performance—that is, rewarding
   managers according to how they were rated on the second leg of
   the stool.

The notion of a stool with three legs was meant to convey that if one leg
were removed the stool would collapse. All three legs together were critical to the process of culture change.

Another program was to train all human resources staff within BA on
consulting skills so they would be in a better position to help the MPF
participants apply what they had learned.

A guiding rationale for conducting the MPF program and spending considerable effort with follow-ups to ensure change in the BA culture was sup-
plied by the research work of Ben Schneider and his colleagues. In a series of
studies reported in Schneider (1980, 1990a) and Schneider and Bowen
(1985), this is what has been consistently demonstrated (Burke, 1994):

How "front line" people in a service organization (in this case,
banks, therefore, tellers, loan officers) are treated by their respective

supervisors has a differential effect on customer satisfaction. In bank branches where front-line employees were managed more participatively as opposed to bureaucratically—following procedures strictly, for example—customer satisfaction was significantly higher. (p. 137)

With BA, of course, being a service business, the same principle was applied. Although ticket agents and cabin crew employees needed some technical training in how they served the customer, the primary emphasis was not with them per se but rather with their managers. To be clear, think of it this way: We have two relationships to consider; one is the relationship of the boss with his or her direct report, say, a ticket agent, and the other relationship is the ticket agent's interactions with customers. For sake of argument, let us say that we had to make a choice as to which relationship to try to improve to enhance customer satisfaction—the boss–subordinate one or the ticket agent–customer one. Schneider's research tells us that the boss–subordinate relationship is more important.

The MPF program was therefore designed and conducted to help managers to manage more participatively, openly, respectfully, enthusiastically, and with greater trust in their subordinates. Managers cannot manage the myriad of hour-by-hour contacts that employees who have direct contact with customers encounter every day, those 50,000 "moments of truth," as Jan Carlzon, another successful airline CEO, described in his popular book (Carlzon, 1987). Managers can, however, work with their subordinates in an involving manner that will in turn have a positive effect on customers (Burke, 1994, p. 137).

Many other activities were involved in this large-scale change effort, for example, changing the entire financial function from one of government accounting and reporting to one of providing annual financial statements for stockholders and monthly income statements for managers. Also, Marshall essentially created a marketing function in BA—where, prior to his arrival, for all practical purposes, none existed.

It is now a matter of record that BA transformed itself (Goodstein & Burke, 1991). By the end of the 1980s, BA was one of the most profitable airlines in the world and had improved its service record so much that passengers who had said that BA stood for "bloody awful" now revised the interpretation to "bloody awesome" (Power, 1989).

In summary, the revolution at BA began as a result of a disruption from the airline's external environment. Internally, the initial disruption was the huge reduction of BA employees by more than 20,000. Then, through a planned series of activities and interventions, the culture (deep structure) was gradually shifted from a militaristic, bureaucratically driven way of doing things to one that was focused significantly more on service to customers and on being competitive in the marketplace. The organization in a span of some six to seven years had fundamentally changed, had transformed itself. And the refreeze stage of Lewin's three was largely realized by 1990 when BA became the most profitable airline in the industry.

You Don't Change Culture by Trying to Change the Culture

Now let us review some important principles, concepts, and theory that are applicable to the BA story and help to explain culture change. First, consider the title of this section, which sounds contradictory and may even seem inane if not ridiculous. But stay with me.

If I were to ask you to rank order the following three terms

- values

- attitudes

- behavior

from most difficult to change to least difficult, you would quickly say, "In the order listed." And I would agree. Values, norms, deeply held beliefs, and attitudes, as well as long-standing historical precedence constitute primary aspects of culture. So why would you begin with trying to change the most difficult aspects? Thus, you begin with the easiest of the three to tackle—behavior. And as I stated earlier:

> Of course, you can begin by determining what you want the new culture to be (in the case of British Airways, it was to become more service oriented and customer focused), followed by an identification of the behaviors required to realize that new and different culture; such as, for example "Communicating with others in an open and frank manner," or "Involving subordinates in decisions that directly affect their work." Next you train managers in these behavioral practices primarily via feedback and role or skill practice. Then you include these new practices in managers' performance appraisals

and incorporate pay for performance so that the more managers actually use the practices the more incentive pay they receive. To summarize, first you announce the change regarding the culture. Second, you get managers' attention by training them in the practices. Third, you measure their degree of use of the practices. And, finally, you reward them when they employ the practices. These were the steps followed in the British Airways change effort. (Burke, 1994, p. 157)

If this quote sounds easy to do then I have been misleading. Remember the change at BA took well over five years. Also recall that Schein has argued persuasively that the "real" culture, so to speak, is embedded in basic underlying assumptions that are largely buried in the collective unconscious of organizational members. How do you get to this level? You cannot "see" assumptions. It is largely a matter of inference, considering artifacts, listening to people espouse their beliefs, and, in general, observing behavior over time. At BA it came down to issues of power and authority. The BA culture had been about command and control, but by the 1980s that militaristic quality had evolved. Top-down behavior was not as evident nor was it accepted as it had been 20 years before. Power in the culture was more about information and who had the most. Managers played their cards close to their vests, as the saying goes. Like Iago, Shakespeare's villain in the *Othello* tragedy, he chided the open and trusting Othello as being foolish. Secrecy was to be valued far more than transparency. For Iago, Othello was extremely naïve. And while not as tragic, information at BA was to be held tightly, rarely if ever shared.

A primary focus of the change effort at BA, therefore, was behavior change in the direction of openness, more trusting of others, and greater teamwork. And in line with the James–Lange theory (see Chapter 7), it was behavior—that is, movement—first then cognitive processing, a reordering of values would follow.

Here is a final thought about diagnosing culture at the level of basic underlying assumptions. The thought is triggered by Lewin's admonition long ago. Although not exactly the way he probably stated it, he said something like "If you really want to understand an organization, try to change it." An intervention into a system causes disequilibrium, and the normal reaction is to seek equilibrium. This may take the form of resistance. In any case, Lewin was telling us to observe closely organizational members' reactions to the attempt to change the "way we do things." It is in the nature of these reactions that give us at least a glimpse into the unconscious. Metaphorically it is like tossing a pebble into a pond. The ripples are far more important than the pebble.

A Theoretical Summary of the British Airways Story

The BA story began with Prime Minister Margaret Thatcher's policy of stopping what she considered to be the continuing yet unacceptable movement toward socialism and a return to her country's strength—free enterprise. A primary initiative to enact this policy was to privatize many of Great Britain's government agencies. Privatizing BA was an early, significant step in this tsunami of societal change. For BA, this action was a huge jolt to the system, punctuating its equilibrium (Gersick, 1991) and what Tushman and Romanelli (1985) referred to as a perturbation. Thus, change at BA was revolutionary, not evolutionary. And as Tushman and Romanelli pointed out, revolutionary change is a consequence of a perturbation from the organization's external environment. This jolt to the BA system led the CEO, Marshall, and his key executives to question the organization's "way of doing things"—its culture that somehow had to be "unlocked" (Foster & Kaplan, 2001) and become more responsive to its marketplace.

The culture-change work at BA involved all three of Schein's (2004) levels. With respect to *artifacts*, early in the change effort (a) all pilots, cabin crew, and customer service personnel (for example, ticket agents) received new uniforms, (b) all of BA's fleet of aircraft were repainted with brighter colors including new, artful patterns on the fuselage and tail, and (c) new, more comfortable seats were installed along with attractive interior fabrics. *Espoused beliefs and values* were changed and expanded to a value system focused on the competitive marketplace, in general, and customer service more specifically. And regarding *basic underlying assumptions*, tackling what Gersick (1991) calls the deep structure, plus following the principles of the James–Lange theory (behavior first), the effort toward change at this more latent or unconscious level took considerable time (the better part of five years) and effort. The focus was on behavior that was intended to counter the basic assumptions that strict, hierarchical procedures are to be followed; information and holding on to it is power; and managing subordinates in a one-on-one manner was the best way. Therefore, the new emphasized behaviors included communicating in a more transparent way, managing more participatively, trusting others, and stressing collaboration and teamwork.

The direction toward what the new culture at BA should be was quite clear and straightforward—customers and safety were top priorities. But what if organizational executives know that culture change is needed but what a different and better culture should look like is not so clear?

Captured in their book, Kotter and Heskett (1992) have provided an important and groundbreaking study of the relationship between corporate culture and organizational performance. They were among the first to show how the culture of a corporation influences its economic performance, for better or worse. They studied more than 200 companies and then concentrated on 10 that had made culture change to draw their conclusions. Some of these organizations they studied were Bankers Trust, BA, ConAgra, General Electric, Imperial Chemicals Industry, and Scandinavian Airlines System. Of interest here is their conclusion about the *adaptive* culture, those organizations that had the highest performance and the ability to make changes when needed. From their work, then, what does an adaptive culture look like?

CHARACTERISTICS OF AN ADAPTIVE CULTURE ACCORDING TO THE WORK OF KOTTER AND HESKETT (1992)

1. Willingness to make changes in culturally ingrained behaviors

2. Emphasis on identifying problems before they occur and rapidly implementing workable solutions

3. Focus on innovation

4. Shared feelings of confidence about managing problems and opportunities

5. Emphasis on trust

6. Willingness to take risks

7. Spirit of enthusiasm

8. Candor

9. Internal flexibility in response to external demands

10. Consistency in word and action

11. Long-term focus

This list represents worthy norms and goals to pursue for most any organization. Attempting to have an organization that looks like this would no doubt help to prevent what Foster and Kaplan (2001) called "cultural lock-in" (see Chapter 2).

Summary

In order to change an organization's culture one must first understand it. This understanding comes from three primary sources or concepts as Schein (2004) has labeled them—*artifacts, espoused beliefs and values*, and *basic underlying assumptions*. Artifacts are what we encounter first: symbols (e.g., a company's logo), the way offices are arranged and how open or closed they may appear, how members of the organization dress, and the nature and characteristics of the organization's products and services. Artifacts are what are "on the surface," and with these observations, we begin to get a feel for the culture, but it is just that, a feel, an interpretation that may be a clue to an accurate understanding of the culture but may not.

With more time and experience in the organization we begin to learn about their espoused beliefs and values, how organizational members express themselves, particularly concerning what they say about their organization—"what we stand for," "why our products do so well in the marketplace," "how we treat our customers," and so forth. These beliefs and values give us more depth of understanding the culture (i.e., beyond artifacts), yet we must be diligent in our quest for an accurate picture of the culture by discerning possible differences between what the organizational members *say* about their beliefs and values and what they do, how they actually *behave*.

And with a lot more time and effort we may begin to understand what the culture truly is all about by getting at the basic underlying assumptions—those unspoken rules mostly below the conscious level of organizational members who guide behavior. When asking a member a question about why certain things in the operation of the organization are done the way they are, the response may be something like "Gee, I don't really know. We simply have always done it that way." Culture, then, is a set of basic assumptions that serve as guideposts for how we are supposed to behave in the organization.

To change the, culture we spin our wheels when we attempt to change at the outset espoused beliefs and values and basic underlying assumptions we cannot see, much less understand. We must first identify the behaviors that when practiced will lead us to the new vision and the change goals. Then as organizational members begin to react to these new behaviors—some embrace them, others resist—we pay attention to these "ripples" and attempt to realign them, if necessary, toward the change goals. The BA story helped to illustrate how these principles drawn from research and theory can work.

TWELVE

Understanding and Working with Loosely Coupled Systems

As we learned in Chapter 11, changing an organization's culture can be a daunting undertaking. It can be done, nevertheless, as the British Airways (BA) story demonstrated. Change at BA did occur. It took at least five years and required talented, dedicated people; considerable resources; and enormous energy and perseverance on the part of leaders in the organization. Most observers of the change at BA would no doubt agree that it was successful.

The story of organization change described in this chapter was also successful but only for a short period of time, no more than two years, and therefore would have to be classified as a failure. There was a short-term change, but in the end, the organization reverted back to what it was before the change effort was initiated. What happened—and an attempt to explain why it happened—are the themes of this chapter as well as what was learned as a result.

The Case of Change at the A. K. Rice Institute

First, let us consider the organization itself, the A. K. Rice Institute (AKRI), briefly described in Chapter 2 as a nonprofit organization that was insufficiently attuned to and aligned with its external environment. Our coverage here will begin with the AKRI's founding purpose, its history, and the problem that was addressed regarding the change effort.

The full story of the attempt to change AKRI is told in the article by Noumair, Winderman, and Burke (2010). What now follows is a synopsis of that story.

AKRI is a network of some eight centers that span the United States from California to the East Coast with a small headquarters located in Florida that helps to coordinate these rather autonomous entities. There is a president and board of directors elected by the AKRI members who oversee the headquarters and the institute as a whole and from time to time establishes policy. AKRI began rather informally in 1965 when Margaret Rioch, Pierre Tourquet, and Ken Rice decided to conduct in the Washington, D.C.–Baltimore area a group relations (GR) conference designed and conducted according to principles and practices of such conferences under the auspices of the Tavistock Institute in the United Kingdom. About five years later, these so-called "Tavi conferences" were taking hold in the United States and later, in 1975, AKRI was incorporated as a nonprofit educational institution. By 2000, AKRI had grown from a small center in Washington, D.C., to a much larger network of eight centers with a paid administrator.

Based on the Tavistock GR tradition of open-system and psychodynamic theories, AKRI produced GR conferences, training programs, scientific meetings, and publications for the general public through its qualified members. By 1990, membership had stabilized at about 225 volunteers, mental health professionals predominating. The modest revenue generated from AKRI-sponsored GR conferences and publications and member dues enabled the Institute to hold an annual meeting of the board of directors and cover administrative expenses (Noumair et al., 2010, pp. 475–476).

As AKRI grew and became a more complex organization, its original purpose seemed to be lost or at least not as clear as it was in the days of Margaret Rioch's leadership. There was ongoing confusion about AKRI's mission and its ultimate purpose, and questions emerged concerning who were the customers—people who attended GR conferences, the broader general public, or AKRI members themselves those who conducted the conferences? Moreover, there was fragility among the eight centers, not to mention their relationships with the headquarters and overall leadership, and the board of directors' work tended to be internally focused instead of outward looking.

Due to these worrisome issues, particularly confusion about purpose, by 1997 the board decided to focus on changing AKRI and launched three major initiatives:

1. To establish broader connections with more focus toward the external environment

2. To strengthen the infrastructure of AKRI

3. To shift more toward a learning culture

Action to undergird these initiatives was the launching of two ad hoc committees: one on strategic planning and the other on training—that is, professional development for members and a clearer set of standards for qualifying members to conduct GR conferences, which, in essence, were certification programs. Additional efforts were made to strengthen communication channels between the AKRI president and the center presidents, and member caucuses were held and surveys conducted to facilitate more focus on mission and core values. These actions culminated in a membershipwide meeting in 2000 with approximately 75 attending. Most agree that change was needed.

Following the thinking of Gersick (1991), there are, at its most basic level and understanding, two requirements for launching an organization change effort: (a) a sense of urgency and (b) a vision for the future. While most AKRI members believed that change was needed, it was not clear at the time that this need was urgent. As it happened, a crisis erupted shortly after the membershipwide meeting that created a clear sense of urgency.

A GR conference was conducted by AKRI leaders but outside the auspices of the institute—in other words, a kind of renegade movement. This act created competition with AKRI and its centers. Moreover, since AKRI leaders designed and conducted this conference, board members were extremely upset and felt betrayed. The board halted its strategic planning effort and sought outside help.

Enter External Consultant (Yours Truly)

My initial diagnosis based on extensive interviews with the board members indicated the institute, certainly at the board level, was quite insular and out of touch with its external environment. This insularity contributed to AKRI's decreasing impact as an educational institution. At the heart of this insularity was in reality two missions—(a) educational, yes, but also primarily (b) a mission of serving members' desires, that is to staff conferences, to enjoy the process of conducting these conferences according to the Tavi approach (focusing on issues of power, control, and authority), and to make some money (albeit not exactly astronomical amounts of compensation). In my judgment, the latter mission, even though not in AKRI's charter, was a reality and contradicted and worked against the educational and original mission. To my way of thinking, it was hard to have it both ways. Also, to my surprise, board meetings were not unlike GR conferences. After all, interpreting members' behavior according to power and authority issues was more fun than dealing with the mundane tasks of the board working on budget issues, committee work, planning for the future, etc. In other words, the real work of the board was often left undone.

> The problem then was the dual and somewhat conflicting missions of the Institute, that is, to be a membership organization and serve its members and centers, while at the same time having an educational mission for the public at large. Membership and center issues often prevented effective accomplishment of the educational mission. To be effective at the latter, AKRI's external environment needed to be monitored and responded to more directly, instead of indirectly via its centers and members, who were often conflicted between an individual desire to seek status or power through conference work and a desire to give back and to serve AKRI with organization needs superseding, at least some if not most of the time, individual needs. (Noumair et al., 2010, pp.478–479)

Faced with these issues and contradictions, the board voted unanimously to adopt the educational mission; they began to engage members and centers in a change process.

Action Steps

To provide focus and to undergird the reality of change, I suggested that a transition task force (TTF) be formed in parallel to the board to plan and lead the change effort, and that the president serve dual roles of remaining head of the board and the overall director of TTF. My job was to work closely with both the board and TTF by serving as a facilitator, a change expert, and executive coach—especially for the president. I used the Burke–Litwin model (see Chapter 10) as the framework for guiding the overall change effort.

The TTF focused on the following:

- Creating a name change from the A. K. Rice Institute to the A. K. Rice Institute for the Study of Social Systems
- Crafting a new mission statement
- Forming a reconstituted board to included three outside members to help the institute stay in better touch with the external environment
- Modifying governance procedures—for example, board elected by members at large
- Establishing a fund-raising effort
- Exploring potential strategic alliances with other like-minded organizations
- Conducting competitor analysis
- Changing centers to affiliates with AKRI becoming more of a whole system as opposed to a simple network.

Special attention was given to crafting the new mission for the institute. Guided by the eight components of effective mission statements identified by Pearce and David (1987), the mission statement clearly reflected the new change direction. See Table 12.1 for the complete statement.

Further accomplishments as a result of the change effort included the following:

- Executive director hired
- Publication of *Group Relations Reader 3* (Cytrynbaum & Noumair, 2004)
- Produced The Forum Special Scientific Conference
- Training and certification process well under way
- Affiliates delivered their signed agreements
- Launched strategic partnerships
- Established global community connections fund

By 2004, I was no longer consulting with AKRI, and although not everything had changed, much had. It was time for AKRI to continue on its own. Yet as we now know, the most difficult aspect of any organization

Table 12.1   Mission Statement of the A. K. Rice Institute for the Study of Social Systems (2002)

The A. K. Rice Institute for the Study of Social Systems is a national educational institution that advances the study of social systems and group relations. It seeks to deepen the understanding and the analysis of complex systemic, psychodynamic, and covert processes, which give rise to non-rational behavior in individuals, groups, organizations, communities, and nations. Using experiential and participatory theories and methodologies which derive from the Tavistock tradition, the Institute encourages people from all walks of life to participate in its group relations conferences, research and publications, professional meetings, and training and application events. Participants have the opportunity to learn the multiple ways in which they more successfully can take up roles as leaders and followers; exercise authority and accountability; and enhance their organizations' effectiveness.

Target Customers and Markets—individuals interested in leadership and organizations in both the private and public sectors

Geographic Domain—we are interested in working with organizations and individuals throughout the world to generate global interest in using this theory base

Core Technologies—methods of understanding the whole group through conferences that offer "real time" experiences, application and training events

Survival, Growth and Sustainability—depend on building successive generations of associates and learners to carry out our educational mission

Organizational Philosophy—outreach to multiple sectors of society to effect social and political systems and the exploration of multiple identities

Organization Self-Concept—we are an educational organization

Desired Public Image—we want to make a difference; acting as guides for those who seek a kind of learning that will promote transformation for themselves and their worlds

SOURCE: Noumair, Winderman, and Burke (2010).

change effort is to sustain it once under way. The changes that were launched began to unravel. There was significant turnover of board members, many issues remained unchanged, many wanted the membership mission not only to remain but to become primary, the changes brought about required increased expenses, and the economy was not exactly favorable. Most important, apparently collective resentment among members toward the transformation process had grown. Furthermore, in retrospect, the basic culture, the underlying beliefs and values, had not changed. By 2007, the turnover at the board level was complete, and these new members reversed the mission decision with membership becoming primary and education incidental. In fact, the final death knell for the change was when the board abandoned the 1975 certificate of incorporation and became solely a membership organization, a club rather than an educational institution. In the Introducing the Discussion section of the paper, we stated the following:

> There are multiple reasons as to why the transformation of AKRI from club to organization did not hold. In this article, we propose five contributing factors: implications of a volunteer organization; a loosely coupled system; trying to change deep structure; management of resistance to, and ambivalence about, change; and insufficient attention to integration of GR and OD approaches to organization change (Noumair et al., 2010, p. 486).

Even though all of these five factors help to explain the change failure and are useful for our understanding, the one that was most powerful for me regarding implications for organization change and for my own learning was the concept of a loosely coupled system. The remainder of this chapter will be devoted to understanding and working with a loosely coupled system, and AKRI is an excellent example of looseness. But before we plunge into loosely coupled systems, let us at least summarize the other four, beginning with the implications of a volunteer organization.

A Volunteer Organization

AKRI is not only an organization run by volunteers; it functions virtually for the most part. The 80–20 rule also applies to AKRI—that is, about 20% of the members do 80% of the work. Busy people are reluctant to volunteer their time especially to undertake a leadership position. This succession of board members not to mention standing for election as president is problematical. A succession plan is rare, and without successions, there is usually a lack of widespread commitment to any kind of change. Such a vacuum can lead to a situation in which those who step up to responsibility are those who opposed the organization change from the beginning. In any case, this kind of succession problem was true for AKRI.

Changing Deep Structure

Deep structure is Gersick's (1991) term for the core of an organization's culture. She explains it in terms of initial choices that members of a group or organization make in the formative stages—choices about how the group is going to work together to accomplish the task at hand. These choices concern such decisions as who will do what and how to organize (division of labor) and decisions about procedures such as how decisions will get made. Once these choices are made they remain tentative decisions so that members can determine if they work well enough for the group or organization. If so, these choices then become systematic, taken for granted, and stick, so to speak. These ideas of Gersick's were covered in Chapter 5. Applying to AKRI, some choices were indeed explicit, some implicit about how the institute was going to carry out its mission such as focusing almost exclusively on small groups not organizations per se and emphasizing authority relations (Rioch, 1975). Group dynamics became the core (deep structure) with Bion's theory providing the rationales for learning objectives and procedures in the GR conferences. With group dynamics at the core, a focus on organizations was clearly secondary, a different level of phenomena (see Chapter 6), and changing AKRI as an organization required modification of its culture, which was quite naturally resisted.

Dealing With Resistance and Ambivalence

Recall that we addressed resistance to change in Chapter 6 and covered Hambrick and Cannella's (1989) three distinctions—(a) blind, (b) ideological, and (c) political. With respect to AKRI, the resistance that occurred was primarily political—that is, many members felt that they were going to lose something of value to them: their identity as a member of an exclusive club that provided opportunities to serve as staff for GR conferences accompanied with feelings of status and prestige, which was more important than the money they might make.

Organizational members in times of change may be viewed as resistant when in reality they are not all that opposed to the change. They simply may be ambivalent, "on the fence" as it were, perhaps skeptical, and have a desire for more information that might convince them. This distinction between resistance and ambivalence has been explained by Piderit (2000) and summarized in Chapter 6. As change leaders for AKRI, we may have concentrated more on countering resistance than on addressing ambivalence. We also embraced a we–they attitude—it's us against those baneful, rigid resisters. This we–they attitude and approach causes a vicious cycle and can significantly contribute to change failure. Recent and more sensible coverage of resistance to change is provided in Chapter 16.

Group Relations Versus Organization Development

As we pointed out in the article (Noumair et al., 2010) there are similarities between a GR perspective and organization development (OD). They both rely on open system theory and their respective value systems overlap—humanism, resolving conflict intrapersonally and interpersonally, and building a better world. But there are differences: the main one being covert versus overt. GR individuals emphasize unconscious processes coupled with interpretations of the overt behavior, what is the intention and meaning underneath, whereas OD people's focus is on the overt behavior itself taking at face value what people say and do. We can compare the two on at least four dimensions: (a) theoretical focus—Bion for GR and Lewin for OD; (b) diagnostic focus—group unconscious for GR and norms and values for OD; (c) the concept of the "invisible leader," Mary Parker Follett's (1996) notion that the "leader" to be followed is *purpose*, which is consistent with OD, whereas for GR individuals the "leader" is the *task*; and (d) the primary concern for GR is authority and authorization, whereas for OD it is power and politics. The point is that the two parties hold different perspectives and the external consultant in this case being an OD type rather than a GR person was a cultural misfit. "From a GR perspective, we failed to analyze the full meaning of intentionally selecting an OD consultant and the extent to which we were enamored with the OD perspective" (Noumair et al., 2010, p. 494).

These four factors—(a) volunteer organization, (b) deep structure, (c) resistance, and (d) ambivalence—and GR versus OD help to explain the failure ultimately to change AKRI. The fifth factor, loosely coupled systems, however, became the most important explanation for me primarily because in retrospect it seems so obvious, yet by sticking to my past, I failed to see what was indeed right in front of me. In other words, often to see is not to see.

Organizational Structure and Loosely Coupled Systems

Although hierarchy and the interdependence of work units remain as critical characteristics of large, complex organizations—that is, tightly coupled systems—with the advent of the Internet, globalization that often includes virtual units, greater use of temporary systems formed to solve a particular problem and then disbanded, and networks of all kinds, means that organizational forms that are more loosely coupled demand our attention more than ever before. Networks, the webs that hold cells together, are especially important.

As executive director of the Organization Development Network for 8 years (1966–1974), I learned about how a network without hierarchy (except perhaps for myself and an advisory board at the center or hub) can accomplish tasks. Key was the fact that our purpose was clear, and therefore, we had clarity of tasks in the service of that purpose. Networks are composed of nodes, where pivotal people serve as connectors (remember Gladwell's [2000] tipping points) and gatekeepers, those who facilitate or impede entry and participation in the network.

With the help of the Internet, networks today are more sophisticated and complex. Consider the following commentary (Rothstein, 2001):

> But terrorist organizations are generally referred to as networks, which can be quite varied. Instead of being built around a controlling hub surrounded by terrorist cells, a network can be a sprawling, decentralized arrangement. In fact, the declaration that Americans are engaged in a different sort of war than ever before may have to do with this structure and not just with terrorism itself. Disabling a network often requires different strategies from those used to attack a nation or a hierarchical organization. . . . For better or worse, the world has entered an era of networks. (p. A13)

Networks that are highly effective are unusually focused and have a structure and process that are built on trust—that is, political and emotional connections among people who must rely on each other to accomplish tasks.

Thus, I am arguing that we need to gain considerable background on networks, to take the points made here and dig deeper by reading articles and books such as the one by Arquilla and Ronfeldt (2001) and to interview experts such as Kathleen Carley, director of the Center for Computational Analysis and Organizational Systems at Carnegie Mellon University.

We also need to formulate the questions and hypotheses for research, such as "The degree of effectiveness (high performance) of a network is a function of the clarity of purpose—the greater the clarity, the higher the performance" or "The degree of effectiveness is a function of the extent of trust among members—the greater the trust, the higher the performance." And we would explore questions such as "What are the key roles and responsibilities in an effective network?" "How do decisions get made?" "What is the nature of accountability in a network?"

One might naturally ask where did my sense of urgency about this learning need come from.

My motivation and learning direction was precipitated by the intensive organizational consulting experience that began positively but ended unsuccessfully: the AKRI organization change case. I had a need to make sense out of this experience. On reflection, if I had known then what I know now, the outcome might have turned out differently.

Although I knew about the work of Karl Weick on loosely coupled systems, I had not diligently studied this literature. Now that I have, what follows are some key summaries of what is most important to learn and know.

Loosely Coupled Systems

When considering the concept of loosely and tightly coupled systems, we typically think in a unidimensional way with loose on one end of the dimension and tight on the other end. The concept of interdependence is a term that helps to define "looseness": the more units of an organization are interdependent, the tighter the system, and the less there is interdependence, the more likely the system is characterized as loosely coupled. Hierarchy is another term that comes to mind to describe tight (steep hierarchy) and loose (flat hierarchy). The Google Corporation is closer to a loosely coupled system than is the U.S. Marine Corps.

Although attractive to help us describe and understand organizations, this unidimensional way of thinking is an oversimplification. According to Orton and Weick (1990), a dialectical interpretation of loose–tight is a more useful and realistic concept. Their argument is that a system can be both loose and tight. This argument is not unlike the question of whether an organization should be centralized or decentralized—a point that was raised earlier in the chapter. The answer to the question is "yes." In other words, the more appropriate question is what functions or which components of an organization should be centralized and what functions should be decentralized, for example, finance centralized and operations decentralized.

To elaborate on and understand the dialectical nature of loosely coupled (and tightly coupled) systems, Orton and Weick (1990) combed the literature, citing more than 100 references and categorized their findings into the following:

> Five recurring voices that focus separately on causation, typology, effects, compensations, and outcomes . . . [The authors] first use the five voices to review the loose coupling literature and then to suggest more precise and more productive uses of the concept. (p. 203)

These "voices" from Orton and Weick's (1990) review of the literature help to explain the meaning of loosely coupled systems. A summary of their work follows.

Voice of Causation

What causes loose coupling? At least three factors cause it: (a) causal indeterminacy, which concerns unclear means-end connections—for example, efforts to improve product or service quality do not seem to lead to higher customer satisfaction; (b) fragmented external environment—for example, a proliferation of market niches and specialties that demand varied responses from the organization; and (c) fragmented internal environment, which can take many forms, one example being when few organizational members are involved in or even care about the larger system or its many operations (Pfeffer, 1978); a university would be an appropriate case in point.

In summary, factors that differentiate the organization further tend to produce in kind differentiated responses—that is, loose coupling.

Voice of Typology

This category is not about causation; rather, it concerns different types of loose coupling. Orton and Weick (1990) identified at least eight that have emerged most often—that is, loose coupling among (a) individuals, (b) subunits, (c) organizations, (d) hierarchical levels, (e) organizations and their environments, (f) ideas, (g) activities, and (h) intentions and actions. The value of this voice is that it "captures descriptions of ongoing actions" (Orton & Weick, 1990, p. 210) that are based on certain decisions in organizations such as adopting some new software system or something as simple as declaring a "dress-down" day on Fridays.

Voice of Direct Effects

This voice is one of advocacy—loose coupling is a good thing; it is or should be a clear management strategy. Such a strategy can eliminate unnecessary relationships, register inputs from the external environment accurately (i.e., more avenues of direct connections to the environment with less filtering), and create more opportunities for autonomous information gathering and making sense of the information.

Voice of Compensation

In a sense, this voice is the opposite of the preceding category: direct effects. Loose coupling is not a good thing; therefore, tightening is in order. "The three most frequently recurring managerial strategies," according to Orton and Weick (1990), "are enhanced leadership, focused effort, and shared values" (p. 211). To compensate for the problems of too much looseness is (a) to provide stronger more direct leadership; (b) to focus more attention on carefully selected targets for improvement and thereby increase efficiency and control resources more rigorously, with management simply acting more forcefully; and (c) to emphasize shared values—that is, working on an agreement about preferences and priorities and what is most important for realizing success over time.

"In summary, this voice preserves a dialectical interpretation when it builds on the premise that looseness on some dimensions should be complemented by coupling on other dimensions" (Orton & Weick, 1990, p. 213).

Voice of Organizational Outcomes

This category is a study of the effects that loose coupling has on organizational performance. To quote Orton and Weick (1990) again for purposes of capturing as clearly as possible what they mean, let us consider the following two sentences:

> Because of the causal distance between loose coupling and organizational outcomes, the voice of organizational outcomes requires the consideration of more independent variables than does the voice of direct effects. The outcome voice, consequently, is less forceful then the voice of direct effects in advocating loose coupling as a managerial strategy, and it focuses on five organizational outcome: persistence, buffering, adaptability, satisfaction, and effectiveness. (p. 213)

To bring about stability or organization change, usually tightening of a loosely coupled system, requires *persistence* (see Chapter 14 using a similar concept: perseverance). As Orton and Weick (1990) pointed out, Wilson and Corbett (1983) found evidence to support the idea: See Firestone (1985), who found "that tightly coupled systems are more conducive to systemwide change than loosely coupled systems" (p. 213). *Buffering* means that loosely coupled systems tend to isolate and prevent problems from affecting the entire organization, which can often be a positive outcome but can also be a negative outcome—recall the National Aeronautics and Space Administration's (NASA) *Challenger* accident referred to in Chapter 11. *Adaptability* is more often than not a positive outcome of loose coupling—and so is job *satisfaction*. Organizational *effectiveness* is harder to pin down. Loose coupling can lead to greater effectiveness but can also lead to the opposite. Studies differ, and as might be expected, it depends heavily on how effectiveness is defined and measured.

The loose–tight conundrum is in the same sphere as many other organizational forces that appear to be opposites—freedom and constraint, autonomy and connection, and differentiation and integration, to name some of the most obvious ones. Orton and Weick (1990), as noted earlier, believed that a dialectical interpretation of loose coupling is more useful than a unidimensional interpretation. From a research standpoint as well as an organizational diagnostic perspective, dialectical thinking leads to qualitative as well as quantitative methodologies and as a consequence enriches our understanding of organizations as systems.

Orton and Weick (1990) concluded their article by raising some key questions:

> To state that an organization is a loosely coupled system is the beginning of a discussion, not the end. What elements are loosely coupled? What domains are they coupled on? What domains are they decoupled on? What are the characteristics of the couplings and decouplings? (p. 219)

Slightly more than a decade later, Weick (2001) was still pursuing his quest for understanding loosely coupled systems. Focusing on change in such systems, he took the position that change is continuous rather than episodic, occurred on a small scale rather than a large one, was more improvisational than planned, was accommodative rather than constrained, and was local rather than cosmopolitan (p. 390). He noted further that change in loosely coupled systems happens slowly and rarely promotes diffusion of innovation.

For a deliberate, planned effort at changing loosely coupled systems, Weick (2001) chose five targets: (a) presumptions of logic, (b) socialization of processes, (c) differential participation, (d) constant variables, and (e) corruptions of feedback. A synopsis of each of these change targets follows.

Presumptions of logic: Highly important ingredients of loosely coupled systems are the beliefs that organizational members maintain about what holds loose events, activities, and units in the organization together. Cause–effect beliefs illustrate this point: Autonomy and independence lead to higher job satisfaction and, in turn, to positive organizational outcomes. Planting a seed of doubt about such a belief can be a precursor to change.

Socialization of processes: As we know, an organization's culture can be a powerful force for conformity of beliefs and behavior. Recall the Procter & Gamble example in Chapter 11. Focusing on aspects of the culture that "resocialize" organizational members can lead to organization change. The BA story described in Chapter 11 is a case in point.

Differential participation: Different degrees of participation are more common in loosely coupled systems. Recall the earlier reference to Pfeffer (1978) where he noted that few organizational members are all that involved in or even care about the overall organization. Thus, a force for systemwide organization change can be to equalize more effectively participation across the organization. Making sure that everyone attends his or her respective meetings in the organization, for example, is a step toward this equalization effort.

Constant variables: Over time subunits within a loosely coupled system, being in large measure independent of other subunits, can become "set in their ways" about how they work together both within their respective units and across units. This behavioral rigidity can cause long-standing conflict—that is, insufficient cooperation especially across units. Distracting this constancy can lead to change (i.e., focusing on a different way of relating and working together can lead to organizational change). For an example, see Burke's (2006) description of managing intergroup conflict between two functional units—(a) manufacturing and (b) engineering— within a manufacturing plant of a large corporation.

Corruptions of feedback: Weick (2001) argued the following:

> In loosely coupled systems, flawed feedback is often a major source of looseness. Consequently, feedback is often suspect when it is introduced, and sometimes people are not even clear how to use it. Loosely coupled systems often learn to make do with minimal feedback because feedback is unavailable, meaningless, or discredited. When feedback is offered by a change agent, people wonder why they should believe it and how they should use it. (pp. 398–399)

For effective change, then, dependability of feedback is imperative such as ensuring that the feedback is explicit, immediate, accurate, and relevant to organizational members' work and to actions that need to be taken.

Summary

It may be that in this day and age with change being constant, the external environment for organizations being almost too fragmented and complex for executives to cope with effectively, and "virtualness" a way of life, the notion of looseness in and across organizations will become more dominant than tightness.

Considering OD, a field of practice about change, it is interesting to note that most of the work by consultants since 1960 has been focused on loosening tight organizations with most having been corporations. But times have changed significantly since 1960 with looseness now surrounding us. The tragic and devastating oil spill in the Gulf of Mexico in 2010 by British Petroleum (BP) is illustrative. The practice of OD, in particular, and more broadly organization change, in general, needs to concentrate more than ever before on loosely coupled systems—how to understand them and at times ensure that looseness is maintained yet also to learn how to tighten them when such action is called for. We know a lot about loosening tightly coupled systems. We have a long way to go to match that level of knowledge about tightening loosely coupled systems. And for more on Weick's contribution, see his book (Weick, 2009).

THIRTEEN

Transformational
Leadership

A psychologist friend and colleague, Dale Lake, years ago learned to fly an airplane, now a primary hobby for him. Flying in the copilot seat with him over and seemingly through the Colorado mountains was a thrill I will never forget. He told me at the time that a primary reason he loved to fly was the precision required and the joy of accurately navigating a chosen destination. He elaborated by saying that for him, flying served as an antidote to the lack of precision in psychology. The antidote for me is boating. Charting a course in the Gulf of Mexico, cruising through the water, and then seeing on the horizon a buoy or lighthouse at the place and time it was supposed to appear is highly satisfying and indeed fun. In planning the trip, one must take into account environmental factors such as tide changes, strength of the current, wind and other weather-related elements (such as the potential for fog), as well as internal factors, such as engines (I prefer motors, not sails) and instruments (radar, radio, etc.). Are they in good working order?

Although not as precise, using an organizational model in the manner described in Chapter 10 is not unlike charting the course and reading the navigational signs. The organizational model serves as a navigational chart that helps us to account for environmental factors both external and internal to the organization. And if we have (1) measures over time, which are automatically provided in boating and flying and in the organization are a matter of comparing the Time 1 with Time 2 measures, as in the Dime case in Chapter 5, and (2) multiple time measures, being even better, then we can determine whether we are on course and, if needed, which is usually the case, take corrective steps.

But who is the "royal we" in the previous statement? Staying with the comparison for one more moment, the "we" is the pilot or the captain. Without this person at the controls or at the helm, the destination will never be reached. Without leadership, planned organization change will never be realized. The leadership box in the Burke–Litwin model is therefore critical. It is the leader who articulates and brings together the external environment with the organizational mission, strategy, and culture and then provides a vision for the future: the destination, the change goal(s).

The purpose of this chapter, then, is to define what leadership is, especially executive leadership, and explore the role of the organization change leader.

First, let us return to a phrase stated previously: Without leadership, planned organization change will never be realized. This is a strong declaration. I am not the only one to make such a statement. For example, one of the concluding remarks that Kotter and Heskett (1992) made as a result of their extensive study of organization change with many corporations, particularly with respect to culture change, was "The single most visible factor that distinguishes major cultural changes that succeed from those that fail is competent leadership" (p. 84).

The question that is implied here is this one: Does leadership really matter? Evidence will be provided beyond the Kotter and Heskett (1992) declaration. Next, we will address a definition with an attempt to clarify the nature and characteristics of leadership. And, in the next chapter, we will discuss the role of the change leader in the context of phases of planned organization change. Thus, this chapter is about the what of leadership. Especially transformational, and the following chapter is about the how, leading a change effort.

Does Leadership Matter?

Before moving too far along on the assumption that leaders do indeed make a difference, perhaps we should pause for a moment and examine the assertion. There is, after all, a school of thought that embraces the argument that leadership is exaggerated and that leaders are not exactly influencing organizational performance. An organizational theorist who takes a sociological perspective would claim that the success of an organization depends largely on external factors—economic conditions, historical forces, technological changes, and so forth—that are beyond the control of an organization's CEO. Salancik and Pfeffer (1977), for example, have argued that organizational leaders do not affect organizational performance in any appreciable way. Others argue, as Zaccaro (2001) has noted, "that organizational performance is strictly a function of environmental characteristics and contingencies" (p. 5); for example, see Aldrich (1979), Bourgeois (1985), Lawrence and Lorsch (1967), and Romanelli and Tushman (1986). Others in this camp have argued that precedence plays a large role, and so do organizational culture and previous organizational decisions and activities (Miles & Snow, 1978; Starbuck, 1983).

These arguments questioning the influence of leaders are heavily dependent on definitions, the measurements and methods used, and the kinds of statistical analyses employed. In other words, some of their conclusions can be questioned on the basis of their methods. To be fair, however, leaders do not account for all or even most of the variance in explaining organizational performance.

But leaders do make a difference, especially in terms of organization change. Anecdotal evidence and common sense need to be considered. As Hogan, Curphy, and Hogan (1994) have pointed out in their answer to this question: "The fact that Lincoln's army was inert until Ulysses S. Grant assumed command and that some coaches [e.g., Phil Jackson in basketball and Bill Parcells in football] can move from team to team transforming losers into winners is, for most people, evidence that leadership matters" (p. 494). Hogan and his colleagues also offer interesting reflections on the damaging side of leadership; that is, leaders can have a harmful effect, for example, Hitler and Stalin. And Hogan et al. also cite evidence from the consumer side—a manager's direct reports or a leader's followers—that leaders make a difference. For further support of the proposition that leaders make a difference, see the work of Bass (1990), Hughes, Ginnett, and Curphy (1993), and Yukl (1998). Furthermore, as Hogan et al. (1994) noted,

Conversely, reactions to inept leadership include turnover, insubordination, industrial sabotage, and malingering. R. Hogan, Raskin, and Fazzini (1990) noted that organizational climate studies from the mid-1950s to the present routinely show that 60% to 75% of the employees in any organization—no matter when or where the survey was completed and no matter what occupational group was involved—report that the worst or most stressful aspect of their job is their immediate supervisor. Good leaders may put pressure on their people, but abusive and incompetent management create billions of dollars of lost productivity each year. (p. 494)

For more on leaders' negative influence, see Dixon's (1976) book on military incompetence and more recently, Hornstein's (1996) book on "brutal bosses."

In addition to the report of Hogan et al. (1994), Zaccaro (2001) has cited convincing evidence that leaders do matter. For example, a study by Weiner and Mahoney (1981), which covered 193 companies across 19 years, showed that leadership accounted for about 44% of the variance in profits and 47% in stock price. Additional evidence can be found in studies by Barrick, Day, Lord, and Alexander (1991), who show that high-performing executives when compared with average performers accounted for an additional $25 million in value to their organizations, and Hambrick (1989) and Hitt and Tyler (1991) have argued that executives do indeed influence organizational strategy. Also, Joyce, Nohria, and Roberson (2003) provided evidence showing that CEOs account for approximately 14% of the variance in the financial performance of their organizations. We can conclude with reasonable confidence now that leaders of organizations can and do make a difference.

What has not been as clear from the literature is the impact of leadership on organization change. There are numerous cases that anecdotally support the argument that leadership matters in times of change; see, for example, Burke and Trahant (2000). But there has been little evidence that scientifically demonstrates the leader's impact. It seems reasonable to assume, nevertheless, that because there is mounting evidence that leaders affect organizational performance in general, surely they have an impact on organizational change in particular. We will proceed in this chapter, in any case, with the assumption that leaders have a significant influence on organization change and in the following chapter describe how this influence can occur.

On Defining Leadership

Defining and attempting to clarify leadership is a lot like trying to define and describe love. First, we know it when we see it and feel it, but finding accurately descriptive words for what we see and feel is not easy. Second, there may be as many and as diverse definitions for leadership as there are for love. Rost (1991), in his book on leadership, devotes two chapters just to definitions, a total of 58 pages. And finally, definitions and descriptions depend on who you are talking with and what your respective experiences have been. All of us have experienced leadership, good and bad, starting with parents, and most of us have experienced some form of love, also beginning with parents. These experiences and forms, after all, differ.

These caveats aside, some initial clarification is warranted, starting with the concepts of power and leadership.

Power is the capacity to influence others; leadership is the exercise of that capacity. In social psychology, a definition of the exercise of power is when Person A is able to get Person B to do something that B might not otherwise have done. Leadership can be defined accordingly, that is, the act of making something happen that would not otherwise occur. The operative phrase here is "making something happen." This chapter is dedicated to that definition.

Before tackling the "making something happen," however, we need some further clarification.

Toward Further Definition

The Leader–Manager Distinction

First, leadership is not the same as authority and is different from management. With respect to the latter, Zaleznik (1977) was one of the first to specify differences between leaders and managers. Leaders, for example, are more personal about organizational goals; that is, they see no distinction between one's own goals and the organization's, whereas managers are more impersonal about goals. With respect to relations with others, especially followers, leaders relate more intuitively than managers do, whereas managers relate more according to role, as Zaleznik sees it. He specified other differences as well—see Table 13.1.

One year later, James McGregor Burns (1978) introduced the concepts of transformational and transactional leadership, defined earlier in Chapter 10. Using different terms, his distinctions between these two forms of leadership were nevertheless very similar to Zaleznik's (1977), that is, Zaleznik's leader was much like a transformational leader for Burns, and Zaleznik's manager

Table 13.1   A Comparison of Leaders and Managers According to Zaleznik (1977)

Dimension for Comparison	Leaders	Managers
Attitude toward goals	Personal, active	Impersonal, reactive, passive
Conceptions of work	Project ideas into images that excite people; developing options	An enabling process of coordinating and balancing; limiting options
Relations with others	Prefer solitary activities; relate intuitively and empathetically	Prefer to work with people; relate according to roles
Senses of self	Feel separate from their environment; depend on personal mastery of events for identity	Belong to their environment; depend on memberships, roles, and so on, for identity

was quite similar to Burn's transactional leader—see Table 13.2 for a summary of the differences that Burns has delineated.

Having read at the time the article by Zaleznik and the book by Burns, I was captured by their contributions and later wrote about these ideas in an attempt to understand the notion of empowerment more thoroughly (Burke, 1986). Around that time I also made a presentation in Tokyo on leadership to an audience of about 100 managers from Japanese firms. All that the audience knew in advance was my topic. They had not read Zaleznik's article nor Burns's book. (I verified this later.) I was curious. So, I began my session with the request that they in small groups discuss the question of whether there were differences between a leader and a manager. If they saw no difference please give their reasons, or if they believed there were differences, please state them using adjectives or language that would express their beliefs and perspectives. After about 40 minutes or so, the walls were covered with their responses on easel-pad paper—all in

Table 13.2   A Comparison of Transformational (Leaders) and Transactional Leaders (Managers) According to Burns (1978)

Dimensions for Comparison	Leaders	Managers
Emotional involvement	With the institution and with ideals/vision	With the task and the people associated with the task
Personal life	Work and personal life not that distinguishable	Work is separate from personal, private life
Achieves commitment via	Inspiration	Involvement
Holds people accountable via	Guilt induction; want whole person	Contractual transactions; want task accomplishment
Value emphasis	Terminal; end state	Instrumental; means
Problems	Create them	Fix them
Plans	Long-range	Short-range
Appreciates from followers/ subordinates	Contrariness	Conformity
Engenders in followers/ subordinates	Intense feelings—love, sometimes hate; desire to identify with; turbulent	Feelings not intense but relations smoother and steadier

Japanese. I asked my interpreter to translate the responses verbatim from Japanese to English. Table 13.3 is a sample of their responses.

It should be obvious when looking at Table 13.3 that the Japanese way of thinking about the leader–manager differences is very similar to that of Zaleznik and Burns. Two other brief examples should clarify that this way of thinking travels across cultures.

I conducted the same exercise some years later for a smaller group of high-level government executives from China; see Table 13.4. A close look

Table 13.3   Sample of Leader-Manager Distinctions From Japan

Leader	Manager
Starter of change	Administrator of change
Risk-taking	Security
Long-term	Short-term
Inductive	Deductive
Develop options	Limit options
Heavy smoker	Gave up smoking
Revolution	Conservative reformation
Rush	Calm
Change gears	Step on the accelerator
What	How
Intuitive	Logical
Passionate	Cool

Table 13.4   Leader-Manager Distinctions From China

Leader	Manager	Leader	Manager
Strategic	Tactic	Giving ideas	Working the idea
Spiritual	Practical	Leader chooses manager	Manager reports to leader
Overall	Specific	Reward via intrinsic	Reward via intrinsic and extrinsic
Aggressive	Passive	Long-term	Short-term

(Continued)

Table 13.4   (Continued)

Leader	Manager	Leader	Manager
Directing	Implementing	Giving orders	Carrying out orders
Giving orders	Giving methods	Decision making	Decision implementing
Political	Business	Analytical	Problem solving
Idealism	Practicality	Controlling	Measuring
Broader contacts	Limited contacts	Thinking	Doing
Stimulating	Enthusiastic	Abstract	Concrete
Policy making	Execution	Guidance	Management

should indicate that these 15 executives see the leader as a bit more top-down and in charge than do the Japanese or Zaleznik and Burns, but the nature of the distinctions are again very similar.

And finally let's consider the perspective of the British. In 1994, I conducted the same exercise with 10 executives from the BBC. Their comparisons are shown in Table 13.5. Displaying perhaps a bit of British culture with their terms, for example, leader as a romantic and manager as prosaic, their distinctions are again close to others' perspectives from the United States and Asia.

These comparisons from my group exercises with the audiences I was addressing are anecdotal and not exactly scientific. The similarities I found fascinating nevertheless.

In the mid-1990s, Bass (1997) conducted a more scientific and rigorous study of these distinctions in all but one continent around the world. In Bass's language, "there is universality in the transactional-transformational paradigm" (p. 130). His evidence comes not only from a variety of cultures but from a variety of organizations in business, military, government, education, and the independent sector. Today, then, these distinctions are more or less taken for granted; see, for example, Kotter (1990).

Table 13.5 Leader-Manager Distinctions From Great Britain

Leader	Manager	Leader	Manager
Motivates	Instructs	Hands-off	Hands-on
Inspires	Orders, compels	Romantic	Prosaic
Visionary	Status quo	Principled	Pliable
Personal authority	Titular authority	Innovative	Directed
Staff respond	Staff comply	Inspirational	Mechanistic
Maximum	Minimum	Visionary	Strategic
Open to ideas from team	Closed to ideas from team	Intuitive	Logical
Earns respect	Demands obedience	Outward	Inward
Rewards for success of team	Claims credit	Charismatic	Controlled
Inspirational	Organizational	Tomorrow	Today
Instinctive	Calculating	Single-minded	Adaptable
Visionary	Goal seeking	Risky	Safe
Self-starting	Externally directed	Overview	Single view
People-oriented	Task-oriented	Global	National

Authority and Leadership

Authority concerns the "right to": the right to make decisions that are binding on others, to use and distribute resources, and to perform certain functions (e.g., hire and fire). Obholzer (1994) differentiates three sources of authority—from above, from below, and from within. Authority from above is derived from a particular role in a social system, for example, within an organizational hierarchy in which the "right to" is authority according to the position that one holds. Authority from below, whether formal or informal, is given (authorized) by subordinates (followers) or colleagues—one's authority is either sanctioned or withheld from below. Authority from within derives from one's individual capacity to assume his or her own authority (formal, informal, or personal) from his or her personality (e.g., charismatic qualities, personal history).

Leadership is more associated with authority from below and from within and less with authority from above. Leadership has more to do with the person and less to do with role and position. Leadership is about influence, not command and control. To be successfully influential requires personal skills such as active listening, persuasion, empathy, and an awareness of how one as leader is affecting others and in turn how one is being personally affected by others.

Second, leadership requires followership. A person may think that he or she is a leader, but if there is no one to follow, it does not matter what the person's self-concept may be: Without a follower, a person is not a leader. Thus, leadership is about influence, but that influence is a reciprocal process. Leadership occurs when a potential follower exists and wants direction.

Third, as noted previously and in Chapter 10, Burns's (1978) two categories of leaders, transformational and transactional, also correspond to the two categories of organization change, discontinuous and continuous, respectively. Transformational leadership is therefore more likely to be required for discontinuous change, and transactional for continuous change.

Transformational Leadership According to Bass

Bass (1998) has developed a measure of these two leadership categories, the Multifactor Leadership Questionnaire (MLQ). From research with this instrument, several components of transformational leadership have emerged:

Charismatic leadership (or idealized influence)

They are role models, admired, respected, and trusted.

Followers identify with and want to emulate them.

As leaders, they are willing to take risks and are consistent.

As leaders, they have high standards of ethical and moral conduct.

Inspirational motivation

The leader provides meaning and challenge.

A team spirit is cultivated.

The leader communicates clear expectations that followers want to meet.

There is a strong commitment to goals.

Intellectual stimulation

The leader urges followers to be innovative and creative, to question assumptions, to reframe problems, and to approach old situations in new ways.

When followers make mistakes, the leader does not criticize them in public.

Individual consideration

The leader pays close attention to followers' needs for achievement.

The leader often serves as a mentor and coach.

Individual differences are recognized by the leader.

The leader practices MBWA ("management by walking around").

The leader follows up with tasks and responsibilities that have been assigned and delegated without followers feeling as if they are being monitored.

Bass (1998) points out that charismatic and inspirational motivation usually form a combined single factor that he labels charismatic-inspirational leadership.

The point is that a significant part of transformational leadership in Bass's MLQ involves charisma. Although Bass (1998) does not equate transformational with charisma, one gets the impression, nevertheless, that the two go together more often than not. Moreover, Bass and his colleagues summarize considerable research evidence that transformational as compared with transactional is a superior form of leadership (Avolio, 1999; Bass, 1998). Bass and his colleagues would probably agree that one can be a successful transformational leader without being charismatic (although they might also argue that such a leader is rare). In any case, Colin Marshall was such a person, that is, a highly successful change agent as CEO of British Airways (BA), yet not charismatic, at least not in the classical sense. Marshall led a transformation of BA from a command-and-control, bureaucratic, insular culture to one that became market-oriented, customer-focused, and more nimble than bureaucratic in its day-to-day operations; see Chapter 5 in this volume, Chapter 6 in Burke and Trahant (2000), and Goodstein and Burke (1991) for more on the BA story.

An opposite example to Marshall, one that fits more with Bass's contention regarding transformational leaders and charisma, is the case of Roger Goldman, who led a significant organization change at NatWest Bancorp from 1991 to 1996; see Chapter 12 in Burke and Trahant (2000). Goldman led much of the change by the sheer force of his personality. For example, he maintained a special phone line direct to his office (the phone was bright red and labeled "Call Roger") that any employee could use to ask him personally any questions he or she desired. In other words, Goldman answered the phone himself.

Goldman, then, is an interesting contrast to Marshall, yet what the two had in common as they led their respective change efforts was persistence. They stayed the course, kept people focused on the mission and strategy, dealt directly with resistances, and bounced back when mistakes were made. The point is that charismatic leadership, though potentially helpful, is not required for successful organization change. What is required includes qualities such as persistence, as already noted, having a clear vision about the desired future state, and self-awareness, also noted previously. We will focus more on the kind of leader behavior and qualities that are needed for successful organization change in Chapter 13.

With respect to the transactional leadership components, Bass (1998) has three:

1. Contingent reward, in other words, pay for performance

2. Management by exception

3. Monitoring of deviances from the standard, mistakes, and errors

Bass (1998) considers the last component of transactional leadership less effective than contingent reward.

Transactional leadership is not the same as laissez-faire management, an avoidance or absence of leadership that represents "nontransaction," that is,

Necessary decisions are often not made.

Actions are typically delayed.

Authority remains unused.

Bass (1998) provides evidence that transformational is superior to transactional leadership. Considering how he defines and measures transactional leadership, one can see why. In the earlier thinking and writing, neither Zaleznik (1977) nor Burns (1978) painted the manager/transactional side of leadership as negatively as Bass. Considering the original distinctions, there is a time and place for both leadership and management. Leadership more often concerns change, which is what the term transformational means, and management is concerned more with solving problems, maintaining efficient and effective operations, and simply keeping the organization running. An organization can survive for some period of time (not long, however) without leadership but can hardly survive at all without management.

Characteristics of Executive Leadership

Finally, our concern in this chapter is with executive leadership, the senior people at the top of the pyramid or at the nexus of a network in organizations. We are less concerned with leadership in the middle or at the first-line supervisory level. Not that leadership is unimportant at these lower levels, quite the contrary. In fact, as organization change progresses, these middle and lower levels become even more critical to the success of the overall effort. But for purposes of this chapter, our concentration is more at the top of the organizational hierarchy because these executive-level individuals in the early phases of organization change are essential to the effort's ultimate success.

With his rather comprehensive book, Zaccaro (2001) has provided a useful compendium of executive leadership. At the outset, he appropriately points out that, broadly speaking, an executive has two primary responsibilities or functions:

1. Boundary management—monitoring the organization's external environment, making choices about what to pay most attention to,

analyzing the amorphous and complex information to make as much sense out of it as possible, and communicating this analysis to organizational members, particularly those in management roles.

2. Organizationwide coordination—making certain that units within the organization communicate with one another, determining what decisions need to be made and who should make them, and monitoring overall performance.

The first function is largely external and the second internal.

Zaccaro (2001) then provides a thorough review of the literature and identifies four primary conceptual perspectives on executive leadership.

Conceptual Complexity

The conceptual complexity theory of leadership is based on the premise that organizations operate within highly complex environments and will do so even more in the future:

> [This] complexity results in the stratification of organizations, wherein higher levels of leadership are characterized by greater information-processing demands and by the need to solve more ill-defined, novel, and complex organizational problems. To thrive, executive leaders require significant conceptual capacities that allow them to make sense of and navigate successfully within such complex environments. (Zaccaro, 2001, p. 17)

A prominent example of this perspective is the work of Elliott Jaques (1978, 1986) and his colleagues; see, for example, Jacobs and Jaques (1987) and Jaques and Clement (1991) in their work on what is referred to as stratified system theory (SST). Interesting and useful components of SST are (1) an emphasis on the executives or "causal map" as the rationale for collective action, that is, making sense of the complexities in the external environment and explaining how to respond for the good of the organization; (2) stratifying the organization according to hierarchical levels (and seven "layers" should be the maximum regardless of organizational size); (3) SST's strong alignment with open-system theory; and (4) the requisite leader characteristics.

With respect to the fourth component, Jaques (1986) specified three primary leader characteristics—technical, interpersonal, and conceptual. At the lower ranks of management, the technical and interpersonal are most important, but the higher one goes in the hierarchy, the more conceptual qualities become important to one's success, with the technical characteristic gradually becoming less important. Although the nature of what a leader-manager deals with day to day and interpersonal characteristics may differ somewhat as a function of level in the hierarchy, the need for this leader characteristic remains critical regardless of level.

This brief digression into Jaques's and his colleagues' contributions was only to provide an illustration of a model of conceptual complexity, not to explore their contributions comprehensively. Other examples of theories and models of conceptual complexity include Mumford, Zaccaro, Harding, Fleishman, and Reiter-Palmon (1993) and Streufert and Swezey (1986).

Behavioral Complexity

The behavioral complexity theory of leadership focuses on the multiple roles the leader plays and the multiple constituencies to be served. With these many and diverse demands, the leader must be capable of behaving in a variety of ways in a variety of situations. Moreover, the leader, at times, must be capable of balancing competing demands, such as mentoring and developing subordinates, yet at the same time having to deliver difficult feedback on, say, poor performance.

It should be noted that behavioral complexity theory is not independent of conceptual complexity. Both theories involve the leader's ability to deal with all kinds of complexities. And both theories involve intelligence, just different forms. Conceptual complexity is more about analytical and thinking skills, and behavioral complexity is more about what we refer to these days as emotional intelligence; see, for example, Goleman (1995). Another way of differentiating the two theories is that conceptual complexity is more about formulating plans for action and behavioral complexity is more about implementation of plans, the action itself. Examples of behavioral complexity theory include Mintzberg's (1973) categories of managerial roles, Quinn's (1988) competing values framework, and Tsui's (1984) multiple constituency model.

Strategic Decision Making

The strategic decision-making theory of leadership stresses the importance of a congruence between the organization and its environment;

thus the primary tasks of senior leaders in the organization are to monitor the environment, analyze potential problems, seek opportunities, form policies and strategies, and implement and then evaluate these policies and strategies. This theory of executive leadership is also about promoting stability and certainty in the short run and flexibility and adaptation in the long run. With respect to leader qualities, emphasis is given to cognitive abilities, functional expertise, and motives, such as need for achievement and self-efficacy, risk taking, and locus of control. Finally, models of strategic decision making are largely about how leaders make the strategic decisions. Examples of this perspective include the work of Bourgeois (1985), Lawrence and Lorsch (1967), Thompson (1967), and Wortman (1982).

Visionary and Inspirational

The visionary and inspirational theory of leadership emphasizes charismatic, transformational, and visionary qualities. The primary role of the leader is to develop a vision that will focus and motivate collective action by followers in the organization. Important leader qualities include cognitive abilities, self-confidence, risk taking, and emotional intelligence. Examples of this perspective include Bass (1998), Bennis and Nanus (1985), Burns (1978), Conger (1989), House (1977), and Sashkin (1988).

Summary

As Zaccaro (2001) pointed out, even though there are different emphases, these perspectives about executive leadership overlap in that all emphasize the importance of long-term goals, organizational directions, and boundary management. With respect to our purpose in this chapter, it is important to understand that, although the language of the Burke–Litwin model might lead us to believe that executive leadership is the same as the transformational and visionary perspective, there is more to it than that. As we proceed, let us bear in mind that the senior leader's roles and qualities in leading change are complex and demanding. All four of these executive leadership perspectives are relevant.

To illustrate this point, at least in part, we will now consider the work of Howard Gardner and others as a way of combining some of the theories from Zaccaro, primarily conceptual complexity and visionary-inspirational.

An additional objective of this final section for the chapter is to highlight the importance of the executive leader's need to provide vision and direction for the organization and to achieve this need with inspiration and contagion.

Howard Gardner's *Leading Minds*

A cognitive psychologist, Gardner (1995) has studied successful leaders, 11 rather intensively, to understand their thinking abilities and patterns—the generation of ideas, thoughts, images, or mental representations and how they are stored, accessed, combined, remembered, and rearranged. Then Gardner wants to know how these leaders transmit their ideas. His 11 illuminaries included Eleanor Roosevelt, Martin Luther King Jr., George C. Marshall, Margaret Thatcher, Mahatma Gandhi, and Alfred P. Sloan. Some commonalities among these leaders for Gardner are they were leaders by choice—not imposed on followers—and they were motivated more by a desire to effect change than simply by a lust for more power.

One of Zaleznik's (1977) leader dimensions or characteristics was empathy. At the same time, he stated that a leader was more of a loner than a manager. How can a leader be a loner and empathetic simultaneously? Gardner (1995) sheds some light on this question. From his perspective, successful leaders empathize collectively. They seem to sense and deliver what followers already desire. They provide what Gardner calls "mental structures" that activate followers' desires. These mental structures are ideas about identity, who we are as an organization—what we believe, what we want, and how we prefer to be seen by the outside world. Gardner goes on to state that the successful leader conveys these mental structures in the form of a story. The leader tells a story about who we are, our aspirations, and the direction we need to take for the future.

Leaders, accordingly to Gardner (1995), can be differentiated according to one these types of stories:

- Ordinary—the leader relates a traditional story. In a corporation, the CEO's story might focus on winning, beating the competition with better quality and customer service, being excellent, being the best at what we do, treating our employees with care and respect, and providing for our stockholders superior returns on their investments. A similar type of story could also be related by the head of a government agency, a health-care institution, or a nonprofit organization. The story comes as no surprise. Followers expect words like winning, improvement, respect, and the rest. This kind of story is therefore common, ordinary.

- Innovative—the leader surfaces a latent story. The leader has a sense of what followers need and want; it is simply that these desires are not in their conscious awareness. It is about beliefs and values that people hold but do not necessarily discuss. They are implicit and tacit. Gardner's (1995) examples of this type of story are Ronald Reagan when he was president of the United States and Margaret Thatcher when she was prime minister of the United Kingdom. They both, Gardner has argued, tapped into latent beliefs and desires of their respective constituents, beliefs and values that support a free-market system, that oppose socialism and prefer capitalism, and that provide people with a feeling of freedom and choice. In the corporate world, innovative leadership might surface a strong desire on the part of employees to be more collaborative as opposed to competing with others in the organization, to be more involved and engaged in the business, or to be a participant in changing the organization.

- Visionary—the leader creates an entirely new story. Gardner's (1995) examples include Mohandas Gandhi and Martin Luther King Jr., who established social movements and eventually social systems that previously did not exist. In the corporate world, this type of story is most associated with creative entrepreneurialism, for example, Steve Jobs at Apple, Bill Gates and Microsoft, and Fred Smith at FedEx.

For Gardner (1995), then, the story is central. Successful leaders have a story that works for them. It is dynamic, not just a headline or a sound bite; in other words, the story constitutes a journey that leaders and followers take together. The story concerns issues of identity, who we are and what we believe, and must fit at a particular historical moment. With respect to this last point, two illustrative examples come to mind: Churchill not being reelected as prime minister after World War II, and Jack Welch would not have been selected to succeed Reginald Jones at General Electric if Jones and other board members had believed that the company at that time needed stability and should proceed as before.

Beyond Gardner, there is at least one other source on the importance of storytelling that warrants our attention. Remember that what I am attempting to do here is (1) concentrate on executive leadership and (2) combine two categories or models/theories of executive leadership, namely, conceptual complexity and visionary-inspirational. My objective, then, is to provide ways of enacting these very important dimensions of leadership, particularly at the outset of organization change.

McKee—A Master Storyteller

Robert McKee is a noted screenwriter and screenwriter coach. He has been interviewed by editors of the *Harvard Business Review* about the importance of storytelling and persuasion (McKee, 2003). Although McKee (2003) does not refer to Gardner's work, he would no doubt suggest that the ordinary story that Gardner describes is indeed ordinary. McKee's point would be that there are two problems with this form of rhetoric. First, organization members have their own set of statistics, authorities, and experiences (what to do to win against competitors) and are arguing in their heads with the leader's attempts to persuade. This kind of reaction is especially relevant to a company's sales force. Second, if the executive does succeed in persuading organizational members to his or her point of view, the commitment will only be intellectual. McKee states that people are not inspired to do something differently by reason alone. Emotion must be engaged, and the best way to do so is with a compelling story. What does McKee consider to be a story?

McKee (2003) states at the outset that "a story expresses how and why life changes" (p. 52). A story begins with life being in balance, things are good, and daily activities occur more or less according to the way that our people of interest want them to occur. But then something happens. There is an event. McKee calls it an "inciting event," an event that throws life out of balance—a key executive dies, a competitor comes up with a new unanticipated product that is clearly a winner, or a major customer threatens to buy from someone else. The leader then discovers a story by asking four primary questions:

1. What must be done to restore balance?

2. What is keeping us from doing this?

3. How should we act to achieve this desire for restored and renewed balance?

4. Do I as the leader and storyteller believe this? Is it truthful? Is it believable and not just hype? Can I come across with integrity?

So, what makes a good story? It begins with a desire, an aspiration, and then the story continues with a description of the forces, the barriers that could prevent achieving the desire. In McKee's (2003) words, "Stories are how we remember; we tend to forget lists and bullet points" (p. 52). The story is about the struggle between expectation and reality. McKee provides a hypothetical example of a CEO of a pharmaceutical company who wants his researchers to discover a chemical compound that could prevent heart attacks. He suggests that the CEO personalize his story somehow. Perhaps his father died prematurely of a heart attack. So, nature itself is a force against the CEO's aspiration. He therefore wants a new drug that will be preventive. A second force to contend with is the Food and Drug Administration (FDA). So, experimentation and clinical trials must be conducted to get a patent for the new drug. A central piece of the CEO's story, then, is how many lives potentially could be saved with this new drug. But capital is needed for the research, for the long road to patenting the drug, and for bringing it to market. The story ends with the CEO stating in emotional terms that millions of lives each year could be saved. McKee then states that bankers and investors will "just throw money at him [the CEO]" (p. 53). The point that McKee makes is that an executive's vision, direction, and inspiration is a story with passion and desire and not a list of tables and statistics. It is a story with a protagonist, say, our CEO, and antagonists, in his example, the forces of nature, the FDA, and people who may be skeptical.

Gardner (1995) emphasizes the importance and potential power of the leader's story for purposes of simply leading people and more specifically for creating the rationale and basis for change. McKee (2003) then helps us to learn how to do it, that is, the ingredients of what a real story is all about. Another article, also from the *Harvard Business Review,* that can be helpful to leaders about storytelling is the one by Denning (2004).

Summary

Gardner (1995) concludes his analysis of 11 carefully selected and successful leaders with a list of what an exemplary leader looks like. His exemplary leader is one who

Is a skilled speaker

Has a strong interest in and understands people

Is energetic

Shows early in life that he or she will accomplish something

Is willing to confront individuals in authority

Is concerned with moral issues

Often is competitive

Enjoys a position of control

Establishes relationships in ever-widening circles

Travels outside her or his homeland

Has completed the necessary apprenticeships

Is attuned to issues on people's minds, particularly issues of identity

Adjusts his or her story to accommodate changing circumstances while still adhering to basic principles and remaining an individual of conviction

Attaches herself or himself to an institution or organization—or creates one (e.g., Gandhi or King)

Seeks opportunities for reflection

- to review, take stock
- to perceive the big picture
- to "unclutter" his or her mind
- to assess failures, resistances, opponents, and so on, and not be permanently set back
- to renew and return to the fray with energy and positive, revised plans and ideas

Is more optimistic than pessimistic

Many scholars and writers of popular books on leadership have their own list of the successful leader's qualities. Some are grounded in research and theory; most are not. One might argue that Gardner's (1995) exemplary list takes some liberties, since it is based on just a few people, exemplary though they may be. After all, the list was not equally applicable to all 11, with some being more or less exemplary on some of the list's characteristics than the other ten. In any case, although small in number of cases, Gardner's analysis of these 11 is grounded in theory from cognitive psychology and his conclusions have a ring of credibility.

Let us now consider further, more recent work by Gardner. This later work, again grounded in cognitive psychology, serves as a segue to the next chapter on the how of leading, particularly leading organization change.

Beyond the act of storytelling and more specific, how do change leaders persuade people to their point of view, to see the need for and embrace change? How do they change people's minds?

Howard Gardner's *Changing Minds*

In his book *Changing Minds,* Gardner (2004) identified seven factors or levers that provide (1) a way of thinking about how one can lead change, and (2) useful action steps for helping to persuade people to one's point of view. All seven factors begin with the letters r-e-:

1. Reason: Many organizational members can be reasoned with. The change leader can use a rational approach that involves logic, analogies, metaphors, and taxonomies. The change leader might also give a list of advantages and disadvantages for each proposal that she or he makes. These rational approaches have appeal for thinking, reflective people.

2. Research: This lever for change complements the reason factor with the collection and presentation of supportive data. The research does not have to be formal and can involve, for example, the use of cases. The more scientifically oriented organizational members may be, however, the more the change leader would need to use data that were derived in a rigorous and persuasive manner. The arguments made by Foster and Kaplan (2001) about "cultural lock-in" in their book (see Chapter 2 in this text for a summary) represent a powerful example of how this second factor of Gardner's (2004) can be leveraged. Another example of combining reason with research is the one at British Aerospace that described how the two top executives made their case for organization change—see Chapter 13 in this text and the more extensive coverage in Evans and Price (1999).

3. Resonance: Does the argument for change feel right; does it resonate with organizational members? Reason and research appeal to

the cognitive, rational, thinking aspects of one's mind, but what about the affective component? Do the change leader's proposals and arguments seem to fit the current situation, what is needed at this time, and convince organizational members that further persuasion and data are actually not necessary? As Gardner points out, it may be that resonance simply follows from the use of reason and research; yet it is also possible that organizational members, at least some of them, are persuaded mostly at an unconscious level. In fact, the reason and research factor, the fully rational considerations, might conflict with what some organizational members believe and feel is more important, like, for example, their respect for and the integrity of the change leader. Organizational members may view the change leader as reliable, consistent, and honest. These qualities of the change leader may be sufficient for changing minds and to go along with what is being proposed. Hard data are simply not necessary. Of course, the leader's story is the primary component of this lever.

4. Redescriptions: A change leader can often be more persuasive when relying on a number of different forms of presenting one's points and ensuring that these forms reinforce one another. A singular point or argument can be made in a number of linguistic, numerical, and graphic ways—telling a story or two, making an argument supported by numerical trends, say, using simple percentages, and then showing a figure that is a bar or line graph that makes the same point. Engineers and scientists in particular love these latter two forms. They love a story too, but a story for them may be interesting enough but just not "data based."

5. Resources and Rewards: This lever might be called enticement, but the term doesn't begin with r-e. Changing organizational members' minds is more likely to occur when the change leader is in a position to provide resources that will facilitate the change being proposed, say by an expanded budget, additional staff, or more space, and subsequently reward organizational members with, say, an additional bonus when their behavior supports the change effort.

6. Real-World Events: Occasionally events in the external environment can change the minds of organizational members—terrorist attacks, economic depression, a hurricane, or more positively, a breakthrough in medical research, or the creation of an entirely new

technology, such as digitization. These kinds of events can be so powerful that a change leader's attempt to make a case for organization change is not really required.

7. Resistances: Gardner, after all, is realistic. He is well aware of the power of resistances. Changing organizational members' minds is most likely when the first six levers are mutually reinforcing and when resistances are not very strong. But if the first six levers are inconsistent with one another and resistances are strong, changing minds will be highly unlikely. As the reader knows, resistances are covered rather extensively in Chapter 5 of this text.

To illustrate the use of these levers for changing minds, Gardner (2004) describes the case of a successful change leader, James O. Freedman. In 1987 the trustees of Dartmouth College hired Freedman as president. Freedman came to Dartmouth from the University of Iowa, where he had served as president for 5 years. The trustees of Dartmouth wanted Freedman to turn the place around. Although an Ivy League member, Dartmouth was known as a party school; had dropped significantly in its scholarship; had a college student publication, the *Dartmouth Review*, that was heavily right-wing, which Freeman, a more liberal thinker, wanted to influence; and had alumni and students who worshipped football far more than academic achievement. These were some of the many problems that Freedman faced.

Gardner's coverage of Freedman's tenure as president is quite comprehensive. Suffice it to say that while Freedman did not change the institution overnight, eventually he did. By a number of different performance indices, Dartmouth changed—and for the better. For example, SAT scores for incoming students increased; a larger number of students received Rhodes, Marshall, and Truman scholarships and Fulbright fellowships; rankings climbed steadily upward over the years in *U.S. News & World Report*; and scholarly publication by the faculty increased.

The four factors that Gardner (2004) believed contributed the most to Freedman's successes were:

- *Research*—the way Freedman was able to learn from other successful examples
- Exemplars of change in many *redescriptions*—presenting his message in many different ways and reaching a wide range of Dartmouth constituents

- *Resources and rewards*—initiating new practices to reinforce the achievement of higher standards and, when achieved, recognizing and rewarding people
- *Resistances*—directly challenging Dartmouth constituents who took an anti-intellectual stance

As a well-trained lawyer, Freedman also used skillfully the reason lever and apparently he resonated with many, especially the faculty, but the four factors listed above, Gardner believed, were the ones that contributed the most to Freedman's success.

Gardner (2004) also covers briefly two other cases that illustrated poor use of the changing minds levers—John Chambers of the Cisco Corporation and Robert Shapiro, CEO of Mansanto. Chambers, Gardner contended, did not pay sufficient attention to research about business cycles, and he underestimated the resistances he faced. Shapiro underestimated resistances as well, and he did not seem to resonate with the powerful constituents of the company. These cases are documented in the popular business press.

Now that we are in the process of trying to understand more thoroughly how to lead and bring about organization change, let us pursue this deeper understanding by moving ahead to the next chapter.

FOURTEEN

Leading Organization Change

As noted and documented in the previous chapter, leadership matters. Evidence shows that leaders can either hurt an organization badly or destroy it completely. The Enron case is clearly a significant example. Evidence also shows that leaders can measurably help their organizations and can add value. Examples of change leaders that made positive differences for their organizations are described in this chapter. Also described and what serves as the structure for the chapter is a simple phase model for planning and leading organization change. The purposes of this chapter, therefore, are to (1) provide a framework, a phase model, for planning and leading change, (2) describe actual cases examples of organization change emphasizing the leader's role, and (3) suggest with the model and case examples that large-scale transformations of organizations, although fraught with potential peril, can indeed be accomplished.

Phases of Organization Change and the Leader's Role

The following descriptions of *how* to bring about organization change are derived from theoretical ideas and from experience in consulting with CEOs who were serving as change agents. What follows is written in a prescriptive fashion for the sake of clarity. Caveats are therefore not presented.

An interesting paradox about organization change, as noted in Chapter 2, is that we plan as if the process is linear when, in reality, it is anything but linear. It is useful, nevertheless, to think about the planning process in terms of phases. After all, phases are not totally discrete; they overlap. But we must bear in mind that as planned organization change is implemented, (1) more than one phase occurs at the same time; that is, they are not temporally mutually exclusive; and (2) contingency plans need to be in place, because rarely does anything turn out as planned. Unanticipated consequences occur. It's not possible to think of everything!

The Prelaunch Phase

Leader Self-Examination

Leadership is personal. The process concerns the use of self, how to be persuasive, how to deal with resistance, and how to be political, in the best sense of the phrase: how to embody the vision of where one wants the organization to go. It is important, therefore, for the leader who is about to begin a significant change effort to take some time at the outset to reflect. This reflection can be considered in three categories: self-awareness, motives, and values.

Self-Awareness. There is growing evidence that self-awareness is related to performance; that is, high performers tend to have a greater overlap between how they see themselves and how others see them than do moderate and low performers (Atwater & Yammarino, 1992; Church, 1997). It behooves leaders who want to bring about a successful change effort to be as cognizant as possible of themselves in personal domains such as the following:

- Tolerance for ambiguity: The courses that organization change will take are not exactly predictable; being able to live with this kind of ambiguity is important.
- Need for control: It is difficult to be a "control freak" and lead change effectively; organization change is messy, sometimes chaotic, and seemingly out of control; thus, being clear about what one can control and needs to control and what one is not likely to be able to control is critical.

- Understanding how feelings affect behavior: What is one's typical reaction when others disagree or challenge or when others resist the change that the leader feels strongly about? Knowing oneself in these ways helps the leader manage himself or herself more effectively, especially in trying circumstances.
- Personal dispositions: Most people know whether their preference is extroversion or introversion, but what about other dimensions, such as need for closure and intuition compared with sensing? (These are components of the Myers-Briggs Type Indicator [MBTI] measure, based on Jung's personality theory.) There is some evidence, for example, that intuition (trusting one's hunches, future orientation, and conceptual tendency) is more related to leader behavior than is sensing (being fact-based, concrete, and practical); see, for example, Van Eron and Burke (1992). When the MBTI was used with the top team of a large global corporation a few years ago, 9 of the 11 scored intuitive, including the CEO. For a brief account of this team-building activity, see Burke and Noumair (2002).
- Decision making: It is highly valuable to understand the differences between times when one as a leader needs to take the reins and decide and times when one needs to loosen control and involve others as a part of self-knowledge.

Additional examples could be catalogued here, but the point was to give a flavor of some of the more important aspects of self-awareness for leadership purposes, not to provide an exhaustive list.

Motives. Knowing one's motives is of course a part of self-awareness, but for this section, the emphasis is on which motives are the more important ones for leading change.

O'Toole (1999), one of our paramount thinkers and writers in the arena of organization change, makes the interesting point that ambition is the "only inherent character trait [that] is essential for effective leadership" (p. 1). This word, for some, maybe most people, conjures up negative feelings. An ambitious person, especially one with high ambition, is to be avoided. But O'Toole argued that a certain amount of ambition is good. O'Toole used the words "appropriately ambitious." As he stated, "Even the saintly Mohandas K. Gandhi had ambition" (p. 2). Gandhi even admitted it himself. So, let us agree with O'Toole that having the appropriate amount of ambition is not only a good quality but may also indeed be a necessary motive for effective organization change leadership. Of course, the important issue here is, what is appropriate? O'Toole did not define *appropriate*, but he stated that the change leader needs to have a "healthy dissatisfaction with the status quo" (p. 2) and then change it. He also points to the importance of having this ambition in the service of an organization change goal. In a sense, then, he was agreeing with Zaleznik's (1977) idea that a leader is one who experiences no difference between personal goals and those of the organization.

Using McClelland's (1965, 1975) three major motives—need for achievement, power, and affiliation—as discussion points, we can proba-bly agree, first, that having at least a moderate (if not high) need to achieve is critical to success as a leader of change. Second, McClelland's need-for-power concept is not unlike O'Toole's notion of ambition. In this case, a certain amount of need for power would seem to be necessary for change leadership. If one does not want to influence others, one is not likely to be very effective at it. The McClelland and Burnham (1976) study puts the need for power into context. Using subordinates' ratings of their organization's degree of clarity and amount of team spirit as indices of successful management, McClelland and Burnham found that if a man-ager was high in power motivation, low in need for affiliation, and high in inhibition (that is, the power need was socialized, mature, and not expressed for self-aggrandizement), the organization's degree of clarity was greater (subordinates knew the goals and what was expected of them) and the team spirit was higher.

There are good reasons for this. Managers who have a high need for affiliation usually want to be liked and to be popular. As a result, their decision making tends to be impulsive, being done to please someone at the moment rather than in rational support of the overall good of the organization. Managers with a high need for power that is personally oriented are not builders of the institution, according to McClelland and Burnham (1976). They tend to demand personal loyalty from their subordinates—loyalty to them as individuals rather than to the organi-zation. The institutional managers are the most successful because they encourage loyalty to the institution rather than to themselves. As a result, the successful manager creates a climate with clarity, team spirit, and opportunities for accomplishment.

The profile of the desirable institutional manager thus has three major elements: high need for power, low need for affiliation, and high inhibi-tion. In addition, successful institutional managers like organizations and are oriented toward them. They typically join more organizations and feel greater responsibility for developing them than others. They enjoy work, they like the discipline of work, and they have a preference for getting things done in an orderly fashion. They place the good of the organization above self-interest. They are judicious; that is, they have a strong sense of fairness. They are generally more mature, less ego-centered and less defensive. They are also more willing to seek advice from experts, and they have longer and broader vision of the future.

Finally, McClelland and Burnham (1976) pointed out that successful managers tend to have a style of management characterized by participative and coaching behavior; that is, they are concerned with the needs and development of their subordinates. In summary, according to McClelland and Burnham:

> The general conclusion of these studies is that the top manager of a company must possess a high need for power, that is, a concern for influencing people. However, this need must be disciplined and controlled so that it is directed toward the benefit of the institution as a whole and not toward the manager's personal aggrandizement. Moreover, the top manager's need for power ought to be greater than his need for being liked by people. (p. 101)

Finally, effective change leaders need to have an above-average level of energy and be capable of (1) working long hours when needed, (2) interacting with lots of people, and (3) energizing others. Of the thousands of citations in Stodgill's (1974) and later, Bass's (1990) handbook on leadership, one of the few consistent findings was that effective leaders are typically high-energy people.

Values. As noted with the explanation of the Burke–Litwin model in Chapter 10, the alignment of individual needs and values with the organization's culture (norms and values) is likely to enhance motivation and in turn performance. This alignment is all the more important for the CEO and other change leaders in the organization. But what if we are attempting to change the culture? Then, it is a matter of modifying current values or establishing an entirely new set of values. Establishing these values to undergird and provide direction for the change effort is the responsibility of the CEO–change leader. Not that the values need to come directly from the CEO; the establishing process can involve many people. But in the end, the values must be compatible with the CEO's personal values because he or she must embody them and live them daily in the organization. In the Dime Bancorp case summarized in Chapter 11, it was a matter of establishing new values (drawn from the mission statement). An internal Dime task force did the work of drafting the new mission statement, but the CEO, Larry Toal, was highly involved. He attended many of the meetings and in the end was committed to the mission statement, and because the new values were elicited from the mission statement, Toal's commitment to the values was easily achieved.

In another merger, that of SmithKline Beecham, values were created to help establish the new culture, as with Dime. In this case, the top team of the global company initiated the work of establishing the values. Bob Bauman, CEO of the newly merged company (SmithKline from the United States and Beecham from the United Kingdom) at the time, 1989, described in his own words the value-generation process (Burke & Trahant, 2000):

> So the executive committee and I went away again, this time to define the values that would make up that culture. Obviously, there were certain values that were critical to our company. Innovation, for example, was critical. We didn't have much trouble getting people to agree on that. . . . There was no disagreement that customers were critical and that our customer base was changing. . . . HMOs were coming in, which brought up the question, "Who's the buyer now, the HMO or the doctor?" and "How do we bridge this gap?" So we knew we had to start thinking more about customers and had to do a better job—not just in providing good drugs but also in how we managed and serviced our customers.
>
> We extended our discussion of customers incidentally to include not just the outside world but also our own organization. Because we thought it important to say that everyone in the company has a customer. I had a customer on the Board. I had customers in dealing with members of the executive committee. We agreed that people on the manufacturing line, in R&D—people everywhere inside the company—had customers. . . . Another value we believed in was winning. We wanted to create a winning attitude inside the company, so we thought performance was important. And there was some feeling in our early discussions that we weren't driving as hard in the area of performance as we needed to. . . . We agreed we wanted to be winners and perform better than our competitors. . . .

Another value that was clearly agreed to but harder to articulate was people. We knew we had to have the best people we could find and that they were key to our competitive advantage. So as part of articulating this value, we emphasized that people needed to contribute to the goals of the organization; we wanted to give everyone a chance to influence and participate in how work was done and how it got measured. And we wanted people to feel ownership for continuously improving the ways they worked on the job.

Finally we agreed to the value of integrity. It's something we felt we possessed and that was important to the nature of our industry. We felt five values was the right number. We believed that if we got too many it would be very hard to drive them all through the organization. (pp. 64–66)

The Dime example was a bottom-up process of determining mission and values, whereas the SmithKline Beecham case was more top-down. Both worked because each organization operationalized its set of values by putting them into behavioral language and then building a multirater feedback program so that all key managers received feedback on behaviors that reflected the values. For more detail on the SmithKline Beecham example, see Bauman, Jackson, and Lawrence (1997), Burke (2000b), Burke and Jackson (1991), and Wendt (1993).

The External Environment

Another critical element of the prelaunch phase is for the CEO and other top leaders in the organization to monitor and gather as much information about their organization's external environment as possible. This includes information such as changing customer needs, changing technology in one's industry, changing government regulations, what competitors are up to, and what is occurring in the general economy both domestically and worldwide. And according to strategy guru Michael Porter (1985), it also includes understanding the bargaining power of customers, suppliers, and unions, and threats of (1) new entrants into the marketplace and (2) substitute products or services. The CEO and his or her team must then determine how to respond to what the environment is telling them and how to establish a more effective alignment for their organization.

This prelaunch activity conforms, of course, to (1) the reality that for their survival, organizations are dependent on their external environment and (2) the theoretical principles of open-system theory. Moreover, organization change occurs primarily as a reaction to some change in the environment. Rarely, if ever, do board members, CEOs, and their executive colleagues sit around a boardroom table together and decide to change the organization without regard to the organization's position in or degree of alignment within its external environment. Reading that environment accurately and reacting accordingly is indispensable.

Several decades ago, in their classic paper on the causal texture of organizational environments, Emery and Trist (1965) discussed four kinds of environment for organizations:

1. Placid, randomized

2. Placid, clustered

3. Disturbed, reactive

4. Turbulent fields

They stated that the world seemed to be moving more toward the turbulent type. They were quite correct, of course; today, most organizational environments are turbulent. Their point further stressed the importance of reading the environment as accurately as possible so that timely and appropriate organizational responses could be made to ensure survival.

The CEO–change leader's responsibility here is to prepare for organization change as thoroughly as possible, by taking the time and expending the effort to gather environmental information carefully and accurately and then to analyze this information before jumping into the change process too quickly. Impulsive behavior by the CEO at this stage of the change process is to be avoided, if not at all other stages as well.

Establishing the Need for Change

If people in the organization see or feel no need for change, they are not likely to embrace the idea. CEOs and other senior executives are often in a better position to monitor the external environment and therefore are likely to see the need for change sooner and more clearly than the majority of organizational members. They are often in a better position, but not always. Technical people down in the organization may see a technological change coming before senior management does. Often, the sales force and others in the organization who have direct contact with customers see a need to serve them differently before senior management does. Regardless of where the awareness of a need for change originates, it remains the CEO's responsibility to communicate that need to organizational members. And the communication must be convincing. An example helps to clarify these points.

British Aerospace (BAe), a multibillion-dollar aircraft and defense industry enterprise, was formed in 1977 by putting together six defense and aerospace organizations under one corporate roof. The firm at that time was a government-owned company, but two years later, Prime Minister Margaret Thatcher declared that BAe would become a private, stock-owned corporation, as she later did with British Airways and other nationalized industries during the 1980s. BAe was Thatcher's first nationalized company to become privatized. In a sense, BAe was a holding company with six previously autonomous organizations, which had rich histories dating back to World War II and before and possessed quite different corporate cultures. Richard Evans (now Sir Richard), having grown up in one of the six firms of the British aircraft corporation, became CEO on New Year's Day, 1990. He inherited six baronies, each of which viewed itself with considerable pride. After all, "that beautiful bird," as Evans called the Concorde, came from the earlier parts of BAe, as did other highly regarded aircraft (e.g., the Comet, the world's first commercial jet) and sophisticated defense weaponry. Also, by 1990, BAe had a number of joint ventures with French and German companies in the manufacture of the Airbus commercial aircraft. So, Evans took over a healthy organization from the standpoint of sales, profit, and future customer orders.

One year later, however, things were considerably worse. The stock price had plummeted, orders were down (after all, the cold war was over), and capital, especially cash, was badly needed. Evans began to cut costs—he laid off thousands of employees, for example—to divest of some of the businesses, and to take severe write-offs. But productivity and innovation remained strong, at least in most of the former six companies, and there were many talented people in the ranks. But for some reason, these strengths could not be fully realized.

Monitoring BAe's external environment, Evans saw three large "blips on the radar," as he called them. One came from Boeing, a major competitor. They produced a new version of their 737 that was superior to the Airbus, at least at that time. A second blip was the fact that the capacity of European aerospace and defense firms far exceeded demand. And finally, there was the abysmal performance of BAe's shares on the stock market.

These "blips" caused Evans to act yet again; he believed this time that a significant change needed to occur within the company to respond effectively. There were other needs for change as well, for example, correcting the silo effect of the six baronies that made up BAe. Evans believed that a major culture change was the right action to take. To use Gersick's (1991) language, change in the "deep structure" of BAe was in order. To use Evans's words (Evans & Price, 1999):

> Why did I think that a culture change was the answer? There were of course many operating and strategic fixes that we could do (and did) to improve our competitive standing and our share price. But when you added all these up, and when you looked at the competitive abilities of rivals, there was a shortfall. I couldn't quantify it. I simply had a gut feeling, a conviction that the underlying reason for our deficiencies lay in the culture of the company. (p. 10)

The new culture desired was one that would integrate the various businesses so that, for example, consistent, common approaches could be taken across the corporation. Another change objective was to lessen the rivalries that existed among the former six companies.

So, relying on the wisdom and experience of his new nonexecutive chairman of the board, Bob Bauman, who knew a thing or two about large-scale organization change (recall that he had led the merger of SmithKline Beecham a few years earlier), and the expertise of external consultants, Evans launched the change effort. Working with his top 100 or so executives, Evans's initial work was on crafting a new mission statement with an appropriate list of corporate values. This early work went fairly well, but some of the executives were simply not convinced that all this effort and the occasional angst were worth it. Many of them had been through "culture change" before. Again, to quote Evans (Evans & Price, 1999):

> In the eyes of many of BAe's top managers, the lack of a "burning platform" weakened my argument that change was urgently needed. How could I make them see that the present good times were not symptomatic of the way things would be five years hence? The easier way was to present them with scenarios of likely futures. For this job I turned to one of our top line executives, John Weston, then managing director of Military Aircraft, now my successor as Chief Executive. I seconded him from his regular duties and gave

him carte blanche to analyze the company from end to end and then report his findings.

With characteristic thoroughness, John documented "The Case for Change." His report probed every single part of the business, its macroeconomic environment, its competitive structure, the state of technology, and so forth. Time and again he documented a stark conclusion: Our business units' rate of progress and future prospects of performance gains were inadequate, given the emergent threats in the external environment. What's more, even if we took a whip to them to urge them to improve sales and profits and squeeze the cash flow, any conceivable improvement would not change the analysis substantially. At the end of the day, BAe would be trailing and not setting the industry tempo.

Because John Weston was the divisional head of our largest and most profitable business unit, his call to action could not easily be dismissed. If he saw the writing on the wall, so might everyone else. "We wanted to give them the macroeconomic and geopolitical picture right between the eyes. The paradigm for defence and aerospace markets was changing dramatically, and we had to learn superior skills and ways of reacting," says Weston. (p. 17)

The case was indeed made and the culture change at BAe went forth. The rest is history. Later, BAe became quite successful, its stock price more than triple what it had been in 1993. One of its major products, the Airbus, became a formidable competitor with Boeing. Moreover, Evans was knighted in 1996 for his role as CEO in the turnaround of BAe. For the full story of how a CEO may make the case for change and other aspects of successful organization change, see Evans and Price (1999) and Chapter 9 in Burke and Trahant (2000).

Providing Clarity of Vision and Direction

The final point of the prelaunch phase is to craft a vision statement and, in so doing, to provide clear direction for the organization change effort. One of the best statements about vision has been articulated by James O'Toole (1999):

A robust vision mobilizes appropriate behavior. It uses memorable, simple concepts that make clear what needs to be different about tomorrow. It describes the distinctive competencies needed to deliver on the desired end state (for example, "Here's what we have to do differently in order to succeed"). Often, a vision will make choices clear by making the case for change as either an opportunity or a burning platform (for example, "If we don't change in this way, the company won't survive"). That's not asking much, is it?

Leaders don't even have to create visions themselves (although many do). But, at a minimum, they must initiate a process for developing a vision and then engage themselves fully in generating buy-in. Shared commitment to a vision can be built either through wide-scale participation in the act of its creation or through involvement immediately thereafter in its dissemination. . . . We're not talking quantum mechanics here. This is simple stuff—so simple that many leaders gloss over the basics. For example, by definition, vision has to do with "seeing, sight, and sensing with the eyes." Recognizing that simple fact, effective leaders make their visions, well, visual. Remember Ronald Reagan's budget message when he explained that a trillion bucks amounts to a stack of dough as high as the Empire State building? By using that visual reference, he got Americans to see that federal spending amounts to real money! In doing so, he changed the terms of the national debate and, for the first time, created a majority in support of lower taxes. It was his most effective moment as a leader. (pp. 302–303)

Perhaps the paramount vision statement was delivered by Martin Luther King Jr. in his "I have a dream" speech on the steps of the Lincoln Memorial. He used striking imagery, for example, of children holding hands, that his listeners could "see." The following are short examples of vision and direction provided by change leaders who have been referenced already:

- At the time of the SmithKline Beecham merger, chairman of the board Henry Wendt's (1993) conceptualization of what a truly global corporation looks like and his and CEO Bob Bauman's crafting of "The Promise" (the merged company's mission statement) provided both the vision and the mission for the future. Their clarity of direction was critical to the success of the change that was, at the time, the largest cross-border merger ever. For the full story, see Bauman et al. (1997), Burke (2000b), and Chapter 4 in Burke and Trahant (2000).

- At British Airways, it was Colin Marshall's clear emphasis on what the new culture should be—one that was customer focused and market driven—that provided the necessary vision for what needed to be reached.
- Dime Bancorp (see Chapter 5) was the newly crafted mission statement.
- At British Aerospace, it was Dick Evans's resolve to see that a mission and vision statement was crafted by the top 100 executives that set the stage for organization change. As O'Toole (1999) noted, the CEO may not write the vision and mission statement himself or herself, but the responsibility for seeing that the job is done is clearly the CEO's. The way Evans did it took time, to be sure, but "at the end of the day," as the British are fond of saying, he had commitment.

By way of a quick summary, recall that in the description of the Burke–Litwin model in Chapter 10, a distinction was made between mission and vision, with vision being associated more with the leadership box or model category. But it is the change leader's or CEO's responsibility to see that both mission and vision are crafted, because both set the tone and the clarity of direction. Without direction, both in terms of who we are and who we want to be in the future, desired organization change will not occur.

The Launch Phase

Communicating the Need

Usually, the CEO is the one who delivers the message about the need for change—but not always. In the BAe example, Dick Evans called on his number two person, John Weston, to deliver the case for change. He made this decision for at least two reasons. First, he had already launched the organization change by involving the top 100 executives in the crafting of a new corporate mission statement and in making the choices of values for the corporation as a whole. Although these executives did the work he asked them to, Evans was not convinced that their hearts were in it. And besides, some of them seriously questioned the whole process. In other words, Evans wasn't certain that his credibility as the change leader was as solid as it needed to be. Moreover, some of his executives had been through culture change in their respective businesses and were not exactly sanguine about going through the whole process again unless there was a compelling reason to do so.

Second, in making the case for change and communicating the message, Evans believed that Weston would have more credibility because, unlike Evans, who came from marketing and sales, he was an engineer and a "numbers guy," as were many of the BAe executives. It would be abundantly clear that Weston had done his homework and knew what he was talking about. This decision by Evans did indeed work, and the buy-in for the organization change began to emerge. The point is that although the CEO does not necessarily have to be the message deliverer, seeing that the delivery occurs, especially by another change-leader colleague, is nevertheless his or her responsibility.

In the British Airways case, it was Colin Marshall, the CEO, who delivered the message. In fact, he delivered it again and again, making certain that he came across as consistent with the message each time he gave it and that he was absolutely serious and committed.

Initial Activities

A significant activity to conduct at the outset of organization change is an event that will capture attention, provide focus, and create the reality that the change effort now launched is not merely an exercise. A quote from Marshall, of British Airways, gives first his rationale and then an example of an initial activity (Burke & Trahant, 2000):

> But to get people to work in new ways, we needed a major change in the company's culture. That meant refocusing everyone on the customer, on the marketplace, and away from the exclusively engineering and operations focus we'd had. That had to be done, of course, without sacrificing safety, technical, or maintenance standards. And that proved tricky. People had difficulty understanding why I kept hammering away at the need to focus on customers while also saying, "We've got to fly these aircraft at a very high technical standard, too." The focus before had always been on the technical side alone, but I made the point repeatedly that we had to do both. It was at this point that we saw the explicit need for a culture-change program. ... The first thing we did was to launch a program called "Putting People First" ... a two-day seminar. We took roughly 150 employees at a time and drew people from various departments

within BA and from various geographical areas. The program focused on how one creates better relationships with people, with one's fellow employees, with customers, even with members of one's own family. (p. 95)

Another example comes from a venerable British organization, the BBC. John Birt, the CEO ("director general" is the proper title), authorized a one-day workshop on "Extending Choice," the new mission and vision for the corporation. The day was devoted to, first, an overview and explanation of extending choice, and second, to small-group meetings so that questions could be raised and discussions could be held about how this new "extended" mission affected each of them in their respective roles.

At BAe, the initial activity, as noted, was the off-site meetings of the top 100 executives to craft the corporate mission statement and to choose the values.

At SmithKline Beecham, the initial activity to help shape the newly merged culture for the CEO, Bob Bauman, and the 10 executives directly reporting to him was working on the mission and value decisions and team building. The team building at the top had two purposes: to get this top group to work together more effectively and, what was perhaps more important, to serve as role models for the rest of the global corporation. Part of the team-building process was (1) use of the MBTI to help the executives learn about their own and their colleagues' communicating, information processing, and decision-making preferences and (2) participation in a multirater feedback process on leadership practices to obtain a clearer understanding of how their self-perceptions of their leadership compared with the perceptions of others, particularly peers and those directly reporting to them. Subsequently, both the MBTI and the multirater feedback process permeated the entire managerial population of the company.

Finally, at Dime Bancorp, the initial activities that launched the organization change (a result of a merger; see Chapter 5) consisted of (1) establishing a task force of 15 people who represented all business units and all levels in the hierarchy to draft a new corporate mission statement, (2) determining a new business strategy led by the CEO, and (3) team building for the newly formed top team.

It should be obvious from these examples that the early activity of organization change can take a variety of forms. The point is that a focused symbolic and energizing event (or multiple events occurring at about the same time) is a highly useful way of launching large-scale and planned organization change.

Dealing With Resistance

Recall that in Chapter 6, organization change was considered at three levels: individual, group, and the larger system, and the nature of resistance to change at each of these levels was discussed. The prudent change leader will be well aware of the nature of resistance to change and the forms that resistance behavior can take at each organizational level. Recall further that at the individual level, it is important that the change leader be wary of imposing change on people and find ways for organizational members to have choice and be as involved in the process as possible. Also, the change leader needs to differentiate among the various types of resistance—blind, ideological, and political—so as to respond to and interact with people in the organization appropriately.

At the group level, recall that protecting one's turf, closing ranks, and demanding a new structure or leadership can be common forms of resistance. Seeing to it that activities in a group setting to achieve closure with the past (for example, having a symbolic funeral) can help in dealing with resistance. Also, recomposing a group with new membership can help and, of course, so can any activity that involves people in key decision making. For example, a highly influential group early in the merger process of SmithKline Beecham was the "merger management committee." Selected by the CEO, this group had the responsibility of selecting who the executives would be for the key positions in the corporation, and the rule instituted by Bauman, the CEO, that no member of the committee could be named for any of these executive jobs was unique. Objectivity was therefore more assured in the decisions of who was selected. Even though none of these committee members could have any of the plum positions they were working with, they were highly motivated and strongly committed to the task. After all, they were involved in an activity that would have far-reaching effects on the corporation. A delayed reward for these members was Bauman's making certain that they were eventually placed in important roles and positions for the corporation. The purpose of this brief case was to provide an example of how to involve people in the change process.

At the larger-system level, recall that resistance can take the forms of "This too shall pass"; that is, "We've seen this kind of initiative, or fad, before and it won't last this time, either." Also, there are diversionary tactics, for example, "Other mainstream business needs are far more important than this change thing." It was suggested earlier that coping with these forms of resistance might involve making a strong, compelling case for the change (as in the BAe example) and exerting strong leadership—not in a dictatorial way but leading with persistence and with clarity of direction, passion, and vision, a point to be emphasized in the next section.

Postlaunch: Further Implementation

Once the organization change has been launched, it becomes quickly apparent to the change leader that so-called change management is an oxymoron. This particular phase of organization change—postlaunch—is difficult for many CEOs. After all, they typically have control needs that are considerably above average, and now matters seem out of control. CEOs can easily experience feelings of (1) anxiety ("What have we unleashed here?") and (2) ambivalence in decision making; some organizational members feel the excitement of change unleashed and want to run free, whereas others are asking for the CEO to step in and exercise control, usually taking the form of a cry for structure ("What's my new job?" "Who will be my boss?"). When control needs are aroused by such pleas for structure, many CEOs will want to step in and establish the new order. Because followers are asking for an antidote for all this uncertainty, the advice of Ronald Heifetz (1994) is most appropriate. In essence, he suggested three actions. First, to hold the collective feet to the fire, that is, to be persistent about what it is going to take to make the change successful (e.g., living with ambiguity about exactly how everything is going to work out). Second, draw the system out of its comfort zone but attempt to contain the associated stress so that it does not become dysfunctional (recall the work of Bridges, 1986; see Chapter 6). Third, deal with avoidance mechanisms that usually emerge during this time, such as blaming, scapegoating, and appealing to authority figures for answers.

During the postlaunch phase, it may also seem to the change leader that the process has taken on a life of its own. In fact, theory associated with living systems holds that when disturbance occurs (the launch phase), "the components of living systems self-organize and new forms and repertoires emerge from the turmoil" (Pascale, Milleman, & Gioja, 2000, p. 6) The CEO–change agent must persevere but be patient at the same time so that creativity and innovation "can do their work" or "magic," as some might call it, and allow for new forms to emerge. New forms may mean any number of things, including new ways of doing work; different values; new structures, new products, services, or business lines; getting into, if not establishing, new markets; acquiring a business never considered before; and so on.

Some more specific actions need to be considered for this postlaunch change implementation phase as the change leader begins to deal with (1) his or her feelings of both excitement and anxiety, (2) follower behaviors of all varieties, and (3) seeming disorder. Though not exhaustive, the following five points are some key actions change leaders need to bear in mind.

Multiple Leverage

In large organizations particularly, change is too complicated for one action (intervention) to do the job. Many managers believe, for example, that changing the organizational structure will suffice. In a study of organization change some years ago, failure was most often associated with change of structure when that was essentially all that occurred (Burke, Clark, & Koopman, 1984). Moreover, in recent coverage of seven case studies of successful organization change, two of the summary points that are relevant here were as follows (Burke, 2000a):

- Time and again, these cases illustrate the absolute necessity of strong leadership for change to occur. We see change leaders in living color here. There is no substitute for visionary leadership in times of change. By definition, if there is leadership, there are followers.
- In addition to demonstrating how the phases of organization change work, all these cases show the deployment of multiple interventions. True organization change is too complicated for one intervention. Multiple sources of influence are required. (pp. 9–10)

Examples of levers for change from these case studies included process reengineering, crafting mission statements, developing a new process of supply-chain management, training and development, crafting corporate values and leadership behaviors that were manifestations of the values, implementing a new pay-for-performance system, developing a "safety" culture, changing a plant in a chemical company, team building, and establishing self-directed work groups.

Taking the Heat

When organization change is launched, it is safe to say that not everyone will be happy with the idea. In fact, some may be quite upset and angry, looking for a target, a person or a group to blame "for this mess we're about to get ourselves into." The change leader is the most obvious target. Recently, a college president, who had launched an organizational change five years earlier, sat through two meetings with full professors, listening to—and absorbing—their wrath about how poorly the change had been led and why it was such a stupid idea in the first place.

Dick Evans, of BAe, described one of his heat-receiving episodes this way (Burke & Trahant, 2000):

> But I got a lot of pushback from people. People asked, "Why do we need to do this? We're operating perfectly well. We all have big change programs to deal with in our own businesses. Why do we need to do all this other stuff?" Many seriously thought and believed that I had some sort of hidden agenda and simply wanted to be told what to do so they could go away and do it. (p. 146)

Pushback, as Evans and Price (1999) described it, is to be expected—not from everyone, perhaps only a minority, but heat is generated nevertheless, especially if those who are pushing back are opinion leaders in the organization. These are the times when the change leader must use as much self-control as she or he can muster, working hard (1) to listen, (2) not to be defensive, and (3) to display the patience of Job.

Consistency

During the early days of change, the change leader's behavior is scrutinized by followers. Does the change leader really mean it? Is this for real? Or is this initiative like all the rest, just another fad that will soon pass? In a recent change at a large nonprofit organization, the most frequently asked question by followers in the hallways or at lunch has been "Does he (the change leader) really mean it?" This is, of course, a question about consistency and about perseverance (see the next section). The point here is about trust. Can we (followers) trust the leader? Trusting the leader, of course, means believing that he or she is open and honest and tells the truth.

Behaviorally, what may be even more important to followers is the extent to which the leader's behavior matches her or his words. This is the essence of consistency in an organization change effort—despite Ralph Waldo Emerson's derogatory comment about consistency, to wit, "A foolish consistency is the hobgoblin of little minds adored by little statesmen and philosophers and divines." The key to this quote, however, is Emerson's adjective *foolish*, and consistency of word and deed by the change leader in the organization's change process is anything but foolish.

Perseverance

"Staying the course" is essentially what is meant by this term. Many potential change leaders falter when the going gets tough. A whimsical but illustrative comparison is that organization change is like losing weight. The first 5 or 10 pounds are easy, but the next 5 or 10 are much, much tougher. The early days of organization change, compared with later, are easy. People are excited and say things like "Finally, things are going to get better around here." But a year later, the change effort may have bogged down, the excitement is gone, and fatigue has set in. This is time for considerable perseverance on the part of the change leader. Perhaps the master of perseverance was Colin Marshall, at British Airways. Here's a perfect example, in his own words (Burke & Trahant, 2000):

> I made a particular point of attending every one of these "Managing People First" sessions. I spent two to three hours with each group. I talked with people about our goals, our thoughts for the future. I got people's input about what we needed to do to improve our services and operations. The whole thing proved to be a very useful and productive dialogue. We found it so valuable, in fact, that in cases when I was away, we offered people the opportunity to come back and have a follow-up session with me. So I really did talk to all 110 groups in that five-year period. (p. 99)

A part of leadership in an organization change effort, then, is to stay the course, to continue to encourage people, to exude energy and enthusiasm for continuing down the change path, and to find ways to continue communicating the message.

Repeating the Message

First, what is it that you repeat? The message is the vision and mission, but to be most effective, a story needs to be told that incorporates the vision and mission and values. The work of Howard Gardner (1995), summarized in the previous chapter, is decidedly helpful in this regard. He deliberately uses the term *story* or *narrative* instead of *message* or *theme* because, as he states, he wants to accomplish the following:

> To call attention to the fact that leaders present a dynamic perspective to their followers: not just a headline or snapshot, but a drama that unfolds over time, in which they—leaders and followers—are the principal characters or heroes. Together they embarked on a journey in pursuit of certain goals, and along the way and into the future, they can expect to encounter certain obstacles or resistances that must be overcome. . . . The most basic story has to do with issues of identity. And so it is the leader who succeeds in conveying a new version of a given group's story who is likely to be effective. Effectiveness here involves fit—the story needs to make sense to audience members at this particular historical moment, in terms of where they have been and where they would like to go. (p. 14)

The change leader tells the story time and again, because people need to be reminded of what it is that we are doing—and why. In addition to the reminding, it is critical that the change leader tell the story to followers in person, face-to-face, not over the web, in a video, on a written document, or on a CD-ROM. Why? Dialogue with followers is essential. Questions need to be answered or at least responded to, and nuances may need elaboration. In the SmithKline Beecham merger, Henry Wendt, the chairman, and Bob Bauman, the CEO, traveled all over the world meeting with employees face to face to tell their story, which was the SmithKline Beecham "Promise": the company's promises to customers, employees, and stockholders.

Another example of a change leader telling the story personally, face to face, to 5,000 people, is the case of Roger Goldman, who turned around a retail banking situation that was not only in the red, but overall moribund in its performance. In his words (Burke & Trahant, 2000):

> I went on the road for a year to explain my vision of the bank to over 5,000 people in 800 profit centers and support offices. I did this to get people's support and to explain what we needed them to do if we

were to be successful. In our case, it was about serving customers, communities, and our fellow employees. "Everyone has to give 110 percent," I told employees. "We're going to reinvent people's jobs and hold everybody more accountable for results." (p. 193)

By way of summary, consider the wonderful children's television show, *Blue's Clues*. The same episode is repeated four times after the initial presentation on Monday of each week. The creators of this program have discovered that for the 4- or 5-year-old, repetition is critical for the child's learning. By Friday, the child "gets it." To learn something, adults in organizations may not need four iterations. Actually, they may need more! The point is this: Organization change with all its complexities and nuances needs to have focus, proper emphases on priorities, and explanation, particularly of "why we are doing these highly disruptive activities." Repeating this story time and again (message/vision/mission) is one of the most important functions of the change leaders.

Finally, we shall conclude this section on further implementation, the postlaunch phase, with a cautionary note from Dick Evans, CEO of BAe (Evans & Price, 1999):

> One danger that besets change programmes is the curse of superficiality, or too much faith in the power of positive thinking. One day top management says, "Let's have a change programme." And after cranking out mission and vision statements, backed with a heavy communications programme, hey presto, they've done it. What are omitted from these narratives are the tensions, ambiguities, conflicts, and frustrations that inevitably arise in the implementation phase. These difficulties get swept under the rug, only to return later—most likely in a more virulent form. (p. 16)

To mitigate the danger that Evans emphasizes, change leaders need to use multiple levers for the transformation, take the heat from followers from time to time, provide consistency in terms of words and deeds, persevere even to the point of risking being called stubborn, and repeat the message again and again.

Sustaining the Change

Before considering thoughts about sustaining organization change once things are fully launched and under way (such as unanticipated consequences, momentum, and further new initiatives), let us examine some recent thinking that is highly relevant and applicable. Earlier, in the section "Postlaunch: Further Implementation," a short quote was cited from the book by Pascale et al. (2000). The overall premise of the book is that recent knowledge, particularly in the life sciences, can inform our understanding of organizations in general, and management, leadership, and organization change in particular. Their premise is quite similar to the reasoning underlying the present book. Pascale et al. made the point that so-called chaos theory is not applicable to organizations, for they are not chaotic. But organizations are complex, that is, complex adaptive systems, and what they label as "the new science of complexity" is the applicable theory. These ideas are congruent with nonlinear complex system theory discussed in Chapter 7, Svyantek and Brown (2000); Gersick's (1991) concept of deep structure; and Capra's (1996) ideas covered in Chapter 4 of this book. Pascale and his colleagues have distilled from complexity theory and the life sciences (biology, medicine, and ecology) "four bedrock principles" (p. 6) that they consider to be applicable to organizations, especially business enterprises. These principles are as follows:

1. *Equilibrium* is a precursor to death. When a living system is in a state of equilibrium, it is less responsive to changes occurring around it. This places it at maximum risk.

2. In the face of threat, or when galvanized by a compelling opportunity, living things move toward the *edge of chaos*. This condition evokes higher levels of mutation and experimentation, and fresh new solutions are more likely to be found.

3. When this excitation takes place, the components of living systems *self-organize*, and new forms and repertoires emerge from the turmoil [referred to earlier].

4. Living systems cannot be *directed* along a linear path. Unforeseen consequences are inevitable. The challenge is to *disturb* them in a manner that approximates the desired outcome. (Pascale et al., 2000, p. 6)

These principles are useful for our thinking about the importance of sustaining an organization change effort. This thinking is organized according to four considerations: unanticipated consequences, momentum, choosing successors, and launching yet again new initiatives.

Unanticipated Consequences

Referred to earlier in this chapter and in Chapter 2 was the paradox of planning organization change in a linear, phased way of thinking, yet realizing that the change process itself is not linear. This means that when the change is launched, equilibrium is disturbed, and seeming chaos occurs; that is, many different reactions to the disturbance happen simultaneously, and the system moves to the edge of chaos, as Pascale et al. (2000) put it. Some examples of this kind of reaction include the following: (1) different organizational units interpret the change vision and direction to fit their needs, and therefore, the implementing of their part of the change becomes different from that of all other units (this is not necessarily bad but is often unanticipated); (2) some people who were expected to resist actually embrace and become champions of the change—and vice versa; and (3) desired and expected outcomes for a part of the overall change effort simply do not occur. The scary part is going to the edge, but the main point to remember here is that living systems are quite capable of evoking new forms and solutions and of self-organizing with gradual movement (however, not linear) to a new state of equilibrium. Reaching a new state of equilibrium is essentially what Lewin (1947) meant with his third stage of organization change, refreeze (see Chapter 8). Also recall Weick and Quinn's (1999) reconceptualizing of Lewin's three-stage model calling for unfreezing after a rebalancing to ensure innovation and finding new ways of ensuring continuous change, which is applicable to our thinking here (see Chapter 7). The point is that after a disturbance, living systems again seek equilibrium, and Pascale et al. warned that equilibrium "is a precursor to death." The important word in their phrase is precursor, which means that death is not necessarily immediate. There is some allowable, if not necessary, time for things to resettle after the disturbance. But for the organization change to maintain momentum, resettlement must not be allowed to last.

Momentum

Writing in 1991 about the successful change effort at British Airways, Goodstein and Burke stated:

It may be that BA's biggest problem now is not so much to manage further change as it is to manage the change that has already occurred. In other words, the people of BA have achieved significant change and success; now they must maintain what has been achieved while concentrating on continuing to be adaptable to changes in their external environment—the further deregulation of Europe, for example. Managing momentum may be more difficult than managing change. (p. 16)

A few years later, BA's performance began to deteriorate in part from the lack of maintaining sufficient momentum and in part because of Colin Marshall's successor—choosing successors being the subject of the following section.

Maintaining the change momentum is critical because the natural movement toward equilibrium has to be countered. Finding new ways to recognize and reward change champions in the organization and celebrating achievements clearly helps to maintain momentum. The broader principles, however, are as follows: To counter equilibrium, Pascale et al. (2000) state rather provocatively that two forces—the threat of death and the promise of sex—can prevail. The desire to survive is powerful. If you question this, think how difficult it is to end a committee in your organization that was supposed to be ad hoc. Darwinian principles suggest that living systems do not evolve on their own but change as they respond to forces in the external environment. Living systems that survive do so because they mutate; that is, they adapt to the changing forces in their respective environments.

To maintain momentum, then, the change leader must constantly monitor the organization's external environment, being alert to changing forces that require adaptation to ensure survival.

The "promise of sex" leads us to the third ingredient for sustaining the change effort.

Choosing Successors

Another form for countering equilibrium is to prevent homogeneity, according to Pascale et al. (2000):

Sexual reproduction maximizes diversity. Chromosome combinations are randomly matched in variant pairings, thereby generating more permutations and variety in offspring. [This] benefits a living system [because] harmful [bacteria] find it harder to breach the diverse defenses of a population generated by sexual reproduction than the relatively uniform defenses affected [by a process such as mitosis or cloning]. (p. 29)

This principle from the science of living systems suggests that change leaders would do well to counter equilibrium and sustain the change effort by infusing "new blood" into their organizations, that is, not cloning themselves. The point is that although a complete overhaul of the people involved in the change would be absurd, having some proportion (20%? 30%?) who are new to the effort (hired from the outside or shifted over from other parts of the organization) counteracts the support equilibrium such as tired thinking, solidified norms, and "group-think."

One of the reasons that Colin Marshall's successor at British Airways, Robert Ayling, did not succeed as CEO was that he had been with the organization for a long time and was peripheral to the change effort that had proceeded under Marshall's leadership. In other words, Ayling was not one of the change leaders and had remained tied to the old system. Examples of effective succession include the one at BAe from Evans to Weston and the more recent change at GE from Welch to Immelt.

Much has been written about problems of succession and infusing new thinking into an organization. For an overview of some of the central issues, see Levinson (1994).

Launching Yet Again New Initiatives

Finally, it is critical to identify and implement new initiatives that will renew organizational members' energy, spark new ways of thinking, and continue to propel the organization farther down its path of change after some unspecified time into the change effort. These new initiatives, of course, need to be in line with the original change objectives, provided the external environment is not signaling to the organization that something more drastic needs to happen to ensure survival.

Examples of new initiatives in the service of sustaining the overall change effort might be the following:

- Acquiring another organization or business
- Creating a new business line or new product, or both
- Establishing a strategic alliance or joint venture with another organization (which might even be a competitor or former competitor)
- Starting a new program that will help to improve quality and reduce costs

- Deploying current products and services into markets not yet pene-trated; for example, a chemical, metal, or ceramic product that has been sold and marketed only to other businesses can now be consid-ered as a product sold directly to an individual customer

The important point is for the change leader to be clear and deliberate about disturbing the system with new initiatives so that equilibrium does not take over. Incidentally, it is imperative for the change leader to cause these disturbances even if the organizational members plead for the change to come to some end point or conclusion. Conclusion needs to occur only for specific initiatives, not for the overall change process.

Summary

To specify what leaders actually do and what they need to do as change leaders, contrasts and comparisons were made between leadership and management, and power and authority. Leadership was considered in terms of transformational (more related to organization change that is discontinuous) and transactional (more associated with continuous change).

An additional refinement of what was being considered as leadership in the previous chapter addressed the distinction of organizational levels, the point being that the executive was our primary focus. For this emphasis, the work of Zaccaro (2001) was particularly helpful. In his survey of the literature, he delineated four different yet overlapping conceptual perspectives about executive leadership: (1) conceptual complexity, having to deal with ever more complex and changing environments; (2) behavioral complexity, the leader's multiple roles in dealing with multiple constituencies; (3) strategic decision making, stressing the importance of congruence between the organi-zation and its environment; and (4) visionary-inspirational, emphasizing the charismatic, transformational, and visionary aspects of leadership. The point was made that what is required to be an effective change leader is highly com-plex and demanding; therefore, all four of these perspectives are relevant.

In this chapter the leader's role and function in organization change was specified according to four primary phases:

1. The prelaunch phase
   - Leader self-examination
   - Gathering information from the external environment
   - Establishing a need for change
   - Providing clarity of vision and direction

2. The launch phase

   - Communicating the need for change
   - Initiating key activities
   - Dealing with resistance

3. Postlaunch phase or further implementation

   - Multiple leverage
   - Taking the heat
   - Consistency
   - Perseverance
   - Repeating the message

4. Sustaining the change

   - Dealing with unanticipated consequences
   - Momentum
   - Choosing successors
   - Launching yet again new initiatives

It should be clear by now that we have attempted to address a great many interesting and complex ideas and practices about organization change. Recall Figure 2.1 that was an attempt to represent some of these complexities with the fall-back loops symbolizing unanticipated consequences that must be addressed and corrected for the overall change effort to keep moving forward.

Perhaps it is also clear that with respect to leading organization change, this chapter has emphasized application and practice more than theory and research. Recall that in introducing the large section "Phases of Organization Change and the Leader's Role," the point was made that these ideas came from theoretical concepts, for example, Lewin's (1947) three steps of unfreeze, change, and refreeze, which have been expanded by others from consulting experience, and that caveats would not be presented. Now, to a couple of caveats.

One reason for the greater emphasis on practice was to stay with the earlier promise that the latter half of this book would stress practice more than theory. A second reason for the practice emphasis is the fact that theory and research about leading organization change is rather sparse. This is why, for example, Zaccaro's (2001) recent book was described as helpful. So, if this chapter sparks some ideas for further research and theory development, I will be delighted.

FIFTEEN

Organization Change

Summary and Integration

In this chapter, the purposes are to (a) do a bit of summarizing and integrating; (b) consider some successful processes of organization change, also as a way of summarizing and integrating, that O'Toole (1995) has accumulated; and (c) take a closer look at what we are attempting to accomplish when launching an organization change effort by summarizing the work of Lawler and Worley (2006) on how to build an organization for change not merely for survival. In the next and final chapter, we will address the future not in a predictive way but instead to make suggestions for what we need to pursue to enhance our knowledge about organization change—that is, some things we still need to know and address.

To begin our summarizing and integrating, let us consider Gladwell's (2000) book, *The Tipping Point*, which has some key principles that we can apply to planned organization change.

Applying *The Tipping Point* Principles to Planned Organization Change

The ideas in Gladwell's (2000) book suggest ways of understanding (a) organization change more thoroughly, for example, his concept of contagiousness and the fact that small events or activities can have large consequences, and (b) ways of planning the process—that is, how to spread a "virus" and cause an epidemic. In short, we must find *the few* that help us (connectors), make certain that our change message (vision, directions, goals) sticks, and find ways to change the context so that our message becomes a reality and our goals become attainable. At the same time, we need to bear in mind, of course, other principles of organization change that we have addressed already, such as open-system theory, causing disequilibrium, dealing with resistance and with unanticipated consequences, and ways of sustaining the change process.

Following our phase framework from the previous chapter—prelaunch, launch, postlaunch, and sustaining the change—we will now apply Gladwell's (2000) ideas and principles to planned organization change.

Prelaunch

Determining the message, or the virus or epidemic, that we want to spread is the first step. This, of course, is our content (see Chapter 8); it's the vision, providing clarity in the organization change purpose and direction. We want to make the message stick, so it is cast in the form of *a story* that can easily be remembered. We also want to consider a variety of ways to communicate the story—that is, not rely on a singular form or medium.

Also, during the prelaunch phase, we search for our highly *important few*: connectors, mavens, and salesmen, those few who have social power, the ones who will be, according to Gladwell (2000), "responsible for starting word-of-mouth epidemics, which means that if you are interested in starting a word-of-mouth epidemic, your resources ought to be solely concentrated on those three groups" (p. 256).

The further point here is that the effort is on selection, or finding the *right few*, not so much on training them. Once they have the story straight and accept it, they will know what to do—that is, they will use their natural motives and abilities. Oreg (2003) made a similar point in a slightly different way. He demonstrated with his research on resistance to change that there are individual differences—some people simply tend to be resistant regardless and others are more likely to embrace change. Oreg's suggestion was to seek out this latter group, the *right few*, to help lead the change.

The Launch

For this phase, our connectors, mavens, salespeople, and those who support the change effort go forth to spread the message, or the story. Our connectors get people together for common tasks, such as helping to plan an initial event. Our mavens facilitate the transactive memories—that is, help people to learn what, where, and how they can be connected. Our salespeople help to persuade people that this change is indeed the right thing to do—that is, they communicate powerfully the need for change.

The launching of initial, key activities is essentially, in Gladwell's (2000) language, an effort to change the *context*. Recall that in the case of British Airways (BA) it was a one-day event—"Putting People First"—stressing that now their primary concerns were customers and the marketplace, with less emphasis on protocol, bureaucracy, and seniority. The Dime Bancorp launch was the formation of a task force of about 15 people to craft a mission statement for the newly merged organization. Also, recall that with respect to the size of these launch events, they included 100 or fewer people at a time, and an early stage of the Dime Bank change effort was to focus on the top 125 executives and managers. In other words, the size in all of these cases was not more than 150. See Dunbar (1992) and Wegner (1991) for the theoretical ideas and research that undergird the importance of this concept regarding size of units and groups.

Postlaunch

From previous coverage, remember that multiple leverage is critical—that is, one should not rely on a singular change intervention, such as a structural change, to do the job. Moreover, Gladwell's (2000) admonition is to do things that are not all that obvious, such as tinkering with the message to find ways to make it stick by communicating the story in multiple ways and determining which way(s) works best, at least for a particular period of time.

Repeating the message is imperative. Remember the lesson from *Blue's Clues:* Repetition, as well as a captivating story, made the message stick. Sir Colin Marshall, CEO and the change leader for BA over the five-year period I was involved in the change effort, must have repeated the story several hundred times.

And in dealing with resistance to the change effort, we relied heavily on our selected few—connectors, mavens, and salesmen—without necessarily telling them that their job is to overcome resistance. As stated earlier, they will know what to do.

Sustaining the Change

It may very well be that the most important ingredient in sustaining organization change is the process of dealing with unanticipated, unforeseen consequences of initiatives and interventions. This is especially true when launching the change process. Gladwell (2000) suggested that we proceed with our intuitions about new initiatives, but he also cautioned that when we act on them, we should get data quickly on the consequences and change to another approach as needed to keep the change going. A brief case should help illustrate this point.

Approximately 18 months into a major organization change at NatWest Bancorp from 1991 to 1996, the change leader, Roger Goldman, conducted an organizationwide employee opinion survey as one of the ways to monitor progress (for details on the survey, see Chapter 12 in Burke & Trahant, 2000). Using the Burke–Litwin model as the framework for structuring the questions and for analyzing the responses to the survey, the results showed that the transformational factors in the model—perceptions of the external environment, mission and strategy, leadership, and culture—were rated highly. Goldman and his executive team members were elated. A few moments later, when the remainder of the survey results were presented, their elation plummeted to depression and then to anger. Some of the transactional factors in the model showed low ratings, for example, a 2 on a 5-point Likert-type scale, particularly in the systems and motivation boxes. To put it in the vernacular, morale at the bank (as reflected in the motivation ratings) was "in the tank." This outcome was *not* anticipated. Goldman and his team were somewhat distraught and wondered what action to take.

The consultant presenting the survey results suggested that they further examine these outcomes by considering other categories of the model and how they related to the problem. He pointed out that two boxes of the model were pertinent here, one transformational and one transactional: the mission and strategy box and the task requirements and individual skills and abilities (job-person match) box. Recall that in the model, these two boxes are connected by a two-way arrow (see Figure 10.2 in Chapter 10). By referring to this link, the consultant argued that the fact that ratings in both of these categories were high should not be overlooked when further examining the survey results. In other words, it was likely that most employees saw a clear connection between what they were doing in their jobs and the bank's mission and strategy. In fact, statistical analysis of the results supported this argument. This linkage, it was further argued, would eventually influence motivation in a positive way, provided some other actions were taken. A key element contributing to the success of organization performance in general and organization change in particular is when people see how their day-to-day actions relate to and support the organization's mission and strategy. So, this part of the survey results was strong support for the ultimate success of the organization change effort.

The problem was actually within the *systems* box. Further examination showed that low ratings in this category were associated with information technology—out-of-date computer hardware and software that did not support the needs of the change goals and the new vision and mission of the bank. In other words, most employees did not feel that they had adequate technical support. In a manner of speaking, the employees were saying, "We understand and believe in the vision, mission, and strategy of the bank. We see how our jobs support this direction and these goals. We would very much like to 'get on with it.' But how can we do it with such outmoded technology? We cannot respond to customers in the ways desired, that is, with speed and accurate information. It is extremely frustrating!" Thus, morale was low.

Goldman and his colleagues then proceeded with a new initiative, which would take time and cost money, but updating the information technology aspect of the bank's work was now an imperative. After about another 18 months, a second, Time 2, survey was conducted. Although other problems had emerged, some unanticipated, of course, motivation and systems were rated higher than at Time 1.

Sustaining change means in large measure (a) to understand that many consequences of interventions cannot be anticipated, (b) to *not* allow these unforeseen outcomes to become barriers to the change effort, and (c) to take swift action with different initiatives and tactics to ensure momentum on new paths toward the change goals.

In summary, Gladwell's (2000) tipping-point principles do not address all aspects of organization change. That was not his intent. But these principles do help us to understand certain change phenomena more thoroughly. Also, Gladwell's book is explanatory in nature, not a recipe for planned organization change. How to apply his explanations has been our intent, at least in part, and how to think about planning organization change in new and different ways.

Changing the Organization

In an attempt to summarize and integrate, let us consider the key questions to raise and some of the critical tenets about organization change. Six major points are summarized as follows:

First, we must begin with the external environment. Actually, the more astute leaders constantly monitor the organization's environment. But are they asking the right questions, gathering the appropriate information, and seeking opinions and ideas from their primary constituents?

The critical questions are as follows:

- What are the customers telling us? How satisfied are they with the quality of our products and services, the timeliness of our delivery, and the degree to which we listen to them? Asking our customers questions and then listening to what they tell us is highly valuable for many reasons, the primary reason being what they may not be saying directly but only hinting at or alluding to. It is not as if our customers are trying to mislead us. It is more a matter of their not quite knowing what they may need, especially for the future. In other words, we must listen to their notions of what is next for them, where they're going, what they may need or want next year and the year after. For more about what customers value and the inherent difficulties in obtaining such information, see Goodstein and Butz (1998).
- What are the capital markets telling us? Recall from Chapter 2 how critically important this question is. If we are a publicly owned company, how is our stock price doing? Are large investors buying shares? What are analysts saying about us? How easy or difficult is it for us to raise money for activities such as acquisitions, invest in new technology, and expand certain business lines, particularly globally?
- If we are a nonprofit organization, the fundamental questions are related but somewhat different. The basic question concerns mission. How relevant is our mission today? After all, nonprofit organizations have customers, government regulators, and professional

audiences. Are we responding appropriately to our constituents? Do we listen sufficiently to those whom we serve?

- What about our competitors? Where do we rank in our industry vis-à-vis our competition? Do we have adequate information (in the military it would be called "intelligence") about what our competitors are doing—where they may be expanding, what their research and development (R&D) objectives are, or where they are investing (new business, new technology, new domains geographically, etc.)? Are they attempting to be low-cost providers, highly differentiated in the marketplace, or niche players?

- What about the people we attract, select, place, and retain in our organization? Do they see us as an attractive organization to join? Do they believe that they will be recognized and rewarded according to merit? Do they believe that they will have challenging work, be able to make a difference, learn and grow, have good colleagues to work with, and even enjoy what they will be doing?

And what about *technology*? Are we up to date, on the cutting edge, or falling behind? Do we even have the right technology? It may be that our products or services are so dated that we need to change to an entirely new technological base, for example, changing from metals to ceramics or from a physical science base to a bioscience base.

There are additional questions about the external environment that need to be raised, such as the possibility of changing government regulations, what is happening in the general economy, demographic shifts, relations with our key supplies and suppliers, social trends, organized labor trends, shifts in educational level of our potential workforce, natural environmental factors, politics, and so on. For some industries and unique organizations, some of these additional questions may be more important than the previous bullet points.

Second, we must take a hard look *inside* our own organizations. Are we still in the right business or set of businesses? This is where an article such as Peter Drucker's (1994) can be very helpful (see Chapter 8 for brief coverage of this article). Drucker indeed raised the right questions. Other questions for an outside and inside look include the following: Do we need to change our industry and technology base? DuPont, for example, has been basically a chemical company for at least a century. Because many of their products have reached maturity and sales have flattened (e.g., nylon), the CEO and other thought leaders in the company are strongly considering shifting from science based on chemistry to a bioscience foundation. This shift would cause a significant change in the kinds of products DuPont might offer in the future.

Do we change some of the business lines and remain with our core, or is there a need to change our business altogether? Perhaps not changing overnight, but moving down a different path for the longer term may be the proper course of action.

And again, if we are a nonprofit organization, the priority question would be as follows: What is the level of commitment to or passion about our organization's mission and purpose on the part of our board members, our senior executives, our employees, and our members?

Third, assuming that some degree of change is needed, how *ready* is our organization for what will be required? The question typically is not whether to change but the following: How quickly and how deeply should the process occur? Should the change be evolutionary and continuous (transactional in nature) or revolutionary and discontinuous (transformational in nature), or should the change be *both*—that is, slower and continuous for certain areas in the organization and revolutionary in other areas? With respect to readiness on the part of organizational members, it will depend in part on how much change has been occurring already and how many initiatives have been thrust on the organization. With the announcement of yet another change, people in the organization have been known to say, "We've been there, done that—even have a T-shirt to prove it!" Under such circumstances, change leaders will have to stress the difference and uniqueness of the current initiative to help organizational members, especially the jaded ones, to get beyond their fatigue and perhaps cynicism.

Fourth, assuming that the change required is transformational, how *locked into* (to use the language of Foster & Kaplan, 2001; see Chapter 2) our culture are we to our way of doing things? After all, a transformation means fundamental change of the culture to support the significantly revised mission, if not a new mission altogether, and of course, a new strategy. It will not be business as usual. As we know, culture change, when done correctly, requires new behavior that leads to new attitudes and beliefs and eventually to different values. Strong cultures are at best difficult to change, and, if the organization is large and complex, it can take years. But change they must, should the external environment demand it—that is, when the capital markets and other factors are incongruent with the organization's current direction and performance.

Fifth, we must make the case for change: *why* we need to transform ourselves. The most immediate response can be something like the following: "We've been successful for more than 70 years; why do we need to take such drastic, even draconian, steps now?" So, if dramatic change is indeed required, the case must be made. The parlance in today's organization change world is the creation, or establishment, of a "burning platform": the implication being that our very survival is at stake. The section titled "Establishing the Need for Change," in the previous chapter, provides an actual case example of establishing a "burning platform."

And *finally,* we follow the sequence, spelled out in Chapter 14, of *prelaunch, launch, postlaunch,* and *sustaining the change.* Staying with this sequence and how we "do things," we would be wise to apply our theoretical and research knowledge about the following:

- Open-system theory: This is bearing in mind principles such as the system's survival being dependent on the external environment; thus, our constant objective is to create negative entropy, and when we change one aspect of the organization, eventually all other aspects will be affected.
- Capra's (1996) ideas about patterns' autopoiesis, structure, and process: The parallels between a cell, a human being, and an organization are not perfect but are sufficient to warrant our understanding so that we are better informed about how organizations change and can be changed.
- The differences between continuous and discontinuous change: These differences have implications for how we plan organization change: If it is discontinuous, we are focusing on transformational factors such as mission, leadership, and culture, and we are attempting to affect the deep structure (Gersick, 1991) of the system; if continuous, our focus is on factors such as structure, systems, and climate.
- Understanding level differences in organizations: This understanding is important because we plan change and deal with resistance differently according to whether our focus is the individual, the group, or the system as a whole.
- Understanding of what comes first: It is behavior before cognition (Chapter 7).
- Measurement: This is being clear that an alpha change is different from beta and gamma changes; in other words, alpha change is a difference along some relatively stable dimension of reality, beta is a

recalibration of the intervals along the dimension, and gamma involves a reconceptualization of some domain. Exactly what we are measuring to determine change progress is critical to our understanding (Chapter 7).

- The distinction between content (what to change) and process (how to change) is key to knowing where and how to focus the change effort (Chapter 8).
- Organization models: It is useful to have a framework for categorizing as many of the primary dimensions of an organization as possible so that we can plan, implement, and track the change as effectively as possible (Chapters 9 and 10).
- If our change effort is transformational, it means that organizational culture is deeply involved and will no doubt need to be changed (Chapter 11).
- Studies of leadership are highly relevant, particularly with an emphasis on executive leadership and the variety of roles and functions, from prelaunch to sustaining the change (Chapter 14).
- The principles of change explained by the writings of Pascale, Milleman, and Gioja (2000; see Chapter 14) are very helpful as is Gladwell's (2000) work briefly described earlier.

Would that everything about organization change could be summarized in seven (plus or minus two) clear and straightforward steps. But surely we have learned one thing clearly: Organization change is entirely too complex and nonlinear to summarize that easily. Thinking about organization change in the sequential terms of prelaunch to sustaining is about the best we can do.

Moreover, if organization change were cast in terms of seven steps or limited to seven principles, we would be fooling ourselves. The complexity of it all is what makes the study and practice of organization change so challenging, so meaningful, so exciting, and so worthwhile.

As a way of further integrating, let us briefly examine what O'Toole (1995) found from his study of change leaders and the organizations they changed. Then we will move on to take a look at what we are seeking when trying to change an organization.

Successful Processes of Organization Change

James O'Toole (1995), in his book *Leading Change,* focused largely on leaders who had led successful organization change, for example, Max

DePree at the Herman Miller company, James Houghton of Corning, Robert Galvin of Motorola, Jan Carlzon at Scandinavian Airlines, and Bill Gore of W. L. Gore & Associates. In studying the changes that they led, O'Toole found eight commonalities:

1. *Change had top-management support:* Organization change, especially change of culture, takes a long time, thus leaders must make a long-term commitment. Colin Marshall of BA knew this, and he clearly made the commitment.

2. *Change was built on the unique strength and values of the organization:* While values for the organization may change, it is imperative that leaders understand what the organization's *core* values are that should not change and serve as anchors for organizational members as they deal with everything else that may be changing.

3. *The specifics of change were not imposed from the top:* The broader vision and overall direction for the change is top management's responsibility, but in terms of implementing the change, all levels in the organization should be involved in all stages of the effort.

4. *Change was holistic:* This commonality is, of course, consistent with open-system theory—that is, that all organizational parts are interrelated and changing one will eventually have consequences for all other parts of the system.

5. *Change was planned:* The long-term process was drawn up and followed by a period of education for all employees. Moreover, implementation was planned and carried out in detail.

6. *Changes were made in the guts of the organization:* Changes in authority and power relationships were made, access to information became easier, and the reward system was modified to support the overall change effort.

7. *Change was approached from a stakeholder viewpoint:* These change leaders started with the external environment, considering such primary stakeholders as customers and the organization's owners. Attempts were made to meet the needs of all the organization's stakeholders.

8. *Change became ongoing:* The external environment is more dynamic than ever before and remains in a constant state of change. The

organization must be adaptive and built to change, which is related to the work of Kotter and Heskett (1992) (see Chapter 11) and Lawler and Worley (2006), which will be covered later in this chapter.

These successful aspects of organization change tend to put us in a positive frame of mind. So let us continue with this theme by pursuing *positivity* in more depth. We will now consider the relatively recent trend in psychology and how this movement relates to organization change.

Positive Organization Change

In recent years, there has been a movement in psychology toward the positive with less emphasis than in the past on pathology and negative aspects of life. A watershed publication a decade ago demonstrated that the positive movement had arrived and was having an impact. A special issue of the *American Psychologist*, edited by Seligman and Csikszentmihalyi (2000), consisted of 15 articles devoted to positive psychology. In their introduction, Seligman and Csikszentmihalyi referred to the movement as a science of positive subjective experience emphasizing such topics as hope, wisdom, creativity, courage, spirituality, and optimism. From the standpoint of research, the movement has been counter to the dominance of negative emphases in psychological research. Studies often begin with a statement of "the problem." Moreover, negative findings are more powerful than positive ones in most studies. In other words, a large effect (e.g., R^2) can usually be detected by accounting for negative phenomena compared with positive phenomena, and the more powerful effects are the ones that are more likely to get published. As Baumeister, Bratslavsky, Finkenauer, and Vohs (2001) put it, the bad is stronger than the good.

Kim Cameron, for one, has taken the lead in applying the positive psychology movement into the organization science domain by focusing both on leadership (Cameron, 2008b) and organization change (Bright & Cameron, 2010; Cameron, 2008a). Basing his organizational change article on more than 160 references, Cameron has provided a solid foundation for understanding what he refers to as the "paradox of positive organizational change"—the positive versus the negative yet how important both are for effective change in organizations.

Cameron (2008a) pointed out that the term *positive* has many definitions and a wide range of connections, but for organization change purposes, he settled on equating positive with *exceptional performance.* Consistent with the positive psychology movement, nevertheless, positive in the context of organizational change refers to an affirmative bias in change efforts with an emphasis on strengths, capabilities, and possibilities rather than problems, threats, and weaknesses. And positive refers to an assumption that all human beings are inclined toward goodness for its own intrinsic value.

In reviewing much of the literature on our natural tendencies toward the positive, Cameron pointed out that studies (see Cameron's article for the specific references) have shown the following:

- Positive words are learned faster than negative words.
- People judge positive phenomena more accurately than negative phenomena (e.g., managers are more accurate in rating subordinates' competencies and proficiencies when they perform correctly than when they perform incorrectly).
- People are simply more accurate in processing positive information.
- People more frequently recall positive life experiences than neutral or negative ones.
- Positive memories tend to replace negative memories.
- We tend to forget the bad and exalt the good in thought, judgment, emotion, and language.

Some explanations for these natural tendencies include the fact that most information we are faced with is disregarded, being too overwhelming, and what we select and retain tends to be life giving rather than life depleting. Moreover, people expect (a) to live longer than average, (b) positive things to happen in the future even when there is no evidence to support such expectations, and (c) to win more than lose in randomized tasks. And most people (a) underestimate the likelihood of getting a divorce, (b) overestimate their prospects for success in the job market, and (c) overrate themselves when compared with how others rate them.

Even with all of these positive tendencies and biases, however, negative factors have a stronger impact on behavior—the paradox. Consider some of the paradoxical effects of the negative. (Again, specific references supporting the following points may be found in Cameron's [2008b] article.)

- Positive change can also result from problems, traumas, challenges, losses, and so forth.
- Negative news sells more than positive news.
- People pay more attention to negative feedback than positive feedback.
- "Bad is stronger than good."
- Living systems respond strongly and quickly to stimuli that threaten their existence.
- When equal measures of good and bad are present, the psychological effects of bad ones outweigh those of the good ones.
- Negative feedback has more emotional impact.
- Negatives tend to disrupt normal functioning longer.
- A positive event is remembered more accurately and longer, but a negative event has more effect on immediate memory and salience in the short run.
- People tend to spend more thought time on threatening personal relationships than on supportive ones.
- Bad reputations are easy to acquire but difficult to lose, whereas good reputations are difficult to acquire but easy to lose.
- To illustrate from a study by Bolster and Springbett (1961), in initial hiring decisions, 3.8 unfavorable bits of information were required to shift a decision to rejection, whereas 8.8 favorable pieces of information were necessary to shift an initial negative decision toward acceptance.

To help explain these paradoxical effects, Cameron (2008a) stated that both inclinations—positive and negative—are evolutionarily adaptive but operate in different ways particularly with respect to intensity. And since most of life's events are positive, a negative event is somewhat unique. Cameron put it this way:

> Just as movement in a still room attracts attention, so negative (novel) events capture more attention than positive (normal) patterns. Furthermore, negative events often indicate maladaptation and a need to change, (and) one single negative thing can cause a system to fail, but one single positive thing cannot guarantee success. (p. 15)

For positive organization change to occur, both positive and negative interventions are important. Recall that Gersick (1991) argued that for change in organizations to succeed both a sense of urgency should be embraced (negative) *and* a vision for the future endorsed (positive). Cameron (2008a) cautioned that overemphasis on either the positive or the negative can be dysfunctional; overly emphasizing the negative is likely to cause defensiveness—for example, paranoid feelings; and too much of the positive can come across as "sugarcoating" and unrealistic.

So both positive and negative interventions are needed for ultimate effectiveness regarding organization change. The problem, we need to be reminded, is the fact that the negative has a far greater impact than the positive. The challenge is to concentrate on processes and practices that will generate life-giving behaviors and, as a consequence, produce positive change in organizations. Most encouraging are findings demonstrating that when positive dominates the negative, such human factors as mental capacity, personal resilience, intellectual complexity, knowledge, the capacity to explore, and physiological functioning are all enhanced (Cameron, 2008a). The point is that for the future, more research and practice that emphasizes the positive is warranted. The payoff of such efforts is likely to be highly significant.

In the next section, again as a way of integrating material from this book yet at the same time including new thinking, we will now consider what a "change" and a "changing" organization might look like.

The Look of Change

The change effort for any organization is unique to that organization. BA needed to become more customer oriented; SmithKline Beecham, Ltd., and Dime Bancorp were about making a merger work; and the A. K. Rice Institute (AKRI) was about a change in its core mission. Commonalities across these four organizational change efforts were there—managed from the top, a holistic approach, the change was planned, and changes were made in the guts of the organization—but in the end, each change looked very different from all the others. These differences were largely in the *content* of the change and, of course, the differences in the end were a function of the nature of the businesses each represented, both profit and nonprofit.

Yet today, with the constancy of change surrounding us, one might argue that all organizations, to ensure long-term survival, effectiveness, and success, should be attempting to change in the same direction—that is, to be nimble, flexible, and adaptive and, in short, to be changed so that the norm, the culture, is one that constantly is in a state of change. Some scholars and practitioners have addressed the idea.

The book by Kotter and Heskett (1992) was a study of the relationship between corporate culture and organizational performance.

As mentioned earlier, their list of 11 characteristics represents worthy norms and goals to pursue for most any organization.

Corporate Culture in the Work of Lawler and Worley

A more recent work in this genre is the book *Built to Change,* by Lawler and Worley (2006). Although these authors give a respectful nod to the Collins and Porras (1994) book, *Built to Last,* they see their book as a kind of sequel and that the way to *last* is for the organization to be designed and operated for *change.* For Lawler and Worley, stability is essentially the opposite of effectiveness. They cover a number of organizational dimensions—external environment, mission and identity, strategizing, organization design and structure, measurement, human capital, and reward systems—and address them in terms of the design and operation of each of these dimensions to ensure that an organization will be built for change. Brief examples of how Lawler and Worley consider these organizational dimensions follow.

External Environment

In the built-to-change organization, the external environment is addressed in terms of "environmental scenarios." Organizational members, senior management, particularly, involve themselves in a process of describing a range of possible future business conditions, not simply the current environment. These scenarios then drive strategizing and how to think about and measure organization effectiveness. Scenarios respond to such questions as the following:

- How will technologies, user interest, and social trends play out or change over the next 3 to 5 years?
- What are our competitors likely to do? Join with a larger provider (IBM, Pfizer, General Electric [GE], etc.), for example?

It's a matter of making reasonable guesses about the future and being prepared to respond accordingly.

Identity

This dimension concerns the organization's statement about how it will achieve its long-term mission and specifically the organization's dominant approach to business, for example, as a low-cost provider? An energy company? A transportation company? A distributor? In other words, what is the core identity of the organization and its business model? Identity comes from the organization's culture—what and how we do things and what we will be rewarded for. Microsoft, for example, is all about being persistent; for Goldman Sachs, it is about making the deal; and for GE, it is about good if not superior management. A built-to-last organization should be able to change, and change quickly, practically all its dimensions—except for its identity, which provides the core and anchor to hold on to for organizational members. The analogy here for Lawler and Worley (2006) is as follows: Identity is like individual personality and strategizing is like individual behavior. Identity is not likely to change, but behavior can change considerably.

Strategizing

Note that Lawler and Worley (2006) used the gerund form for this dimension, not the more static terms of strategic planning or simply strategy. They wanted to convey with the "-ing" that strategy is a process and constantly in motion. For example, they stated that companies need to develop temporary competitive advantages and therefore be prepared for changing this aspect of their strategy overnight if necessary. Strategizing concerns intent—how does the organization intend to accomplish its mission and objectives? There are five elements of strategic intent in strategizing:

1. Breadth—range of products and services offered, different markets served, different technologies supported, different segments of the value chain occupied, and so on

2. Aggressiveness—*how* does the company develop new products, grow its business, and battle its competitors, for example, with highly active acquisitions of smaller companies, tough advertising, large budget for R&D to create new products and services?

3. Differentiations—*how* the company's products and services are unique in their respective industry—for example, how is a Toyota different from a Nissan or a Honda?

4. Strategic logic—the company's business model; is it based on capturing ever larger market share, lowering unit costs, small margin across many units (high volume), economies of scale, globalization?

5. Orchestration—a planning process for how breadth, aggressiveness, and differentiation are sequenced and managed as well as for how communication, actions, decisions, and events to implement change are coordinated

Implementation of strategy is about creating value through *competencies* and *capabilities*. Organizational competencies are a combination of technology and production skills that underlie the product lines and services offered—for example, Sony's miniaturization of technology. Organizational capabilities are what the organization can do and are difficult to copy: managing knowledge, developing new products and services, responding quickly to changes in the business environment, and serving customers, to name a few. It's about competitive advantage.

Organization Design and Structure

Lawler and Worley (2006) contended that the era of job descriptions should be history. They argued for "structures without jobs," meaning that (a) job descriptions rapidly become outdated, (b) people should be assigned responsibility on a temporary basis, (c) people's skills change as well as organizational needs, and (d) it is better to think project-to-project than job-to-job. The authors also are advocates for teams and business units. They discussed the advantages of multidisciplinary teams, temporary project and problem-solving groups, self-managing teams, and virtual groups that are useful for organizations with multiple sites and locations. They found business units to be useful for (a) more direct customer contact and focus on the external environment; (b) getting more people to understand "the business"; (c) adding and subtracting units of an organization more easily, thus making it easier to pursue new business opportunities; and (d) making judgments about the degree of autonomy and independence for these units—that is, executives are forced to think through the degree of independence they wish to support in this structural feature of the organization. Lawler and Worley also covered two other structural features that they found useful:

1. Matrix (combinations of business units or project management groups with functions such as engineering)
2. Front–back structures (customer-facing units, like sales combined with "back" units that produce products and services)

Front–back structures are easier to manage than matrix structures; they involve primarily only two sets of operations: (a) directly dealing with customers and (b) those who serve or back up these front-line individuals and groups. The authors also discuss the pros and cons of business process outsourcing, joint ventures, acquisitions and mergers, and alliances. They are not favorably disposed toward steep hierarchies and related structural traditions because they tend to prevent change and rapid action.

Measurement

Lawler and Worley (2006) are strong advocates of constantly gathering performance information at the business unit and organizational level by scanning the environment, measuring individual performance at all levels, and using simple and objective assessments. At the organizational level, they argued for not only financial data but for intangibles as well— employee motivation and satisfaction and measures represented by the balanced score card, such as innovation and customer satisfaction.

Human Capital

Besides the usual admonitions for finding the right talent (use interviews, consider past behavior, and lean toward temporary and contract employment where possible), the authors stressed keeping the right people by rewarding learning and developing person descriptions for selection and placement along the lines of (a) thinking like a customer and (b) developing talent.

Reward System

This dimension is, of course, Lawler and Worley's (2006) strong suit. Two chapters in the book are devoted to reward systems. Briefly, suffice it to say that the authors address such topics as the impact of goals on motivation; job satisfaction; linking reward to skills, knowledge, and organizational performance; the need to reward change initiatives; and something they call "reward attractiveness," which means providing rewards that are not the usual (not to say boring) types—fringes, big offices, stock options, recognition awards, as important as these may be for most people—but in addition giving out such unusual rewards as "private rodeos with mechanical bulls, fly fishing on Western ranches, flights in a fighter plane, river rafting, sabbaticals, forty-two kinds of free drinks, and a lifetime supply of Ben and Jerry's ice cream. Any of these rewards can be effective motivators if they are valued by individuals" (p. 238).

Built to Change

Built to Change is more than 300 pages, and obviously I have only touched on its considerable content. My intent was to give a flavor of what the authors consider to be the significant dimensions of a flexible, adaptive organization and what a desired organization for these times of constant change should look like. To ensure survival, effectiveness, and long-term success, organizations today and for the future need to be built to change, not built to last.

The purposes of this chapter were to summarize and integrate. The four phases of change leadership—(a) prelaunch, (b) launch, (c) postlaunch, and (d) sustaining the change—covered in Chapter 14 were reviewed but this time by relating ideas about change from Gladwell's (2000) book, *The Tipping Point*, to the phases. The point was to broaden our thinking about how to implement these four phases more effectively.

The Changing the Organization section was an attempt to highlight the most important questions to answer—from customers we serve whether profit or nonprofit to changing technology—when planning an organization change. Also summarized were the critical sources of knowledge regarding organization change from theory and research.

O'Toole's (1995) list of successful processes of change was useful if not encouraging (we *do know* some things from experience!), and the positive psychology movement applied to organization change is also encouraging and expands our perspective about the complexities of change.

And, finally, the Lawler and Worley book on change provides coverage on the key component of an organization that will help us to sustain change.

And now let us turn to the future, not in a predictive sense but in terms of what we need to know more about or at least to know in more depth.

SIXTEEN

Organization Change

What We Need to Know

S ome years ago, I wrote an article on what I thought we knew about organization change and what we needed to know (Burke, 1995). With respect to what we needed to know, I chose eight areas to cover. What follows is a synopsis and brief update of these eight areas regarding what we need to know more about now and in the future.

The Process of Organization Change

Momentum

Recall from the previous chapter that the fourth phase of organization change—sustaining the change—is the most difficult. We must learn more about "organization change momentum," or how to sustain the change once we are under way. Some specific suggestions for what to research and learn more about include keeping people informed, measuring and celebrating achievements, and experimenting with new and different ways of rewarding people for the appropriate changes that they make. See Lawler and Worley (2006) for a start on different ways of rewarding.

Chaos During Transition

Remember two important phenomena about chaos theory: one is that even when not apparent in the midst of change, patterns do exist. Figure 2.1 in Chapter 2 was an attempt to represent this phenomenon. Understanding more about pattern is a fruitful avenue for research. A second phenomenon is the likelihood of innovation and creativity at the "edge of chaos" (Pascale, Milleman, & Gioja, 2000). How long should the change leader allow chaos to continue, hoping for a breakthrough? And how does creativity emerge?

Communication

It is easy to state that during organization change, leaders need to communicate. More important than this simple admonition, however, is the need to understand more about the timing of communication and the amount to communicate at any given time.

Organization Change Leadership

Personality and Culture

Because leadership is such a personal matter, understanding more about the proper match between the leader's personality and the desired organizational culture is critical to successful change. Moreover, charismatic leaders can play important roles during times of crisis, but what about afterward? The classic case of Winston Churchill during and after World War II remains puzzling. Why was he not reelected? More recently and similarly, Rudolph Giuliani, the former mayor of New York, was superb during the aftermath of September 11, 2001, but perhaps not so superb during times of relative normalcy. Successors to charismatic leaders often have a difficult time because charismatic leaders rarely leave adequate infrastructures and systems to maintain what they initiated during their tenures. We need to understand more about leadership in such key areas as personality, self-awareness, charisma, crisis versus noncrisis leadership, and succession.

Power and Politics

Understanding more about power—the leader's capacity to influence—is needed. Classic works remain informative; for example, see French and Raven (1959) on basic sources of power (reward, coercive, legitimate, expert, and referent) and Kipnis (1976) on the question of whether power corrupts (under certain conditions, power does corrupt). But what about the use of power during change? Revolutionary change requires strong, powerful leadership, the transformational type. What is the proper balance between powerful leadership and involving organizational members in decisions that directly affect them? These and related questions are ripe for research.

The Change Leader

Building on these questions, how does change leadership differ from leadership during times of relative stability? I have made the claim that self-awareness is necessary for effective change leadership, as well as the need for high emotional intelligence. Am I correct?

Organizational Structure

Self-Directed Groups

As a result of organization change, the trend continues toward flatter hierarchies in large systems, with the consequences of greater spans of control for managers. Work units in organizations now operate more on their own, with less supervision. Hackman (1992) has contributed to our understanding of self-directed groups, but we need to know much more.

Centralization–Decentralization

It used to be a question of one versus the other. This is no longer the question; it is rather what functions to centralize (finance?) and what functions to decentralize (human resources?). Learning more about how to do both simultaneously is needed.

Cells

These self-managed groups have been prevalent in manufacturing organizations for quite some time now, but we still do not know enough about how to change to this mode of operating effectively and how to make them work well over time.

Networks

A network is a structural form that has been around for a long time. There are actually many different types of networks. When is one type, a loosely coupled professional association, for example, more effective than another form, a network of, say, computer scientists within the same organization? How do you move effectively from a hierarchy to a network, or vice versa? (This topic was addressed in more depth in Chapter 12 on loosely coupled systems).

Formal and Informal Rewards

Incentives

We know about pay, bonuses, and fringe benefits, but we do not know enough about applying them: the conditions for when they work well and when they do not. Pay for performance remains an issue. As soon as it becomes expected, any pay-for-performance scheme loses the characteristic of incentive. If pay for performance is an incentive, how long does it last? And how can such schemes be used to support organization change?

Intrinsic Rewards

I believe we need to know much more than we do about intrinsic motivation and reward. We know that "it's the work itself," but what, in more depth and with more specificity, do we know? Such thinking as Csikszentmihalyi's (1990) work on flow is helpful here, especially his distinction between joy and pleasure. We need to know more about how to make work more satisfying, how to experience flow from time to time, and how to make change more accepted and enjoyable. The growing positive psychology movement is likely to be helpful in this arena.

Training and Development

Training in the Service of Change

Too often, training in organizations is conducted because competitors are doing it or because some executive believes that conducting a certain program would be a good thing to do, regardless of whether any evidence exists that the program actually works. Training is, indeed, capable of helping organizational members to learn and develop, but training targeted at supporting and enhancing organization change can have considerable payoff. Recall the British Airways (BA) case from Chapter 11 and how training was deployed for culture change. Learning more about the use of training at individual and group levels in the service of ultimate organization change is needed.

Action Learning

This form of training and development combines actual problem solving in organizations with learning about how to work together better, how to solve organizational problems more efficiently and effectively, and how to improve the learning process in general—learning about learning. Even though action learning is reasonably well known, it is not practiced very often. This form of learning can be a powerful vehicle for organization change; see, for example, Tichy and Sherman (1993). We need to know more about the intricacies of this problem-solving and learning process and why it is not used more often.

Teams and Teamwork in Organizations

There are good sources about teams and teamwork. Katzenbach and Smith's (1993) *The Wisdom of Teams* is one of them, as is *Organizing Genius* by Bennis and Biederman (1997) and *Leading Teams* by Hackman (2002). What surprises me, however, is why this collective wisdom is applied so seldomly? Yes, here in the United States, we are an individually focused culture, but we know that teamwork can benefit organization change and performance. I believe now as I did earlier (Burke, 1995)—that is, we need to know more about such things as follows:

- Why there is so much talk about teamwork, with so little real action
- What the elements are of a high-performing team
- What kinds of goals for teams are those that provide "demanding

performance challenges"—and I do not mean going over a wall or climbing a mountain together (i.e., "ropes and slopes")

- What it takes to achieve a high degree of personal commitment among team members
- What synergy is, really, and what the conditions are for achieving it
- The kinds of assumptions that organizational members hold about teamwork
- How to instill a team culture in an organization and make it last through structural and management changes as well as changes in the reward system? (pp. 167–168)

Organizational Size

Large and Small Simultaneously

The main thesis of Naisbitt's (1994) book, *Global Paradox,* is that in the face of global expansion for nations, there is at the same time a strong emphasis worldwide on ethnic groups, local community, and subparts of countries as the basis for one's primary identify and loyalty. If Naisbitt's thesis holds for large organizations, what does this mean for organization change? Supposedly, the organizational whole should be more than the sum of its parts, but in thinking about organization change in the future, should we consider the opposite—that is, strengthening parts more than the whole? Of course, the answer to this question is "It depends." But what are the pros and cons? These are interesting questions for research.

Silos and Boundary Spanning

This is the newer language for differentiation and integration. Obviously, any large organization needs both. It seems, however, that silos win over cross-functional teams. Is this a phenomenon? If so, don't we need to know more? And how can change toward a greater boundary-less way of working be promoted and realized?

Size of Organizational Units

The evidence for an organizational unit's being no larger than 150 people is compelling. Following Wegner's (1991) lead to understand more about how this works and its importance for organization change would be a fascinating stream of research.

Organizational Performance

As part of his review of Jim Collins's (2001) book about how some "good companies become great," Holstein (2001) made the following point:

> Whatever contributions the book offers are called into question by an intellectual assumption that runs throughout: The only way to define a great company is in its return to investors over a continuous and prolonged period. Such a standard doesn't consider how a company could have changed society or the world, how it benefited customers, how it conquered international markets, or how it treated employees. (p. 6)

The point is that defining the degree of greatness of a company according to its stock price, even if measured over time, is a very limited index of performance. The time is overdue for us to consider organizational performance in multiple ways; yes, financial is one measure, but as Kaplan and Norton (1996) have explained (and earlier noted in Chapter 10), there are at least three other ways to measure performance. Moreover, measures of organization change are far too complex to be left only to financial measures. Thus, we need to learn much more about how to define and measure organizational performance than we now know.

Learning Priorities Moving Forward

The coverage in the previous section on "what we need to know" consisted of eight categories—(a) process, (b) leadership, (c) structure, (d) rewards, (e) training and development, (f) teams and teamwork, (g) organizational size, and (h) organizational performance. The point was that we know some things in these eight areas but need to know more. What follows now is coverage of four areas where we need to know *much more* because mistakes are being made. The *first* area concerns structure with concentration on loosely coupled systems and especially networks. Since I considered this area to be of critical importance, an entire chapter (12) is now devoted to it. The *second* is to call our attention to the nature of resistance to change. We have been living with a fairly narrow understanding of this phenomenon. The *third* area is again leadership but this time to address the two primary issues— (a) selection and (b) development. The *fourth* area is the relatively new ideas about something called learning agility. And finally, although briefly, we will touch on the importance of trust in times of change.

Not too long ago I was asked to write a perspective article on the field of organization development (OD) and change. In that paper (Burke, 2011), I discussed four areas that I believed needed considerable attention in order for the field to move forward. Two of these areas were covered in the third edition of this book—(a) culture changes (see Chapter 11) and (b) loosely coupled systems, which is now covered in Chapter 12. The other two areas from the perspective article of 2011 will also be discussed in this closing chapter—(a) resistance and (b) leader selection and development. The two additional areas for brief coverage are (a) learning agility and (b) trust.

Resistance Isn't What It Used to Be

People always resist change. We know better. People do not *always* resist change. Some embrace change and make remarks like, "It's about time" or "What took them (management) so long?" or "We've been needing to address this problem for a long time." Yet when in a position to lead and manage change in an organization, we act as if that opening statement is true. I have been no exception. After all, one of the first articles I read as a graduate student was the classic Coch and French (1948) study titled "Overcoming Resistance to Change." Shortly thereafter, I was influenced by Goodwin Watson's (1966) thoughtful paper on resistance, and I learned from Paul Lawrence (Lawrence, 1954) about how to deal with resistance. The main learning was that resistance was something to "overcome."

Yet we have learned that resistance is not as simple as I have portrayed it so far in the previous paragraph. In Chapter 6, we learned that people do not necessarily resist change itself but will resist the imposition of change—that is, taking away our freedom of choice. And we know that change, whether positive or negative, means a loss of something, particularly a loss of familiar routines. We also know that not all forms of resistance are the same: one form can be blind, another ideological, and another political, and we should not attempt to treat the different forms in the same way. Moreover, O'Toole (1995) made things even more complicated by identifying 33 hypotheses about why people resist change. And Piderit (2000) cautioned us that what looks like resistance may be nothing more than ambivalence, and the person or group simply needs more convincing evidence for the idea to "sink in." Piderit (2000) went on to point out that responses to change are "neither consistently negative nor consistently positive" (p. 783). I was influenced by her thinking. Also, at about the same time, Dent and

Goldberg (1999) challenged my earlier thinking, which they characterized as a mental model—that is, resistance is consistent and must be overcome. Furthermore, my mental model was "anti Lewin" (sheer heresy on my part) by limiting my perspective to the person who is resisting and not to the combination of the individual and his or her context, the larger system. Their argument was that many of us in the change business were making resistance totally psychological and not a systematic issue. Being a Lewinian, this argument made perfect sense to me. And to others.

More recently, Jeffrey Ford and his colleagues have added to the notion that resistance isn't what it used to be. These change scholars view resistance more as a resource to be deployed in the service of change rather than a barrier to be overcome. In other words, their perspective is one of broadening our thinking about and working with perceived resistance. Perceived resistance is just that, a perception, and is rarely seen by change leaders as rational, thoughtful, or reflective. Ford, Ford, and D'Amelio (2008) then went on to suggest three ways to expand our thinking:

Sensemaking

Relying on Weick's (1995) thinking, Ford and colleagues see dealing with resistance as a matter of problem solving. What's the problem? The change leader's need to implement change compared with the change recipients' need to understand what the change means personally for him or her. The goal then is trying "to make sense" of the situation and trying to solve a problem of differing needs rather than assuming resistance and attempting to overcome it.

Change Leader Contributions to Resistance

We know from research and from stories in the media that when change leaders (a) say one thing then do another, (b) misrepresent the chances of success, and/or (c) ignore ideas and suggestions from change recipients, resistance is bound to occur. In other words, the causal agent for change resistance can easily be the change leader.

Resistance as a Resource

Where there is resistance there is energy. People who resist care about something. What is worse? Apathy. Resistance after all is a form of engagement. Change leadership, then, concerns movement of energy; think of it as movement from resistance to ambivalence to acceptance.

Easy to state, not so easy to do, but the leadership is about working with that energy, that engagement, rather than ignoring or attempting to gain submission from change recipients.

To summarize, the changing conception of resistance concerns avoiding a we–they process between change leaders and change recipients, avoiding a misinterpretation of change recipients' reactions as resistance rather than ambivalence, and treating at least perceived resistance as a resource rather than a barrier to overcome.

Allow me to repeat a story from my earlier perspective article that illustrates our need to reconceptualize resistance:

> Several years ago in my role as director of our graduate programs in social organizational psychology, I (read "change agent/leader") proposed that we initiate a new MA program in addition to the two programs (MA and PhD) that we had been providing for well more than 20 years. I explained (I thought patiently) the market, the need, and our capabilities of delivering such a program successfully. When I finished, there was a long silence followed finally by a faculty member's raising questions rather than cheering me on. I perceived the questions to be resistance, and I became rather belligerent and withdrawn. A rather heated debate then ensued. I later learned that my colleague was not necessarily opposed to the idea; her behavior could more accurately be labeled as ambivalent (Piderit, 2000). In fact, we as a faculty did decide to proceed with the new program. As the change agent, I came close by my own behavior to fulfilling a prophecy about my colleague who was not necessarily resistant, only questioning. As the agent, I needed to have treated these questions as important concerns, reasons to explore in more depth the rationale and potential hazards for such a program.
>
> This short story captures and illustrates the primary points that Ford et al. (2008) make—the role and behavior of the change agent, the change recipient, and the interaction between the two. It is this dynamic, to use Ford and his colleagues' term, that needs to be understood in more depth and used as a framework for learning and skill development. (Burke, 2011, p. 158)

Getting Leadership Selection and Development Right

Over two decades ago, it was documented that the failure rate for individuals in positions of leadership was, on average, 50% (Hogan, Curphy,

& Hogan, 1994). One of every two did not accomplish the goals set forth for them as leaders. I suspect that this outcome has not changed all that much. This is a costly and unacceptable situation. Do we have a selection problem in the first place, or once selected, is it a matter of development? The answer appears to be yes.

Selection

With respect to the issue of selection, we have at least three biases that influence us. If the leader nomination process comes from senior managers and executives, there appears to be a strong cloning effect even though scholars such as Bennis and O'Toole (2000) and Levinson (1974) have given us due warning of the consequences.

A few years ago, some colleagues and I were working with a high-tech firm on leader development. We designed and delivered a two-day intensive program to enhance self-awareness. We had convinced the client of the importance of conducting such a program since there was strong evidence of the relationship between self-awareness and leader–manager performance, see, for example, Atwater and Yammarino (1992), Church (1997), and the section on self-awareness in Chapter 13. The individuals attending the program were supposedly "high potentials" for leadership in the company and were selected by their bosses. An important part of the program was multirater feedback, which, of course, included supervisor ratings. Over time we began to see a pattern—the people selected for the program had behavioral profiles that looked a lot like their direct supervisors' profiles. This example is only one company, and our "high potentials" number in the hundreds not the thousands, but at the risk of overgeneralizing, I would wager nevertheless that cloning is alive and well. Senior executives in this company have espoused the importance of diversity among their employees, but it would seem that this is more preaching than practicing.

A second selection bias is an explicit one that is largely based on the big five factors of personality (Hogan et al., 1994). We like people for leadership roles who are (a) mentally and emotionally stable, (b) agreeable, (c) conscientious, (d) outgoing and extravertive, and (e) open to new ideas and experiences. We also prefer leaders who are tall, over six feet. There is nothing inherently wrong with this bias; it is more a matter of our not quite knowing as yet if people who are high on these qualities or characteristics make effective leaders. The bias hearkens back to trait theory in leadership studies.

A third bias is implicit theory, also noted by Hogan and colleagues (1994). With the possible exception of the big five bias, we seem to have "in the back of our heads" a picture of what a successful leader looks like. And if our search committee is composed of, say, eight members we then have eight different pictures. I have been known to win money on the veracity of this so-called theory. As noted in my recent perspective article (Burke, 2011), I ask an audience to list what each person believes are the five most important characteristics of a successful leader. Then I propose a wager of 5 dollars that there will be no two people in the room who will have the same list. Some people will take the bet. With the audience being no more than 40 individuals, I have never lost. If the audience is more than 40, I simply do not propose a wager. The more the number is over 40, the poorer my odds. The point is this: With all of these different pictures, it is difficult to agree on one person who looks like what each of us prefers. Thus, we often end in a stalemate or compromise and the "right" person to fit the position and context is overlooked.

The point has also been made that in selecting leaders we want them to have a reasonably high degree of self-awareness, and we would like to see the relationship between self-awareness and performance verified. In the Church (1997) study, performance was defined at the individual level—performance appraisal ratings, merit awards, promotion rate, etc. But what about performance, or at least an outcome (dependent variable), at the group level? An arena and framework for exploration is via the Burke–Litwin model (Chapter 10) and testing, say, the relationship between dimensions such as management practices and climate. Although insufficiently rigorous due to small numbers, such a study informally has been done. In other words, does self-awareness predict performance at the work unit level, the group's assessment of their work climate?

In an unpublished study of work unit climate and multirater feedback in the National Aeronautics and Space Administration (NASA) in the early 1990s, we compared managerial behavior ratings of NASA middle managers by boss, peer, subordinate, and self with their subordinates' ratings of work unit climate, our outcome variable. Table 16.1 is a display of the entire set of 39 work unit climate items (e.g., "the work unit goals are clear") organized according to the six primary categories derived from earlier statistical methods such as factor analysis. The overall work unit climate rating was a simple mean score for all 39 items rated by the subordinates of a given manager.

The managerial practices ratings were 37 behavioral statements organized into five primary categories. These five categories with an exemplar for self-ratings for each one follows:

1. Planning and controlling: You establish work unit goals.

2. Promoting achievement: You encourage subordinates to initiate innovative approaches to tasks or projects.

3. Understanding and supporting others: You pay close attention and seek to understand subordinates when interacting.

4. Evaluating subordinates: You face up to and take appropriate action regarding poor performance on the part of subordinates.

5. Managing interfaces: You present bad news in a constructive manner.

While the study was based on small sample sizes that somewhat limit the conclusions that can be drawn, it is reviewed here to (a) stimulate similar research on manager behaviors as antecedents linked with climate and (b) illustrate how climate can be used as an outcome variable in change work.

In this study, managers' self-ratings of his or her practices were categorized as high or low based on whether they were above (high) or below (low) the 50th percentile when compared with all self-ratings provided by managers. Their self-ratings (M) were also compared to how they were rated, in aggregate, by their subordinates (Sub). Thus, some managers rated themselves: higher than their subordinates rated them, which is often the case (M > Sub), about the same as their subordinated rated them (M = Sub), or lower than their subordinates rated them (M < Sub). The following table shows the comparisons:

Manager Self Ratings	High	Climate	Climate	Climate
	Low	Climate	Climate	Climate
		M > Sub	M = Sub	M < Sub

Our informal prediction was that the highest climate ratings would occur in the upper middle box of our 2 x 3—that is, in work units led by managers whose self-ratings were high relative to those of their peers (interpreted as reasonable self-confidence perhaps) and whose ratings of themselves were roughly the same as how their subordinates perceived

Table 16.1 Work Unit Climate

Clarity	Recognition	Participation	Standards	Intraunit Relations	Interunit Communications	Interunit Relations
1 Work unit members know what tasks others in the work unit expect them to perform	**8** When a person does good work, other work unit members individually communicate their appreciation to him/her	**14** Subordinates have an opportunity to contribute to the setting of their work unit goals	**20** Performance standards in the work unit are high	**25** Members of the work unit trust one another	**31** Day-to-day work unit activities are well integrated with other work units	**35** Conflicts that arise with other work units are dealt with effectively
2 Operating procedures in this work unit are clearly understood	**9** When a person does good work, he/she is appropriately recognized for their contribution	**15** Work unit members have an opportunity to influence each other's work objectives	**21** Work unit members continually strive to do the best possible work	**26** Work unit members have friendly relationships with one another	**32** The work unit is quick to respond to the needs of the other work units	**36** People in the work unit believe that identifying problems between units will increase organization effectiveness
3 Work unit members are expected to achieve tasks that are reasonable	**10** The most recognition goes to the best performer in the work unit	**16** Thoughts and opinions of other work unit members are solicited from one another	**22** Work unit goals are challenging	**27** The manager is not distant or generally unapproachable in relating with work unit members	**33** Other work units are quick to respond to the needs of this work unit	**37** Higher management rarely has to deal with conflicts between this work unit and other units
4 The work unit is well organized to perform its tasks			**23** Performance of work unit members is not overly constrained by a fear of failure	**28** When a work unit member needs help, others in the work unit are quick to respond	**34** Ideas, thoughts and suggestions are freely communicated between work units	

(Continued)

Table 16.1 (Continued)

Clarity	Recognition	Participation	Standards	Intraunit Relations	Interunit Communications	Interunit Relations
5 The work unit's productivity is not hampered by the way projects are planned and organized	**11** Work unit members do not overly criticize each one another's performance	**17** Subordinates have an opportunity to influence the overall direction of the work unit	**24** Members of the work unit are inspired to perform at a higher level	**29** People take pride in being a member of the work unit		**38** Relationships between this work unit and other units would not be characterized by suspicion and distrust
6 The work unit goals are clear	**12** Recognition for performance is given in a timely fashion in the work unit	**18** Manager and subordinates sit down to review performance		**30** The manager supports the subordinates when he/she believes they are right		**39** There is little competitiveness between this work unit and other units
7 The informal, personal relationships between work unit members combines well with the formal, task relationships	**13** Subordinates hear from the manager at times other than when things go wrong	**19** Work unit changes *are* jointly planned between the manager and members of the unit				

them (interpreted as an above average degree of self-awareness). We were not quite perfect with our prediction. The outcome of our study was as shown in the following table:

Manager Self Ratings				
	High	3	2	1
	Low	6	5	4
		M > Sub	M = Sub	M < Sub

That is, the highest rated work unit climate was the #1 box (upper right) where the managers rated themselves above the 50th percentile yet rated themselves less favorably than their subordinates rated them. I call this the "slight humility effect." The most "out-of-touch" managers (the #6 box) were those who rated themselves below average but at the same time rated themselves higher than their subordinates rated them.

Again, the purpose of presenting this research here is twofold: (a) to stimulate further climate research that focuses on antecedents particularly with the leader and management practices dimensions and illustrate how climate can be used as an outcome variable in change work—that is, at the group level—and (b) to advance further the hypothesis that self aware-ness predicts performance, in this case, by way of climate, and in turn, motivation, then performance, as the Burke–Litwin model sets forth.

Finally, we want self-awareness at the top of our list as criteria for selec-tion, more specifically an individual who has self-confidence, and an above average level of self-awareness (as measured by the degree of con-sequence between self and others' ratings of our individual leader) yet also having a dose of humility. Incidentally, this earlier tentative finding of ours is consistent with the research of Jim Collins reported in his *Good to Great* book (Collins, 2001) that Level 5 leaders are unique in two ways— (a) persistence and (b) humility.

Returning for a moment to our work with the high-tech firm and their issue of cloning, we believed that "accusing" them of a problem without an alternative was not fair. Thus, I put together for them a set of 10 criteria for selection of potential leaders (see Table 16.2).

Development

Notice that the concept here is *development* not training. If we revisit for a moment Chapter 12 and consider the distinctions between a leader and

Table 16.2   What Criteria Should Managers Use to Negotiate and Select High-Potential Individuals for Important Positions of Leadership?

What Follows Are the 10 Fundamental Criteria (One Is as Important as the Other):

1. Above average on general mental ability yet does not need to be brilliant. But does need to be capable of thinking in complex ways—that is, to understand complexity yet can explain complicated matters in simple language

2. Satisfactory technical skills and abilities but does not need to be the highest rated technician or professional in the organization

3. Highly motivated to want to make a difference, to make things better; ambitious; never quite satisfied with the status quo

4. Strong people skills; emotionally intelligent and mature or at least has high potential for growth and development in this domain

5. Loves to learn and finds multiple ways to do so; enjoys ideas and concepts; above average curiosity

6. Reasonably self-aware: understands own strengths and limitations; knows how other people view him or her

7. High self-confidence and esteem without being arrogant. Does not take oneself overly seriously

8. Has high energy; gets things done

9. Has integrity; tells the truth; honesty is a paramount value

10. And, in general, more optimistic than pessimistic

a manager, and even bearing in mind that there is overlap, it should be apparent that one can train a person for management more easily than one can train an individual for leadership. While both require skills, the ones required for management are simply more trainable than those for leadership. Management concerns such skills as planning and forecasting, analyzing competitors in one's marketplace, reading an income statement, and budgeting, whereas leadership is more about setting a course of direction, convincing people that change may be required, thinking long-range of what might be, inspiring people, and having emotional intelligence. I cannot imagine getting an MBA degree in leadership.

Morgan McCall's earlier work at the Center for Creative Leadership, see, for example, McCall, Lombardo, and Morrison (1988), set the stage for his more recent conclusions about developing potential leaders (McCall, 2010). He concluded that leader development stems largely from different job experiences. As the cliché goes, "experience is the best teacher" but not just any experience and not just experience alone. Some experiences are more important than others. McCall stated that a number of studies show the following:

> Successful managers [my word would be leaders] describe similar experiences that shaped their development. These experiences can be classified roughly as early work experiences, short-term assignments, other people (almost always very good and very bad bosses or supervisors), hardships of various kinds, and some miscellaneous events like training programs. (McCall, 2010, p. 4)

The experiences that produce the greatest opportunities for learning about leadership are therefore nonroutine, challenging and demanding, stressful, and often require tough decision making. McCall estimated that 70% of leadership learning comes from these kinds of experiences. Others agree; see, for example, Yost and Plunkett (2009). McCall (2010) went on to declare that effective leader development needs to follow the 70–20–10 rule; specifically, that is 70% varied and challenging assignments, 20% learning from others—good and bad bosses and the same for mentors and coaches—and 10% learning from programs that focus on specific skills such as public speaking and the art of storytelling. An important point should be added regarding programs: the more they are stand-alone events, the less effective they are for leader development. In other words, they work best when designed to support directly the potential leader's job experiences, mentoring, and coaching.

Thus far, we have considered the importance of *how* learning should be provided for effective leader development. But *what* should potential leaders learn? Again, based on the work of McCall (2010) and others, and as I (Burke, 2011) summarized recently, what leaders need to know can be boiled down to five basic demands of the leader role:

1. Setting and communicating direction—determining purpose and vision goals and establishing support for these endeavors

2. Aligning critical constituencies—making sure that those who need to support these endeavors are "on board"

3. Developing an executive temperament—being able to cope with complexity, ambiguity, and the pressures of the leadership role

4. Setting and living values—clarifying what to believe in and stand for and making sure that as leader, one's words match one's actions

5. Growing of self and others—practicing and supporting in others' lifelong learning, growth, and change (p. 161)

In an attempt to summarize and conceptualize leader development based on the work just presented, I have suggested a framework of four stages or phases—see Table 16.3. *First,* is selection (see Table 16.2 for suggested criteria). *Second,* is to provide opportunities for learning from varied and challenging job assignments. *Third,* is reinforcing the learning from the second phase. Simply having an experience is not sufficient for learning. We must connect our experience to language, to concepts that help us to *understand* what we have experienced, and be able to apply that learning to new challenges in the future. Thus, reflection is key. Mentors and coaches can be helpful in this third phase. And finally in the *fourth* phase we need to determine if the first three phases have been effective. Having an evaluation process all along—that is, not waiting for Phase IV to begin, would be ideal. Such indices as multirater feedback, job performance indicators, promotion rate, awards received, etc., can be useful for the evaluation process.

One final point or perhaps caveat has not been addressed—the issue of performance versus development. Developing potential leaders as just outlined requires an investment in a deliberate plan for learning over an extended period of time. Executives must be willing to reassign their high potentials and performers for some period of time—six months to a year perhaps—to another position. From the executive's point of view, he or she would be making a sacrifice to allow one or more high performers to be seconded to another assignment. His or her "bottom line" could easily be affected. Moreover, just as stated before, the following applies:

With the pressure that executives face in our rapidly changing world putting an inexperienced person, regardless of how bright and able the individual may be, into a tough, risky assignment requires a strong commitment to development, a commitment that most executives are

Table 16.3 A Phased Program of Leadership Development

Phase I, Selection	Phase II, Job Assignments	Phase III, Reflection	Phase IV, Evaluation

• Based on the criteria that are grounded in the organization's current or future desired state
 	
• Avoid cloning of bosses
 	
• Emphasize diversity—heterogeneous executives outperform homogeneous executives
	• Provide challenging assignments such as
	
	  ○ Turn-around, fix-it
	  ○ A leap in scope, e.g., from middle manager to general manager
	  ○ Line to staff switch
	  ○ Start from scratch, e.g., new business line
	  ○ Task force and project management
		• Provide support for learning via
		
		  ○ Mentoring
		  ○ Coaching with emphasis on learning and introspection
		  ○ Specific skill-based training, e.g., public speaking
			• Before and after assessments based on multirater systems
			
			  ○ Performance appraisal
			  ○ Promotion rate
			  ○ Extent to which a person is selected for further challenging assignments

SOURCE: Burke (2011).

unwilling to make. McCall (2010) addressed this issue and suggested, among other ideas, to "embed development seamlessly in the business strategy" (p. 11). In short, he argued that it is better to "join with" executives than to confront them about the development versus performance issue. Whether to fight or join, we as change consultants nevertheless have a lot to learn about how to ensure that evidence-based knowledge regarding leadership development gets used appropriately in the organizations we serve. (Burke, 2011, p. 162)

Learning Agility

It may be that those high potential leaders who perform well and learn the most in a variety of job experiences are highly agile with respect to their modes of learning. These are early days for understanding and conducting research on learning agility but the future looks promising and exciting. Moreover, if a reliable and valid measure of the concept can be realized, learning agility would then be added to the criteria for selection of potential leaders. Claims have been made regarding measurement (DeMeuse, Guangrong, & Hallenbeck, 2010; Eichinger & Lombardo, 2004; Lombardo & Eichinger, 2000), but confusion about the concept itself and what is being measured remains. A major article by DeRue, Ashford, and Myers (2012) highlights the confusion by pointing out that the measures that exist may be assessing learning *ability* not *agility*. These authors offer a definition of learning agility that emphasizes both *speed*—gaining understanding of an issue, problem, situation, or idea quickly—and *flexibility*—can see patterns and make connections across a variety of situations and ideas. DeRue and colleagues then moved from definition to a model of learning agility that is, (a) comprehensive, including such variables as individual differences, contextual and environmental factors, and (b) complex, defining learning agility as speed and flexibility but in two different ways or processes—cognitive and behavioral. All of these factors then lead to outcomes—that is, learning in and across situations and positive performance and change over time.

Over a period of some four years, doctoral students and I have been working on defining learning agility and attempting to measure it but only behaviorally not cognitively—see our commentary piece in the same journal issue as the DeRue and colleagues' (2012) article (Mitchinson, Gerard, Roloff, & Burke, 2012). We recognize that eventually to understand fully what learning agility is all about, we must account for both behavior and how people think, but, for now, our focus is on behavior. Currently we are exploring six categories of behavior. These six are listed with a behavioral example for each one:

- Exploring—taking on challenges outside one's area of expertise
- Experimenting—trying out new practices and approaches
- Exploiting—becoming aware of unconscious habits
- Being flexible—adapting to new situations rapidly
- Presencing—not being tied to the past
- Reflecting—examining critical advice to improve

These behavioral categories and measurement items written in observable, behavioral terms is our beginning. We have only scratched the surface conceptually; for example, we need to be as clear about learning as we are about agility, and behaviorally—that is, to end up with measurement items that can support both self-rating and others' ratings of the target individual. Our quest is to operationalize behaviorally what is meant by learning agility. Stay tuned.

Trust

The purpose of this last section of the book is simply to call our attention to a serious issue between people individually, between groups, in and between work organizations, and in and between nations. Problems of trust seem to be pervasive and deeper than ever before. Maybe this problem is no worse than it was in Shakespeare's day and before. It just seems worse perhaps because our planet is occupied by so many more people and organizations. In any case, the problem, nevertheless, is with us. We know a lot about mistrust and conflicts; we know less about how to resolve conflict and restore trust once broken. The following brief description of a case of broken trust should illustrate my point.

The Department of Energy (DOE), a primary agency within the U.S. government, is the parent organization for most of the research and development (R&D) laboratories within the federal system, ranging from the many laboratories that serve the Department of Defense to those that serve other agencies such as those that are health related and the DOE itself. Examples of the latter are the three national nuclear laboratories located in the West: (a) Los Alamos and (b) Sandia in New Mexico and (c) Lawrence Livermore in Los Angeles with a satellite operation in

Berkeley, California. The primary mission of these laboratories is to oversee and protect the stockpile of nuclear materials, especially pertaining to weapons for the U.S. military. The laboratories also conduct basic and applied research in a variety of areas such as materials science and laser fusion. For many decades, these laboratories have been managed contractually by the University of California charging DOE a dollar a year for their services. Around the turn of the 21st century, Congress decided that DOE's relationship with the University of California had run long enough plus the fact that some incidents had recently occurred that frightened some members of Congress such as a Los Alamos scientist taking his computer home for a short period. It was time for new management—some thought—and time to put the management contract out for public bid. Winning the contracts for all three laboratories were private corporations such as Lockheed Martin, Bechtel, and Babcock & Wilcox. Thus, new management took over with bonus systems for senior managers and closer scrutiny and supervision for practically everyone. According to a number of laboratory employees who complained to their local representatives in Congress, the culture of the laboratories was being affected in a deleterious manner. Congress then commissioned the National Research Council of the National Academies of Science to conduct a review (if not investigation) of the situation at all three of the laboratories. I served on the 12-person committee of scientists—most of whom were nuclear physicists (read: intimidation on my part). I was the only psychologist and person on the committee with an organization and change management background.

We pursued our charge for the better part of a year concluding with a written report of some 120 pages (*Managing for High-Quality Science and Engineering at the NNSA National Security Laboratories*, 2012; Shank & Patel, 2012). Numerous issues were explored, but the one that seemed to loom large and most pressing was labeled as "broken relationships," which had emerged between DOE and the three laboratories. In other words, mistrust was everywhere but especially at the nexus of the parent DOE and the management of the laboratories. It wasn't that the laboratories were poorly managed but more a matter of heavy if not oppressive oversight that challenged local expertise, experience, and autonomy, a precious commodity especially for a scientist.

One of my contributions, perhaps my only one, was to write a one-page document titled "On the Psychology of Trust" (see the sidebar), which was incorporated within the chapter of our report on "Broken

Relationships." One of the recommendations in the report was essentially the last paragraph of this one-page document shown in the sidebar.

The message of the "broken relationships" story was to illustrate the point made in the opening statement of this section on trust. Mistrust and broken trust are very difficult to restore. We know precious little about how to do it. I am not the only one hoping for innovation in this critical arena of human relationships. Ford and colleagues (2008) and Tomlinson, Dineen, and Lewicki (2004) have pointed out that we have few tools that help us to repair damaged trust that has resulted from broken agreements.

But there is encouragement. Trust is getting more attention. In addition to writing a book about leading a high-trust organization, Bob Hurley (2011) also designed and conducted a "Summit on Restoring Trust in Business" in the fall of 2011, sponsored by Fordham University, that was well attended and generated spirited dialogue. Also see Dirks and DeCremer (2011) for coverage on repairing trust. So, maybe with more concerted attention to the issue of mistrust and restoring trust as well as putting the issue more centrally in our attention span, like holding a conference on trust as Hurley led at Fordham University, progress can be made.

ON THE PSYCHOLOGY OF TRUST

We can consider trust in two somewhat different ways: one concerning *reliance* and the other *confidence.* Reliance means believing in the other person's character and ability. Can I believe what the other person tells me? Does he know what he's talking about? Do I have faith in her expertise, her knowledge? The other form of trust—confidence—means believing that I can depend on something in the future regarding another individual (or group perhaps). Can I rely on the other person to do, to deliver what he said he would? If I rely on her, for example, to keep a confidence, will she? Can I confide in her?

This latter form of trust is more about the dynamics of interpersonal relationships, hence, more complicated. The remainder of this brief treatise addresses this form of trust.

First, let us by comparison consider the opposite. *Mistrust* is very stable, whereas trust between people is delicate, ephemeral, like gossamer wings, and to maintain requires diligence.

(Continued)

(Continued)

Mistrust can last centuries (think, e.g., the Middle East, China, and Japan) and take the form of what we refer to as "intractable conflict." Trust, on the other hand, can be broken in a nanosecond.

To repair broken trust requires considerable time and effort. Attempting to fix things all at once and quickly is naïve and highly likely to fail.

To repair broken trust requires first an understanding of what the antecedents are. Being open, transparent, straight, and direct usually breeds the potential for trust. These behaviors do not in and of themselves guarantee trust; in other words, they are necessary but not sufficient, yet they do set the stage for trust to ensue.

To repair broken trust, it is best to take small steps. Initially one needs to take a trust risk that is relatively inconsequential—that is, if the other person violates the trust one has initiated, the outcome is not dire. If trust is not broken with this first step, then one can try a second step, a risk that again is fairly small, and if violated, no babies will die. If with a second step trust is not violated, then continue the process, and with an accumulative effect over time trust can eventually be restored. Bear in mind that this process of restoration requires motivation, perseverance, and patience.

Summary Statement

My main objective with this final chapter was to highlight areas of organizational dynamics that can have considerable influence on the success or failure of organization change efforts. These six areas—(a) culture change (covered in Chapter 11), (b) loosely versus tightly coupled systems (let me clarify that my treatise on culture change in Chapter 11 was aimed primarily at highly coupled rather than loosely coupled systems, which would be treated differently), (c) resistance, (d) leader selection and development, (e) learning agility, and (f) trust—are strong candidates for deeper learning. While not the only areas in need of more attention, I nevertheless believe that if we poured more of our learning energy and focus into these six, we could likely reduce the failure rate of over 70% regarding organization change efforts to a less embarrassing figure.

Conclusion

How do you end a book about change? After all, as some wise people stated long ago, change is ongoing. Reaching for my trusty *Bartlett's Familiar Quotations* (Bartlett, 1968), I found at least three that captured this thought:

> *Nothing endures but change.*
>
> —Heraclitus (540–480 BC)

> *Nothing in the world lasts save eternal change.*
>
> —Honorat de Bueil, Marquis de Racan (1589–1659)

> *There is nothing in this world constant, but inconstancy.*
>
> —Jonathan Swift (1667–1745)

Also, I have continued to read things, such as the article by Pettigrew, Woodman, and Cameron (2001) and the extensive review by Oreg, Vakola, and Armenakis (2011). They relied on much of the same literature I did, which was nice confirmation. Friends kept telling me about interesting articles and books they had read that needed to be included. And I realized that, like change, this process could go on for the rest of my life. So, we are not ending; it is merely a matter of stopping—for now.

Appendix

Annotated Bibliography

Burke, W. W., & Trahant, W. (2000). *Business climate shifts: Profiles of change makers.* Boston: Butterworth-Heinemann.

This book is about examples of organization change and, more particularly, about change leaders. The first two chapters (a) set the stage for the external environment for organizations, especially corporations, in this early part of the 21st century and (b) provide a framework—the Burke–Litwin model—for how each chapter is positioned, in other words, which dimensions (boxes) of the model are emphasized as the primary levers for change. Each remaining chapter is then devoted to an interview, including summary comments at the end, with a senior executive who is, in most cases, the CEO of a large, complex organization and had the primary responsibility for leading a significant transformation of his or her enterprise. These executives included Mac McDonald, head of Royal Dutch Shell, South Africa; Bob Bauman, of SmithKline Beecham; Lee Griffin, of Bank One, Louisiana; Lord Colin Marshall, British Airways (BA); Bill Henderson, postmaster general, U.S. Postal Service; Sir Richard Evans, British Aerospace; Jane Garvey, Federal Aviation Administration; and Roger Goldman, NatWest Bank.

Capra, F. (1996). *The web of life.* New York: Anchor Books. [Issued in paperback by Doubleday (1997).]

Fritjof Capra was originally trained in theoretical physics, and as a writer, he has significantly contributed to our understanding of modern science. With his expansive mind, he has drawn from the variety of research and theory in biochemistry, biology, and other life sciences, by luminaries such as Prigogine, Maturana, Varela, Margulis, and Kauffman, to provide a new scientific understanding of life at all levels, from organisms to social systems to ecosystems. He explained how we are shifting paradigmatically from a mechanistic world based on physics to an ecological world based on the life sciences and systems theory. Capra helps us to see the world as an integrated whole rather than as an aggregation of dissociated parts and to realize that all phenomena are fundamentally interdependent. Moreover, he showed how all of us—organisms, individuals, organizations, societies—are embedded in and are ultimately dependent on the cyclical processes of nature.

Capra, then, is an integrator, his book being a synthesis of recent theories: complexity, Gaia, and chaos theories. It is useful to consider how organizations fit within the larger ecosystem and at the other end of the spectrum, how organizations are like and imitate organisms but also differ—that is, in that they are creations of humans, not of nature.

Duck, J. D. (2001). *The change monster: The human forces that fuel or foil corporate transformation and change.* New York: Crown Business.

Jeanie Daniel Duck is a senior vice president at the Boston Consulting Group and has years of experience as an organization change consultant. The premise of her book is the notion that during organization change, and especially early in the process, human emotions and social dynamics "emerge like a dragon surfacing from the ocean depths" (p. xi). This emerging dragon is the "change monster." All organization transformations (OTs), of course, involve people, and that means emotions are rampant and egos are on the loose. This notion is another way of explaining what Pascale, Milleman, and Gioja (2000) referred to as "being on the edge of chaos." These emotional aspects are scary for change leaders, and they tend to avoid them. The purpose of Duck's book, therefore, is to help executives deal with seemingly uncontrollable and irrational responses to organization change.

Duck provided a sequenced set of actions to deal with the change monster. The first is to confront *stagnation*—that is, to deal with denial that change is needed. The second is preparation, in which change leaders engage in planning and communication. Duck advised going slowly at first and then going faster later. Third is implementation, which means to form new habits, and fourth is determination, or staying the course. The final set in the sequence is what Duck called fruition, when emotions are the most intense. The payoff comes with new behavior and deep change. Duck provided many examples that clarify how meaningful organization change occurs.

Foster, R. N., & Kaplan, S. (2001). *Creative destruction: Why companies that are built to last underperform the market—and how to successfully transform them.* New York: Currency and Doubleday.

These two McKinsey consultants argued that with the rapid rate of change that occurs now, unlike in the past, organizations that are successful and "built to last" will not. Nothing breeds failure like success. The better the company, the more efficient its operations and the more "locked in" to their culture, to use their words, they become—and thus, resistant to deep change. Foster and Kaplan were rather blunt about how wrong they believed the message is in *Built to Last,* by Collins and Porras (1994). The message by Foster and Kaplan, incidentally, is much like that in Drucker's (1994) *Harvard Business Review* article "The Theory of the Business"; that is, frequent examination of and questioning what business you are in is imperative for long-term survival.

   Creative Destruction is based on a straightforward theory of how capital markets work and how they are more amorphous and change more rapidly than do corporations. The mission of the corporation is to adapt as rapidly as possible to these forces and to fight against the rigidities of thinking by executives. It is interesting that the authors drew on research from cognitive psychology to explain how executives make decisions when they are faced with the "enigmas, dilemmas, paradoxes, puzzles, riddles, and mysteries" (p. 62) of the marketplace. Changing the mental sets of these executives is the challenge.

Gladwell, M. (2000). *The tipping point: How little things can make a big difference.* Boston: Little, Brown.

A writer for the *New Yorker*, Malcolm Gladwell was intrigued with the phenomenon of how and why major changes in society frequently happen suddenly and unexpectedly. Why did crime in New York City decline as suddenly as it did during the mid-1990s? Why did Hush Puppies shoes all of a sudden make a comeback? Why was Paul Revere's ride so successful when William Dawes's ride in another direction—but with the same warning about the British—was so unsuccessful? Gladwell compared these social epidemics to viral epidemics and points to the parallels—that is, when they reach a critical mass, they take off. They have reached the *tipping point*.

Parallels can also be drawn between the ideas and facts that Gladwell presented and organization change. The perspective that needs to be maintained is the difference between change that simply occurs and *planned* change. Gladwell's notions can indeed be applied to planned organization change.

Lawler, E. E., III, & Worley, C. G. (2006). *Built to change: How to achieve sustained organizational effectiveness.* San Francisco: Jossey-Bass.

Foster and Kaplan criticized the *Built to Last* premise and stated that "cultural lock-in" is the problem—that is, organizations, to last, must change their cultures and must continue to do so over time to succeed in the long term. But Foster and Kaplan did not necessarily tell us how to do it, to unlock the culture. Enter Lawler and Worley from the University of Southern California. These authors also referred to the Collins and Porras (1994) book, *Built to Last*, and used their reference to it as a taking-off point. In order for organizations to last today, especially in the commercial sector, they must be built to change. To last, they argued, organizational leaders must ensure that their organizations are agile and adaptable and constantly monitor their external environments. *Built to Change* is very much about design, identifying and adopting practices, structures, and processes that support and foster *continuous* change. Organization change is not so much a goal but more a process, a way of organizational life.

For Lawler and Worley, designing organizations for change should concentrate on such dimensions as (a) performance and defining organizational effectiveness, (b) strategizing, (c) structuring for effectiveness and change, (d) developing the right information, measurement, and decision-making processes, (e) acquiring the right talent, (f) managing human capital, and (g) designing the right reward system—that is, the one for performance and change. To give a couple of examples of how these authors address these dimensions, they argued that it is far more important for organizational executives to construct environmental scenarios that describe a range of possible future business conditions than simply to assemble an array of facts about the current environment. These scenarios should then drive strategizing and define effectiveness. A second example is their use of the term *strategizing* rather than strategy or strategic planning. Strategizing should occur every day rather than developing a plan that is done once a year. Lawler and Worley also emphasized the continuous development of a *temporary* competitive advantage for a business, that is, what may be an advantage today may not be one next week. The authors provided many additional examples for how to think about design on these dimensions and cite illustrative cases from such companies as Procter and Gamble, Johnson and Johnson, Limited Brands, and Toyota.

Pascale, R. T., Milleman, M., & Gioja, L. (2000). *Surfing the edge of chaos: The laws of nature and the new laws of business.* New York: Crown Business.

These authors, like Capra, chose an organism as the best metaphor for an organization. In fact, they argued that because an organization is a living system, the organism notion is more a reality than a metaphor. They drew from the life sciences what they referred to as "four cornerstone principles," which are just as valid for organizations as they are for species. These cornerstone principles are (a) equilibrium leads to death, (b) innovation often occurs "on the edge of chaos," (c) self-organization and emergence happen quite naturally, and (d) organizations can only be disturbed ("perturbed"), not directed. Using examples from well-known organizations, including Sears, Hewlett-Packard, and the U.S. Army, Pascale and his colleagues demonstrated one important way that organizations act like species: They either respond to change and evolve—or die.

These authors claimed by means of their parallels with the life sciences that change for organizations is a constant and those that survive learn how to adapt themselves to the perpetually changing external environment.

Note: The following five books and a video served as general background sources for this book.

Buchanan, M. (2000). *Ubiquity: The science of history . . . or why the world is simpler than we think.* London: Weidenfeld & Nicolson.

This book is in same genre of books as those cited already by Capra, Gladwell, and Gleick—that is, writings about science for the broader public. In this case, Buchanan, a science writer with a PhD in theoretical physics, began like Gladwell (2000) in his *The Tipping Point* by pointing out that sudden upheavals, such as world wars, earthquakes, gigantic forest fires, and stock market crashes, all erupt from very different roots but have at the same time an intriguing similarity. In each instance, the organization of the system made it possible for a small triggering event to cause reactions far out of proportion to the event itself. Such small triggering events are called by physicists the *critical state,* an "unstable and unusual condition that arises only under the most exceptional circumstances" (p. 13)—a slight grain of sand falling into a pile of sand that causes an avalanche, a slight shift in the earth's surface that causes an earthquake, one stockowner's decision to sell that causes a market crash, the butterfly effect, and so on. Buchanan's book is loaded with such examples, and the examples indeed make his conclusions persuasive. It is interesting to speculate about the applicability of these ideas for organization change. A small lever in the direction of the desired change—for example, a brief exchange between the CEO and a few key people—could cause a revolution.

Capra, B. (1990). *Mindwalk: A film for passionate thinkers.* Hollywood, CA: Paramount Pictures.

Based on Fritjof Capra's (1982) book, *The Turning Point,* this movie is an extensive conversation among three people—an academic (played by Liv Ullmann), a politician (played by Sam Waterston), and a poet (played by John Heard)—who happen to be on a respite of sorts at the same location, the beautiful island abbey of Mont Saint-Michel. The academic waxes eloquent and philosophical about organisms, patterns, ecosystems, the whole earth, and the universe, while the politician scoffs at the impracticality of it all and the poet provides some levity on occasion but mostly perspective—and a bit of poetry. Not quite two hours in length, the movie is a useful medium for introducing ideas from the new science: chaos and complexity theories, self-organization, patterns, autopoesis, and open-system theory. This movie is not for your average 10-year-old but for "passionate thinkers" who are somewhat older. It can be a worthy alternative to heavy tomes on the same subject matter.

Gleick, J. (1987). *Chaos: Making a new science.* New York: Penguin Books.

The introduction to chaos theory, at least for us neophytes, is this book by James Gleick. He provided for us the fundamentals of chaos theory as well as how it evolved. Gleick's manner of writing is most helpful in two primary ways. One, he simply is an excellent writer. He took incredibly complex ideas and explained them in such a way that nearly anyone can understand. Two, Gleick told stories about the scientists in the field, which, of course, makes the reading all the more interesting. Last, there are pictures—some in beautiful colors!

As Gleick stated, "Where chaos begins, classical science stops" (p. 3). The implication is that classical science is about order, predictability, and regularity. Chaos theory is the opposite. By the 1970s, a handful of scientists in the United States and abroad began to see "things" within disorder and irregularity that had not been seen before. These things, to name a few, became known as the *butterfly effect, nonlinearity, fractals, attractors, bifurcation, arrhythmia, the Mandelbrot set,* and the phenomenon we have all experienced, especially in airplanes, *turbulence.* And the beauty of it all, and certainly for those of us who need some closure, is that underlying apparent chaos is often order, pattern, and even at times symmetry.

Kauffman, S. (1995). *At home in the universe: The search for laws of self-organization and complexity.* New York: Oxford University Press.

Kauffman, a biologist, clearly stated that although Darwin's theory of evolution has been "spectacularly successful," it was not sufficient to explain much of life. Evolutionary theory, after all, is steeped in scientific reductionism—that is, breaking complex systems into their respective parts. But the whole often, if not always, has properties that cannot be explained by understanding the parts. This kind of complexity and whole-system way of thinking is not new. Yet Kauffman, using as his base biology and mathematics, provided compelling evidence with examples that show dramatically that we can understand systems without knowing all the details. He pointed out that one needs to know which properties of a system are important and which properties of a system are less so. Then one is in a position to independently explain the details of what the nature of a system is. An effective organizational model can have these characteristics. In chapter after chapter, Kauffman validated his point. Implicitly, we have believed for quite some time that a group and an organization are more than the sums of their parts. Now there is hard evidence. Kauffman also helps us understand more about principles such as self-organization, the edge of chaos, and complexity. Recall that Capra (1996) in his book, *The Web of Life*, drew on the work of Stuart Kauffman.

McClure, B. A. (1998). *Putting a new spin on groups: The science of chaos*. Mahwah, NJ: Lawrence Erlbaum.

The initial premise of this book is that the models and theories of small-group development from the 1950s and 1960s, when put to use, are really not very valid. They tend to be overly linear and too static; for example, groups go through stages such as "forming, storming, and norming" (p. 34). McClure did not argue that these ideas should be discarded; he preferred to add new concepts from chaos theory and from the evolution theory work of Arthur Young (1976) to build a new model of group development. McClure's model is neither linear nor unidimensional, and he emphasized the central function of conflict. Although there is a progressive quality to his model, the focus is more on how groups change, evolve, and mature. McClure is not as comprehensive as Gleick in his coverage of chaos theory, but he did introduce us to the terminology and to some of the primary ideas and concepts, particularly those that he found most applicable to group development, such as self-organization and behavior in systems far from equilibrium. Based on Young's ideas of how evolution occurs— that is, nonlinearly—McClure derived an "arc" of group development having seven stages and beginning and ending with *performing*. After the initial performing stage comes *unity*, then *disunity*, followed by the central focus or nadir of his arc, *conflict and confrontation*, followed by *disharmony, harmony,* and ending with a new version of *performing*. His model is more complex than my description may sound and does indeed reflect thinking from chaos theory and Young's work.

Stickland, F. (1998). *The dynamics of change: Insights into organisational transition from the natural world.* London: Routledge.

As Stickland has pointed out, many books have been written about how to manage change but few about the nature of change itself, the *what*. His book, therefore, addresses the content; that is, he explored what organization change is as a phenomenon. Stickland's fundamental question is this: How can we really understand the process of leading and managing organization change if we are not sufficiently clear about what it is in the first place? He then proceeded to explain systems thinking—that is, general systems theory, or metaphorical ways of understanding organization change. Then he summarized much of the relevant literature, referring to familiar names such as Kurt Lewin, William Bridges, and Andrew Pettigrew. Seeking a definition of organization change, Stickland then explored various perspectives, particularly from the social sciences and the physical sciences. For the remainder of his book, Stickland used the perspective of the natural and physical sciences to examine the nature of change and how to apply this kind of understanding to organizations. In his final chapter, he explored two interesting questions: "What constitutes successful change, and when does a change metaphor become reality?" (p. 155). In the scholarly tradition, at the end, Stickland suggested areas for further research in the quest for a deeper understanding of the nature of organization change itself.

References

Adizes, I. (1979). Organizational passages: Diagnosing and treating life cycle problems of organizations. *Organizational Dynamics, 8*(1), 3–25.

Alderfer, C. P. (1977a). Group and intergroup relations. In J. R. Hackman & J. L. Suttle (Eds.), *Improving life at work: Behavioral science approaches to organizational change* (pp. 227–296). Santa Monica, CA: Goodyear.

Alderfer, C. P. (1977b). Organization development. *Annual Review of Psychology, 28,* 197–223.

Aldrich, H. E. (1979). *Organizations and environments.* Englewood Cliffs, NJ: Prentice Hall.

Alexander, Y. (2002). *The impact of cross-cultural differences on the relationship of management practices, organizational climate, and employee satisfaction.* Unpublished doctoral dissertation, Columbia University, New York.

Alinsky, S. (1946). *Reveille for radicals.* Chicago: University of Chicago Press.

Allport, F. H. (1962). A structural conception of behavior: Individual and collective. I. Structural theory and the master problem of social psychology. *Journal of Abnormal and Social Psychology, 64,* 3–30.

Allport, G. W. (1945). *The nature of prejudice.* Cambridge, MA: Addison-Wesley.

Amburgey, T. L., & Dacin, T. (1994). As the left foot follows the right? The dynamics of strategic and structural change. *Academy of Management Journal, 37,* 1427–1452.

Amis, J., Slack, T., & Hinings, C. R. (2004). The pace, sequence, and linearity of radical change. *Academy of Management Journal, 47,* 15–39.

Anderson-Rudolf, M. K. (1996). *A longitudinal study of organizational change: How change in individual perceptions of transformational and transactional constructs predicts change in organizational performance.* Unpublished doctoral dissertation, Columbia University, New York.

Argyris, C. (1964). T-groups for organizational effectiveness. *Harvard Business Review, 42*(2), 60–74.

Argyris, C. (1970). *Intervention theory and method.* Reading, MA: Addison-Wesley.

Argyris, C. (1971). *Management and organizational development.* New York: McGraw-Hill.

Argyris, C., Putnam, R., & Smith, D. M. (1985). *Action science.* San Francisco: Jossey-Bass.

Argyris, C., & Schön, D. (1978). *Organizational learning: A theory of action perspective.* Reading, MA: Addison-Wesley.

Argyris, C., & Schön, D. (1982). *Theory in practice.* San Francisco: Jossey-Bass.

Armenakis, A. A., & Bedeian, A. G. (1999). Organization change: A review of theory and research in the 1990s. *Journal of Management, 25,* 293–315.

Arquilla, J., & Ronfeldt, D. F. (2001). *Networks and netwars: The future of terror, crime and militancy.* Santa Monica, CA: RAND Corporation.

Ashkanasy, N. M., Wilderom, C. P. M., & Peterson, M. F. (Eds.). (2000). *Handbook of organizational culture and climate.* Thousand Oaks, CA: Sage.

At Emery Air Freight: Positive reinforcement boosts performance. (1973). *Organizational Dynamics, 1*(3), 41–67.

Atkinson, J. W. (1958). *Motives in fantasy, action, and society.* Princeton, NJ: Van Nostrand.

Atwater, L., & Yammarino, F. (1992). Does self-other agreement on leadership perceptions moderate the validity of leadership predictions? *Personnel Psychology, 45,* 141–164.

Audia, P. G., Locke, E. A., & Smith, K. G. (2000). The paradox of success: An archival and a laboratory study of strategic persistence following radical environmental change. *Academy of Management Journal, 43,* 837–853.

Avolio, B. J. (1999). *Full leadership development: Building the vital forces in organizations.* Thousand Oaks, CA: Sage.

Bachman, J., Smith, C., & Slesinger, J. (1966). Control, performance, and satisfaction: An analysis of structural and individual effects. *Journal of Personality and Social Psychology, 4,* 127–136.

Bargh, J. A., & Chartrand, T. L. (1999). The unbearable automaticity of being. *American Psychologist, 54,* 462–479.

Barrick, M. R., Day, D. V., Lord, R. G., & Alexander, R. A. (1991). Assessing the utility of executive leadership. *Leadership Quarterly, 2,* 9–22.

Bartlett, J. (1968). *Bartlett's familiar quotations* (14th ed.). Boston: Little, Brown.

Bass, B. M. (1990). *Bass and Stodgill's handbook of leadership* (3rd ed.). New York: Free Press.

Bass, B. M. (1997). Does the transactional-transformational leadership paradigm transcend organizational and national boundaries? *American Psychologist, 52*(2), 130–139.

Bass, B. M. (1998). *Transformational leadership: Industrial, military, and educational impact.* Mahwah, NJ: Lawrence Erlbaum.

Bateson, G. (1979). *Mind and nature: A necessary unity.* New York: Dutton.

Bauman, R. P., Jackson, P., & Lawrence, J. T. (1997). *From promise to performance: A journey of transformation at SmithKline Beecham.* Boston: Harvard Business School Press.

Baumeister, R. F., Bratslavsky, E., Finkenauer, C., & Vohs, K. D. (2001). Bad is stronger than good. *Review of General Psychology, 5,* 323–370.

Beckhard, R. (1967). The confrontation meeting. *Harvard Business Review, 45*(2), 149–155.

Beckhard, R. (1972). Optimizing team-building efforts. *Journal of Contemporary Business, 1*(3), 23–32.

Beckhard, R. (1997). *Agent of change: My life, my practice.* San Francisco: Jossey-Bass.

Beckhard, R., & Harris, R. T. (1977). *Organizational transitions: Managing complex change.* Reading, MA: Addison-Wesley.

Beckhard, R., & Harris, R. T. (1987). *Organizational transitions: Managing complex change* (2nd ed.). Reading, MA: Addison-Wesley.

Beer, M. (1980). *Organization change and development.* Santa Monica, CA: Goodyear.

Beer, M., Eisenstat, R. A., & Spector, B. (1990). *The critical path to corporate renewal.* Boston: Harvard Business School Press.

Beer, M., Spector, B., Lawrence, P. R., Mills, D. Q., & Walton, R. E. (1984). *Managing human assets.* New York: Free Press.

Beer, M., & Walton, A. E. (1987). Organization change and development. *Annual Review of Psychology, 38,* 339–367.

Bennis, W., & Biederman, P. W. (1997). *Organizing genius: The secrets of creative collaboration.* Reading, MA: Addison-Wesley.

Bennis, W. G., & Nanus, B. (1985). *Leaders: The strategies for taking charge.* New York: Harper & Row.

Bennis, W. G., & O'Toole, J. (2000). Don't hire the wrong CEO. *Harvard Business Review, 78*(5/6), 171–176.

Bernstein, W. M., & Burke, W. W. (1989). Modeling organizational meaning systems. In R. W. Woodman & W. A. Pasmore (Eds.), *Research in organizational change and development* (Vol. 3, pp. 117–159). Greenwich, CT: JAI.

Bion, W. R. (1961). *Experience in groups.* New York: Basic Books.

Blake, R. R., & Mouton, J. S. (1964). *The managerial grid.* Houston: Gulf.

Blake, R. R., & Mouton, J. S. (1968). *Corporate excellence through grid organization development.* Houston: Gulf.

Blake, R. R., & Mouton, J. S. (1978). *The new managerial grid.* Houston: Gulf.

Blake, R. R., Shepard, H. A., & Mouton, J. S. (1964). *Managing intergroup conflict in industry.* Houston: Gulf.

Block, P. (1981). *Flawless consulting: A guide to getting your expertise used.* San Francisco: Jossey-Bass/Pfeiffer.

Blumberg, M., & Pringle, C. D. (1983). How control groups can cause loss of control in action research: The case of Rushton Coal Mine. *Journal of Applied Behavioral Science, 19,* 409–425.

Bolster, B. I., & Springbett, B. M. (1961). The reaction of interviewers to favorable and unfavorable information. *Journal of Applied Psychology, 45,* 97–103.

Bonabeau, E., & Meyer, C. (2001). Swarm intelligence: A whole new way to think about business. *Harvard Business Review, 79*(5), 106–114.

Bossidy, L., & Charan, R. (2002). *Execution: The discipline of getting things done.* New York: Crown Business.

Bourgeois, L. J., III. (1985). Strategic goals, perceived uncertainty, and economic performance in volatile environments. *Academy of Management Journal, 28,* 548–573.

Bower, M. (1979). *Perspective on McKinsey.* New York: McKinsey.

Bowers, D. G. (1964). Organizational control in an insurance company. *Sociometry, 27,* 230–244.

Boyatzis, R. E. (1982). *The competent manager.* New York: Wiley.

Boyatzis, R. E., Smith, M. L., & Blaize, N. (2006). Developing sustainable leaders through coaching and compassion. *Academy of Management Learning & Education,* 5(1), 8–24.

Bracken, D. W. (1996). Multisource (360-degree) feedback: Surveys for individual and organizational development. In A. I. Kraut (Ed.), *Organizational surveys: Tools for assessment and change* (pp. 117–143). San Francisco: Jossey-Bass.

Brehm, J. W. (1966). *A theory of psychological reactance.* New York: Academic Press.

Bridges, W. (1980). *Transitions: Making sense of life's changes.* Reading, MA: Addison-Wesley.

Bridges, W. (1986). Managing organizational transitions. *Organizational Dynamics, 15*(1), 24–33.

Briggs, K. C., & Myers, I. B. (1943). *Myers-Briggs Type Indicator.* Palo Alto, CA: Consulting Psychologists Press.

Bright, D. S., & Cameron, K. (2010). Positive organizational change: What the field of POS offers to OD practitioners. In W. J. Rothwell, J. M. Stavros, R. L. Sullivan, & A. Sullivan (Eds.), *Practicing organization development* (3rd ed., pp. 397–410). San Francisco: Pfeiffer/Wiley.

Brooker, K. (2001). The chairman of the board looks back. *Fortune, 143*(11), 62–76.

Buchanan, M. (2000). *Ubiquity: The science of history . . . or why the world is simpler than we think.* London: Weidenfeld & Nicolson.

Bullock, R. J., & Lawler, E. E., III. (1984). Gainsharing: A few questions and fewer answers. *Human Resource Management, 23,* 23–40.

Bunker, B. B., & Alban, B. T. (1997). *Large group interventions: Engaging the whole system for rapid change.* San Francisco: Jossey-Bass.

Bunker, D. R., & Knowles, E. S. (1967). Comparison of behavioral changes resulting from human relations training laboratories of different lengths. *Journal of Applied Behavioral Science, 3,* 505–524.

Burck, G. (1965, December). Union Carbide's patient schemers. *Fortune,* pp. 147–149.

Burke, M. J., & Pearlman, K. (1988). Recruiting, selecting, and matching people with jobs. In J. P. Campbell, R. S. Campbell, & Associates (Eds.), *Productivity in organizations* (pp. 97–142). San Francisco: Jossey-Bass.

Burke, W. W. (1974). Managing conflict between groups. In J. D. Adams (Ed.), *New technologies in organization development* (Vol. 2, pp. 255–268). San Diego: University Associates.

Burke, W. W. (1980). System theory, Gestalt therapy, and organization development. In T. G. Cummings (Ed.), *Systems theory for organization development* (pp. 209–222). Chichester, UK: Wiley.

Burke, W. W. (1982). *Organization development: Principles and practices.* Boston: Little, Brown.

Burke, W. W. (1986). Leadership as empowering others. In S. Srivastva & Associates (Eds.), *Executive power: How executives influence people and organizations* (pp. 51–77). San Francisco: Jossey-Bass.

Burke, W. W. (1994). *Organization development: A process of learning and changing* (2nd ed.). Reading, MA: Addison-Wesley.

Burke, W. W. (1995). Organization change: What we know, what we need to know. *Journal of Management Inquiry, 4,* 158–171.

Burke, W. W. (1997). Leadership development. In L. J. Bassi & D. Russ-Eft (Eds.), *What works: Training and development practices* (pp. 1–25). Alexandria, VA: American Society for Training and Development.

Burke, W. W. (2000a). The broad band of organization development and change: An introduction. In D. Giver, L. Carter, & M. Goldsmith (Eds.), *Best practices in organization and human resources development handbook* (pp. 5–10). Lexington, MA: Linkage.

Burke, W. W. (2000b). SmithKline Beecham. In D. Giver, L. Carter, & M. Goldsmith (Eds.), *Best practices in organization and human resources development handbook* (pp. 103–118). Lexington, MA: Linkage.

Burke, W. W. (2006). Conflict in organizations. In M. Deutsch, P. Coleman, & E. Marcus (Eds.), *The handbook of conflict resolution: Theory and practice* (2nd ed., pp. 781–804). New York: Wiley.

Burke, W. W. (2011). A perspective on the field of organization development and change: The Zeigarnik effect. *Journal of Applied Behavioral Science, 47,* 143–167.

Burke, W. W., & Biggart, N. W. (1997). Interorganizational relations. In D. Druckman, J. E. Singer, & H. Van Cott (Eds.), *Enhancing organizational performance* (pp. 120–149). Washington, DC: National Academy Press.

Burke, W. W., Clark, L. P., & Koopman, C. (1984). Improve your OD project's chances for success. *Training and Development Journal, 38*(8), 62–68.

Burke, W. W., & Coruzzi, C. A. (1987). Competence in managing lateral relations. In J. W. Pfeiffer (Ed.), *The 1987 annual: Developing human resources* (pp. 151–156). San Diego: University Associates.

Burke, W. W., & Jackson, P. (1991). Making the SmithKline Beecham merger work. *Human Resource Management, 30,* 69–87.

Burke, W. W., Javitch, M., Waclawski, J., & Church, A. (1997). The dynamics of midstream consulting. *Consulting Psychology Journal: Practice and Research, 49,* 83–95.

Burke, W. W., Lake, D. G., & Paine, J. W. (Eds.) (2009). *Organization change: A comprehensive reader.* San Francisco: Jossey-Bass.

Burke, W. W., & Litwin, G. H. (1992). A causal model of organizational performance and change. *Journal of Management, 18*(3), 532–545.

Burke, W. W., & Noumair, D. A. (2002). The role and function of personality assessment in organization development. In J. Waclawski & A. H. Church (Eds.), *Organization development: Data-driven methods for change* (pp. 55–77). San Francisco: Jossey-Bass.

Burke, W. W., Richley, E. A., & DeAngelis, L. (1985). Changing leadership and planning processes at the Lewis Research Center, National Aeronautics and Space Administration. *Human Resource Management, 24,* 81–90.

Burke, W. W., & Schmidt, W. H. (1971). Primary target for change: The manager or the organization? In H. A. Hornstein, B. B. Bunker, W. W. Burke, M. Gindes, & R. J. Lewicki (Eds.), *Social intervention: A behavioral science approach* (pp. 373–385). New York: Free Press.

Burke, W. W., & Trahant, B. (2000). *Business climate shifts: Profiles of change makers.* Boston: Butterworth Heinemann.

Burns, J. M. (1978). *Leadership.* New York: Harper & Row.

Burns, T., & Stalker, G. (1961). *The management of innovation.* London: Tavistock.

Cameron, K. S. (1980). Critical questions in assessing organizational effectiveness. *Organizational Dynamics, 9*(2), 66–80.

Cameron, K. S. (2008a). Paradox in positive organizational change. *Journal of Applied Behavioral Science, 44,* 7–24.

Cameron, K. S. (2008b). *Positive leadership: Strategies for extraordinary performance.* San Francisco: Barrett-Koehler.

Cameron, K. S., & Whetten, D. A. (1981). Perceptions of organizational effectiveness over organizational life cycles. *Administrative Science Quarterly, 26,* 525–544.

Cameron, K. S., & Whetten, D. A. (Eds.). (1982). *Organizational effectiveness: A comparison of multiple models.* New York: Academic Press.

Campbell, J. P., & Dunnette, M. D. (1968). Effectiveness of T-group experiences in managerial training and development. *Psychological Bulletin, 70,* 73–104.

Capra, B. (1990). *Mindwalk: A film for passionate thinkers.* Hollywood, CA: Paramount Pictures.

Capra, F. (1982). *The turning point.* New York: Simon & Schuster.

Capra, F. (1991). *The Tao of physics* (3rd ed.). Boston: Shambhala. (Original work published 1975)

Capra, F. (1996). *The web of life.* New York: Anchor Books.

Carlzon, J. (1987). *Moments of truth: New strategies for today's customer-driven economy.* Cambridge, MA: Ballinger.

Carnall, C. A. (1982). *The evaluation of organizational change.* Brookfield, VT: Gower.

Chandler, A. (1962). *Strategy and structure.* Cambridge: MIT Press.

Chin, R., & Benne, K. D. (1985). General strategies for effecting changes in human systems. In W. G. Bennis, K. D. Benne, & R. Chin (Eds.), *The planning of change* (4th ed., pp. 22–43). New York: Holt, Rinehart & Winston.

Church, A. H. (1997). Managerial self-awareness in high-performing individuals in organizations. *Journal of Applied Psychology, 82,* 281–292.

Church, A. H., Waclawski, J., & Burke, W. W. (2001). Multisource feedback for organization development and change. In D. W. Bracken, C. W. Timmreck, & A. H. Church (Eds.), *The handbook of multisource feedback* (pp. 301–317). San Francisco: Jossey-Bass.

Coch, L., & French, J. R. P. (1948). Overcoming resistance to change. *Human Relations, 1,* 512–532.

Collins, J. (2001). *Good to great: Why some companies make the leap and others don't.* New York: HarperCollins.

Collins, J. C., & Porras, J. I. (1994). *Built to last: Successful habits of visionary companies.* New York: Harper Business.

Conger, J. A. (1989). *The charismatic leader: Behind the mystique of exceptional leadership.* San Francisco: Jossey-Bass.

Cooperrider, D. L., & Srivastva, S. (1987). Appreciative inquiry in organizational life. *Research in organizational change and development, Vol. 1,* (pp. 129–169), Greenwich, CT: JAI Press.

Coser, L. (1967). *Continuities in the study of social conflict.* New York: Free Press.

Costa, P. T., & McCrae, R. R. (1985). *NEO-Personality Inventory.* Odessa, FL: PAR Psychological Assessment Resources.

Crockett, W. J. (1970). Team building—One approach to organizational development. *Journal of Applied Behavioral Science, 6,* 291–306.

Csikszentmihalyi, M. (1990). *Flow: The psychology of optimal experience.* New York: Harper & Row.

Cytrynbaum, S., & Noumair, D. A. (Eds.). (2004). *Group dynamics, organizational irrationality, and social complexity: Group relations reader 3.* Jupiter, FL: A. K. Rice Institute.

Davis, S. A. (1967). An organic problem-solving method of organizational change. *Journal of Applied Behavioral Science, 3,* 3–21.

Deal, T. E., & Kennedy, A. A. (1982). *Corporate cultures: The rites and rituals of corporate life.* Reading, MA: Addison-Wesley.

DeMeuse, K. P., Guangrong, D., & Hallenbeck, G. S. (2010). Learning agility: A construct whose time has come. *Consulting Psychology Journal: Practice and Research, 62,* 119–130.

Denis, J.-L., Lamothe, L., & Langley, A. (2001). The dynamics of collective leadership and strategic change in pluralistic organizations. *Academy of Management Journal, 44,* 809–837.

Denning, S. (2004). Telling tales. *Harvard Business Review, 82*(5), 122–129.

Dent, E. B., & Goldberg, S. G. (1999). Challenging "resistance to change." *Journal of Applied Behavioral Science, 35,* 25–41.

DeRue, D. S., Ashford, S. J., & Myers, C. G. (2012). Learning agility: In search of conceptual clarity and theoretical grounding. *Industrial and Organizational Psychology: Perspectives on Science and Practice, 5,* 258–279.

Deutsch, M. (1969). Conflicts: Productive and destructive. *Journal of Social Issues*, 25, 7–40.

Deutsch, M. (1985). *Distributive justice: A social psychological perspective.* New Haven, CT: Yale University Press.

Dickson, W. J., & Roethlisberger, F. J. (1966). *Counseling in an organization: A sequel to the Hawthorne researchers.* Boston: Harvard Business School, Division of Research.

Dime Savings Bank. (1997). *Our vision; our mission.* New York: Dime Bancorp.

Dirks, K. T., & DeCremer, D. (2011). The repair of trust: Insights from organizational behaviour and social psychology. In D. DeCremer, R. Van Dick, & J. K. Murnighan (Eds.), *Social psychology and organizations* (pp. 211–230). New York: Routledge.

Dixon, N. F. (1976). *On the psychology of military incompetence.* London: Futura.

Drucker, P. F. (1969). *The age of discontinuity: Guidelines to our changing society.* New Brunswick, NJ: Transaction.

Drucker, P. F. (1974). *Management: Tasks, responsibilities, practices.* New York: Harper & Row.

Drucker, P. F. (1994). The theory of the business. *Harvard Business Review, 72*(5), 95–104.

Druckman, D., Singer, J. E., & Van Cott, H. (Eds.). (1997). *Enhancing organizational performance.* Washington, DC: National Academy Press.

Duck, J. D. (2001). *The change monster: The human forces that fuel or foil corporate transformation and change.* New York: Crown Business.

Dunbar, R. I. M. (1992). Neocortex size as a constraint on group size in primates. *Journal of Human Evolution, 20,* 469–493.

Duncan, J. R. (1979). What is the right organization structure? *Organizational Dynamics, 7*(3), 59–80.

Dunnette, M. D. (1969). People feeling: Joy, more joy, and the slough of despond. *Journal of Applied Behavioral Science, 5,* 25–44.

Dunnette, M. D., & Hough, L. M. (Eds.) (1992). *Handbook of industrial and organizational psychology* (Vol. 3, 2nd ed., p. 722). Palo Alto, CA: Consulting Psychologists Press, Inc.

Dyer, W. G. (1987). *Team building: Issues and alternatives* (2nd ed.). Reading, MA: Addison-Wesley.

Easterby-Smith, M. (1997). Disciplines of organizational learning: Contributions and critiques. *Human Relations, 50,* 1085–1103.

Eichinger, R. W., & Lombardo, M. M. (2004). Learning agility as a prime indicator of potential. *Human Resource Planning, 27,* 12–16.

Emery, F. E., & Trist, E. L. (1965). The causal texture of organizational environments. *Human Relations, 18,* 21–32.

Evans, R., & Price, C. (1999). *Vertical take-off: The inside story of British Aerospace's comeback from crisis to world class.* London: Nicholas Brealey.

Faucheux, C., Amado, G., & Laurent, A. (1982). Organizational development and change. *Annual Review of Psychology, 33,* 343–370.

Firestone, W. A. (1985). The study of loose coupling: Problems, progress, and prospects. In A. Kerckhoff (Ed.), *Research in sociology of education and socialization* (Vol. 5, pp. 3–30). Greenwich, CT: JAI Press.

Flamholtz, E. (1979). Organizational control systems as a managerial tool. *California Management Review, 22*(2), 50–59.

Fleishman, E. A. (1953). Leadership climate, human relations training, and supervisory behavior. *Personnel Psychology, 6,* 205–222.

Follett, M. P. (1996). The essentials of leadership. In P. Graham (Ed.), *Mary Parker Follett—Prophet of management: A celebration of writings from the 1920s* (pp. 163–181). Boston: Harvard Business School Press.

Ford, J. D., & Ford, L. W. (2012). The leadership of organization change: A view from recent empirical evidence. In A. B. Shani, W. A. Pasemore, & R. W. Woodman (Eds.), *Research in organizational change and development* (Vol. 20, pp. 1–36). Bingley, UK: Emerald Group.

Ford, J. D., Ford, L. W., & D'Amelio, A. (2008). Resistance to change: The rest of the story. *Academy of Management Review, 33,* 362–377.

Fordyce, J. K., & Weil, R. (1979). *Managing with people* (2nd ed.). Reading, MA: Addison-Wesley.

Foster, R. N., & Kaplan, S. (2001). *Creative destruction: Why companies that are built to last underperform the market—and how to successfully transform them.* New York: Currency.

Fox, M. M. (1990). *The role of individual perceptions of organization culture in predicting perceptions of work unit climate and organizational performance.* Unpublished doctoral dissertation, Columbia University, New York.

French, J. R. P., & Raven, B. H. (1959). The bases of social power. In D. Cartwright (Ed.), *Studies in social power* (pp. 150–167). Ann Arbor: University of Michigan, Institute for Social Research.

French, W. L., & Bell, C. H., Jr. (1995). *Organization development: Behavioral science interventions for organization improvement* (5th ed.). Englewood Cliffs, NJ: Prentice Hall.

Friedlander, F. (1970). The primacy of trust as a facilitator of further group accomplishment. *Journal of Applied Behavioral Science, 6,* 387–400.

Friedlander, F., & Brown, L. D. (1974). Organization development. *Annual Review of Psychology, 25,* 313–341.

Galbraith, J. R. (1973). *Designing complex organizations.* Reading, MA: Addison-Wesley.

Galbraith, J. R. (1977). *Organization design.* Reading, MA: Addison-Wesley.

Galbraith, J. R. (1995). *Designing organizations: An executive briefing on strategy, structure, and process.* San Francisco: Jossey-Bass.

Gardner, H. (1983). *Frames of mind: The theory of multiple intelligences.* New York: Basic Books.

Gardner, H. (1995). *Leading minds: An anatomy of leadership*. New York: Basic Books.

Gardner, H. (2004). *Changing minds: The art and science of changing our own and other people's minds*. Boston: Harvard Business School Press.

Georgiades, N., & Macdonell, R. (1998). *Leadership for competitive advantage*. Chichester, UK: Wiley.

Gersick, C. J. G. (1988). Time and transition in work teams: Toward a new model of group development. *Academy of Management Journal, 31*, 9–41.

Gersick, C. J. G. (1991). Revolutionary change theories: A multilevel exploration of the punctuated equilibrium paradigm. *Academy of Management Review, 16*, 10–36.

Gilley, A., McMillan, H. S., & Gilley, J. W. (2009). Organizational change and characteristics of leadership effectiveness. *Journal of Leadership and Organizational Studies, 16*, 38–47.

Giuliani, R. (2002). *Leadership*. New York: Hyperion.

Gladwell, M. (2000). *The tipping point: How little things can make a big difference*. Boston: Little, Brown.

Gleick, J. (1987). *Chaos: Making a new science*. New York: Penguin Books.

Goleman, D. (1995). *Emotional intelligence*. New York: Bantam.

Golembiewski, R. T., Billingsley, K., & Yeager, S. (1976). Measuring change and persistence in human affairs: Types of change generated by OD designs. *Journal of Applied Behavioral Science, 12*, 133–157.

Goodman, P. S., Devadas, R., & Griffith-Hughson, T. L. (1988). Groups and productivity: Analyzing the effectiveness of self-managing teams. In J. P. Campbell, R. J. Campbell, & Associates (Eds.), *Productivity in organizations* (pp. 295–327). San Francisco: Jossey-Bass.

Goodstein, L. D., & Burke, W. W. (1991). Creating successful organizational change. *Organizational Dynamics, 19*(4), 5–17.

Goodstein, L. D., & Butz, H. E. (1998). Customer value: The linchpin of organizational change. *Organizational Dynamics, 27*(1), 21–34.

Gordon, G. G. (1985). The relationship of corporate culture to industry sector and corporate performance. In R. H. Kilmann, M. J. Saxton, R. Serpa, & Associates (Eds.), *Gaining control of the corporate culture* (pp. 103–125). San Francisco: Jossey-Bass.

Gould, S. J. (1977). *Ever since Darwin*. New York: Norton.

Gould, S. J. (1980). *The panda's thumb*. New York: Norton.

Greiner, L. (1972). Evolution and revolution as organizations grow. *Harvard Business Review, 50*(4), 37–46.

Gronn, P. (2002). Distributed leadership as a unit of analysis. *The Leadership Quarterly, 13*, 423–451.

Guzzo, R. A., Jette, R. D., & Katzell, R. A. (1985). The effects of psychologically based intervention programs on worker productivity. *Personnel Psychology, 38*, 275–291.

Gyllenhammar, P. G. (1977). *People at work*. Reading, MA: Addison-Wesley.

Hackman, J. R. (1992). The psychology of self-management in organizations. In R. Glaser (Ed.), *Classic readings in self-managing teamwork* (pp. 143–193). King of Prussia, PA: Organization Design and Development.

Hackman, J. R. (2002). *Leading teams: Setting the stage for great performances.* Boston: Harvard Business School Press.

Hackman, J. R., & Oldham, G. R. (1980). *Work redesign.* Reading, MA: Addison-Wesley.

Haken, H. (1981). Synergetics: Is self-organization governed by universal principles? In E. Jantsch (Ed.), *Toward a unifying paradigm of physical, biological, and sociocultural evolution* (pp. 15–23). Boulder, CO: Westview.

Hall, J., & Williams, M. S. (1966). A comparison of decision-making performances in established and ad hoc groups. *Journal of Personality and Social Psychology, 3,* 214–222.

Hall, J., & Williams, M. S. (1970). Group dynamics training and improved decision making. *Journal of Applied Behavioral Science, 6,* 39–68.

Hambrick, D. C. (1989). Guest editor's introduction: Putting top managers back in the strategy picture. *Strategic Management Journal, 10,* 5–15.

Hambrick, D. C., & Cannella, A. A., Jr. (1989). Strategy implementation as substance and selling. *Academy of Management Executive, 3*(4), 278–285.

Harvey, J. B. (1974). The Abilene paradox: The management of agreement. *Organizational Dynamics, 3*(1), 63–80.

Harvey, J. B. (1977). Consulting during crises of agreement. In W. W. Burke (Ed.), *Current issues and strategies in organization development* (pp. 160–186). New York: Human Sciences Press.

Hayakawa, S. I. (1941). *Language in thought and action.* New York: Harcourt, Brace, & World.

Heifetz, R. A. (1994). *Leadership without easy answers.* Cambridge, MA: Belknap Press of Harvard University Press.

Herold, D. M., Fedor, D. B., Caldwell, S., & Liu, Y. (2008). The effects of transformational and change leadership on employee commitment to change: A multilevel study. *Journal of Applied Psychology, 93,* 346–357.

Herzberg, F. (1966). *Work and the nature of man.* Cleveland, OH: World.

Herzberg, F., Mausner, B., & Snyderman, B. (1959). *The motivation to work.* New York: Wiley.

Hewlett-Packard (2013). Culture. *Wikipedia: The Free Encyclopedia.* Retrieved from http://en.wikipedia.org/wiki/Hewlett-Packard#Culture.

Higgs, M., & Rowland, D. (2005). All changes great and small: Exploring approaches to change and its leadership. *Journal of Change Management, 5*(2), 121–151.

Hitt, M. A., & Tyler, B. B. (1991). Strategic decision models: Integrating different perspectives. *Strategic Management Journal, 12,* 327–351.

Hofstede, G. (1991). *Cultures and organisations: Intercultural cooperation and its importance to survival.* Glasgow, UK: Harper & Collins.

Hogan, R., Curphy, G. J., & Hogan, J. (1994). What we know about leadership: Effectiveness and personality. *American Psychologist, 52*(2), 130–139.

Hogan, R., Raskin, R., & Fazzini, D. (1990). The dark side of charisma. In K. E. Clark & M. B. Clark (Eds.), *Measures of leadership* (pp. 343–354). West Orange, NJ: Leadership Library of America.

Holstein, W. J. (2001, November 25). Three user's manuals for modern management. *The New York Times*, p. 6.

Homans, G. C. (1950). *The human group.* New York: Harcourt Brace.

Hornstein, H. A. (1996). *Brutal bosses and their prey.* New York: Riverhead Books.

Hornstein, H. A., Bunker, B. B., Burke, W. W., Gindes, M., & Lewicki, R. J. (1971). *Social interventions: A behavioral science approach.* New York: Free Press.

Hornstein, H. A., Callahan, D. M., Fisch, E., & Benedict, B. A. (1968). Influence and satisfaction in organizations: A replication. *Sociology of Education, 41*, 380–389.

House, R. J. (1977). A 1976 theory of charismatic leadership. In J. G. Hunt & L. Larson (Eds.), *Leadership: The cutting edge* (pp. 189–204). Carbondale: Southern Illinois University Press.

How mergers go wrong. (2000, July 22). *Economist*, p. 19.

Huber, G. P. (1991). Organizational learning: An examination of the contributing processes and a review of the literature. *Organization Science, 2*, 88–115.

Hughes, R. L., Ginnett, R. A., & Curphy, G. S. (1993). *Leadership: Enhancing the lessons of experience.* Homewood, IL: Irwin.

Hunter, J. E., & Schmidt, F. L. (1982). Fitting people to jobs: Implications of personnel selection on national productivity. In E. A. Fleischman & M. D. Dunnette (Eds.), *Human performance and productivity: Human capability assessment* (Vol. 1, pp. 233–284). Hillsdale, NJ: Erlbaum.

Hurley, R. F. (2011). *The decision to trust: How leaders create high-trust organizations.* San Francisco: Jossey-Bass.

Huselid, M. A., Jackson, S. E., & Schuler, R. S. (1997). Technical and strategic human resource management effectiveness as determinants of firm performance. *Academy of Management Journal, 40*, 171–188.

Jacobs, T. O., & Jaques, E. (1987). Leadership in complex systems. In J. Zeidner (Ed.), *Human productivity enhancement.* New York: Praeger.

James, W. (1890). *Principles of psychology* (Vols. 1 & 2). New York: Holt.

Jaques, E. (1978). *A general theory of bureaucracy.* Exeter, NH: Heinemann.

Jaques, E. (1986). The development of intellectual capability: A discussion of stratified systems theory. *Journal of Applied Behavioral Science, 22*, 361–384.

Jaques, E., & Clement, S. D. (1991). *Executive leadership.* Arlington, VA: Cason Hall.

Jick, T. D. (1990). *The recipients of change.* (Teaching materials). Boston: Harvard Business School.

Johnson & Johnson (2013). Our credo values. *Johnson & Johnson Homepage.* Retrieved from http://www.jnj.com/about-jnj/jnj-credo.

Johnson, S. (1998). *Who moved my cheese?* New York: Putnam.

Jordan, P. C. (1986). Effects of an extrinsic reward on intrinsic motivation. A field experiment. *Academy of Management Journal, 29,* 405–412.

Joyce, W. F., Nohria, N., & Roberson, B. (2003). *What really works: The 4 + 2 formula for sustained business success.* New York: Harper Business.

Joyce, W. F., & Slocum, J. W. (1984). Collective climate: Agreement as a basis for defining aggregate climates in organizations. *Academy of Management Journal, 27,* 721–742.

Kanter, R. M. (1982). Dilemmas of managing participation. *Organizational Dynamics, 11*(1), 5–27.

Kaplan, R. S., & Norton, D. P. (1996). *The balanced scorecard: Translating strategy into action.* Boston: Harvard Business School Press.

Katz, D., & Kahn, R. L. (1978). *The social psychology of organizations* (2nd ed.). New York: Wiley.

Katzell, R. A., & Thompson, D. E. (1990). Work motivation, theory and practice. *American Psychologist, 45*(2), 144–153.

Katzenbach, J. R., & Smith, D. K. (1993). *The wisdom of teams: Creating the high-performance organization.* Boston: Harvard Business School Press.

Kauffman, S. (1995). *At home in the universe: The search for laws of self-organization and complexity.* New York: Oxford University Press.

Kavanagh, M. H., & Ashkanasy, N. M. (2006). The impact of leadership and change management strategy on organizational culture and individual acceptance of change during a merger. *British Journal of Management, 17,* 81–103.

Kerr, J., & Slocum, J. W. (1987). Managing corporate culture through reward systems. *Academy of Management Executive, 1,* 99–108.

Kimberly, J. R., Miles, R., & Associates. (1980). *The organizational life cycle.* San Francisco, CA: Jossey-Bass.

Kimberly, J. R., & Nielsen, W. R. (1975). Organization development and change in organizational performance. *Administrative Science Quarterly, 20,* 191–206.

King, D. (1972). Selecting personnel for a System 4 organization. In W. W. Burke (Ed.), *Contemporary organization development: Conceptual orientations and interventions* (pp. 201–211). Washington, DC: NTL Institute for Applied Behavioral Science.

Kipnis, D. (1976). *The powerholders.* Chicago: University of Chicago Press.

Koch, C., & Laurent, G. (1999). Complexity and the nervous system. *Science, 284,* 96–98.

Kotter, J. P. (1990). *A force for change: How leadership differs from management.* New York: Free Press.

Kotter, J. P. (1996). *Leading change.* Boston: Harvard Business School Press.

Kotter, J. P., & Heskett, J. L. (1992). *Corporate culture and performance.* New York: Free Press.

Kotter, J. P., & Rathgeber, H. (2005). *Our iceberg is melting.* Boston: Privately Published Edition 1.5 (www.ouricebergismelting.com).

Kraemer, K. L., King, J. L., Dunkle, D. E., & Lane, J. P. (1989). *Managing information systems: Change and control in organizational computing*. San Francisco: Jossey-Bass.

Kraut, A. I. (Ed.). (1996). *Organizational surveys: Tools for assessment and change*. San Francisco: Jossey-Bass.

Kubler-Ross, E. (1969). *On death and dying*. New York: Macmillan.

Kuhn, T. S. (1970). *The structure of scientific revolution* (2nd ed.). Chicago: University of Chicago Press.

Laird, J. D., & Bresler, C. (1990). William James and the mechanisms of emotional experience. *Personality and Social Psychology Bulletin, 16,* 636–651.

Lange, C. G. (1922). *The emotions* (I. A. Haupt, Trans., pp. 33–90). Baltimore: Williams & Wilkens. (Original work published 1885)

Lawler, E. E., III. (1973). *Motivation in work organizations*. Monterey, CA: Brooks/Cole.

Lawler, E. E., III. (1977). Reward systems. In J. R. Hackman & J. L. Suttle (Eds.), *Improving life at work* (pp. 163–226). Santa Monica, CA: Goodyear.

Lawler, E. E., III. (1990). *Strategic pay: Aligning organizational strategies and pay systems*. San Francisco: Jossey-Bass.

Lawler, E. E., III, & Worley, C. G. (2006). *Built to change: How to achieve sustained organizational effectiveness*. San Francisco: Jossey-Bass.

Lawrence, P. R. (1954). How to deal with resistance to change. *Harvard Business Review, 32*(3), 49–57.

Lawrence, P. R., & Lorsch, J. W. (1967). *Organization and environment*. Boston: Harvard University Business School, Division of Research.

Lawrence, P. R., & Lorsch, J. W. (1969). *Developing organizations: Diagnosis and action*. Reading, MA: Addison-Wesley.

Leavitt, H. J. (1965). Applied organizational change in industry. In J. G. March (Ed.), *Handbook of organizations* (pp. 1144–1170). New York: Rand McNally.

Legge, K. (1984). *Evaluating planned organizational change*. Orlando, FL: Academic.

Levine, A. (1980). *Why innovation fails: The institutionalization and termination of innovation in higher education*. Albany: State University of New York Press.

Levinson, D. J. (1978). *The seasons of a man's life*. New York: Knopf.

Levinson, D. J. (1986). A conception of adult development. *American Psychologist, 41,* 3–13.

Levinson, H. (1972). *Organizational diagnosis*. Cambridge, MA: Harvard University Press.

Levinson, H. (1974). Don't choose your own successor. *Harvard Business Review, 52,* 53–62.

Levinson, H. (1975). *Executive stress*. New York: Harper.

Levinson, H. (1976). *Psychological man*. Cambridge, MA: Levinson Institute.

Levinson, H. (1994). Beyond the selection failure. *Consulting Psychology Journal: Practice and Research, 46,* 3–8.

Lewin, K. (1947). Group decision and social change. In T. M. Newcomb, E. L. Hartley, et al. (Eds.), *Readings in social psychology* (pp. 330–344). New York: Henry Holt.

Lewin, K. (1951). *Field theory in social science.* New York: Harper.

Lewin, K. (1958). Group decision and social change. In E. E. Maccoby, T. M. Newcomb, & E. L. Hartley (Eds.), *Readings in social psychology* (pp. 197–211). New York: Holt, Rinehart & Winston.

Liebovitch, L. S. (1998). *Fractals and chaos simplified for the life sciences.* New York: Oxford University Press.

Likert, R. (1961). *New patterns of management.* New York: McGraw-Hill.

Likert, R. (1967). *The human organization.* New York: McGraw-Hill.

Lippitt, R., Watson, J., & Westley, B. (1958). *Dynamics of planned change.* New York: Harcourt Brace.

Litwin, G. H., Bray, J., & Brooke, K. L. (1996). *Mobilizing the organization: Bringing strategy to life.* London: Prentice Hall.

Litwin, G. H., Humphrey, J. W., & Wilson, T. B. (1978). Organizational climate: A proven tool for improving performance. In W. W. Burke (Ed.), *The cutting edge: Current theory and practice in organization development* (pp. 187–205). La Jolla, CA: University Associates.

Litwin, G. H., & Stringer, R. A. (1968). *Motivation and organizational climate.* Boston: Harvard Business School Press.

Lombardo, M. M., & Eichinger, R. W. (2000). High potentials as high learners. *Human Resource Management, 39,* 321–330.

London, M. (2001). The great debate: Should multisource feedback be used for administration or development only? In D. W. Bracken, C. W. Timmereck, & A. H. Church (Eds.), *The handbook of multisource feedback* (pp. 368–385). San Francisco: Jossey-Bass.

Lundberg, G. C. (1989). On organizational learning: Implications and opportunities for expanding organizational development. In R. W. Woodman & W. A. Pasmore (Eds.), *Research in Organization Change and Development* (Vol. 3, pp. 61–82), Greenwich, CT: JAI.

Luthans, F. (1988). Successful vs. effective real managers. *Academy of Management Executive, 2,* 127–132.

Luthans, F., & Peterson, S. J. (2003). 360-degree feedback with systematic coaching: Empirical analysis suggests a winning combination. *Human Resource Management, 42,* 243–256.

Mann, F. C. (1957). Studying and creating change: A means to understanding social organization. *Research in Industrial Human Relations* (Industrial Relations Research Association, Publication No. 17).

Marrow, A. J., Bowers, D. G., & Seashore, S. E. (1967). *Management by participation.* New York: Harper & Row.

Maslow, A. H. (1954). *Motivation and personality.* New York: Harper.

Maturana, H., & Varela, F. (1987). *The tree of knowledge.* Boston: Shambhala.

McCall, M. W., Jr. (2010). Recasting leadership development. *Industrial and Organizational Psychology: Perspectives on Science and Practice, 3*(1), 3–19.

McCall, M. W., Jr., Lombardo, M. M., & Morrison, A. M. (1988). *The lessons of experience: How successful executives develop on the job.* Lexington, MA: Lexington Books.

McClelland, D. C. (1961). *The achieving society.* Princeton, NJ: Van Nostrand.

McClelland, D. C. (1965). Achievement and entrepreneurship: A longitudinal study. *Journal of Personality and Social Psychology, 1,* 389–392.

McClelland, D. C. (1975). *Power: The inner experience.* New York: Irvington.

McClelland, D. C., & Burnham, D. H. (1976). Power is the great motivator. *Harvard Business Review, 54*(2), 100–110.

McClure, B. A. (1998). *Putting a new spin on groups: The science of chaos.* Mahwah, NJ: Lawrence Erlbaum.

McGregor, D. (1960). *The human side of enterprise.* New York: McGraw-Hill.

McGregor, D. (1967). *The professional manager.* New York: McGraw-Hill.

McKee, R. (2003). Storytelling that moves people: A conversation with Robert McKee. *Harvard Business Review, 81*(6), 51–55.

Meglino, B. M., & Ravlin, E. C. (1998). Individual values in organizations: Concepts, controversies, and research. *Journal of Management, 24,* 351–389.

Miles, R. E., & Snow, C. C. (1978). *Organizational strategy, structure, and process.* New York: McGraw-Hill.

Miller, C. C., & Cardinal, L. B. (1994). Strategic planning and firm performance: A synthesis of more than two decades of research. *Academy of Management Journal, 37,* 1649–1665.

Miller, D. (1996). A preliminary typology of organizational learning: Synthesizing the literature. *Journal of Management, 22,* 485–505.

Miller, E. C. (1978). The parallel organization structure at General Motors: An interview with Howard C. Carlson. *Personnel, 55*(4), 64–69.

Miller, G. A. (1956). The magical number seven, plus or minus two: Some limits on our capacity for processing information. *Psychological Review, 63,* 81–97.

Mintzberg, H. (1973). *The nature of managerial work.* New York: Harper & Row.

Mintzberg, H. (1989). *Mintzberg on management: Inside our strange world of organizations.* New York: Free Press.

Mirvis, P. H. (1996). Historical foundations of organizational learning. *Journal of Organization Change Management, 9,* 13–31.

Mitchinson, A., Gerard, N. M., Roloff, K. S., & Burke, W. W. (2012). Learning agility: Spanning the rigor-relevance divide. *Industrial and Organizational Psychology: Perspectives on Science and Practice, 5,* 287–290.

Morgan, G. (Ed.). (1983). *Beyond method: Strategies for social research.* Beverly Hills, CA: Sage.

Morgan, G. (1997). *Images of organizations* (2nd ed.). Thousand Oaks, CA: Sage.

Mumford, M. D., Zaccaro, S. J., Harding, F. D., Fleishman, E. A., & Reiter-Palmon, R. (1993). *Cognitive and temperament predictors of executive ability: Principles for developing leadership capacity.* Alexandria, VA: U.S. Army Research Institute for the Behavioral and Social Sciences.

Nadler, D. A., & Tushman, M. L. (1977). A diagnostic model for organization behavior. In J. R. Hackman, E. E. Lawler III, & L. W. Porter (Eds.), *Perspectives on behavior in organizations* (pp. 85–100). New York: McGraw-Hill.

Nadler, D. A., & Tushman, M. L. (1989). Organizational frame bending: Principles for managing reorientation. *Academy of Management Executive, 3,* 194–204.

Naisbitt, J. (1994). *Global paradox.* New York: William Morrow.

Noumair, D. A., Winderman, B. B., & Burke, W. W. (2010). Transforming the A. K. Rice Institute: From club to organization. *Journal of Applied Behavioral Science, 46,* 473–499.

Obholzer, A. (1994). Authority, power and leadership: Contributions from group relations training. In A. Obholzer & V. Z. Roberts (Eds.), *The unconscious at work: Individual and organizational stress in the human services* (pp. 39–47). New York: Routledge.

Oreg, S. (2003). Resistance to change: Developing an individual difference measure. *Journal of Applied Psychology, 88,* 680–693.

Oreg, S., Vakola, M., & Armenakis, A. (2011). Change receipients' reactions to organizational change: A 60-year review of quantitative studies. *Journal of Applied Behavioral Science, 47,* 461–524.

Orlikowski, W. S. (1996). Improvising organizational transformation over time: A situated change perspective. *Information Systems Research, 7*(1), 63–92.

Orton, J. D., & Weick, K. E. (1990). Loosely coupled systems: A reconceptualization. *Academy of Management Review, 15,* 203–223.

O'Toole, J. (1995). *Leading change: Overcoming the ideology of comfort and the tyranny of custom.* San Francisco: Jossey-Bass.

O'Toole, J. (1999). *Leadership A to Z: A guide for the appropriately ambitious.* San Francisco: Jossey-Bass.

Pascale, R. T., Milleman, M., & Gioja, L. (2000). *Surfing the edge of chaos: The laws of nature and the new laws of business.* New York: Crown Business.

Pasmore, W. A. (1988). *Designing effective organizations: The sociotechnical systems perspective.* New York: Wiley.

Peabody, G. L. (1971). Power, Alinsky and other thoughts. In H. A. Hornstein, B. B. Bunker, W. W. Burke, M. Gindes, & R. J. Lewicki (Eds.), *Social intervention: A behavioral science approach* (pp. 521–532). New York: Free Press.

Pearce, J. A., & David, F. (1987). Corporate mission statements: The bottom line. *Academy of Management Executive, 1,* 109–116.

Pearson, C. A. L. (1992). Autonomous work groups: An evaluation at an industrial site. *Human Relations, 45,* 905–936.

Peters, T. (2001, December). Tom Peters's true confessions. *Fast Company, 53,* 78–92.

Peters, T. J., & Waterman, R. H., Jr. (1982). *In search of excellence: Lessons from America's best-run companies.* New York: Harper & Row.

Pettigrew, A. M., Woodman, R. W., & Cameron, K. S. (2001). Studying organization change and development: Challenges for future research. *Academy of Management Journal, 44,* 697–713.

Pfeffer, J. (1978). The micropolitics of organizations. In M. W. Meyer & Associates (Eds.), *Environments and organizations* (pp. 29–50). San Francisco: Jossey-Bass.

Pfeffer, J., & Salancik, G. R. (1978). *The external control of organizations: A resource dependent perspective.* New York: Harper & Row.

Piderit, S. K. (2000). Rethinking resistance and recognizing ambivalence: A multi-dimensional view of attitudes toward an organizational change. *Academy of Management Review, 25,* 783–794.

Porras, J. I. (1987). *Stream analysis: A powerful way to diagnose and manage organizational change.* Reading, MA: Addison-Wesley.

Porras, J. I., & Robertson, P. J. (1987). Organization development theory: A typology and evaluation. In R. W. Woodman & W. A. Pasmore (Eds.), *Research in organization change and development* (Vol. 1, pp. 1–57). Greenwich, CT: JAI.

Porras, J. I., & Robertson, P. J. (1992). Organizational development: Theory, practice and research. In M. D. Dunnette & L. M. Hough (Eds.), *Handbook of industrial and organizational psychology* (2nd ed., Vol. 3, pp. 719–822). Palo Alto, CA: Consulting Psychologists Press.

Porras, J. I., & Silvers, R. C. (1991). Organization development and transformation. *Annual Review of Psychology, 42,* 51–78.

Porter, M. (1985). *Competitive advantage: Creating and sustaining superior performance.* New York: Free Press.

Power, C. (1989, October 9). From "bloody awful" to bloody awesome. *Business Week,* p. 97.

Prescott, J. E. (1986). Environments as moderators of the relationship between strategy and performance. *Academy of Management Journal, 29,* 329–346.

Prigogine, I., & Stengers, I. (1984). *Order out of chaos: Man's new dialogue with nature.* New York: Bantam.

Quinn, R. E. (1988). *Beyond rational management: Mastering paradoxes and competing demands of high performance.* San Francisco: Jossey-Bass.

Rajagopalan, N., & Spreitzer, G. M. (1997). Toward a theory of strategic change: A multi-lens perspective and integrative framework. *Academy of Management Review, 22,* 48–79.

Rasiel, E. M. (1999). *The McKinsey way.* New York: McGraw-Hill.

Richter, F. M. (1986). Non-linear behavior. In D. W. Fiske & R. A. Shweder (Eds.), *Meta-theory in social science: Pluralisms and subjectivities* (pp. 284–292). Chicago: University of Chicago Press.

Riegel, K. F. (1976). The dialectics of human development. *American Psychologist, 31,* 689–700.

Rioch, M. J. (1975). Group relations: Rationale and technique. In A. D. Colman & W. H. Bexton (Eds.), *Group relations reader 1* (pp. 21–33). Jupiter, FL: A. K. Rice Institute.

Roethlisberger, F. J. (1980). The Hawthorne experiments. In D. Mankin, R. E. Ames Jr., & M. A. Grodsky (Eds.), *Classics of industrial and organizational psychology* (pp. 29–39). Oak Park, IL: Moore.

Roethlisberger, F. J., & Dickson, W. J. (1939). *Management and the worker: An account of a research program conducted by the Western Electric Company.* Cambridge, MA: Harvard University Press.

Rogers, C. R. (1968). Interpersonal relations: W.S.A. 2000. *Journal of Applied Behavioral Science, 4,* 265–280.

Romanelli, E., & Tushman, M. L. (1986). Inertia, environments, and strategic choice: A quasi-experimental design for comparative longitudinal research. *Management Science, 32,* 608–621.

Rosenberg, R. D., & Rosenstein, E. (1980). Participation and productivity: An empirical study. *Industrial and Labor Relations Review, 33,* 355–367.

Rosenthal, R. (1976). *Experimenter effects in behavioral science* (Enlarged ed.). New York: Halsted.

Rost, J. C. (1991). *Leadership for the twenty-first century.* Westport, CT: Praeger.

Rothstein, E. (2001, October 20). A lethal weapon with no spider. *The New York Times,* pp. A13, A15.

Rubin, I. (1967). Increasing self-acceptance: A means of reducing prejudice. *Journal of Personality and Social Psychology, 5,* 233–238.

Sagie, A., & Elizur, D. (1996). Work values: A theoretical overview and a model of their effects. *Journal of Organizational Behavior, 17,* 503–514.

Salancik, G., & Pfeffer, J. (1977). Constraints on administrator discretion: The limited influence of mayors on city budgets. *Urban Affairs Quarterly, 12,* 475–798.

Sashkin, M. (1988). The visionary leader. In J. A. Conger & R. N. Kanungo (Eds.), *Charismatic leadership: The elusive factor in organizational effectiveness* (pp. 122–160). San Francisco: Jossey-Bass.

Sashkin, M., & Burke, W. W. (1990). Understanding and assessing organizational leadership. In K. E. Clark & M. B. Clark (Eds.), *Measures of leadership* (pp. 297–325). West Orange, NJ: Leadership Library of America.

Schachter, S. (1959). *The psychology of affiliation.* Stanford, CA: Stanford University Press.

Schein, E. H. (1972). *Organizational psychology* (2nd ed.). Englewood Cliffs, NJ: Prentice Hall.

Schein, E. H. (1980). *Organizational psychology* (3rd ed.). Englewood Cliffs, NJ: Prentice Hall.

Schein, E. H. (1983). The role of the founder in creating organizational cultures. *Organizational Dynamics, 12*(1), 13–28.

Schein, E. H. (1985). *Organizational culture and leadership.* San Francisco: Jossey-Bass.

Schein, E. H. (1987). *Process consultation: Vol. 2. Its role in organization development* (2nd ed.). Reading, MA: Addison-Wesley.

Schein, E. H. (1992). *Organizational culture and leadership* (2nd ed.). San Francisco: Jossey-Bass.

Schein, E. H. (2004). *Organizational culture and leadership* (3rd ed.). San Francisco: Jossey-Bass.

Schneider, B. (1980). The service organization: Climate is crucial. *Organizational Dynamics, 9*(2), 52–65.

Schneider, B. (1985). Organizational behavior. *Annual Review of Psychology, 36*, 573–611.

Schneider, B. (1990a). The climate for service: Application of the construct. In B. Schneider (Ed.), *Organizational climate and culture* (pp. 383–412). San Francisco: Jossey-Bass.

Schneider, B. (Ed.). (1990b). *Organizational climate and culture.* San Francisco: Jossey-Bass.

Schneider, B., & Bowen, D. E. (1985). Employee and customer perceptions of service in banks: Replication and extension. *Journal of Applied Psychology, 70,* 423–433.

Schneider, B., & Bowen, D. E. (1995). *Winning the service game.* Boston: Harvard Business School Press.

Schneider, B., & Snyder, R. A. (1975). Some relationships between job satisfaction and organizational climate. *Journal of Applied Psychology, 60,* 318–328.

Seifert, C. F., Yukl, G., & McDonald, R. A. (2003). Effects of multisource feedback and a feedback facilitator on the influence behavior managers toward subordinates. *Journal of Applied Psychology, 88,* 561–569.

Seligman, M E. P., & Csikszentmihalyi, M. (2000). Positive psychology: An introduction. *American Psychologist, 55*(1), 5–14.

Senge, P. (1990). *The fifth discipline: The art and practice of the learning organization.* New York: Doubleday Currency.

Shank, C., & Patel, C. K. N. (Eds.). *Managing for high-quality science and engineering at the NNSA National Security Laboratories.* (2012). Washington, DC: Laboratory Assessments Board, Division on Engineering and Physical Sciences, National Academies of Science Press.

Sherif, M. (1966). *In common predicament.* Boston: Houghton Mifflin.

Sherif, M., Harvey, O. J., White, B. J., Hood, W. R., & Sherif, C. W. (1961). *Intergroup conflict and cooperation: The robbers cave experiment.* Norman: University of Oklahoma, Institute of Group Relations.

Sherif, M., & Sherif, C. W. (1953). *Groups in harmony and tension.* New York: Harper & Row.

Sherif, M., & Sherif, C. W. (1969). *Social psychology.* New York: Harper & Row.

Skinner, B. F. (1948). *Walden two.* New York: Macmillan.

Smith, J. E., Carson, K. P., & Alexander, R. A. (1984). Leadership: It can make a difference. *Academy of Management Journal, 27,* 765–776.

Smither, J. W., London, M., Flautt, R., Vargas, Y., & Kucine, I. (2003). Can working with an executive coach improve multisource feedback ratings over time? A quasi-experimental field study. *Personnel Psychology, 56,* 23–44.

Srinivasan, K. (2001, June 1). FCC chief: Move to digital bumpy but worth it. *Naples Daily News,* p. 6A.

Starbuck, W. H. (1983). Organizations as action generators. *American Sociological Review, 48*, 91–102.

Stickland, F. (1998). *The dynamics of change: Insights into organisational transition from the natural world.* London: Routledge.

Stodgill, R. M. (1974). *Handbook of leadership: A survey of theory and research.* New York: Free Press.

Streufert, S., & Swezey, R. W. (1986). *Complexity, managers, and organizations.* Orlando, FL: Academic Press.

Svyantek, D. J. (1997). Order out of chaos: Nonlinear systems and organizational change. *Current Topics in Management, 2*, 167–188.

Svyantek, D. J., & Brown, L. L. (2000). A complex-systems approach to organizations. *Current Directions in Psychological Science, 9*, 69–74.

Svyantek, D. J., & DeShon, R. P. (1993). Organizational attractors: A chaos theory explanation of why cultural change efforts often don't. *Public Administration Quarterly, 17*, 339–355.

Tagiuri, R., & Litwin, G. H. (Eds.). (1968). *Organizational climate: Explorations of a concept.* Cambridge, MA: Harvard University Press.

Tannenbaum, A. S., & Kahn, R. L. (1957). Organizational control structure: A general descriptive technique as applied to four local unions. *Human Relations, 10*, 127–140.

Tannenbaum, A. S., & Kahn, R. L. (1958). *Participation in union locals.* Evanston, IL: Row Peterson.

Taylor, F. W. (1915). *The Principles of Scientific Management.* New York: Harper & Row.

Taylor, F. W. (1980). The principles of scientific management. In D. Mankin, R. E. Ames Jr., & M. A. Grodsky (Eds.), *Classics of industrial and organizational psychology* (pp. 15–28). Oak Park, IL: Moore.

Thompson, J. D. (1967). *Organization in action.* New York: McGraw-Hill.

Tichy, N. M. (1983). *Managing strategic change: Technical, political, and cultural dynamics.* New York: Wiley.

Tichy, N. M., Hornstein, H. A., & Nisberg, J. N. (1977). Organization diagnosis and intervention strategies: Developing emergent pragmatic theories of change. In W. W. Burke (Ed.), *Current issues and strategies in organization development* (pp. 361–383). New York: Human Sciences.

Tichy, N. M., & Sherman, S. (1993). *Control your destiny or someone else will: How Jack Welch is making General Electric the world's most competitive corporation.* New York: Doubleday.

Tomlinson, E. C., Dineen, B. R., & Lewicki, R. S. (2004). The road to reconciliation: Antecedents of victim willingness to reconcile following a broken promise. *Journal of Management, 30*, 165–187.

Trist, E. (1993). Introduction to Vol. 2. In E. Trist & H. Murray (Eds.), *The social engagement of social science: A Tavistock anthology: Vol. 2. The socio-technical perspective* (pp. 36–60). Philadelphia: University of Pennsylvania Press.

Tsui, A. S. (1984). A multiple constituency framework of managerial reputational effectiveness. In J. G. Hunt, D. Hosking, C. Schriesheim, & R. Stewart (Eds.), *Leaders and managers: International perspectives on managerial behavior and leadership* (pp. 28–44). New York: Pergamon.

Tushman, M. L., & Romanelli, E. (1985). Organizational evolution: A metamorphosis model of convergence and reorientation. In L. L. Cummings & B. M. Staw (Eds.), *Research in organizational behavior, 7*, 171–222. Greenwich, CT: JAI.

Van de Ven, A. H., & Poole, M. S. (1995). Explaining development and change in organizations. *Academy of Management Review, 20*, 510–540.

Van Eron, A. M., & Burke, W. W. (1992). The transformational/transactional leadership model: A study of critical components. In K. E. Clark, M. B. Clark, & D. P. Campbell (Eds.), *Impact of leadership* (pp. 149–167). Greensboro, NC: Center for Creative Leadership.

Von Bertalanffy, L. (1950). An outline of general systems theory. *British Journal of the Philosophy of Science, 1*, 134–165.

Vroom, V. (1964). *Work and motivation.* New York: Wiley.

Wake, D. B., Roth, G., & Wake, M. H. (1983). On the problem of stasis in organismal evolution. *Journal of Theoretical Biology, 101*, 211–224.

Walton, R. E. (1975). The diffusion of new work structures: Explaining why success didn't take. *Organizational Dynamics, 3*(3), 2–22.

Wanberg, C. R., & Banas, J. T. (2000). Predictors and outcomes of openness to changes in a reorganizing workplace. *Journal of Applied Psychology, 85*, 132–142.

Watkins, K. E., & Marsick, V. S. (1993). *Sculpting the learning organization: Lessons in the art and science of systemic change.* San Francisco: Jossey-Bass.

Watson, G. (1966). Resistance to change. In G. Watson (Ed.), *Concepts for social change, Cooperative Project for Educational Development series* (Vol. 1.). Washington, DC: National Training Laboratories.

Wegner, D. M. (1991). Transactive memory in close relationships. *Journal of Personality and Social Psychology, 61*, 923–929.

Wegner, D. M., & Wheatley, T. (1999). Apparent mental causation. *American Psychologist, 54*, 480–492.

Weick, K. E. (1979). *The social psychology of organizing* (2nd ed.). Reading, MA: Addison-Wesley.

Weick, K. E. (1995). *Sensemaking in organizations.* Thousand Oaks, CA: Sage.

Weick, K. E., & Quinn, R. E. (1999). Organizational change and development. *Annual Review of Psychology, 50*, 361–386.

Weick, K. E. (2001). *Making sense of the organization.* Malden, MA: Blackwell.

Weick, K. E. (2009). *Making sense of the organization: The impermanent organization* (Vol. 2). Chichester, UK: Wiley.

Weiner, N., & Mahoney, T. A. (1981). A model of corporate performance as a function of environmental, organizational, and leadership influences. *Academy of Management Journal, 24,* 453–470.

Weisbord, M. R. (1976). Organizational diagnosis: Six places to look for trouble with or without a theory. *Group and Organization Studies, 1,* 430–447.

Weisbord, M. R. (1987). *Productive workplaces: Organizing and managing for dignity, meaning, and community.* San Francisco: Jossey-Bass.

Welch, J. (with Byrne, J. A.). (2001). *Jack: Straight from the gut.* New York: Warner Books.

Wendt, H. (1993). *Global embrace: Corporate challenges in a transnational world.* New York: Harper Business.

Whetten, D. A. (1989). What constitutes a theoretical contribution? *Academy of Management Review, 14,* 490–495.

Whyte, W. F. (1955). *Money and motivation.* New York: Harper & Row.

Wilkens, A. L. (1989). *Developing corporate character: How to successfully change an organization without destroying it.* San Francisco: Jossey-Bass.

Wilson, B. L., & Corbett, H. D. (1983). Organization and change: The effects of school linkages on the quantity of implementation. *Educational Administration Quarterly, 19*(4), 85–104.

Witherspoon, R., & White, R. P. (1998). *Four essential ways that coaching can help executives.* Greensboro, NC: Center for Creative Leadership.

Wortman, M. S. (1982). Strategic management and changing leader-follower roles. *Journal of Applied Behavioral Science, 18,* 371–383.

Yost, P., & Plunkett, M. (2009). *Real time leadership development.* London: Blackwell.

Young, A. (1976). *The reflexive universe.* Lake Oswego, OR: Robert Briggs.

Yukl, G. A. (1998). *Leadership in organizations* (4th ed.). Englewood Cliffs, NJ: Prentice Hall.

Yukl, G. A. (1999). An evaluation of conceptual weakness in transformational and charismatic leadership theories. *The Leadership Quarterly, 10,* 285–305.

Zaccaro, S. J. (2001). *The nature of executive leadership: A conceptual and empirical analysis of success.* Washington, DC: American Psychological Association.

Zaleznik, A. (1977). Managers and leaders: Are they different? *Harvard Business Review, 55*(3), 67–78.

Zuboff, S. (1988). *In the age of the smart machine: The future of work and power.* New York: Basic Books.

Index

About the Author

W. Warner Burke is the Edward Lee Thorndike Professor of Psychology and Education and coordinator for the graduate programs in social–organizational psychology in the Department of Organization and Leadership at Teachers College, Columbia University, in New York. Dr. Burke earned his BA from Furman University and his MA and PhD from the University of Texas, Austin. Prior to Teachers College, he served as chair, Department of Management at Clark University, head of management programs and organization development (OD) at the NTL Institute, and as executive director of the OD Network. Dr. Burke's consulting experience has been with a variety of organizations in business–industry, education, government, religious, and medical systems. A diplomate in industrial-organizational psychology and in organizational and business consulting psychology, the American Board of Professional Psychology, he is also a fellow of the Academy of Management, the Association of Psychological Science, and the Society for Industrial and Organizational Psychology, and past editor of both *Organizational Dynamics* and the *Academy of Management Executive.* He has authored over 180 articles and book chapters in organizational psychology, organization change, and leadership, and authored, coauthored, or edited 19 books. He has received numerous awards, including in 1989 the Public Service Medal from the National Aeronautics and Space Administration (NASA), in 1990 the Distinguished Contribution to Human Resource Development Award, in 1993 the Organization Development Professional Practice Area Award for Excellence—the Lippitt Memorial Award—from the American Society for Training and Development, in 2003 the Distinguished Scholar–Practitioner Award from the Academy of Management, and in 2007 the Distinguished Professional Contributions Award from the Society for Industrial and Organizational Psychology. He has received lifetime achievement awards from the OD Network; Linkage, Inc.; and the Best Practice Institute. His latest book (2009), edited with Lake and Paine, is *Organization Change: A Comprehensive Reader.*

RAMBLES IN CORK CITY AND COUNTY

Joe Cronin has been a keen walker for many years, having walked the remotest hills in Ireland as well as many of the recently-developed long-distance paths. His work has featured in a variety of outdoor magazines and books.

RAMBLES IN CORK CITY AND COUNTY

Joe Cronin

The Collins Press

Published in 2000 by
The Collins Press
West Link Park
Doughcloyne
Wilton
Cork

© 2000 Joe Cronin

Typesetting by The Collins Press Ltd.

Printed by Cox and Wyman Ltd., UK

ISBN: 1-898256-72-1

Walking the Routes

The public has traditionally used the walks included in this book. Indeed many landowners do not object to people following traditional paths and tracks provided that users do not damage property, frighten livestock or abuse crops. It has to be pointed out, however, that a right-of-way may not exist in all cases and accordingly permission should be obtained from the landowner if in doubt. Most of the routes are on public roadways, a few traverse parks where a small entry charge may be made and others meander along riverbanks or coastal paths. A pair of good walking shoes are the ideal footwear to use for maximum comfort and for the longer walks a small day sack might be taken which could include a rain jacket and some refreshments. Remember to include the camera also and a good Ordnance Survey Map (Discovery Series) is a most useful accessory.

Disclaimer

The publisher and author cannot accept any responsibility for accidents suffered or any form of loss by members of the public who follow the routes outlined in this book. This also includes where any trespass might occur. Care and common sense are imperative when walking near waterways, coastal paths and busy roadways and close to unpredictable animals.

This book is dedicated to the warm and wonderful people who live and work hard in the remote mountain valleys of Ireland. Thanks to their generous spirit, many people have been able to experience the charm and splendour of this truly beautiful country.

CONTENTS

WALKS OF DISCOVERY

Why do people like to go for a walk? Perhaps for exercise! Maybe to give the dog an outing! And what of those who after Christmas each year decide to discard that additional weight gained over the eating season? Sadly many good resolutions are short-lived and once again we are back to the same routine.

So what is missing? Discovery! Yes, that is what makes a walk really interesting. To walk blindly without paying attention to what is around you is a bit of a chore and cannot be fulfilling. If, however, you go with an enquiring mind full of enthusiasm, the rewards will be great and the memories lasting.

For more than 21 years I have walked remotest Ireland from the hills of Donegal to the high mountains of Kerry, Wicklow and Connemara. So too have the long distance paths been trodden – the Wicklow Way, Western Way, Dingle Way, Burren Way and many others. All have provided enjoyment and lasting happy memories. All those major walks were shared with enthusiastic walking companions whose pleasant and humorous company helped to make the outings well worthwhile.

This book, however, is not about major mountain or long distance treks. Instead it has been written for short and medium walks, some quite short but interesting. Most of the walks range from 2 to 5 miles with just a few longer.

i

INTRODUCTION

Apart from being the largest county in Ireland, Cork also has been enriched with some of the finest scenery on this island. It's hard to believe (but experts tell us) that Ireland once lay south of the equator about the latitude of South Africa and over the past 500 million years or so it gradually drifted northward to where it is now. Of course it looked very different over that great period to what we know it as today.

For example, the mountains and hills that now exist were created about 300 million years ago, when a major disturbance occurred in the earth's crust which resulted in a mountain-building process taking place in the south of Ireland. Those impressive mountain ranges like the Comeraghs, Knockmealdowns, Galtees, Boggeraghs and MacGillycuddys Reeks were all created. Prior to that event the peninsulas of the southwest would have been much wider and flatter. Over the millions of years the mountains eroded, rapidly at the beginning as there would have been much loosened rock and the terrain would have been subject to landslides just as the Himalayan mountain valleys are today. Mountain streams would have carried off the smaller debris such as grains of sand and soil, rock debris and other materials. Eventually a more stable pattern emerged and the landscape eroded at a less rapid pace, pretty much like what happens today.

Erosion generally occurs so slowly that it is hardly discernible except of course near the coast of south Cork where the sandier cliffs are being demolished by the unceasing action of the sea. This unfortunately is now posing a serious threat to some homes, which are located near the cliffs.

Ireland too has been subject to invasion by the sea and this resulted in a layer of limestone being laid down over the existing rocks – in County Cork this would have been principally over Red Sandstone. The limestone eroded much faster than the sandstone and so it disappeared from the hilltops but remained in the lower valleys. Today the valley of Cork city has a bedrock of limestone but the hill at Cork Airport is comprised of sandstone. If you travel to Carrigaline you are again in a limestone valley.

Cork County has also been subject to the sculpturing of the Ice Ages. Imagine a glacier (a slow-moving river of ice) coming from Kerry, in along the Lee Valley, pushing its way through Cork city and powering its way to Cork Harbour before halting around Garryvoe. Such an event did occur before the city was ever even thought of and it left large deposits of gravel, sand and other debris which have since been of great assistance in supplying material for the construction industry. The ice also shaped the hills. Mountain hollows were deepened to form enclosures for many a mountain lake and knife-edge ridges often formed on mountains as well.

When these geological processes had ceased, something else happened which had a major effect on the landscape. Humans arrived about 9,000 years ago, just after the ending of the last Ice Age. These were a very primitive people and they used stone implements instead of the metal objects we have today. Flint was a treasured substance and it was fashioned into crude objects like knives, scrapers, projectiles, etc., by these early hunter-gatherers, as they were known. Had you been in existence at that time you may have met them on the shoreline just east of Roches Point where they could have been gathering nodules of flint which had been washed ashore. Evidence of their existence has also been found in north Cork near Castletownroche where they fished the Blackwater River and kept a watching brief from a cliff-top perch high above its waters, which was their home.

Later in Neolithic times the first farmers arrived and began to clear the forests so that they could cultivate the land. These were the people who erected the impressive passage tombs such as can be seen at Newgrange in County Meath and elsewhere. Centuries passed and the Bronze Age came with the Beaker people introducing their distinctive pottery.

The time of the stone circles arrived with their mysterious significance. How did these people know when to sow their crops? It had to be connected to the height of the sun at a certain time each year. How was this recorded? Had it a connection with the stone circles and stone alignments?

Later, copper was extracted from the rocks and metal objects came to be. Gold objects were fashioned and decorated with sophisticated designs. Were the peoples of remote Ireland truly primitive? I wonder! The Bronze Age was followed by the Iron Age, which spanned the time of Christ and beyond. Christianity was introduced and ogham script was carved out on standing stones, beautiful manuscripts such as the *Book of Kells* (available to view at Trinity College Dublin) came to be created. So too came the time of the Christian monasteries and oratories which dot the landscape. Many of their ruins now exist in remote areas including offshore islands such as the Skelligs and Blaskets in County Kerry. After the Iron Age, the early Christian times and Medieval Period dawned and ringforts spread across the land. These were the early farmsteads and many of them survive to the present day.

Cork city began to take shape in medieval times after St Finbarr originally founded it in the sixth century. In the twentieth century the city has expanded rapidly, with extensive housing estates to be seen on all sides of it. New roadway systems continue to be developed and learning centres educate a growing number of students each year in a variety of disciplines. Industry continues to expand and develop and the city is now very much in the technological age. The methods of farming have kept pace as well and smaller farms are now fast disappearing to make way for much larger enterprises. Fishing methods have also changed, with large boats fitted with up-to-date equipment leaving ports for days on end and travelling far to rewarding fishing ground

WALK 1
CORK CITY CENTRE

OS Map: No. 87 (Discovery Series)
Distance: 1³/4 miles/2km
Average time: 1¹/2 hours
Location: The walk start is located at the northern end of St Patrick's Street in the city centre by St Patrick's Bridge.

INTRODUCTION

Cork has often been likened to the Italian city of Venice and indeed there is a notable similarity as both possess many bridges as well as central 'thoroughfares' which were created by water and are of similar meandering shape. This walk, best taken on a weekend morning, is especially designed for visitors but will also be of interest to local people.

WALK DESCRIPTION

Commence this stroll by the Fr Mathew Statue (affectionately known to Corkonians as the 'Statcha') and turn left down Lavitts Quay to the left of St Patrick's Bridge. Over the Quay Wall is the northern channel of the River Lee, a river which rises on a mountain slope high above the picturesque valley of Gougane Barra, 43 miles west of here.

Prominent on the hill above the river ahead is the pepper-pot shaped Shandon Steeple and more distant the Church of the Ascension (RC) on the slopes of Gurranebraher.

The bridge at the first junction by the traffic lights is the Christy Ring Bridge, so named in memory of Ireland's

1

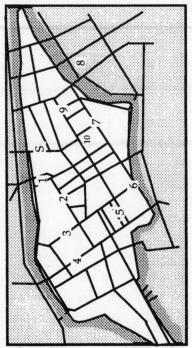

1 Opera House	Monument
2 Paul Street	7 South Mall
3 Coal Quay	8 City Hall
4 North Main St	9 Oliver Plunkett
5 Bishop Lucey	St
Park	10 GPO
6 National	S Statue

2

greatest exponent of the Irish game of hurling. The modern façade of the Cork Opera House stands erect before you. Follow the footpath left by the metal railings alongside the Crawford Municipal Art Gallery – a pleasant place to visit and linger in.

Look out at the end of the street for a sign for Paul Street Shopping Centre, where Paul Street leads to a celebration of enlightened restoration. Just a few years ago the area was run-down but now projects a pulse of commercial energy with its shopping centre, pottery and clothes shops and cafés.

The way leads directly ahead passing St Peter and Paul's (RC) Church on your left and within a short distance turn sharply right down the outdoor market thoroughfare of Cornmarket Street. At the end of the street turn left by the river where if you look right the view extends over an extensive section of the river to Cork's dockland.

Shandon Steeple dominates the skyline as you approach the North Gate Bridge. Turn left at the traffic lights down one of the oldest streets in Cork, the North Main Street, once Cork's main thoroughfare.

You now enter a bustling busy street with an accu-mulation of interesting shops, outfitters, pet shops, super-markets, shoe shops, religious, pottery and sports shops. All offer interesting goods and are worth visiting to get that special Cork bargain. Having reached the junction with Washington Street pass through the traffic lights and shortly on your left a walk down Tobin Street would take you to the interesting gallery of the Triskel Art Centre.

We continue however on South Main Street and just past Christchurch (left) bear down the narrow lane and enter Bishop Lucey Park. This small oasis of rest in the city centre is a welcome respite from the humming purr of city traffic. The park boasts an attractive fountain, ornamental lamps and restful seats. Of more interest to the historian or archaeologist will be the plaques announcing the location of an early medieval city wall exposed during excavations in 1985 and another plaque indicating the remains of a thirteenth-century wall.

The main double-gate archway was formerly the entrance to the city cornmarket in Anglesea Street, built about 1860 but re-erected here in 1985. Leaving the park, bear right on the footpath and look out for a curiosity, an old upturned cannon located on the footpath at the junction with Tuckey Street. In olden times Cork's Grand Parade was a channel of water and boats would tie up at this point.

Further along the street is the City Library and some bow-fronted offices. The southern arm of the river Lee now confronts you but the route turns left down the South Mall. In the small green area on your right the National Monument has been erected to the memory of those who fell in the two World Wars and a stone tablet to the memory of those who lost their lives in the atomic bombing of the Japanese cities Hiroshima and Nagasaki.

Within a short while you reach the eastern end of the South Mall. Parnell Bridge to the right leads over the Lee to the City Hall but our route turns left into Parnell Place where we take the first street on our left, Oliver Plunkett Street. At the General Post Office we bear right into Winthrop Street. Reaching St Patrick's Street, it is only a short distance back to the walk start.

OS Map: Cork City Street Map – Scale 1:15000
Distance: 1 mile/2km
Average time: 1³/₄ hours
Location: This walk begins at the Father Matthew statue in St Patrick's Street in the centre of Cork City.

INTRODUCTION
A stroll through Cork City's north side, passing by some historical buildings and visiting some of the very narrow old streets.

WALK DESCRIPTION
Commence beside the Father Mathew statue in St Patrick's Street in Cork City centre. The noted Father Matthew was an Apostle of Temperance and credited with having brought a more responsible attitude to drinking in the nineteenth century.

Walk north across St Patrick's Bridge observing as you go the Gurranebraher Hills upstream to your left and Cork's dockland downstream on your right. Turn left beyond the bridge into Camden Place with its red-brick buildings. Continue past the Christy Ring Bridge (named in memory of one of Ireland's greatest exponents of hurling). Across the River Lee can be seen the Cork Opera House and the Crawford Art Gallery. Ahead are the stately columns of St Mary's Church but our route turns up the second road on the right beyond the traffic lights. Pass by Knapps Square and bear left

5

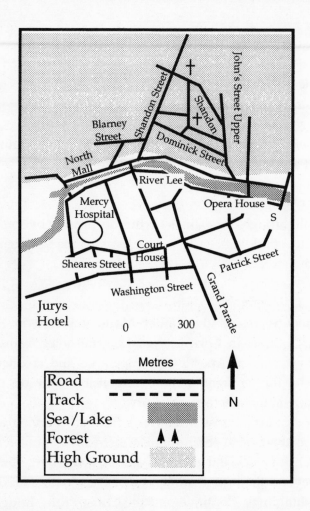

up Dominick Street. Take the first turn right up the narrow Romans Walk and proceed left up to the Butter Market. On the way up you may notice a plaque on a wall in memory of the foundation of the Loft in 1924. This was the Cork Shakespearean Company.

6

Before turning right towards Shandon Steeple you pass the premises of the Butter Exchange Brass and Reed Band. Passing Shandon Steeple, continue up to Easons Avenue and turn left before veering right up Cathedral Avenue. The north chapel stands straight ahead. Turn left at the cathedral and left again at the traffic lights to walk down Shandon Street, formerly called Mallow Lane. This is a very old and famous Cork Street and in years past was frequented by 'shawlie' women – women clad in black shawls who trod its cobbled stones on their way to town.

Near the bottom of the street turn right up Blarney Street, reputed to be the longest street in Cork. Directly behind you the children's play area was once an old graveyard. Walking up hilly Blarney Street take the second turn left which leads down steps to the North Mall. From here there is a fine view of Cork city's southern hills and St Finbarr's Cathedral soars skyward. Reaching the North Mall turn right and at its western end cross the metal footbridge over the river. Around this area one may see mute swans, mallard duck and seagulls. St Vincent's Church stands out boldly on the hill over the water. Continue past the Mercy Hospital (founded 1857). Pass through the traffic lights and note the Maltings Pub, formerly the Lord Mayor's house.

Turn left at Washington Street and proceed eastward past the courthouse to the Grand Parade before winding into St Patrick's Street as a river once did to carve out the principle channel of the city.

OS Map: Cork City Street Map – Scale 1:1500
Distance: 3 miles/5km
Average time: 1¹/₂ hours
Location: This walk begins at the Fr Mathew statue in St Patrick's Street in the centre of Cork City.

INTRODUCTION

Just like the north side the south side of Cork city has some very interesting thoroughfares, buildings and viewing points. This route follows the River Lee most of the time but a few short deviations add extra interest to the ramble. One superb viewing point gives panoramic views over the city.

WALK DESCRIPTION

Begin this walk close to the Fr Mathew Statue in St Patrick's Street and walk south and west (the opposite direction from the river Lee) along Cork city's principle street. Follow its meandering route as a river once did below its now tarmacadam surface. A broad street – 'Pana' as it is known to many locals – contains a fine selection of shops and, combined with bustling traffic, it generates a special atmosphere.

At the top of the street veer left into the Grand Parade from which you turn right at the traffic lights into Washington Street. You are now walking in a westerly direction and soon on your right you pass the imposing courthouse with its striking portico. Erected

8

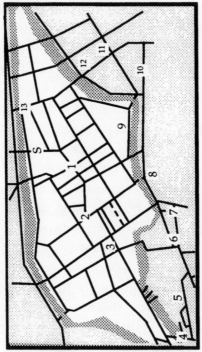

1 St Patrick's St
2 Daunt Square
3 Courthouse
4 UCC Gates
5 Gillabbey
Rock
6 St Finbarres
7 Elizabeth Fort

8 Government
Buildings
9 Holy Trinity
10 South Terrace
11 Gardaí
12 City Hall
13 Merchants
Quay
S Statue

in the 1830s, its sessions are often quite interesting to attend. Making one's way further along the street you soon reach the southern arm of the River Lee on your left. Behind, the striking spires of St Finbarr's Cathedral rise skyward as they have done since 1870 when the cathedral was opened. Nearby on the footpath is an old horse trough. Passing Jury's Hotel you leave the central section of Cork city and ahead on the horizon the tall building of the County Hall is visible.

At the entrance to University College Cork bear left up Donovans Road before taking the second left turn into Connaught Avenue. Again, within a few metres, turn left again into a short roadway which veers right. You pass a large cross which was erected to the memory of Cork people who died in the great South African War of 1899-1902. From this area there is an outstanding view of much of the city skyline and St Vincent's Church prominent on the opposite hillside. The pepper-pot shaped Shandon Steeple and the more rounded dome of St Frances Church can also be observed.

Continue past the metal barrier along the concrete walkway and eventually you reach Gillabbey Street where you bear left down this short sloping street. At the traffic lights cross the busy junction to Dean Street. Towering on your left is the magnificent cathedral of St Finbarr's designed in the French Gothic style by William Burgess. It is open to visitors from 10am each day.

Continue until you reach Barrack Street, a very old Cork thoroughfare. Swing left and again at the first turn on your left. Here one reaches Elizabeth Fort and after passing through the main gate take the steps to the right to the top from which there is a panoramic view of the city, with the southern arm of the River Lee in the foreground. Returning to the fort entrance look out for a narrow stepped laneway with well-kept homes called Keysers Lane. This is one of Cork's oldest passageways and it is but a short traverse down to Proby's Quay where you continue right along by the river ignoring the junction at the bridge. After a short while the prominent Holy Trinity Church rises skyward across the river. Up to a few years ago fishermen were often observed repairing their nets on this quayside.

Leaving the river, continue your journey along the South Terrace before turning left at the traffic lights into Anglesea Street. The modern building on your right is the Cork Garda (Police) Headquarters and beyond it is the Fire Brigade Station. Just further ahead is Cork's City Hall, which opened to the public in 1936. It replaced a previous building, which was burned down during the War of Independence in 1920.

Cross busy Parnell Bridge into Parnell Place and proceed as far as the northern arm of the River Lee where you walk left up Merchants Quay beside the red-bricked shopping centre. Swing left at the traffic lights into St Patrick's Street where the walk started.

WALK 4
SUNDAYS WELL/CLOGHEEN

OS Map: Cork City Street Map – Scale 1:15000
Distance: 3 miles/5km
Average time: 1³/₄ hours
Location: Situated 2 miles/3km west of Cork city centre, it is reached by travelling via Western road or Sundays Well Road.

INTRODUCTION
A walk which offers fine panoramas of the north-west side of Cork city, taking in some hilly roadways and passing through an old neglected boreen before arriving at the western end of the city overlooking the river Lee.

WALK DESCRIPTION
Begin at Thomas Davis Bridge and proceed a few paces along the Lee Road before going up the narrow lane of Rose Hill. Continuing, the hill veers sharply right and a series of steep steps lead the walker quickly up the hillside. At the top your way now turns eastwards by the houses and some ornamental trees are observed over the wall on your left. In season (late autumn) old mans beard decorates the bushes on the right. The old wall on the left is adorned with lichen and behind it is a small deciduous wood. Continue down to Sundays Well Road where you proceed uphill past Shanakiel Road to Sundays Well village.

A few paces beyond the Post Office turn left up Convent Avenue (formerly called City Gaol Road). The route now veers left where the old wall is adorned with moss, ivy and polypody ferns. The former Women's Jail

12

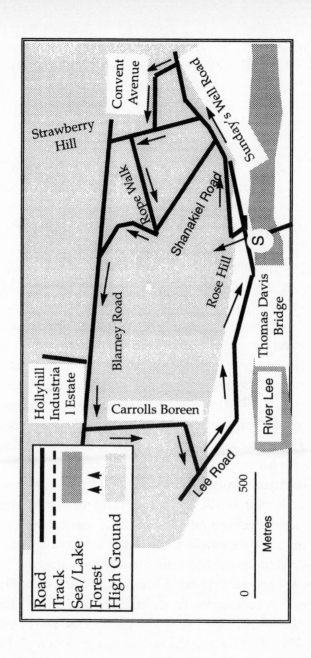

Convent Avenue

Sunday's Well Road

Strawberry Hill

Rope Walk

Shanakiel Road

Rose Hill

Blarney Road

Hollyhill Industrial Estate

Carrolls Boreen

Thomas Davis Bridge

River Lee

Lee Road

S

Road
Track
Sea/Lake
Forest
High Ground

0   500

Metres

13

dominates the right side of the road with its barred windows. Swing right up Strawberry Hill and then enter Rope Walk on your left before reaching the old school on the right. This narrow laneway shortly merges into an old boreen and its walls display many fine specimens of wall pennywort and copious brambles.

Take a right at the end of the laneway beside St Anne's Hospital and continue past the Calvary shrine at the road junction. Care is now required as this road is usually busy. Walk along the footpath on the right side past the premises of St Vincent's Hurling and Football Club.

After passing Hollyhill Industrial Estate you reach a dip in the road known as the 'milestream'. Beyond this point take the first laneway to the left – Carrolls Boreen. Initially it appears somewhat neglected but after a right-hand bend you enter a small haven of nature from which there are fine views south over the city. This old secluded boreen contains many specimens of flora: maidenhair spleenwort, harts tongue fern, foxgloves, wall pennywort, mosses and even a fruitful crabapple tree. Linger here if time permits as such attractive passageways are now rare around the city suburbs.

When you reach its western end at the wall turn left downhill to the Lee Road. At the road junction turn left. Stone tablets are spaced at intervals on the Lee Road to commemorate the fifteen mysteries of the rosary.

Near the end of the walk the stone wall on the left conceals the austere-looking building of the former Our Lady's Hospital. Across the river is the tall County Hall. After a short distance you finish the walk at Thomas Davis Bridge.

WALK 5
THE MARDYKE

OS Map: Cork City Street Map – Scale 1:15000
Distance: 1¹/₂ miles/2km
Average time: 1 hour
Location The walk is located 1 mile/1km west of Cork
city centre.

INTRODUCTION
A famous thoroughfare for all Corkonians that passes by
some noted Cork recreational areas as well as crossing
one of the most attractive sections of the River Lee.

WALK DESCRIPTION
Commence this walk beside the green area across the
road from the entrance gates to University College Cork
on the Western Road.

Turn left up the Mardyke, keeping the grounds of the
Cork County Cricket Club on your right. From its
entrance gate there are good views of St Vincent's
Church high up on the hillside towards the city centre.
Just beyond is the entrance to Fitzgerald's Park, named
after a former Lord Mayor, Sir Edward Fitzgerald. The
inscription on top of one of the pillars – Exhibition 1902
and 1903 – refers to an exhibition held in these grounds
at which British Royalty attended.

Our walk continues past the park entrance and as
you proceed try to identify the young trees such as sil-
verbirch, lime and sycamore planted along this route in
recent years. Beyond the next junction are UCC's playing

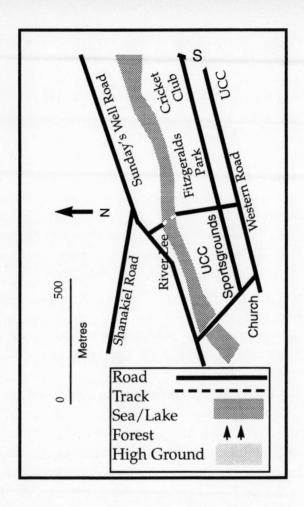

fields and athletic track. Many world famous athletes have competed at his venue.

On reaching the top of the Mardyke the Sacred Heart Church and College face you. Behind it is the tall building of the County Hall. Turn right towards Thomas Davis Bridge, but just short of it on the right, a metal gate leads to a riverside walk. This is only open at certain hours depending on the time of year. If the gate is locked continue across the bridge, turn right and walk east by the river. The roadway eventually slopes upwards and near the top of the incline, steps lead down to the right which will guide you across Dalys Bridge, opened in 1927, and thus to Fitzgerald's Park. Had you taken the riverside walk you would also have arrived at this location. If you glance at the railings by the riverbank you will observe a beard-like creeper, old man's beard, also known as travellers joy. Ahead now is Fitzgerald's Park and one gains access via the small gate a few metres up Ferry Walk on your right.

Having entered the Park turn immediately left along the path towards the notice board and riverbank. This segment of walkway is particularly pleasant, running east along the riverbank, in part beneath some tall shady trees. On the water you may observe an occasional wily moorhen or otter, while graceful homes adorn the northern bank of the river in the company of stately scots pine and poplar trees. At the eastern extremity of the park the path turns sharply right to lead to the main entrance. Several sculptures are placed around this area as well as attractive flowerbeds. The museum is worth a visit and beside its entrance is a large sculpture of the Cork city coat of arms which was salvaged from the Cork City Hall after its burning in 1920.

As you leave the park observe the beautiful sculpture by Seamus Murphy entitled 'Virgin of the Twilight'. Re-entering the Mardyke, turn left and walk east towards the city to reach the walk start.

WALK 6
CORK LOUGH

OS Map: Cork City Street Map – Scale 1:1500
Distance: A short walk of less than a mile
Average time: 20 minutes
Location: Located just 1 mile/2km southwest of Cork city centre the Lough is reached by travelling up Barrack Street from the South Gate Bridge and continuing out along the Lough Road.

INTRODUCTION

Tucked away in a southern suburb of Cork city is a most delightful recreational location. Known to generations of Corkonians as a place to relax or to view its varied wildfowl, one could really enjoy a few hours in its environs. A shallow lake, not greater than 1m in depth, it contains pike and sizeable carp apart from plenty of smaller fish.

WALK DESCRIPTION

This lake of limestone formation offers a short but pleasant walk around its perimeter and a small car park at Glendalough Park on the lake's southern end is possibly the best place to commence.

Immediately one is struck by the amount and variety of bird life, which gather here and indeed this is very much a 'bird walk'. The island on the lake provides an undisturbed haven for the wildfowl and it is interesting to dwell on the various species.

The coot and the moorhen (or waterhen) are rather

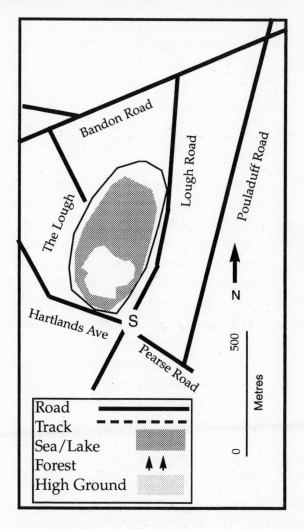

similar in appearance except the coot is slightly larger and bears a white bill and forehead. Both birds give a distinctive nod of the head while swimming and their young in springtime swim in formation behind their parents.

Pride of place in the bird life here must go to the mute swan, a graceful bird admired for its beauty for centuries. Its curved neck and widened rear feathers and the manner in which it glides through the water all combine to give it an aura of regal splendour. But care is required if feeding this bird as the adults regularly display aggressive tendencies. Two black swans also inhabit these waters.

Several ducks are present like the mallard, pochard and shoveller ducks. The male mallard is an impressive coloured bird with a yellow bill, orange legs, grey body and a blue green patch on the wing. The pochard is a winter visitor with a preference for Irish lakes. A huge bill is a distinguishing feature of the shoveller duck and the male of the species is very striking, displaying a black head with white and rust-coloured plumage.

This side of the lake teems with the constant movement of birds and has been further enhanced with several small fountains and bird rests all creating a fascinating display. To help one identify the species an illustrated display board has been erected nearby. Indeed the surrounding area has been appropriately landscaped to blend with the ethos of the lake.

The preferred route is to walk anti-clockwise around the Lough but it is very much a personal choice. Whichever you choose it will be a worthwhile exercise. A favourite place for dog-walkers, joggers, youthful anglers, model boat enthusiasts, etc., the Lough was in former times used as a skating rink when the waters froze in harsher winters. For anyone interested in ornithology it should not be missed.

WALK 7
GLEN PARK

OS Map: Cork City Street Map – Scale 1:15000
Distance: 1¹/₂ miles/2 km
Average time: 1 hour
Location: Situated 1 mile/2km north of Cork city centre, it is reached by travelling via Dillons Cross and Ballyhooley New Road. One can also travel to the Park via Blackpool and Spring Lane.

INTRODUCTION
This walk features a visit to an ice-age carved glen located on the north side of the city. Donated to Cork Corporation in 1967 Glen Park has proved to be a popular rendezvous for many people.

WALK DESCRIPTION
To gain entrance to the Park pass through Dillons Cross and take the second turning left on the Ballyhooley New Road. At the Sunview East entrance follow the narrow pathway beside the sign marked 'The Glen Recreation Area'. Some ornamental bushes have been planted here which include the red-berried Himalayan cotoneaster while a playing area has also been laid out close by for children.

Within a few moments you reach an open area which includes a football pitch. The pathway continues along by a high bank that contains gorse bushes, nettles and brambles while olearia shrubs adorn the other side. At a metal barrier turn sharply left and follow the pathway

21

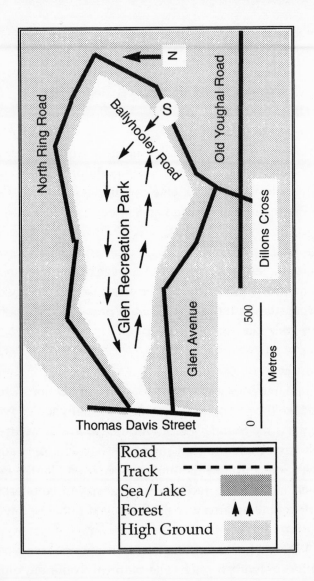

that now leads west. As you walk distant views of Farranree are apparent and close by you may spot mallard duck, coots and seagulls. Some ornamental rose bushes embellish the bank at your left and seats are provided should you care to rest. The second pond on your walk contains plenty of duckweed in late summer. It's an unusual plant as its delicate roots are not anchored in the water. Rushes also are plentiful and amongst them coots scavenge for morsels of food. A sand quarry looms on the northern bank while a wooden pailing at your right offers a protection from the steep slope to the water. Where the water exits from the pond the area has been landscaped with stony banks.

Increasing panoramas of Farranree are observed with the spire of the church particularly prominent. Ignore the metal-railed bridge that crosses the water to your right and continue ahead along the track. Bracken and gorse abound on the nearby cliffy bank. Rushes grow in the water here and as you reach the concrete structure at the water end, leave the track and take a less well-defined pathway uphill which swings to your right. The western exit from Glen Park is only a few paces walk from here. Pause at the top of the hillside as the views are good along the narrow path into the heart of the deep gorge. Behind you (westward), the city's northern suburbs of Farranree and Gurranebraher are apparent. Clearly visible is the large red-brick building, formerly the residence of the Bishops of Cork. In the far distance Mushera Mountain rises in silence from the fertile lands of west Cork. On the ground beside you bell heather grows in small quantities, probably the most beautiful of all wild heathers.

Leave the path and take the very narrow trail down the slope through the dense bracken. Ignore the path further on which slips down the hillside to the solid metal bridge. Eventually you arrive at a bushy area where graceful mature trees have escaped the felling saw. A narrow track leads through a bushy glade and sycamore trees guard the way. As you pass by a sandpit on your left caution is required as there is almost a sheer drop beside the trail. Pause beyond the eastern tip of the pit and admire the vista over the very core of the Glen which boasts two ornate concrete bridges. In the vicinity grow gorse, ragwort, blackberry brambles and, in season, bindweed.

Eventually you attain the eastern perimeter of the park where you drop to the stream. Here a bird of water places, the grey wagtail, is often seen bathing in the weedy water while snowberry and vetch eke out a living on the slope nearby. Several pathways converge around this area but our way now goes right again. Admire the graceful willow tree as you go. Having reached a central T-junction take the earthen steps up the hillside. Pause by the basketball courts on top for another fine view before returning to the nearby walk start.

WALK 8
BLACKROCK MARINA

OS Map: Cork City Street Map – Scale 1:15000
Distance: 4¹/₂ miles/7km.
Average time: 2 hours
Location: Situated 3 miles/5km east of Cork city centre it
is reached by travelling via Blackrock Road and
Ballintemple.

INTRODUCTION
This walk features a stroll by the side of Lough Mahon,
a ramble on the former Cork/Passage railway line and
to finish, a walk along the Marina.

WALK DESCRIPTION
Commence this walk at the car park by the harbour in
Blackrock village. Glancing across the waters one has
fine views of the river Lee and the Tivoli hills. Initially
take the obvious road (Convent Road) southward but
within a few yards turn down the laneway to your left,
Convent Avenue. After having passed some small pretty homes the lane broadens into Rope Walk and then
the walk veers right into Coakleys Row before reaching
Ringmahon Road. Here turn left and soon you pass
Ringmahon House to your left with its ruined 'castle'.
Inside the wall tall Scots pine and beech trees rise skyward. Increasingly good views of Lough Mahon are
apparent as you progress forward. Reaching the end of
the road veer to the left and follow the coastal roadway
where across the water you will observe the now-

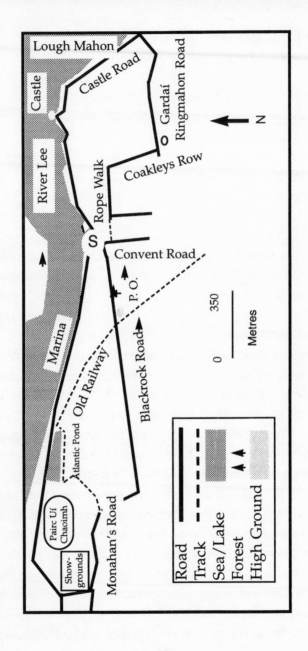

Lough Mahon

Castle Road

Castle

Gardaí

Ringmahon Road

River Lee

O

Coakleys Row

Rope Walk

S

Convent Road

N

P. O.

Marina

350

Metres

Old Railway

Blackrock Road

0

Atlantic Pond

Páirc Uí
Chaoimh

Monahan's Road

Show-
grounds

Road
Track
Sea/Lake
Forest
High Ground

26

industrialised Little Island.

From the mudflats close by the lonesome call of the curlew will often be heard, a familiar cry in wetlands and bogs. Ahead can be seen the Glanmire bypass and the Glanmire valley. On the shoreline you get the first examples of sea life – seaweed, shells and gravel stones. Rounding a bend Blackrock Castle comes into view. This attractive building, designed by J. and G.R. Pain (architects), was completed in 1829. Leaving the castle behind continue your walk along the road which is now in a commanding location over the river.

After 1 hour you should be back at Blackrock village and from there continue straight ahead passing the Ursuline Convent on your left and further up the inclined roadway, St Michael's Church. On the same side of the road look out for Blackrock Post Office, as beside it is a passageway which leads down to the cutting of the old railway line. You now follow this route and turn right at the track passing under two bridges as you move forward. This quite concealed haven of nature is a favourite of walkers and occasional joggers. A delightful mixture of oak, sycamore, hawthorn, ash, dogrose, dandelions and nettles co-exist happily together.

At the top of the track by the boulders turn left down the pathway at the metal barrier which will lead you to the Atlantic Pond. This is a pleasant place to relax as you watch some bird life – seagulls, swans and mallard ducks. The route leads you to Monahans Road where after passing the showgrounds you turn right into Centre Park Road and again another right that takes you to the Marina. Savour each step as you traverse the mile back to Blackrock village. Long a favourite with Corkonians, the Marina is best visited in October when the various colours of the leaves are glorious to behold. The waters here have for many years provided a venue for popular regattas while nearby the stadium of Pairc Uí Chaoimh has witnessed many exciting Gaelic games as well as outdoor concerts.

As you near the walk end it is worthwhile relaxing on one of the riverside seats where you will get the true atmosphere of this hallowed place.

WALK 9
THE LEE FIELDS

OS Map: Cork City Street Map – Scale 1: 15000
Distance: 2 miles/3 km
Average time: Approximately an hour
Location: Situated 2 miles/3km west of Cork city centre it is reached by travelling via the Western Road and Carrigrohane Road.

INTRODUCTION

This walk features a pleasant riverside stroll on the banks of the river Lee and an opportunity to observe some flora and fauna that exist by an inland waterway.

WALK DESCRIPTION

Begin this walk at a metal barrier just beyond the hotel on the Carrigrohane Road. Take the obvious pathway towards the river where, in the early morning, shortly after dawn, many wild birds feed. Amongst these are cormorants and grey herons which take up positions close to the stepped fishpass on the weir. Overhead batches of oystercatchers and mallard duck fly back and forward over the water.

Follow the tarmacadem pathway, which leads west beside the river. On the hillside across the water are the grey and red buildings of the former Our Lady's Psychiatric Hospital, the grey building being one of the longest in Ireland. It is often best to walk this route in early morning to experience the river awakening or in late evening when the setting sun sinks over the distant

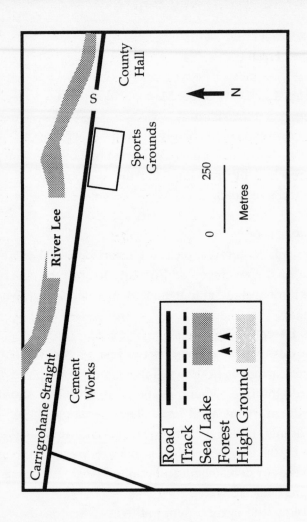

Iniscarra Hills. In recent years the Lee Fields has been the venue for pop concerts and the adjoining Carrigrohane Road has witnessed many motorcycle races as well as speed trials. As you progress along the path many different tree species will be observed – silver birch, ash, willow, maple, alder and oak. About ten minutes into the walk a concrete slipway is reached just at the narrowest section of the fields beside the road. From the slipway canoeists often launch their vessels.

Continuing the ramble, a metal sculpture of a dinosaur stands sentinel in the grass, often in winter a pathetic figure as it stands forlorn in a flooded field. Moving westward the wooded hills beyond the former hospital make a pleasant backdrop to the river Lee. In this area purple loosestrife will be seen flowering in late summer. Amongst the rushes, wily dragon and damselflies dart to and fro and small minnow fish are noticed in the shallow waters.

Shortly you arrive at a small 'beach' area known locally as 'Palm Beach'. A shelter has recently been erected there. Here some people swim all the year round even in harshest winter while dog walkers and joggers are frequent users of the pathway. Along the riverbank there is now a profusion of growth – in September you will notice elegant oak trees laden with acorns. Yellow ragwort and much-maligned bracken struggle in the jungle of brambles, bindweed and nettles while the species of yarrow, knapweed and vetch may be of interest to the botanist. From the open field by the wire fence return back to the walk start.

Walk 10
Nash's Boreen and Holly Hill

O.S. Map: Cork City Street Map – Scale 1:15000
Distance: 2 ¹/₄ miles / 4 km
Average Time: 1¹/₂ hours
Location: Situated 1 miles/2km northwest of Cork city centre it is reached by travelling via Sundays Well and Strawberry Hill

Introduction
This walk features expansive vistas from the north side of Cork city, a blend of urban and rural passageways and a stroll along one of the most attractive boreens remaining in the greater Cork area.

Walk Description
The walk commences at the base of Hollyhill near the top of Strawberry Hill on Blarney Street. This street was once an old route to Kerry and a 'butter' road in past times. Large quantities of butter were transported from west Cork and Kerry to the Butter Exchange near Shandon Steeple in Cork. From there the butter was dispatched to worldwide markets.

Leaving Blarney Street behind, walk up the laneway of Hollyhill, once a popular passage for the sport of road bowling but now a haven for small birds and scented hawthorn bushes. Graceful sycamores, oak and ash trees further up the hill seem to have escaped the cutters' chainsaw whilst polypody ferns lay down their roots on the old walls. Care is required as you reach the

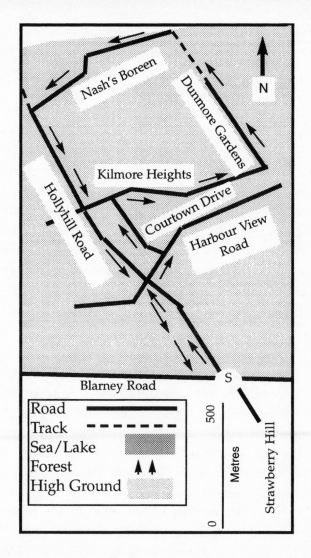

busy Harbour View Road. Cross the road to the Church and take the first turn left by the small roundabout that guides you up Courtown Drive.

Bear right along Kilmore Heights at the T-junction

and from this elevated area fine views of Cork Harbour and the southern city hills are apparent. Take the first turn left beyond the wigwam-shaped water tower and reservoir. The way now angles right into Dunmore Gardens where you should look out for the narrow laneway at the end of the row of houses on your left. Continue to the end of the laneway and then continue to the field edge just left of the old overgrown route. Along this old route was a heap of stones (now concealed by gorse bushes) referred to as the 'Croppy Boy'. This is reputed to be the grave of a youth that was murdered during the 1798 rebellion. It was a practice to throw stones onto the pile and the following lines were associated with it:

> Ladies and Gentlemen as you pass by,
> Fire three stones at the Croppy Boy.

The story goes that in 1798 a youth was pursued by Yeomen from Mallow Lane (now called Shandon Street) and was eventually caught and shot at this spot. Around the fields here in summertime swallows can be observed flying low before they gather on nearby electric wires prior to the annual exodus to Africa.

Continue downhill along the faint track that brings you to Nash's Boreen. Now turn left along this peaceful route where often dogs are exercised by the 'boys of Fairhill'. As you walk gaze west to the groves of famed Blarney and the more distant Mushera Mountain. This boreen must be one of the most attractive within easy reach of Cork city. Many different types of flora can be observed – gorse, nettles, brambles, vetch, tormentil, hawk-bit, tansy, ragwort and the solitary bumble bee or hoverfly will be seen working the scented honeysuckle. Further on, yarrow and wall pennywort will be observed.

After a long straight stretch the boreen turns sharply left and right before continuing west again. Once more impressive views are seen to Clogheen and the townland of Blarney. As you reach the western end of Nash's boreen the route turns left uphill. However the observant walker will notice the narrow path to the right which was known in times past as *Cosán na Piobra*, the path of the piper. It continues down to the field and a place known locally as the 'Watery' before gaining access to the Lower Old Killeens Road.

As we proceed uphill from the junction along the leafy laneway where hawthorn trees abound one notices on the moss-covered walls foxgloves, herb robert and thistles. As you pass the old farmyard on your left you leave the rural section of the walk and the final stages are straight down the hill of Hollyhill Road to reach Blarney Street where you began the walk.

Walk 11
Clogheenmilcon Walk

OS Map: No. 80 (Discovery Series)
Distance: 2¹/₂ miles/4km
Average time: 1 hour
Getting there: Situated 4 miles/6km northwest of Cork city it can be reached by travelling via Blackpool and Killeens or via Sundays Well and Clogheen.

Introduction

In recent years a new walkway combining unbridled nature and modern development has been created a few miles northwest of Cork city. The Clogheenmilcon Wildlife Sanctuary walk, which came into being in conjunction with the construction of the final stage of the N20 Cork to Mallow road, offers a variety of interest to the nature enthusiast, in particular to the ornithologist.

Walk Description

This walk commences at the Wildlife Sanctuary Car Park situated by the newly constructed roundabout adjacent to the N20 Cork/Mallow road and the R617 road to Blarney, being about 1 mile east of Blarney village. Over 100 different bird species have been identified in this area which says a lot for the decision to manage this alkaline wetland. Comprising of approximately 100 acres, the area was once a deep lake. In winter it was used as a shooting area by gun clubs and in summer it was occasionally grazed. Eighteen small islands are scattered throughout the wetland and they provide

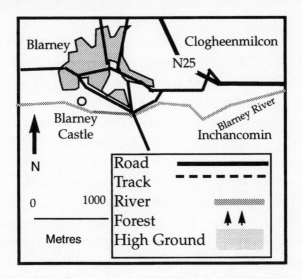

restful habitats for the wildlife. It is hoped that as the area matures in the future migrant birds will decide to stop in the Blarney suburb and overwinter. Generally in Ireland the best time to observe wetland wild birds is in winter (October to March).

Because this walk is on a straightforward tarmacadam pathway which runs more or less parallel to the wetland, some information about the birds observed should be of interest.

The cormorant can sometimes be seen perched solitary on an outcrop with wings outstretched. This unusual posture is interpreted as being the bird's method of drying its wings. Cormorants are large glossy black birds with a long body and a reasonably long neck. It lives in a variety of habitats, including coastal waters, inland lakes and rivers and can be frequently seen on the River Lee immediately west of Cork city. The bird is not a diver but plunges from the water surface to snatch fish from the waters below, often staying beneath for a considerable time before surfacing to swallow its prey.

Another popular inhabitant at this wildlife sanctuary is the mallard duck which utters the distinguished quack, quack, quack, when it flies away after being disturbed. Quite often it is very tame and regularly mixes with ducks in a farmyard. Its habitat is water areas of many types but it is mostly seen in slow-moving rivers and lakes. The male of the species (the drake) is a very fine bird when in full plumage and it sports a greenish head with a white collar on its neck, a brownish breast and greyish body with a green-blue feathered area on its wings.

The largest bird to be observed during this walk is the mute swan, the most common swan to be seen in Ireland and also one of the most graceful and beautiful birds to inhabit Irish waters. The adults possess orange bills with black at the tip and a black knob at the base. Its habitat is usually fresh slow-moving water with nearby vegetation which it uses for nesting or resting purposes. Young swans are brown at first but soon become patchy before emerging as mature birds. However, the male adult can be quite aggressive when approached so care is required.

A solitary bird, the grey heron (*Ardea cinerea*) is often noticed quietly stalking the edges of rivers and lakes. A unique looking bird, the adults have white heads and necks. Their general plumage is mostly grey and they have a slow-moving flight when airborne. The herons diet can consist of frogs, fish – particularly eels, young birds, etc.

Having walked eastwards to the end of the walkway return by the same route to the carpark where you may notice the pied wagtail which attends regularly for morsels of food. This sprightly bird is easily identified with its black and white plumage and constant motion. A lover of insects they often fly up from the ground to snatch their victims in mid-air and can be found in a variety of habitats both urban and rural.

Leaving the car park and continuing to take the path westward (towards Blarney village) beside the busy R617 look out for some other birds like the magpie and reed bunting. The former, a most striking bird but also a very clever one, seeks food opportunities in a variety of locations but it is principally insectivorous. Observed at close quarters it displays plumage of a glossy blue, green and purple and it has a habit of collecting non-edible shiny objects which are often found in its nest of sticks. The much smaller reed bunting possesses a black head and throat with a white breast for the male and brown heads for females with some black markings. It is frequently found at the verge of reed beds or perched on tall grassy stalks and feeds largely on insects and seeds.

Moving towards the western end of the walk as it swings left in conjunction with the link road, a glance towards distant Blarney village will be rewarded with a view of famous Blarney Castle rising skyward behind the housing estate.

Having reached the roadway close to the bridge return along the tarmacadam path to the car park. On the way look out for some of the wetland insects which dart about like the dragonflies and damselflies.

WALK 12
FOTA WILDLIFE PARK

OS Map: No. 80 (Discovery Series)
Distance: Various
Average time: The recommendation is to spend several hours in the park and discover the many walkways of varying lengths.
Location The park is situated 10.6 miles/17km east of Cork city on the road to Cobh. There is a modest admission fee.

INTRODUCTION
A walk around a most attractive wildlife park with a stroll through pleasant gardens and avenues in which many old and uniquely varied trees and shrubs can be observed.

WALK DESCRIPTION
The park, which was officially opened in July 1983 by the former President of Ireland, Dr Patrick Hillery, comprises principally a wildlife park and an outstanding arboretum. To confine the visitor to a particular walk route would be a mistake as there are many hidden treasures around each area and all are worth seeking out.

On entering the Wildlife section of the park it is worth initially viewing the video (15 minutes duration) as it gives a good overview of what is to be seen. A children's play area erected nearby has some swings and roundabouts as well as tame goats, bantam hens and some hamsters. Visitors to the park are requested not to feed the animals or disturb the tranquil atmosphere

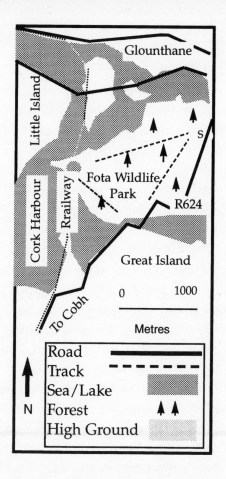

by using radios. As you proceed along the tarmacadem roadway look out for the giraffe and cheetah compounds, the latter being one of the world's fastest animals, having been timed in its run at up to 60mph. Its numbers worldwide are now reducing rapidly largely due to agricultural development. Giraffes are of course the tallest animals on earth and can grow to a height in excess of 17 feet. Other animals that can be

41

viewed are emus, blackbucks, axis deer, guanacos and prairie dogs. Down by the lakeside look out for the ever restless white-handed gibbon apes that move through the trees constantly. Penguins can be observed and ring-tailed lemurs are the small animals with black and white tails. Wallabies and kangaroos also inhabit the park as well as monkeys and peacocks.

The arboretum is a haven for anyone interested in trees and shrubs. In particular attention is drawn to the serenely beautiful cedar of Lebanon tree (planted in 1825) and located on the raised lawn to the rear of Fota House. In October cyclamen plants bloom at its base. Other very impressive trees in the collection are an ever-green oak, an 85-foot tall monterey pine, a gum tree from Tasmania and a tulip tree from China planted in 1936. Other interesting trees and shrubs are the Killarney strawberry tree, camellias, embothrium (chilean fire bush), eucalyptus, fuchsias, forsythias, magnolias, jasmines, laburnums and the curious Chinese ginko tree. It is the mild climate here which helps many delicate species to survive and flourish. Trees and shrubs have been brought from China, South America, Japan, Australia and New Zealand. Some species also exist from the Himalayas and North America. Most of the older conifer trees were planted during the 1840s. The Smith Barry family who once owned the estate collected plants from all over the world and planted them at Fota.

Walk 13
Cobh Town Trail

OS Maps: No. 87 (Discovery Series) plus the map available from the Cobh Tourist Office.
Distance: 1¹/₄ miles/2 km
Average time: ³/₄ hour
Location: Located 15 miles/24km southeast of Cork city it is reached via Dunkettle, Belvelly, and Rushbrooke.

Introduction
Cobh is an attractive town located at the inner end of one of the finest harbours in the world, Cork Harbour. It is an historical place with a population of approximately 8,500, people, yet very much a modern town.

Walk Description
Begin at Casement Square in the town centre and walk west along Westbourne Place keeping the harbour on your left. On the left also is the Yacht Club building which once housed the Royal Cork Yacht Club previously founded in Haulbowline in 1720. It is reputed to be the oldest in the world, originally named the Water Club. Later the club's headquarters was transferred to Crosshaven.

After a short distance the road divides. Follow the road on the right which veers uphill (High Road) an shortly you arrive at a T-junction. Across the road is the former Scots Presbyterian Church erected in 1854, which closed as a place of worship a few decades ago. It has since reopened as Cobh Museum and is worth a visit. It features Irish lace and glass, an Irish naval display, paintings/watercolours from the nineteenth century, models of former ships and old photographs of Cobh in former times.

At the T-junction turn right up Spy Hill and continue along Bishops Road to an elevated position above the town and harbour. As you progress forward it is interesting to reflect on some of Cobh's history. This town expanded rapidly from the time of the Great Famine in 1845-7. Large emigration took place to America and countless adults and children emigrated from Ireland in the years immediately after the Famine. Large numbers left from Cobh, the majority of whom were never to return to their native land.

Earlier during the Napoleonic Wars (1792-1815) the harbour was an important place of rendezvous for commercial and naval ships and several hundred could regularly be seen anchored off Cobh.

A few years after the Famine Queen Victoria visited Ireland in 1849. Accompanied by a naval escort the royal yacht anchored at Cove (as it was then known). To mark the occasion it was decided to change the town's name to Queenstown. It remained so until 1920 when the name reverted back to an Irish version of Cove, i.e. Cobh.

In recent years Cork Harbour has hosted some large cruise liners like the *Q.E.2*, *Royal Viking Queen*, *Vistafjord*, *Crown Odyssey*, etc., and in 1991 the Cutty Sark Tall Ships Race came to Cork for four days.

On 7 May 1915 a German submarine sunk the ill-fated *Lusitania* liner some miles off the Old Head of Kinsale. Many hundreds of the passengers, survivors and those who perished were brought into Cobh. Some who died were interred in the old Clonmel graveyard, located about 1km north of the town.

At the top of Bishops Road continue to Park Lane where you turn right and right again to head downhill towards the striking Cobh Cathedral (RC) which dominates this portal town, particularly when viewed from the sea. The cathedral is named after St Colman, born in the sixth century, and its style of architecture is French Gothic. Its foundation stone was laid in 1868 and the building was completed in 1915. The spire is 300 feet high and the stone used was granite and limestone. The view of Cobh and Cork Harbour is marvellous from this location. Cork's motto is *Statio Bene Fida Carinis* (a safe anchorage for ships) and so it is, stretching from Rostellan in the east to Monkstown in the west and from Cobh to the southerly entrance watched over by Roches Point Lighthouse. Two islands of reasonable size are located within the harbour, Spike Island and Haulbowline Island, the latter being the headquarters of the Irish naval service.

Continue downhill from the Cathedral and pass through the first road junction. At the next junction swing right down a few steps by a postal box (set in the wall) and continue west along East Beach, which after a short distance merges into West Beach. On the way you pass on the left the Town Hall and Clock Tower which was built in 1874 and a little further on the former Cunard Line offices, now a Savings Bank. Just before you end your ramble a visit to the *Lusitania* Monument is worthwhile at Casement Square in the Town Centre close to the start of this walk.

WALK 14
GLENBOWER WOOD

OS Map: No. 81 (Discovery Series)
Distance: 4 miles/6.5km
Average time: 2 hours
Location: Glenbower is located 23 miles/38km east of
Cork city, adjacent to the village of Killeagh. It is reached
by travelling through Midleton and Castlemartyr.

INTRODUCTION
Glenbower Wood, a shady leafy recess located to the
north of Killeagh in east Cork, has quietly attracted visitors and nature lovers for many years with its reclusive
charms. A place of secluded pathways and elevated
viewing points, this haunting glen with its shy and varied wildlife, should not be missed if you seek an afternoon's relaxation.

WALK DESCRIPTION
From the car park follow the path through the trees on
the left ignoring the forest road on the right. This fine
wood formerly contained a very attractive lake but it
was deemed unsafe and was drained in 1988. It is therefore prudent to heed the warning sign about mud flats
in the former lake deemed to be hazardous.

Within a few moments you reach a wider track, formerly a millrace that took water to a mill downstream.
Here turn right and follow the track. On the left bank
grows a small but attractive plant called wood sorrel. A
creeping perennial, it grows throughout Europe and

46

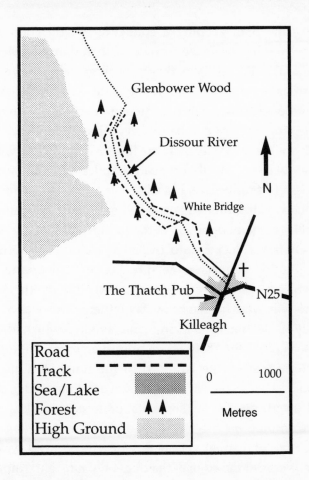

Central Asia even as far as Sakhalin Island, north of Japan. Easily recognised by its large green 'shamrock' leaves which often fold up, it produces a white flower in late spring which balances on a slender fragile stalk.

This pleasant shaded walk of oak and occasional holly trees, smells of wild garlic in May and is an agreeable introduction to Glenbower. At the path junction ahead turn left over the wooden bridge and veer right along the path keeping a conifer grove on your left. Soon you approach the former earthen dam and sluice gate of the drained lake. Before a bridge, take the wooden steps on your left and swing right on a rising pathway. Between here and the forest road ahead several plant/tree species can be observed like rhododendron, holly, oak, ash, violets, bullrush, ferns and bilberry, the latter being a shrub of heaths and lower mountain slopes. It produces a blackish berry in late summer, which was traditionally collected and made into jam.

Having joined the forest road follow it to the right as it penetrates deeper into the glen tracking the former 'lake' until you reach a metal bridge. Up to a quarter of a century ago many people flocked here on the first Sunday in May for the May Day Pattern. This was a celebration of music, dancing and singing which dates back as far as the 1830s when improvements were made to the estate by the landlord of the time, De Cappell Brooke. This metal bridge is known as White Bridge and its four turrets display some elaborate stonework.

Continue on the forest road ahead and as you do take note of a small yellow flower which grows on the grass verge at the edge of the trees on your right. Known as yellow pimpernel it flowers profusely in May and is common in Ireland on moist mountain pastures and in woods as well as finding an occasional home on damp roadside ditches. The flowers have five petals and are a yellow colour.

As you ascend the now hilly road the wood becomes more remote and the view over the valley improves with trees visible on all horizons. Birdsong increases and a kestrel, the only hovering game bird, may be spotted over the valley. Continue to the back of the valley where the path descends to cross the river by a wooden bridge. Here the silence is tangible and the wily fox and grey heron can occasionally be observed. The fox in Ireland dates back to over 5,000 years ago and has continuously been attacked by man. However, this beautiful and clever animal has always been one step ahead of the posse and has survived up to the present, even though many are killed each year in Ireland.

Having crossed the bridge turn right for the return journey to the car park. This will lead you back to White Bridge, which should not be crossed. Instead continue on the ascending forest road which passes beneath some tall conifers. Turn right at the next junction and follow the road to eventually pass over a bridge (known as Metal Bridge) before reaching the car park a short time later.

Walk 15
Ballycotton Cliff Walk

OS Maps: No. 81 (Discovery Series)
Distance: 3 miles/5km
Average time: 1½ hours
Location: The walk start is located about 25 miles/40km east of Cork city and just 7 miles/12 km southeast of the village of Cloyne.

Introduction
In former times many doctors of high repute would prescribe a short stay in this coastal village for patients suffering from stress or other ailments. Its clifftop path, known to some as the Champagne Walk, has long been a special favourite with visitors and locals alike.

Walk Description
Having reached Ballycotton village take the road to the right at the obvious Y junction in the village centre. This road ends abruptly at a metal gate from which the walk starts through an open stone stile a few paces to the left.

The well-worn path guides you westward following the meandering contour of the clifftop from which fetching views are broad and breathtaking. Interesting carpets of wildflowers abound throughout the route and in the early stages yellow gorses and trefoil as well as pink clumps of sea thrift will be observed. A very adaptable plant, thrift is found on coastal cliffs and at the summit areas of mountains.

Behind as you press forward the attractive lighthouse

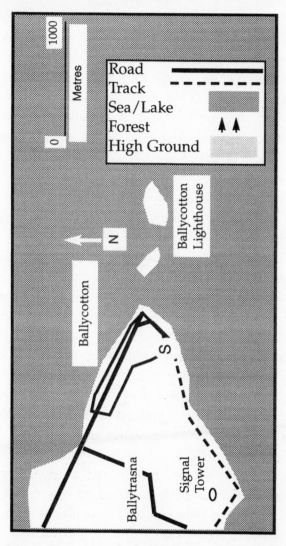

rises skyward having first flashed its light on 1 June 1851. Initially intended to be erected on Capel Island near Knockadoon Head the site was abandoned in favour of Ballycotton Island. The ruthless sea along this coastline has often challenged the resourcefulness of local people and many was the occasion when the Ballycotton Lifeboat had to go to the aid of stricken vessels.

As one continues on the worn path a concrete lookout building looms in a field to the right. These buildings were erected in strategic locations around the Irish coast to observe naval manoeuvres at sea. All along this route sea birds can be observed like the oystercatcher which flies low over water making a high pitched squeaking sound. A large black and white bird with an orange bill, it is generally seen in Ireland during the winter months, often flying inland over the wide surface of larger rivers.

The worn track leads clearly ahead along the clifftop and cautionary common sense is required where it veers close to the cliff. Ireland's only reptile, the viviparous lizard, is occasionally observed sunning itself on the concrete stiles, along the route. It mates in April/May and after three months gestation, young lizards are born. Almost immediately the young are able to fend for themselves and sustain themselves by devouring small insects.

As the walk progresses a series of headlands extend seawards in the distance which in late afternoon light display a generous shaping by nature. Towards the western end of the route views of Ballytrasna beach are apparent and the ceaseless sound of the sea is a constant audible companion. Finally you reach some concrete steps which lead down to a small water channel. From this point return the way you have come to the walk start.

Route 16
Garryvoe Beach Walk

OS Map: No. 81 (Discovery Series)
Distance:
Average time: Very much a personal choice as to what distance you wish to walk but an hour's walk on reasonably level ground at an average walking pace approximates to three miles in distance.
Location: Situated 24 miles/39km east of Cork city it can be reached by travelling via Midleton and Cloyne.

Introduction
Cork County boasts some fine stretches of coastline, with its fair share of beaches. Particularly impressive sandy beaches occur in the east of the county from Ballycotton to Youghal. One of the best for a good summer or winter stroll is Garryvoe beach, fronting onto Ballycotton Bay.

Walk Description
At the outset it is interesting to reflect on some of the geological and archaeological history of the area. Within the past 200,000 years at least two ice ages occurred which sculpted the land. Large ice sheets formed and moved south over Ireland and the Irish Sea. The ice flow which pushed down the Irish Sea turned west along the south Irish coast to reach its limit at Ballycotton Bay. It left a deposit of glacial till, i.e., a mass of gravels, sands and boulder clay. The mountains of Cork and Kerry then developed their own ice-cap which resulted in ice

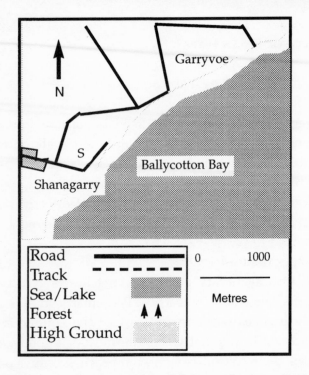

Road

Track

Sea/Lake

Forest

High Ground

0   1000

Metres

Garryvoe

N

S

Ballycotton Bay

Shanagarry

flowing towards the coast and it reached its limit at Garryvoe, its till overlying the previously deposited boulder clay. Therefore, if one looks carefully at the cliff at Garryvoe, different layers are apparent as well as the composition of the stones within the layers. Generally the more angular the stones the closer they are to their source. Another aspect of geological interest in this region are the chalk deposits offshore from which flint nodules occasionally are washed ashore. Flint can be black, grey or brown and the samples usually carry a partial white covering. As flint breaks somewhat like glass it can have very sharp edges and therefore was prized by early inhabitants. These early hunter-gatherers (as they were known) shaped the flint to make primitive tools and some of these have been found along the coastline east of Roches Point which is located at the entrance to Cork Harbour.

Garryvoe, therefore, is more than just a beach. A popular bathing area in summertime it has long been frequented by Cork holiday makers. Walking the beach on a fine day is a pleasant experience. Where sea meets land a variety of activities take place. The continual movement of the seas and the in-rushing waves against the coastline shape the latter and deep inlets are sometimes carved, sheer cliffs are formed, sea arches, sea stacks and islands are created. As the seas move they transport various material and a proportion of this is washed up high on a beach when the waves have a strong onshore wind assisting them. This debris can include many things like cuttlefish bone, sea weeds, shells, man-made discarded junk, odd shoes and plastic containers of every description. Gardeners and farmers collect the rotting seaweed for land nourishment.

As you walk Garryvoe Beach look out for the great variety and colour of the pebbles. Many people collect these and around the Irish coast some places are noted for their variety. Apart from examining the beach glance seaward and skyward as the birdlife is interesting and varied. Coastal birds include the black and white oystercatcher, various gulls, shags, curlews and redshanks.

WALK 17
YOUGHAL TOWN WALK

OS Map: No. 81 (Discovery Series)
Distance: 1¹/₂ miles
Average time: 1 hour
Location: Situated 30 miles/48km east of Cork city it can be reached by travelling via Midleton, Castlemartyr and Killeagh.

INTRODUCTION
Located at the eastern end of County Cork, Youghal is a pleasant coastal town beloved by Corkonians, particularly in summertime when many take their annual holiday there. It is also a town of history. Once defended by thick stone walls it received its first charter in 1209 from King John. Youghal, it has been suggested, comes from the Irish word for a yew tree, *eochaill.*

WALK DESCRIPTION
A prominent feature of Youghal town is its clock tower which straddles the main street. It was erected by the local council more than two centuries ago in 1777. This tower was once a prison and a place of oppression; several inmates were publicly hanged from its windows in order to frighten any potential revolutionaries in the town's population or surrounding countryside.

Approaching from the Cork city side follow the steps (left) immediately beyond the tower. This steep passageway quickly gains height to cross a road and continues up once more on some steps which after a good

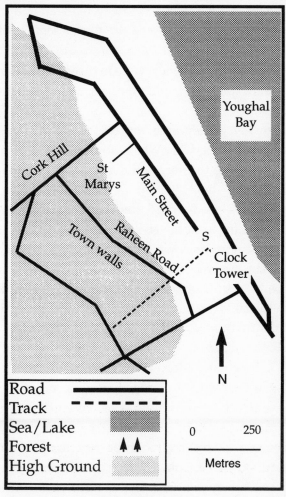

Youghal
Bay

Cork Hill

St
Marys

Main Street

Raheen Road

Town walls

S

Clock
Tower

N

Road	
Track	
Sea/Lake	
Forest	
High Ground	

0   250

Metres

stiff ascent one reaches Raheen Road. Here turn right and from this elevated position fine vistas of the Youghal estuary are apparent. Continuing along the roadway one can view an extensive section of the town wall, part of which dates back to the thirteenth century. Inside the wall common beech trees rise skyward.

Continue on the grassy area close to the wall and if you look closely you will observe the upper section of the wall looks more recent. Much restoration work has taken place. When the walls were first constructed many towers were spaced along their route. Only three towers now remain.

Leave the grassy area towards the wall end and continue on the roadway which now begins to turn and descend. Keep to the verge on the right and try to identify the flora there, vetch, herb robert, stonecrop, hawthorn, hogweed. These flower in the peak summer period. Pass through a well-maintained housing estate before turning right down Lower Cork Hill to reach the main street. Continue right again and within a short distance turn up the narrow passage of Church Street also on the right. Here you pass the public library at the left and further on Shalom House (formerly the Protestant Asylum and originally built in 1838 but renovated in recent years). At the top of Church Street is St Mary's Collegiate Church which now occupies the site of a church which is supposed to have existed before the Norman invasion. The interior of the church is impressive and it contains an east window, which is large and attractive. This window dates from the end of the fifteenth century. Just to the right of the Church entrance is Myrtle Grove, a private residence. At one time it was the home of Sir Walter Raleigh. From Youghal he sailed west to America and returned with the potato and tobacco, it is said. He was mayor of Youghal Town in 1588-9.

Return to the main street and continue right where

you now reach the Alms House erected in 1610 by the Earl of Cork. The architecture is of the Elizabethan period and it was originally built to house old soldiers down in their luck. On your left across the street is Tynte's Castle, an ancient tower built in the fifteenth century by English settlers. Note the amount of flowers growing in its upper section. Just up the street is the Benedictine Priory, which dates from the fourteenth century. Particularly distinctive is its doorway.

As you near the Clock Tower cross the usually busy main street and walk left down O'Rahilly Street. Turn right at the street end and walk directly ahead keeping the harbour on your left. Around this general area in 1954 much of the film *Moby Dick* was made starring Gregory Peck. Directly ahead is Market House and Market Square. Across the way from Market House is the Water Gate under which you pass to reach the Main Street and turn right to arrive at the imposing Clock Tower.

Walk 18
Corrin Hill

OS Map: No. 81 (Discovery Series)
Distance: Over 1¹/₂ miles/1km
Location: Situated 1 mile south of Fermoy it is reached from Cork by travelling via Watergrasshill and Rathcormac.
Average Time: 1¹/₄ hours

Introduction
A hill walk through forested slopes giving panoramic views at its summit where a large cross has been erected in front of a massive cairn and within the circular confines of a prehistoric fort.

Walk Description
Begin this walk by the large car park at the forest entrance close to Fermoy Golf Club. Coniferous trees (lodgepole pine) cover the hill. Lodgepole pine (*Pinus Contorta*) is a native of the Rocky Mountains from Colorado to Alaska and has the capacity to grow up to 25m. Stations of the Cross in the form of stone tablets blend suitably along the forest track with the trees at periodic locations almost as far as the summit. Each year on the last Sunday in September, a religious procession and service is held on Corrin Hill.

Leaving the car park behind, continue along the forest road which winds its way in a gradual ascent to the top of the hill. On your climb ignore the forest tracks which trail to the right except when you come to the

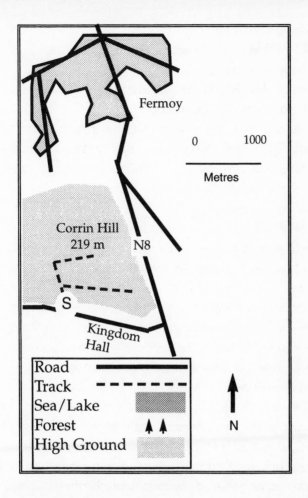

third junction which leads to the summit area. On the upper reaches look out for a typical mountain plant, bilberry (or fraughan), a low-sized shrub sprouting light, bright green leaves. In April and May it flowers and is pollinated by bees. Usually in September it bears fruit, a purple/black berry which is edible and is suitable for jam making. In times past in Ireland bilberry twigs were chopped and made into brooms and the berries were usually picked on a regular 'Fraughan Sunday' when children were brought to collect the fruit.

As you approach the summit area, the Galtee mountain range dominates the horizon to the north. The Ballyhoura hills are visible to the northwest and eastwards rise the Knockmealdown and Comeragh Mountains. Corrin summit offers a bird's eye view of the ever-expanding town of Fermoy. The 30-ft high stone cross was erected in 1933 to commemorate the nineteenth centenary of the death of Christ. The cairn behind the cross is a collection of large loose stones and is almost circular in shape measuring approximately 100 feet by 90 feet by 10 feet high. Knowledge is limited about these cairns. It is generally accepted that they are the burial sites of important people and date from the Iron Age or earlier. In the 1830s this cairn was excavated and a chamber was discovered which contained two urns, one containing ashes.

The other particular item of interest around the summit is the now-broken wall of the Hill Top Fort. There is still a lot to be discovered about hillforts in Ireland but in olden times they offered protection as the valleys were mostly forested. Some of these sites may have been places of religious significance. On the broken wall of the 'fort', bell heather, woolly haired moss, polypody ferns, and polytrichum moss grow profusely.

After completing your tour of the summit area return by the forest road to the walk start at the car park.

OS Maps: Nos 80 and 81 (Discovery Series)
Distance: 3 miles/5km
Average time: 1¹/₂ hours
Location The walk start is located about 23 miles/38km from Cork city in the town of Fermoy.

INTRODUCTION
Extending westward from the town of Fermoy along the bank of the river Blackwater is the locally well-known Barnane Walk but to the curious outsider a gem to be explored and relished.

WALK DESCRIPTION
Commence the ramble by the hotel, close to the bridge in Fermoy town and walk west away from the town along the concrete rampart by the river. Within a few minutes you pass by a metal barrier close to the premises of Fermoy Rowing Club from which you continue along the tarmacadam pathway ahead.

On top of the wall on your left you can identify the herb robert plant by its red hairy stem and small pink flowers. Widespread throughout Ireland, its juices were once used to cure human and animal ailments. Closer examination of the wall on your left will result in the observation of a small fern making its home in a favoured surround. This is known as rusty back fern and on the reverse side of its leaves small overlapping scales display a pronounced rust colour. High in the tall

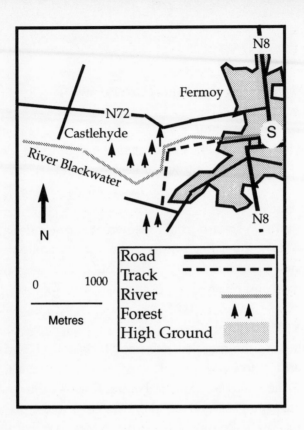

trees choruses of noisy rooks are frequently heard emitting their monotonous raucous cawing sound.

Just beyond a stone shelter on the left is St Bernard's Well and in the secluded alcove coins are often left in the pool by well-wishers. Resuming the riverside walk one soon reaches a concrete stile at which point the tarmacadam walkway ends. The track ahead leads to a wooden stile within a few moments where an abundance of buttercups burst into flower.

Pressing forward views of Corrin Hill to the south

soon become apparent and fishermen often fish for roach and dace along this section of the river where a number of fishing stations (or pegs) are clearly identifiable. After some time following the contour of the meandering river you enter a more overgrown brambly area and care is required as you pass by the riverbank beyond. You now enter a mixed wooded passageway where cow parsley grows abundantly in the company of wild garlic and spearwort. Exiting this you pass through a passage of wire fencing supported by wooden posts. The observant will notice bluebells growing beneath some oak trees on the hillside at the left.

Having walked through a concrete tunnel the way swings sharply left to confront a short line of noble beech trees. Here the red squirrel has been observed. A delightful creature and one of Ireland's prettiest animals, it normally only permits fleeting glimpses as it flits from branch to branch.

Continue along the route ahead which will eventually lead you through a 'jungley' patch before gaining the wall at the roadside where you exit. Here a signpost indicates Fermoy to your left. Follow this route and you will reach Fermoy centre and your walk start.

WALK 20
DONERAILE COURT AND FOREST PARK

OS Map: No. 73 (Discovery Series)
Distance: 2¹/₂ miles/4 km
Average time: 2 hours
Getting there: Doneraile Court is located 30 miles/50km
northeast of Cork city and just a few miles east of the
main road from Mallow to Buttevant.

INTRODUCTION
For over 200 years Doneraile Court was the centre of
social life in the Doneraile area and was the family seat
of the St Leger family for 250 years. Acquired by the
state in 1969 it was later leased to the Georgian Society
and considerable sums of money have been spent in
restoring it so that it can be used by the public as part of
the nations heritage.

WALK DESCRIPTION
Begin this walk at the spacious car park a short distance
inside the estate and take the pathway down to the
water and ornamental bridge. Here in summertime
dragonflies flit about, often in contorted shapes as they
mate. Continue over the wooden footbridge ahead near
which some huge chestnut trees grow including a massive beech tree.

Take the central track uphill, which at first veers
slightly left before swinging right. Ahead is the imposing 40-room mansion of Doneraile Court, a residence
with a long history which is suitably documented in historical journals.

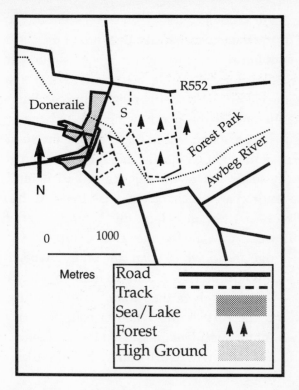

From the mansion take the green track over the meadow back to the left of the house where swallows are often observed skimming low back and forth. Reaching the road turn right over a wooden bridge beyond which a fine view of Doneraile House can be seen to the right. One might also spot a peacock beside the house. Go under the trees where the pungent aroma of wild garlic abounds.

Reaching a clearing there is yet again a view of Doneraile House. Then the path veers left and at the first turn left walk down the long avenue of tall lime trees, surely one of the features of this demesne. Around this quiet glade rabbits can sometimes be seen and to the right inside the enclosure, sika deer are in residence. At the end of the avenue turn left along the fishpond. In the rather still water yellow flag, bogbean and dock abound while the colourful damselfly relishes the combination.

At the end of the pond swing left and then right along a short wooden fenced road keeping the stretch of water on your right. In the distance red deer often graze. The way leads left at the T-junction and behind the rhododendron are beech, oak and ash trees. At the next junction bear right and along this section a variety of wild flowers grow in the meadow. Cross the elegant stone bridge ahead, which spans the pretty Awbeg river, garnished with waterweed. Turn right by the river bank along a broad rough earthen track. After this turn left uphill via the earth ramp where a collection of deer busily hunt for succulent grasses. At the wire fence veer left and this route will return you to the car park.

OS Map: No. 79 (Discovery Series)

Distance: Various

Average time: Very much a personal choice as the complex contains many tracks and trails from the higher levels down to the visitor centre located at the lower level of the park. However, one could start at height and descend gradually and allow at least 3 hours for a visit, perhaps even make it a full day out.

Location: The Millstreet Country park is situated 32 miles/52km northwest of Cork city, as the crow flies. It can be reached by travelling 24 miles/39km via Macroom and then continue northeast for another 8 miles/13km to reach the park. Alternatively, you can travel from Millstreet where you head east towards Mallow. Turn right at the Dairygold Co-op Store, and go right at the second crossroads for the park.

INTRODUCTION

One of the most interesting places to open to the public in recent years is Millstreet Country Park. It could be described as a kingdom of nature as its development has harmonised with the wild, untamed landscape of the Boggeragh Mountains.

WALK DESCRIPTION

Upon arrival at the park one cannot but admire the very fine entrance gates and the adjoining walls of large boulders which prior to their present resting place lay about

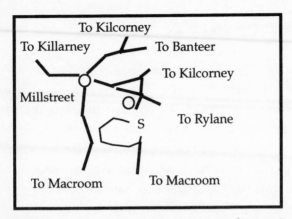

the park area as erratics from the now distant ice ages. Incidentally these boulders were formed as rock about 350 million years ago during the geological period known as the Devonian.

From the entrance gate to the visitor centre there is a drive of 2 miles down into the bottom of the valley. It is worth taking it slowly as the unfolding view is superb on a fine day. Across the broad plain one can see Claragh Mountain towering above Millstreet town. To its left and further west is the large lump of Caherbarnagh Mountain with its broad grassy summit and again left, topped by a communications mast, is Mullaghanish Mountain.

A short distance beyond the entrance hut is Carrig Leabra (Rock of Books). This crag is on an adjoining, private property and was the site of a 'hedge school' in penal times (1695-1829). Travelling teachers came and taught only those who could afford to pay.

Having arrived at the *Turin Na Bláth* Visitor Centre take time to view the large mural map on the wall which will assist in planning your route. There are also very helpful leaflets available as well as audio-visual and touch screen thematic presentations to view. A free park transport system operates throughout the park and you may initially use it to return to the heights near the main entrance and explore the Mushera Ravine Reserve. Some typical mountain and bog flora can be found there, including the three popular heathers, ling, bell and crossleaved heath, as well as bilberry, bog cotton, greater butterwort and the special bog asphodel. Why not rest at the seating by Mushera Ravine Bridge and listen to the sound of the rustling grasses. This area too is a place of cascades plunging into tiered small lakes and gurgling brooks wind their way northward through the steep ravine. Well-constructed stone bridges are a feature of this remote park location.

Animal and birdlife is well represented too with over 600 red deer enclosed in paddocks. You may well observe the fox towards dusk or the hare or rabbit. Hovering kestrels have been spotted eyeing their unfortunate prey from above before dropping like a stone to capture a meal. It also is the home of the crow, woodcock and meadow pipit as well as the heather-loving red grouse. In its streams one may observe the brown trout, eel and lesser creatures.

But there is another aspect to this landscape which is equally fascinating. Reflect on the stone circle, stone alignment, *fullaght fiadh* (cooking place) and the newly constructed *crannóg* hut. More than 80 stone circles have been located in County Cork, the largest concentration of such circles anywhere in these islands. What was their significance? They appear to have been revered places, perhaps of ritual and burial with many, it is thought, having a connection with the old Solar calendar. However, this whole subject is vast and well documented and discussed in books and journals.

At the lower end of the park one can view a meadow, rich in herbs and wild flowers which grow unrestricted as nature intended. The Owenbaun Walk is worth taking as a variety of insect life is apparent. Butterflies are colourful and varied such as the orange tip, speckled wood, peacock, red admiral, small tortoiseshell, painted lady, green-veined white and meadow brown.

There too dragonflies are plentiful and often take a contorted shape while mating as they fly through the air. All of this lesser life attracts the swallows as they fly low by the small stream, which acts as a bubbling water symphony.

Millstreet Country Park has been carefully planned and developed and is a wonderful amenity for the general public. Long may it continue to be so.

WALK 22
THE QUIET ROADS OF MUSHERA

OS Map: No. 79 (Discovery Series)
Distance: 8½ miles/13km
Average time: 3 hours
Location: Situated 32 miles/52km northwest of Cork city
it can be reached by several routes. One is recommended is to travel from Cork to Macroom (24 miles/39km)
and then drive a further 8 miles/13km to the walk start.

INTRODUCTION
One of the quiet localities of County Cork, the Mushera
roads are narrow and seemingly remote but they possess a wealth of interest especially the megalithic
remains. This walk also traverses part of the 'Butter
Road' with a pause at the Kerryman's Table before completing the ramble close to the attractive St John's Well.

WALK DESCRIPTION
The walk begins at the T-junction just west of
Musheramore Mountain close to the entrance to
Millstreet Country Park. A sign points to Knocknakilla
Stone Circle and as you walk generally westward notice
the fine glaciated valley southward (on your left)
drained by the Awbeg River. Many valleys in the south-
west were shaped by the ice and show the might and
power of glaciers which radiated out from their centre at
Templenoe, west of Kenmare in County Kerry.

Leaving this elevated and often wind swept area
we follow the Duhallow Trail, one of the long-distance

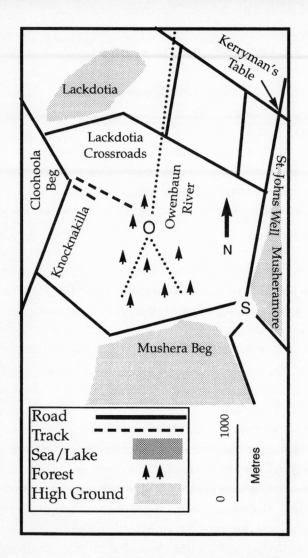

walking routes marked out in Ireland in recent years.
This region too is the home of 'mountainy' sheep, many
of which dot the hill of Musherabeg ahead and
Musheramore Mountain behind. These small black-

faced sheep which often wander about these roads come from stock which are believed to date from the Neolithic period, about 4,000 to 2,000 BC.

The road now veers northwest and expansive views open up across the landscape to Millstreet and north Cork. Dominant is Claragh Mountain towering over Millstreet while to its left is the large hump of Caherbarnagh Mountain and further to the left the famous mountain of Mullaghanish. In the valley down to the right is the privately-owned Millstreet Country Park – the subject of a separate walk in this book.

The keen observer will notice in summertime the greater butterwort plant growing by the roadside stream on the left. This insectivorous plant traps small flies on its sticky base leaves. To the right is a construction used probably for penning sheep when they need to be culled, marked with raddle, sheared or perhaps dosed. Immediately west of it a small stream has carved a significant mini-gorge on its journey to the valley below. This is a classic example of the power of water, which over a long period can erode even the hardest rocks.

Directly ahead prominent standing stones rise from the boggy terrain. This is the Knocknakilla Stone Circle and well worth a visit, being located on a hillock just a short distance from the road. This dates from prehistoric times and is one of many stone circles found in Counties Cork and Kerry. In fact the largest concentration of stone circles in Britain and Ireland is found in Cork and Kerry. What is its significance? Was it a burial site? Perhaps a place of ritual! Maybe even linked to the patterns of the seasons or astronomical orientations.

Whatever the reason one must admit that a marvellous view exists from this lonely site.

Continue northwest along the road which winds its way through a coniferous forestry plantation before eventually arriving at a T-junction. Rather concealed here at the left is a standing stone (also called a pillar-stone), one of many to be found in the Boggeragh Mountain area. Our route continues to the right and for the next kilometre or so gives fine vistas of Musheramore Mountain eastwards. If you walk this road in the period June to September you should be able to identify some of the wayside flowers like ragwort with its cluster of yellow flowers, a member of the geranium family, foxglove with its thimble-like pinky-purple flowers suspended on a tall stalk and, of course, the popular bramble which produces juicy blackberries in late summer.

In the fields carrion and hooded crows can often be seen strutting about amongst the grazing cattle, the peace occasionally interrupted by the noisy magpie. The latter is a beautiful bird but much maligned as it is accused of taking small birds and robbing eggs from other nests. However, it takes far less than the wily sparrowhawk or the stalking cat.

Turn right at Cloghboolabeg and a sign that says 'Trail' points in the direction from which you have come. You are now walking up a slight incline but it levels out after a short distance. A shady section is reached before a steep downhill passage leads to a bridge over the Owenbaun River. Just beyond turn left at the junction and follow the straight road that stretches northward. Eventually you arrive at a crossroads and you turn right. You are now walking east on the 'Butter Road', a great trade route of the eighteenth century. Many a horse and trap traversed this route carrying firkins of butter from distant parts of Counties Cork and Kerry to the butter market in Cork city, from where it was exported to distant lands.

It is a constant gradual climb now to the Kerryman's Table Cross Roads where signs point right to Millstreet Country Park, Knocknakilla Stone Circle and St John's Well. This is the route to follow but before doing so you might like to visit the actual Kerryman's 'Table' which is set in the ditch about 200m ahead through the crossroads. Almost like a standing stone lain on its side, this stone slab is reputed to have been used by Kerry folk for a rest and a bite to eat before continuing their journey to Cork.

Resuming, return to the crossroads and go left in the direction of St John's Well and Millstreet Country Park. After a kilometre you reach the well secluded in a coniferous plantation. Here stations were erected in 1982 while the grotto was constructed earlier in the 1950s. Tradition has it that the waters of the well can cure warts.

From St John's Well it is just a short distance further along the road to the walk start.

WALK 23
GOUGANE BARRA

OS Map: No. 85 (Discovery Series)
Distance: Various
Average time: Since this glen contains a variety of low and high level walks the suggestion is that you spend several hours there and take your pick of the trails. For the more adventurous a trek to the source of the River Lee is recommended.
Location: Gougane Barra valley is located 43 miles west of Cork city. It is reached by travelling through Inchigeelagh and Ballingeary.

INTRODUCTION
Just 4 miles beyond Ballingeary in west Cork, the secluded wild glen of Gougane Barra is one of Ireland's most beautiful locations. Relatively unspoilt, it is wrapped in a web of history and folklore as well as being a home to special plants and fauna. The name Gougane Barra refers to St Finbarr who built a monastery here in the sixth century and who is credited with founding the city of Cork where he later resided.

WALK DESCRIPTION
Begin this walk by the hotel at the lakeside and continue along the road, which leads into the valley. This awe-inspiring depression was shaped and deepened during the Ice Age of more than 10,000 years ago. Rocks and boulders were dragged from the head of the valley by a glacier, to be deposited as mounds of gravel and other

78

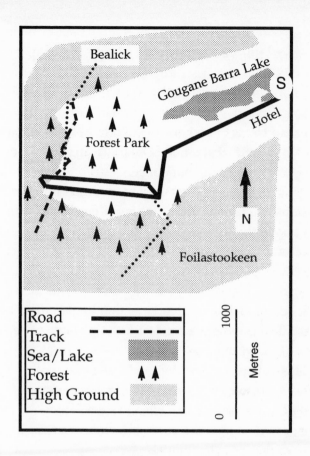

material at the eastern edge of the lake and beyond.

Just a short distance after starting the walk and at a level above the road is the small graveyard where the remains of two famous local people lie buried. The widely-respected Tailor and Ansty were made famous in a book of the same name, the subject of bitter controversy and banned soon after its publication in 1942. On their headstone is the intriguing inscription 'A star danced and under that was I born'.

Across the way on the small island is the chapel built about 1900 in the Irish Romanesque style. Its interior contains some fine stained glass windows. Close by is the stone court with eight cells built around 1700 by Reverend Denis O'Mahoney who retired here to a life of self-denial and abstention. On the walls of the court pennywort grows in abundance.

Leaving the island the route now leads into the valley along the tarred road with the cliffs of Bealick rising high above the lake waters to the north. After a period of wet weather the waterfalls from these cliffs are particularly impressive. Pass the pretty thatched building (a public convenience) on your left and continue along the road, bearing left at the road junction to gain the official park entrance where a modest fee is payable at certain times of the year.

This valley, acquired by the Forestry Service in 1938, has been planted with several species of coniferous trees, lodgepole pine, Japanese larch and sitka spruce. All three have grown well on the poor soil whereas broad-leaved trees would not have flourished.

Having entered the official park continue along the forest road which will take you to the end of the valley. As it turns eastwards again you could continue along and eventually return to the walk start. However, the more adventurous may like to climb to the source of the River Lee which rises high on the hillside above you. Care should be taken in the ascent and more importantly the descent of the hill as the ground is rough in its upper stages. Follow the Slí Sleibhe trail up through the wood, which crosses pretty wooden bridges and pathways of exposed tree roots (these roots are often slippery so care is necessary). Higher on the hillside the track becomes less defined but white arrows on trees guide you and eventually you reach the treeline, the point where the trees meet the open hillside.

Continue right along the track at the treeline and look out for a small stream, which comes down the slope on the left with the Irish words *An Laoi* painted on a boulder just outside the wire fence. Follow the stream up the slope until you eventually reach its source, a small bubbling pool which is the birthplace of the river Lee. From this high elevation there is a breath-taking panorama of the surrounding hills and sweep of distant countryside.

Return back to the treeline using the stream as your navigational aid. Then veer left along the track and continue eastwards. As you descend, distant views of the lake are observed, the wandering path avoids too steep a descent and eventually reaches the forest road on the floor of the valley. Here turn left and continue out of the glen until you finally reach the walk start by the hotel.

WALK 24
THE GEARAGH

OS Map: No. 79 (Discovery Series)
Distance: 2 miles/3km
Average time: 1 hour
Location: The Gearagh is located just over 25 miles/40km west of Cork city and about 1 mile south of Macroom on the route to Inchigeelagh.

INTRODUCTION

One of the most unusual habitats on the Irish landscape, the Gearagh is an ancient forest system located on a very broad channel where the river Lee extends into an alluvial plain formed after the conclusion of the last Ice Age. Nowhere in Ireland is there a place like this, with its deep water channels, varied wildfowl and some rare plants.

WALK DESCRIPTION

Commence this walk at the gateway with the half-circle parking area on the northern shore of the Gearagh. This is located about one mile on the Inchigeelagh/Gougane Barra road from the junction on the main Cork road just before Macroom.

A sign nearby indicating that bathing in the area is dangerous should be heeded. The Gearagh, derived from the Irish *an gaoire*, means the wooded river and to make the walk more enjoyable it is important to acquaint oneself with the wildlife and other interesting features of this noted and unique place.

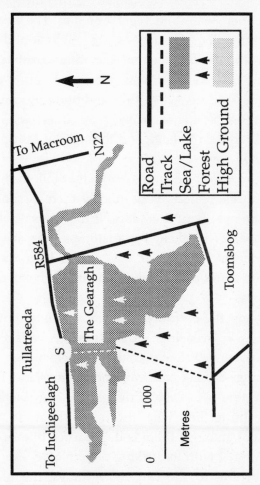

In springtime a chorus of birdsong is heard while the woodland flora begins to develop. Summertime brings the dragon and damselflies as well as swallows and swifts. Mute swans arrive in large numbers when summer flowers are in bloom. Autumn is the time for birds to migrate but winter birds take their place and nuts appear on the hazel trees. Finally winter ushers in the whooper swans and vegetation dies. The woodland is generally flooded, mosses are obvious and ducks adopt a vibrant plumage for the mating season to come.

In 1987 the Gearagh was declared a nature reserve under the Wildlife Act of 1976 and brought to national consideration as an area of enormous interest. Its woodland is unique in Ireland, and throughout Europe, such a habitat is now very rare.

Accordingly, as one sets forth on a walk through the Gearagh, one realises very quickly there is something very different about this place. If the water is at a low level, hosts of blackened tree stumps give an idea of how extensive the wood was before large-scale tree felling occurred prior to the flooding of the area in the mid 1950s.

Leaving the entrance gateway, continue out along the causeway over three old bridges, the walls of which contain several different colours of lichen. Beyond the third bridge a small pathway leads to an island. In summertime this is a place of delightful wild flowers and feeding butterflies who flit from bloom to bloom. Prominent amongst them is the peacock butterfly, visible in August with its striking pattern of 'eyespots'.

Returning to the causeway follow the old road over the water towards the wooded area where sally trees abound and the rarer spindle tree can be observed. Care should be exercised in straying too far from the pathway as the waters are rather deep, particularly on the left side. Large pike may on occasions be seen jumping out of the deep to snatch flies that hover over the waters.

Having passed through the somewhat spooky wooded area the track continues southward and now a sense of solitude and isolation prevails. On the right, stems of the greater reedmace stand triumphant while luxuriant gorse leads on the left.

The track eventually ends by a bridge at the roadside in a grove of alder trees where occasional clumps of bluebells can in season be observed. From this point you return back on the same route from which you came.

Walk 25
Farran Forest Park

OS Map: No. 80 (Discovery Series)
Distance: 2¹/₂ miles/4km.
Average time: 1¹/₂ hours
Location The park is located 15 miles/25km west of Cork
City a short distance off the main Cork/Killarney road.

Introduction
The forest park covers 130 acres – an area that was once
owned by a Captain Clarke, a name associated with a
well-known tobacco. Later on it passed to a Captain
Matthews who was responsible for converting pastureland into woodland with suitable shrubs introduced to
act as cover for game birds. This spacious forest park
offers much variety to the visitor. A rich selection of
trees and shrubs, a wildlife enclosure and riverside vista
all combine to make this a very pleasant place to visit.
The Forest and Wildlife Service acquired the property in
1962.

Walk Description
Begin this ramble at the car park near the wooden scale
map. The observant will notice the stately scots pine
trees which grow in the proximity. Pass by the red-and-
white metal barrier and continue down the gentle sloping forest road. After walking about 50m turn right
along the shaded walkway keeping the wire fence on
your left. Deer can often be seen amongst the trees –
either red or fallow, the two species in the park. Continue

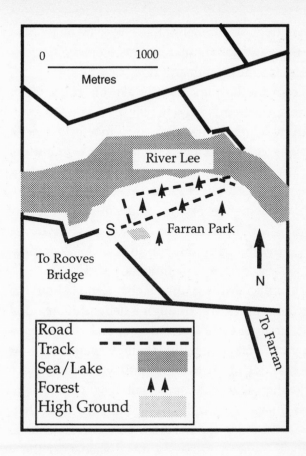

0   1000

Metres

River Lee

S

Farran Park

To Rooves
Bridge

N

To Farran

Road
Track
Sea/Lake
Forest
High Ground

along the trail that will take you around the wildlife enclosure. Many species of wildfowl make their home here such as teal, barnacle geese, mallard duck, shelduck, etc.

Towards the end of the enclosure, look out for a stone building on your right at a junction. This is the Display Centre and was once a shooting lodge. The building now contains a nature display that includes a stuffed badger and otter as well as photographs of several trees. A number of tree cones are on display also and these include monterey pine, Norway spruce, sitka spruce, Japanese larch and douglas fir.

From the Display Centre take the route on its left running eastwards which will lead you into remoter environs of the park that are embellished with the decaying colours of bracken and maple in autumn. At its eastern extremity a narrow pathway leads down through a pretty silver glade to secluded Mallard Cove. Here the water levels rise and fall as a result of the damning of the river Lee further east at Inniscarra. Notice too the cliffy outcrop to your left, comprised of Old Red Sandstone, a sedimentary rock.

Take the narrow pathway above and behind the outcrop that guides you through a delightful area down to the shoreline. Plenty of old chopped tree stumps rise like giant crabs from the shallow waters. Follow the aforementioned path west until you reach the forest road where close by some tall magnificent oak trees stand guard. Veer right along the park road that contours west along the northern boundaries of the estate. Along the way you pass a metal shed near the water from which rowing boats are launched.

Around this locality at twilight one can hear the call of the curlew or view the cormorant fishing in the waters or perhaps see a group of long-tailed tits fly from shrub to shrub making a 'whispering' noise as they go. Expansive views now extend uninterrupted over the waters to distant Rooves Bridge and the west Cork hills on the horizon.

Further on, the roadway swings sharply left and

then right again at a junction. A large area of open ground extends up the slope from the riverbank and in just a short distance one arrives at a large parking area on the road from which a concrete slipway leads to the river. Water-skiing takes place along this stretch of water and the riverbank is a prime location for a picnic.

Resuming the forest road it gradually climbs uphill to its most westerly point before swinging left. A secluded path runs off to the right to Bracken Point which is aptly named as you traverse through a jungle of bracken and oak saplings in order to reach it. The forest road leads you quickly back to the car park which you reach after passing by a metal barrier held by two stone pillars.

WALK 26
BALLINCOLLIG REGIONAL PARK

OS Map: No. 80 (Discovery Series)
Distance: 2¹/₂ miles/4km.
Average time: 1¹/₂ hours
Location: The park is located 8 miles/13km west of Cork city close to Inniscarra Bridge and is reached by travelling through Carrigrohane and Ballincollig.

INTRODUCTION
Ballincollig (or Coll's Town) derives its name from a former owner of Ballincollig Castle, Robert Coll. To the north of this constantly-expanding town lies a delightful recreational area by the banks of the River Lee. This is Ballincollig Regional Park, home to dog-walkers, joggers, anglers, footballers, orienteers and pony trekkers. It also contains the remains of the Gunpowder Mills.

WALK DESCRIPTION
From the car park at the western end of the park follow the pathway east over the bridge beside the sluice gates and continue along by the river where wooden seats offer rest. A short distance further on, the sound of churning water announces the weir on the river where many enjoy a swim in summertime.

Continue on the path between the water and the football pitches which picks up a large stone wall a short distance further on the left. In autumn the way ahead is a pathway of fallen crunchy leaves while further along on the right, stagnant pools lurk among the tangled undergrowth. Occasional clumps of marsh marigolds,

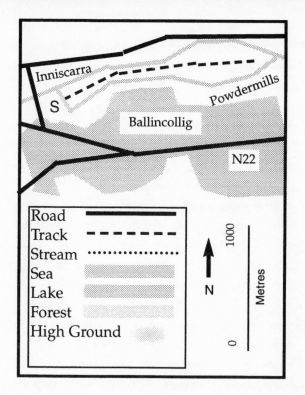

a relative of the buttercup family, are spotted here from February to April. In shady places this plant can be quite large and impressive.

Pass over the unrailed bridge where the path angles to the right before it swings left again. Around this area you may observe the light red/brown silver-washed fritillary butterfly. Large in size, it measures about 62mm across its wings and lays its eggs in tree trunks. Its caterpillars descend from the trees in springtime and feed almost exclusively on dog violet plants.

Your route stays along the riverbank where untamed nature abounds in a lavish jungle of ferns, brambles, bracken ivy and hawthorn. A sunken ruined building is passed on the right which was an isolated magazine of the former gunpowder mills. The path ahead leads to a sports field known as Goats Island but follow the narrow track to the left by the river Lee. With occasional muddy patches in winter it leads to another ruined building further along on the left, home to a surprising number of plants like harts tongue fern, herb robert, maidenhair spleenwort, nettles, etc.

Continue eastwards through an attractive tree-lined trail where a stagnant waterway lies on the right. At the junction of the two water channels ahead, bear right along the narrow riverside track which will bring you to a bridge. Having crossed the bridge continue along the track slightly ahead to the right by the high fence which will eventually lead to an open area of ruined buildings. This is the main centre of the former gunpowder mills.

Originally established in 1794 by Charles Henry Leslie, the British Board of Ordnance later purchased the mills and developed their productive capacity. In the 1830s a Liverpool company acquired the mills and from then on their rapid expansion resulted in a peak of 500 being employed. Towards the end of the nineteenth century demand for gunpowder declined leading to the closure of the mills in 1903. In recent years Cork County Council has been restoring various sections of the mills as part of its development programme for the regional park.

Return the short distance back to the bridge which you previously traversed. However, do not cross it but follow the path to its left along the side of the waterway. This will lead you on a pleasant route back to the car park.

WALK 27
KILNAGLERY CIRCUIT, CARRIGALINE

OS Map: No. 87 (Discovery Series)
Distance: 2 miles/3km.
Location: 1 hour
Getting there: Situated about 7 miles/11km southeast of Cork city it can be reached by travelling via Douglas and Carrs Hill.

INTRODUCTION

Carrigaline, *Carraig Uí Leighin* – rock of the son of Laighin, located at the western end of the Owenboy estuary, is a rapidly expanding satellite town of Cork city and apart from being close to the Ringaskiddy ferryport it is also close to Cork Airport.

WALK DESCRIPTION

Begin the ramble at the bridge in the centre of Carrigaline and head east along the Crosshaven Road, which is extremely busy in summertime. As you proceed, a glance over the wall on the left will introduce you to the ways of the Owenboy river as it makes its way to the sea. The mudflats further on are a haven for bird life and here many feed incessantly, including the curlew, oystercatcher, plover and other waders while the heron is often observed standing solitary as if on guard.

Continue along the footpath until it eventually peters out. Care is required crossing the road and after doing so take the road on the right which leads into the industrial estate. This junction is about a mile from

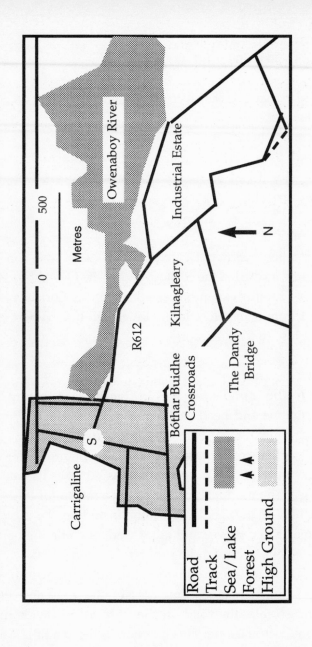

Carrigaline. Continue and near the top of the industrial estate follow the narrow road to the right. Immediately the buzz of traffic is left behind and you are now in a quiet country passage with only the occasional car. The ditches are lined with brambles and ferns with a generous covering of ivy and nettles (in season).

Glancing at the hedgerows one wonders what the country would be like without them. Hedgerows are very special places for the bird population and typical birds are the sparrow, blackbird, thrush, tits, finches, robins, yellowhammers and perhaps the goldcrest, Ireland's smallest bird.

Gradually modern homes appear as you move along the roadway. When you reach a T-junction turn right downhill to the one arch Dandy Bridge which straddles a small stream. In such a stream one might be fortunate to observe a dipper with its bobbing movement. This shy bird flies from rock to rock and frequently dives beneath the waters to hunt on the riverbed.

The road now gently contours along a slight incline as you pass some pastures with cattle often grazing peacefully. Heed any bull warning signs and never enter a field which contains a bull.

After a while you reach Bothar Buidhe Cross Roads where you turn right down Chapel Hill to once again reach the centre of Carrigaline.

WALK 28
COUNTRY ROADS NEAR CARRIGALINE

OS Map: No. 87 (Discovery Series)
Distance: 7 miles/11km
Average time: 2 hours
Location: Situated about 6 miles/10km southeast of Cork city it can be reached by travelling via Douglas and Carrs Hill.

INTRODUCTION
Sometimes country roads close to a population centre can provide an amount of interest and satisfaction. Such an area lies in the roads southeast of Carrigaline.

WALK DESCRIPTION
Begin this walk at the bridge in the centre of Carrigaline and walk south uphill as far as Bothar Buidhe Crossroads where you turn left. The terrain now levels off as you proceed eastwards through some modern housing estates. Shortly the outskirts of Carrigaline are left behind and pastureland stretches out on both sides from the road. From here on a foggy morning you can hear the foghorn sounding from Roches Point.

Pause at the single-arch Dandy Bridge and listen to the stream. These little humpbacked bridges are becoming rarer but this one is especially attractive. Ignore the next turning left and continue uphill. Along the ditches much vegetation is in evidence such as the customary brambles (so popular at 'blackberry time'), a multitude of ivy and plenty of harts tongue fern (which sports a tongue-like leaf).

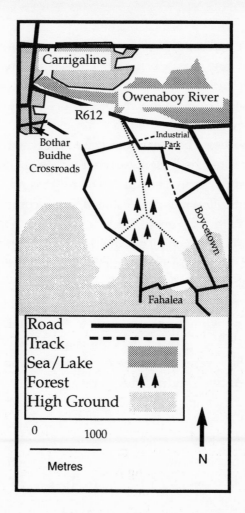

You have now left the precincts of the Owenboy valley behind as you walk along the remote open road. Tall
scots pines rise skyward as a landmark and these noble
trees can grow to heights of 36m (120 feet). Along this
route also are sycamores and holly trees as well as the
occasional crab-apple tree which indicates its presence

in springtime by its blossom and in late autumn when it sheds its crab apples. The road eventually dips down into a hollow and a bridge is crossed before a sharp, short rise uphill. On this bridge there are some distinctive plants like maidenhair-spleenwort, polypody ferns and rusty back ferns. From this elevation there are extensive views both east and west. After a while a road junction is reached. Here turn left opposite a farmstead with a large corrugated shed. The route is now passing through the townland of Fahalea, open country where Friesian cattle and geese work out their existence.

You should be now about 1 hour into the walk. The road eventually turns right and the next turn right (as you walk uphill) should be ignored. At the next road junction turn left into the townland of Boycetown and walk along what I can only name as 'Barking Dog Road' as several dogs greeted me enthusiastically as I passed along. They were not aggressive, however, and a friendly word or two subdued the 'opposition'. This road gently dips downhill after a while and eventually veers to the right opposite large corrugated sheds (left). Do not go straight ahead on the green road.

Walking downhill you reach a road junction with a yield- right of way sign. Here turn sharply left and begin the descent after a short distance northeast towards Carrigaline. The road finally descends more steeply towards Kilnaglery Industrial Estate, which you pass through to reach the Carrigaline-Crosshaven road. At this busy junction turn left and walk the 'short' mile back into Carrigaline.

OS Maps: No. 87 (Discovery Series)
Distance: 2 miles / 3km.
Average time: 1¼ hours
Location: Currabinny Wood is located 13 miles/21km southeast of Cork City and 4 miles/7km east of Carrigaline Village.

INTRODUCTION
Currabinny Wood is a fine example of a mixed coniferous and deciduous wood. The hill itself dates back to links with the Bronze Age, about 1500 BC.

WALK DESCRIPTION
Commence this walk at the car park where a memorial plaque has been erected to the memory of William Warren Baldwin (1775-1844), the grandson of a former mayor of Cork and an ardent advocate of constitutional reform, being particularly remembered in Canadian history.

Leaving the car park take the path to the left of the display board located at the eastern end. After a few paces veer left downhill to the waters of Cork Harbour below. This well-worn path swings right close to the water and follows a route eastwards over many exposed and sometimes slippery tree roots. Across the broad expanse of seawater the town of Cobh (pronounced Cove) is clearly visible with its cathedral a dominant landmark, while the storage tanks of Whitegate Oil Refinery are prominent to the east.

On the shoreline you may find a variety of seashells

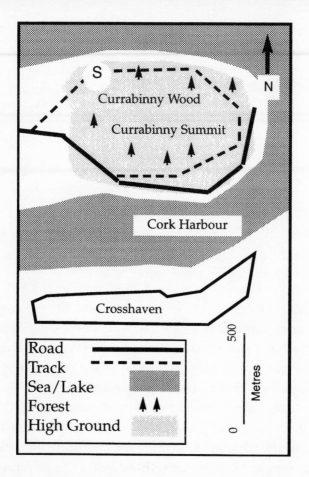

such as whelk and periwinkle as well as barnacle and oyster. Seaweeds include bladder wrack and sea lettuce. Amongst the trees, Ireland's smallest bird, the goldcrest, can sometimes be heard, its call similar to a mouse-like squeak. Look out also for the small blue tit which is noted for its acrobatic feeding habits on suspended food holders in gardens.

In a short while the route is joined by a track from the

right and as you walk ahead bilberry plants dominate the ground flora, with their luxuriant crop of bright green leaves, while on the moss-covered tree branches the curious polypody ferns proliferate. If you visit this location in late March or early April keep an eye out for a large cluster of wood anemones which congregate near the shore. Nearby a small rustic fence is a place to pause and inhale that distinctive freshness of the sea. The trail now passes beneath some fallen trees which overhang the pathway and just a short distance further a wooden rail leads down some steps to the rocky seaweed-covered shore. As this is a remote section of the wood and because the rocks are extremely slippery, great care should be exercised in your descent. A deposit of sea shells are visible here, one of a series around Cork Harbour probably left by people who lived in the vicinity and largely depended on edible shellfish for food. It could also be evidence of stark survival during the great famine times of the 1840s.

Returning to the trail, a wooden barrier blocks your progress but the route continues up the wooden steps to the right. This short steep ascent leads to the principal woodland track. Follow the low wall east (left) until you come to a small gate. Directly across from this some steps lead you to the upper reaches of the wood. Veer left at the arrow sign and the indicated path brings you to a rather forlorn looking gazebo. Many great estates boasted gazeboes, which were ornamental summerhouses that commanded wide views. This particular five-windowed structure served as a tea-house in the relaxed days of the past.

Continuing the journey take the track on the right

101

of the Octagon which, after a few metres, accords an admirable vista of Cork Harbour, one of the finest natural harbours in the world. From this lofty platform distant Cobh and Spike Island stand out. Progressing forward one attains the highest point of Currabinny Hill (264 feet) where about 1,500 years ago hardy Bronze Age people built a great cairn to their dead. This was excavated in 1932 but no human remains were found, though a platform of clay (9ft x 4ft) was discovered at its centre. It is hoped to restore the cairn to its former appearance at some stage in the future.

Take the path to the right, which now begins to descend. Look out for the Portuguese laurel tree at a wooden stump marked 11. This was a most popular tree in old estates, being widely planted for the berries it produced and also for its attractive evergreen leaves. Further ahead on the track the observant walker will spot a birch tree adorned with clumps of densely packed twigs. This unusual arrangement has resulted because a fungus has attacked the chemistry of the tree causing it to sprout densely-packed twigs which in medieval times were known as 'witches broom'.

The way veers sharply right passing through an area of glorious confusion of brambles, bracken and coniferous trees. As you walk the few paces back to the car park you may notice a rather decrepit looking tall European silver fir tree whose native habitat is among the mountains of Central Europe.

WALK 30
CROSSHAVEN CLIFF WALK

O.S. Map: 81 and 87 (Discovery Series)
Distance: $4^1/4$ miles/7 km
Average time: 2 hours
Location: Situated 13 miles/21km southeast of Cork city
it is reached by travelling via Douglas and Carrigaline

INTRODUCTION

For many Corkonians visits to Crosshaven, particularly
in summertime, are a must. A popular coastal village
nestling in the south-western corner of Cork Harbour, it
is very much a yacht centre and indeed has the oldest
yacht club in the world, the Royal Cork Yacht Club,
which was founded in 1720 at Haulbowline. Quite close
to the village are beaches and other bathing places such
as Graball Bay, Church Bay, Myrtleville and
Fountainstown.

WALK DESCRIPTION

Begin this walk at the car park in the centre of
Crosshaven village and head out the Point Road,
which is in a north-easterly direction. When the tide is
out the mud flats act as a feeding ground for the
curlew and other birds as a whiff of seaweed perme-
ates the air. Continue past the amusement field on your
right, a place where much entertainment can be had in
summer months. Glances to your left give fine views of
the village and across the estuary the rising wooded
hill of Currabinny is prominent.

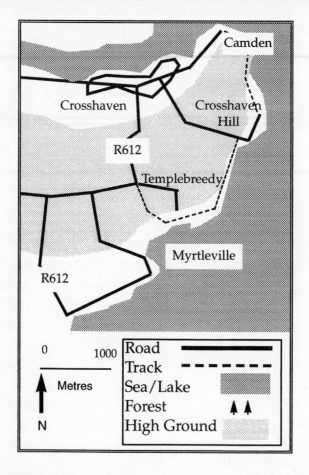

Continuing, one passes Crosshaven Boatyard, which has, amongst many other crafts, built the famous *Gypsy Moth IV* for the late Sir Francis Chichester.

Moving forward Castle Point Seaside Garden comes into view at the seafront and the road tends to narrow as it extends away into the distance. Ever increasing panoramas of Cork Harbour unfold and on this particular ramble you will see how attractive it can be for sea-going mariners and a variety of ocean-going vessels. The town of Cobh is visible in the distance with its prominent cathedral spire. Closer to the shore one may see a variety of sea birds such as the black and white oystercatcher with its bright orange bill, the blackish shag which is strictly coastal and a variety of gulls which all frequent the area. In time you come to the end of the road and reach an area known as the 'Grassy'. Climb the steep path, which contours right to the road above. Close by is the entrance to Fort Meagher (formerly Fort Camden). Various fortifications have existed at the Fort site since about the middle of the sixteenth century. However, it was eventually passed to the Irish Army in 1938 before coming finally into the ownership of Cork County Council. With Fort Carlisle, it served as a defence against unwanted vessels entering the harbour in past centuries.

The next section of the walk to Church Bay contains a few areas where the cliff has eroded as far as the pathway. Accordingly it is not suitable for younger children. If you wish to end the walk, continue along the road to your right (Camden Road) which will take you back to the village.

If you wish to continue, cross the road to the car park and walk on the pathway to the left of the GAA field. The pathway (well worn) leads gently down through tall gorse bushes towards the cliff tops while fine views of the harbour entrance and Roches Point Lighthouse open up. It is now a very pleasant walk along the path to Weavers Point (a peaceful place to pause) before continuing to Church Bay. Here follow the road up to the junction and turn left (seawards) in the direction of Templebreedy Fort. About 100m further on and just before a 'no entry' sign, a narrow road runs up through houses on your right. At the top of this passage continue ahead on a grassy track which leads to a metal gate. Enter the field via the open stile at the right and follow the worn track at the side of the field towards Templebreedy Church (now in ruins) at the top of the hill. Eventually you reach the roadway by the Church and, if time permits, observe some of the headstones in the graveyard which bear dates back to the eighteenth century.

Leaving Templebreedy, walk down the road westward and after a short distance a road leads left down to Fennells Bay. Across from this junction a stone stile permits entry to a field where a pathway is followed into Cruchan Wood before it continues its way, meandering through the fields, back to the village. Back at the Fennels Bay road junction one could also take an alternative route by continuing uphill to the water tower and taking the road to the right which leads back to Crosshaven village also.

WALK 31
KINSALE TOWN WALKING TRAIL

OS Map: No. 87 (Discovery Series)
Distance: 1¹/₄ miles /2km
Average time: 1 hour
Location: Situated 17 miles/27km south of Cork city, Kinsale is reached by travelling past Cork Airport, through Fivemilebridge and Belgooly.

INTRODUCTION
Kinsale is a long-established town with a vibrant history stretching back hundreds of years. It was formerly governed under a charter (1333) of Edward II and for centuries was a most important port on the coast, its harbour being well sheltered and now a haven for fishing boats and sailing enthusiasts.

WALK DESCRIPTION
Begin this walk at Emmet Place in the centre of Kinsale town and proceed out along the Pier Road. You pass the park on your right and the waters of Kinsale Harbour stretch away towards James Fort and beyond. This general area is very much the 'pulse' of the coastal town in summertime, with plenty of tourists, fishermen and yachting folk frequenting the sea front.

Standing sentinel by the quay wall is the anchor monument erected in 1989 by Kinsale Harbour Commissioners to the memory of all seafarers from Kinsale and district who lost their lives at sea. At the yachting marina turn right into Denis Quay which was formerly a waterway before the road's construction

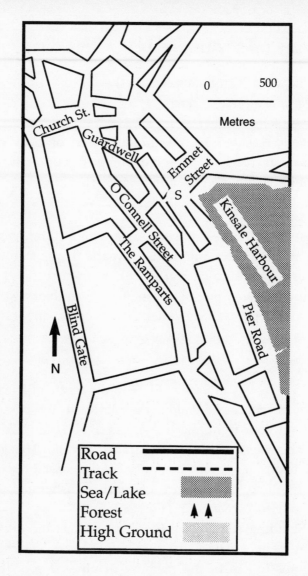

Road ──────

Track ── ── ──

Sea/Lake

Forest ▲ ▲

High Ground

about 1890. Press forward to the T-junction where a left turn is taken and then a right turn uphill (St John's Hill) short of the Pier some distance beyond. Moving upwards the narrow street to your right leads to the Town Hall, Courthouse and Library.

Retrace your steps down the street as far as the Kinsale Outdoor Education Centre beside which a narrow laneway runs right uphill. The keen observer will notice maidenhair spleenwort growing on the stone wall at the left. Pass through two black and yellow bollards and continue up the inclined roadway until it levels out. The views over Kinsale Harbour are very impressive. Return back down the road and walk along The Mall. Rest if you wish on the seats overlooking the bowling-green as you view again the harbour area. Continuing, look out for the Almshouses just before Winters Hill on the left. Erected originally by Sir Robert Southwell in 1682 they eventually went into disrepair but were restored again in the 1960s.

Walking along the Ramparts the Convent of Mercy looms large on the left. Here the nuns established a school for Irish lace in the middle of the last century which brought considerable international fame to Kinsale.

Beyond the Convent walk left up Rampart Lane and right at the T-junction into Blind Gate. Care is required here due to fast moving traffic. Continue through Rose Abbey and bear right into Church Street with Saint Multose Church inside the wall at your right. Why not visit this noble building with its Norman tower? A solid structure with the original building dating back to the thirteenth century, it also possesses some fine stained glass windows. Leaving the Church, continue downhill to Church Square which was the central part of the town in medieval times. At the circular stone flower bed bear left into Cork Street, having passed the Garda station on the corner at the left.

Walk up Cork Street and turn left into Friar Street to the Church of St John the Baptist. Erected after Catholic emancipation, it replaced a smaller chapel and was designed by Brother Augustine Riordan. The walls are composed essentially of local sandstone with some limestone. Its interior is noted for the elaborate candelabra, which was executed by Italian craftsmen.

Return back to Cork Street and turn left where, within moments, you reach the stout structure of Desmond Castle (also called the French Prison). Erected in the sixteenth century the castle was used during the Siege of 1601 as a magazine by Don Juan del Aquila, the Spanish commander. During the eighteenth century, French prisoners of war were incarcerated within its walls, so giving it the alternative name of the French Prison. Tragically, in 1747, more than 50 prisoners died there in an accidental fire and in the early part of the nineteenth century the building was used as the local jail. In 1938 the Irish Government declared it a National Monument.

Leaving the Castle behind walk down the street directly opposite, Chairmans Lane, which leads to Newmans Mall. A right turn will take you to Market Square, the very core of the modern town and oozing with atmosphere. The narrow streets around this area reflect a special charm, quaint and modern, for that is the town of Kinsale – a place where the past meets the present, a town that is cared for by its residents and as a result has won fame as well as justly-earned rewards.

From here it is just a short walk through Market Quay to Emmet Place and the walk start.

Walk 25
Scilly to Charlesfort

OS Map: No. 87 (Discovery Series)
Distance: 2¹/₂ miles/4km
Average time: 1 hour
Location: The walk runs from the Scilly area of Kinsale to the old fortress of Charles Fort. Travel 17 miles/27km south from Cork City via Cork Airport to Kinsale.

Introduction
A popular and pleasant stroll overlooking picturesque Kinsale Harbour, the route winds its way east and south through the scenic district of Scilly before reaching the sturdy and durable Charles Fort.

Walk Description
Begin this walk where a sign 'Scilly Walking Tour' directs one downhill to reveal views of Kinsale Harbour and across the waters to Compass Hill rising above the town. Proceed past the cul-de-sac signs and continue on the tarmacadam surface ahead, to a pleasant walkway overlooking the waters. Several seating areas offer rest to those who wish to linger. Passing the large conifer trees on your left the route rises and a glance to the right across the water will provide excellent views of James Fort. Turn right at the revolving metal stile downhill to Summercove, a picturesque hamlet and a place to pause.

The route now leads uphill to the entrance to Charles Fort on the right. Charles Fort was built in the seventeenth century on a site, formerly occupied by a previous fortress. Shaped like a star, it was designed to

111

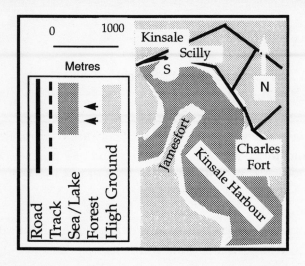

prevent invading forces from entering Kinsale Harbour. Additions were made to the fort in more recent centuries and troops occupied it until 1921. On the other side of the estuary is James Fort, which was built in 1602 just after the Battle of Kinsale.

Return to Scilly via the same route to the walk start.

MORE TITLES FROM THIS PRESS

New Irish Walks and Scrambles

Barry Keane

The walks described in these books vary from pleasant strolls to more strenuous scrambles. Most of these have not featured in previous guidebooks and so provide a range of new options.

1. The Iveragh Peninsula

50 Walks and Scrambles Around Killarney
1 898256 27 6 PB £5.99   1997

2. The Dingle Peninsula

30 Walks and Scrambles
1 898256 28 4 PB £5.99   1997

3. The Beara and Mizen Head Peninsulas

40 Walks and Scrambles
1 898256 29 2 PB £5.99   1998

4. The Galty, Knockmealdown, and Comeragh Mountains

40 Walks and Scrambles
1 898256 48 9 PB £5.99   1998

5. The Burren, Aran Islands and County Clare

1 898256 83 7 PB £5.99   1999

Keane's lifetime knowledge of these magnificent ranges makes the routes he selects spectacular memories for those who walk these trails. He chooses clear, concise routes on Ireland's most challenging summits for both novice and veteran. He suggests sites for pleasant strolls, demanding walks or scrambles where you use your hands and feet to get up the mountain. Each book is illustrated with maps by the author.

> *'well presented and compact'*
> – Irish Mountain Log

Walks Around Cork

Vincent Godsil and John C Morrish

This is an informative guide to the beauty, seren-
ity and scenic grandeur of Cork city and its suburbs, its little known tracks, trails and boreens.
The walks are all within 25 miles of the city, and
each walk tells a story; some tell the history of
the area, with poems to help you along your way.
Each walk is easy to follow, pleasant and rewarding.

*'An informative guide to the city and its surround-
ings'* – The Examiner

1 898256 19 5 PB £7.99 1997

Wild Plants of the Burren and Aran Islands

Charles E. Nelson

The Burren and Aran Islands are renowned for
the beauty of their natural flora. Charles Nelson
has selected 120 of the most widely occurring
plus a number of special plants. Introduced
with background information on the plants and
instructions on how to use the guide, photographs are grouped according to flower
colour and the pages colour coded. Plants are
described simply using the common English
name, followed by the name in Irish and then
the Latin (botanical) name. The flowering period and each plant's distribution are given succinctly.

1 898256 77 2 PB £10.00 1999
Full colour